INTERACT WITH
WEB STANDARDS

A HOLISTIC APPROACH TO WEB DESIGN

 Erin Anderson, Virginia DeBolt, Derek Featherstone, Lars Gunther, Denise Jacobs, Leslie Jensen-Inman, Chris Mills, Christopher Schmitt, Glenda Sims, and Aarron Walter

New
Riders

VOICES THAT MATTER™   1249 Eighth Street Berkeley, CA 94710

InterACT with Web Standards: A holistic approach to web design

Erin Anderson, Virginia DeBolt, Derek Featherstone, Lars Gunther, Denise Jacobs, Leslie Jensen-Inman, Chris Mills, Christopher Schmitt, Glenda Sims, and Aarron Walter

New Riders
1249 Eighth Street
Berkeley, CA 94710
510/524-2178
510/524-2221 (fax)
Find us on the Web at: www.newriders.com
To report errors, please send a note to errata@peachpit.com
New Riders is an imprint of Peachpit, a division of Pearson Education

Project Editor: Michael J. Nolan
Project Manager: Aarron Walter
Development Editor: Jeff Riley/Box Twelve Communications
Production Editor: Myrna Vladic
Techincal Editor: Patrick Lauke
Copyeditor: Doug Adrianson
Proofreader: Rose Weisburd
Indexer: Rebecca Plunkett
Creative Director: Leslie Jensen-Inman
Designer: Jessi Taylor

ISBN 13: 978-0-321-70352-1
ISBN 10:   0-321-70352-9
9 8 7 6 5 4 3 2 1
Printed and bound in the United States of America

InterACT with Web Standards is dedicated to those who give their resources to improve the state of web education and to their families, friends, and colleagues who support their efforts.

Table of Contents

Part III: Implementation—
HTML and CSS Fundamentals, and Accessibility   151

Part I:
Preparation and Background Knowledge

Every creative skill has a certain degree of theory and preparation to go through before you can just jump in and produce a masterpiece, and web design is no different. In this part of the book we will give you the background knowledge you need to start planning and implementing websites with confidence. You will initially learn about the mission of InterACT, and why web standards are so important, then move on to looking at the toolset you'll need for web design.

Chapter 3, "Learning on the Web," then explores how to effectively use the Web as a resource to find learning aids, get help, become a part of the web community, and manage your resources. We then look at internet fundamentals—the basics of how the Web works—before finishing off by learning about writing for the web. Effective web copy is distinctly different from print copy, as people tend to read and learn from the Web in different ways.

To summarize, this part contains the following topics:

- **The InterACT mission**
- **Why web standards matter**
- **The tools you'll need**
- **Finding answers on the Web**
- **Staying up to date with the latest web happenings**
- **Keeping productive**
- **The web community, and contributing to it positively**
- **Web history**
- **Web architecture**
- **How a web server works**
- **Writing good copy for the Web**

Chattanooga,
Tennessee ♀
USA

Leslie Jensen-Inman, assistant professor at The University of Tennessee
at Chattanooga, acts on her passion to improve web education through
initiatives such as Teach the Web, the Open Web Education Alliance, the
WE Rock Summit and Tour, and InterACT. She is an author, speaker, and
creative director who has a unique background in design and business that
includes being the graphic designer for a major motion picture and owning
a design, marketing, and public relations business.

http://teachtheweb.com
http://interact.webstandards.org
http://morellc.com
http://twitter.com/jenseninman

CHAPTER 1
InterACT

by Leslie Jensen-Inman

InterACT with Web Standards brings together ten authors from across the world to focus on front-end web design and development topics. Each author employs her or his unique view, tone, and experience to create a well-rounded and informative collection of techniques and resources. This book is written to aid in the instruction of web education—whether guided in a classroom or self-guided at home or at the office. The authors are dedicated to improving web education.

Who this book is for

Are you learning how to design websites? Are you teaching how to design websites? If you've answered "yes" to either question, this might be the book you are looking for. If you enjoy reading accurate information from a variety of authors in a conversational tone, this book will be a good fit. *InterACT with Web Standards* has been organized with learners and educators in mind. This book is written and designed to enhance learning, to allow learners to easily digest information and practice the skills from the content they've just consumed. Through the guided "Try It Yourself" sections, you are encouraged to regularly pause from reading in order to practice the techniques you've just read, helping you to reinforce the learning by doing and to bolster your skills and confidence.

InterACT with Web Standards approaches front-end web design and development with a focus on web standards. By reading and completing the exercises you should gain a solid understanding of Internet fundamentals, website planning, HTML, and CSS. The book draws upon the experiences of industry experts and extraordinary educators to create chapters that are easy to read and comprehend yet delve into concepts and techniques that empower you to develop a solid grasp of front-end web design and development.

How to use this book

The design and content of this book are intended to make learning front-end web design and development an enjoyable experience. The information builds upon itself. This book should be read sequentially; start from the beginning and stop at the end. We recommend that you read the content and then, when you encounter a "Try it yourself!" section, pause to practice and build your skills. Many of the "Try it yourself!" sections require you to have access to a computer, the Internet, and to specific software. If you do not have access to these items while you are reading the book, be sure to note that you need to return to the "Try it yourself!" section when you have access to these tools.

Tip: Read all the content in the book; do not skip over Tips, Resources, and other areas that are highlighted by color fields. These sections are important to read in order to fully grasp the topics.

Chapter 25 brings together all of the concepts and techniques explained throughout the book. This entire chapter is basically one big "Try it yourself!" section that offers a great way to bring everything you've learned into focus. It will also help you to gauge what information you have retained and what information you may need to review.

In order to truly comprehend the information you are reading, you must employ the techniques that you've just read by putting them into practical application. You will get the most out of this book if you take the time to read *and* to practice. Be sure to review any material that you feel unsure of and keep this book as a resource as you move ahead to utilize your newly acquired/refreshed skills for future projects.

Tip: There are three parts to this book; each part is color-coded and chapters within each part retain the same color-coding. Use the chapter tabs at the edge of the page to navigate quickly to chapters within parts.

Key

We determined that it is really helpful for learners to practice what they learn immediately after they have consumed information about a topic. With this in mind, the book divides information into digestible amounts and uses color to help learners easily understand the information provided. For example, we have color coded the markup (HTML) and presentation language (CSS) throughout the book. HTML tags are orange and CSS rules are purple.

We also used color to highlight specific types of information within the book. These sections have different color treatments and are each paired with icons. The following is the icon key:

Resource

Supplementary sources provided to aid growth of knowledge and skills.

Whenever possible, these resources are also linked on the book's companion website http://interactwithwebstandards.com/. Use these resources to more fully grasp concepts and techniques. Also use these resources as part of your toolkit for future front-end web design and development endeavors.

Tip: Additional information supplied to help improve your comprehension of the material.

Try it yourself!

Complete these exercises to practice the techniques you have just learned.

Warning

Highlighted areas where it is best to proceed with caution.

For Educators

The design and content of this book are not only intended to make learning front-end web design and development an enjoyable experience, but to make teaching these topics enjoyable as well. It is often difficult to find a trade book that works within the classroom; a book that takes into consideration the ways students learn and retain information; a book that considers the way a course is segmented into shorter periods of time; a book that provides the education students need and the support educators must have to truly make the book a successful tool within a course. *InterACT with Web Standards* strives to meet these requirements. This book is organized in a way that is easy to adopt in a classroom environment and designed in a manner that appeals to learners. Every effort has been made to ensure that this book is well suited for both learners and educators. We want to make learning and teaching web design as painless and pleasurable as possible.

One of the ways we are able to make web education simpler is by aligning this book with the InterACT curriculum (http://interact. webstandards.org). InterACT is a living, open curriculum based upon web standards and best practices, designed to teach students the skills of the web professional. On the InterACT website you will find fully developed courses that include: competencies, assignments, exam questions, resources, and learning modules. There are even downloadable rubrics to facilitate the grading of assignments. The InterACT curriculum is created specifically to assist you in developing standards-compliant courses quickly and easily. The courses in the curriculum are organized according to specialized tracks:

- Foundations
- Front-end development
- Design
- User science
- Server-side development
- Professional practice

You may use this information to help supplement and build your courses. The InterACT curriculum is free to use and is licensed under the Creative Commons Attribution 3.0 United States license, which means you may share and remix the work as long as you attribute the work (http:// creativecommons.org/licenses/by/3.0/us/). We encourage you to share the way you incorporate InterACT and your own materials into the classroom, to be part of the InterACT community, and join the discussion on the InterACT forums (http://interact.webstandards.org/forums/). It is important for us all to interact with each other to improve the state of web education.

Opera's Web Standards Curriculum (http://www.opera.com/company/ education/curriculum/) includes more than 50 focused articles about topics such as standards-based web design, HTML, CSS, and JavaScript. These articles support the information in the book and can be used to provide students with additional resources on key web design and development topics.

Tip: The companion website also connects the content of the book with the InterACT Curriculum and the Opera Web Standards Curriculum.

About this book

Learners and educators were taken into consideration with both the creation of content and the design of this book. This book is unique in the way it handles the content and the approach of the design.

This book also helps the future of web education as **25 percent of author proceeds** will be donated to the Open Web Education Alliance (http://www.w3.org/2009/02/owea-xg-charter.html).

Authors

Each author's bio can be found at the beginning of the first chapter of their section. Even though the authors share similar ideals, their tone and voice can be very different. We have preserved the authors' voices in order for you to experience each of their individual personalities. We have maintained regional differences in the English language to also retain each author's voice. For example an author from the United States might use the word *color* while an author from the United Kingdom might use the word *colour*. InterACT is comprised of many individuals from around the world who unite to improve the state of web education. InterACT has the unique ability to fuse a diverse group of people together to support a single cause yet still maintain each person's individuality. *InterACT with Web Standards* is written in the spirit of the group's synthesis while celebrating each author's distinctiveness.

Even though cat hearding ten authors for a single book is no easy feat, Project Manager, **Aarron Walter** has lead the project with style. Aarron is the author of *Building Findable Websites: Web Standards, SEO, and Beyond* (New Riders, 2008) http://buildingfindablewebsites.com and the lead user experience designer for MailChimp. For more than a decade Aarron has been busy building websites for clients, and teaching interactive design courses at colleges and universities in the US. As a member of The Web Standards Project, Aarron is the lead of The WaSP InterACT curriculum

project. You can find more information about Aarron at http://aarronwalter.com or find him on Twitter http://twitter.com/aarron. Aarron recognizes that, "Despite the great influence the Web has upon our economies, politics, culture, and our daily lives, schools around the world are still struggling to find the right place for the study of this young medium in their programs. The Web is arguably the most sophisticated communication conduit in human history, but it's often afforded only one or two courses tacked on to existing degrees, rather than treated as the complex medium that it is, which is worthy of an independent program of study." Aarron believes that, "by improving web education we can make the Web and the industry that drives it sustainable for centuries to come, resulting in communication advancements far beyond our imaginations."

Designers

As a designer, with both print and web experience and as an educator, I was uniquely positioned to lead the creative direction of this book. I worked with one of my former students, Jessi Taylor. You will not find Jessi's bio at the beginning of any chapter but you will find her passion and dedication for design and web education within each element of the book. And just in case you wanted to know a little more:

Jessi Taylor is a graphic designer living and working in the greater Chattanooga area. When she is not designing, you can find her behind a camera lens.

Jessi began designing for The Web Standards Project Education Task Force (WaSP EduTF) as part of a design fellowship when she was a student at The University of Tennessee at Chattanooga. Together Jessi and I created the look and feel for InterACT. Jessi continues her work with WaSP EduTF and helps shepherd the evolution of the InterACT brand. You can also find more information about Jessi at http://www.jessitaylordesign.com or follow her on Twitter http://twitter.com/JessiTaylor.

Austin, Texas
USA

Christopher Schmitt, is the founder of Heat Vision, a small new media
publishing and design firm in Austin, Texas. Christopher is a web design
specialist who has been working with the Web since 1993.

As a sought-after speaker and trainer, Christopher regularly demonstrates
the use and benefits of practical standards-based designs. He is co-Lead of
the Adobe Task Force for The Web Standards Project in addition to being a
contributing member of its Education Task Force.

http://christopherschmitt.com/
http://heatvision.com/
http://environmentsforhumans.com/
http://twitter.com/teleject

CHAPTER 2
Tools

by Christopher Schmitt

To author and manage a website, all you really *need* are the simplest of text editors and an FTP client. However, the more complex your web projects are, the more collaborators are involved with them, and the more sophisticated a developer you become, the more you come to appreciate the efficiency and power of professional-grade tools.

To successfully develop and maintain a website, you need not run out and buy the most expensive and powerful development tools. If you can get by with a free or cheaper version of a product, or one that has fewer features, you should definitely do so.

Not only are they easier on your wallet, but simpler programs involve an easier learning curve and are often more efficient to use.

However, if a more feature-rich application is needed to get the job done, it may be in your best interest to shell out the money and take the time to learn the software.

How do you know what applications and features you need?

Knowing what you want to accomplish

Generally, the smaller and the less complex a website is, the more likely it is you can get away with simpler tools.

If you are developing a five-page site with a handful of images, you can probably use a simpler text and image editor and not notice the difference. But, if you are creating a website complete with a database and hundreds of pages and images, then you'll come to appreciate a good MySQL client and the batch-imaging capabilities of Photoshop.

In short, to know what tools you need, you need to know what the end product of your project is going to look like and what you need to do to realize that end.

You also need to have a good understanding of your own skill set: Someone who is comfortable with hand coding might want a different kind of software than someone who prefers WYSIWYG editing. Someone completely fluent with programming may not need a GUI MySQL client, whereas the rest of us do.

Knowing what tools a particular project needs and understanding the extent of your own skills takes experience. In the meantime, begin by acquiring and learning some basic web-development tools and work from there.

Knowing your tools

You waste a lot of money on Adobe Photoshop if all you know how to do with it is resize and crop. Photoshop has a wealth of professional features, but to use them you need to learn how.

This goes for all of the tools we talk about here. It is all well and good to have the most powerful, sophisticated web-development software, but it does you little good if you don't fully understand how to use it. Knowing your text editor's keyboard shortcuts, how to work with your image editor's layers and masks, and how to debug JavaScript with your web-developer toolbar makes you a more efficient and capable developer. But it also requires you to take the time to learn the software.

Check out the plethora of software tutorials on the Web about the tools at your disposal. Read the manuals. Buy a book on the subject. Most importantly, dive in and use the software. Learning the ins and outs of your application may initially take some time and effort, but the time and effort it saves down the line makes it worth it.

Text editors

A good text editor makes the job easier on the coder. It makes project files easy to manage and code easier to read with code highlighting and indenting, it automates common tasks like auto completing your markup, and makes site changes easy to keep track of and implement. These features are why most coders wouldn't think of using TextEdit to get their work done, and why many are comfortable to using hard-earned money for a text editor that makes their life easier.

Graphics editors

Images play an important role in enhancing your text. From logos for branding to custom icon bullet points, graphics help put the sizzle in web page designs.

You will need a graphics editor that can not only handle the creation of graphics, but also export your images to proper web-friendly formats like GIF, JPEG, and PNG.

FTP clients

After you've created your web masterpiece, you need a way to get it onto the Web. You'll need an FTP client. **FTP** (which stands for **File Transfer Protocol**) does one thing: moves your local files to and from an online server (presumably your web host).

How quickly and reliably it performs this task, and how easy it makes it for you to update and synchronise your files, depends on the FTP client.

Databases

Professional web developers at some point find themselves mucking about with MySQL, the most popular database management system for simple projects. MySQL is most commonly used in conjunction with PHP to create database-driven websites. And, unless you want to interact with MySQL via command-line, you'll need to befriend a GUI client in order to manage your database properly.

Validators

No matter how sophisticated your text editor or web-authoring software is, you're going to make mistakes. And when you do, you need to be equipped with the right tools to make finding and correcting these mistakes easier.

Troubleshooting tools

Getting your web pages to look and behave as they should is not usually as easy as getting them to validate as proper HTML and CSS. Even valid documents may not render as you had hoped, and need further tweaking. Additionally, you may need to debug any JavaScript that is included within, or linked to, your HTML document.

Fortunately, there is a variety of powerful and free tools that help to tweak and troubleshoot web pages. Note that there are comparable tools within some web-authoring applications.

However, if you don't have these applications, or you'd like to use some of these tools within your browser, there are great options for any of the popular browsers.

Managing your work

When working on a complex website, it can become tricky to keep track of your project. You make changes to a set of files, then upload those changed files to your server, while keeping an old version of your site files handy in case the changes don't go over well.

Or, even stickier, you have more than one person working on a website: keeping track of who made what changes when can be a nightmare.

Versioning software

That's when versioning software comes in handy. While version control systems like CVS, Subversion, or Git are often used when a team of coders is working on software, they're also useful in web development.

Versioning systems keep track of changes, store previous versions of a project, and sync the "repository" copy of a project with your local (working copy) files.

Versioning allows collaborators to make changes to website files, test those changes in a safe environment, and then commit all of those changes at once to your server. If things don't work out as expected, you can revert to a previous version of the site. You can see who made changes to a project, and keep and view a detailed log of why those changes were made.

If you start working on large and complex web projects, or you have a whole team of developers working on a site, then versioning software is invaluable.

Tool links and reviews at the book site

We could go on and on about the specific tools and, in fact, we did.

You'll find links to software and detailed reviews of a variety of tools on the companion website, http://interactwithwebstandards.com.

Miami, Florida
USA

Starting with teaching herself HTML in 1996, Denise R. Jacobs has worked with the Web in a range of capacities, from localization project management to instructing web design/development. At present, Denise is a Web Solutions Consultant in Miami, Florida, helping businesses transform their web presence. In addition to writing about the Web, she develops curricula for The Web Standards Project (WaSP) Education Task Force and is an organizing member of Social Media Club South Florida.

http://www.denisejacobs.com
http://www.cssdetectiveguide.com
http://www.papilloneffect.com
http://twitter.com/denisejacobs

CHAPTER 3
Learning on the Web

by Denise Jacobs

Just because you use a tool every day doesn't necessarily mean that you are using it well—especially if you've never learned what using it well means. This is certainly true with computers, as there are countless people who use computers daily but only to the degree of their limited knowledge. The same can be said for the Web, as many—even the generations who became familiar with computers before they were familiar with books—probably don't use the Web and the vast numbers of useful tools contained therein to their fullest extent.

This chapter aims to provide a guide to using the Web better in order to more efficiently find the answers to your own questions, locate new sources of information and retain said new information. Further, we will look at good reasons and venues for getting help, knowing how to participate online, making and maintaining connections, organizing the information found, organizing yourself and expanding your learning through working with others.

About learning

My guess is that if you have started down the path to becoming a web professional, then you are no stranger to learning. However, there is taking in information, and then there is *learning*. What's the difference? I see learning as an enjoyable process, where you actively seek the information that you need, find great sources, and easily incorporate the new knowledge into your current reserve of information, where it has staying power. Unfortunately, so much of what is passed off as learning—such as cramming information that doesn't interest us into our heads to be able to pass a test or engaging in academic activities that don't truly interest us and make us want to acquire more knowledge—doesn't fit that profile.

In my opinion, real learning is pleasurable, and at the core of true learning is following and feeding your natural curiosity and being hungry for more. Being passionate and deeply interested in the subjects where you increase your knowledge will not only give you the capacity to learn more about them, but to have a great time while doing so.

Know your learning style

Knowing how you learn best ensures that you will be able to retain and easily access whatever information you attain—while also enjoying the process. Embarking on an endeavor such as acquiring new skills for a new profession or hobby takes initiative, and is made a lot easier if you know how gather the information for yourself so that you can best absorb it.

Let's take a look at the most basic learning styles, and see which one(s) sounds most like you.

Visual and written learners

Do you find yourself wanting to sit at the very front of the room so you don't miss anything? Do you get a lot from printed text, diagrams, and handouts? Do you tend to think in pictures? Congratulations, you are a visual learner.

Chances are that you remember what things look like and potentially where they are located on the page. You probably also like to take detailed notes, make annotations and write your ideas out to clarify them.

So how do you make this learning style work for you? Here are some suggestions:

- Visualize information that you hear into representative pictures or text.
- Sketch out your ideas as pictures or diagrams.
- Take copious notes and use color to highlight points.
- Read and study in a place with no sound distractions.

Auditory learners

Do you remember what has been said to you, often verbatim? Are you less concerned with where you sit in a classroom, as long as you can hear what is being said? Do you process your thoughts by talking them through, and gain a lot of understanding from discussions? If that sounds like you, then you are an auditory learner.

You probably don't get as much from written text unless it's read to you, and probably love books on tape. You may also be musically inclined and have a good ear for tone, pitch, and key.

So how do you make this learning style work for you? Here are some suggestions:

- Take an active part in discussions and organize opportunities for talking about the subject.
- Record classes or get audio or video recordings of lectures.
- Read text aloud so that you can hear it.
- Express your ideas verbally and accentuate with stories and analogies.

Kinesthetic learners

Do you find it hard to sit still for very long? When in a classroom, are you wishing that everyone would stop reading and talking about subjects and actually *do* something? Do you get easily distracted by movement and gesture while you talk? These qualities mean that you are a kinesthetic learner who learns best through doing, movement and touch.

You may be prone to tapping a foot while sitting down and to being physically active. If someone shows you how to do something once, you have no problem repeating it, and then probably improving upon it.

So how do you make this learning style work best for you?

- Skim through readings once before reading them again in detail.
- Read or study standing up, while doing something physical (like on an exercise machine), or while chewing gum.
- Do something with your hands while learning (like sculpt something, fold paper, etc.).
- Take study breaks where you move around.

Once you know how you learn best, you will have a better idea of the types of sources that you will get the most value out of when looking for information on the Web. However, your learning style is not the only thing that determines how well you take in information. Our brains are naturally wired to learn better when we are engaged, relaxed, when more of our senses are stimulated, and when we follow our natural urge to explore.

Finding the answer

So, now you have something that you want to know more about and you are on the quest for knowledge. Let's take a look at some of the ways you can more easily find the information that you seek.

Effective web searching

I'm sure you have used Google thousands of times at this point, but are you getting the results that you want quickly? Here are some tips on how to effectively search the Web for the answers you seek.

Types of searches

The most common searches use keywords and phrases. However, you can get even more specific results by incorporating search operators or even targeting specific sites. Let's take a look at each of these.

Keywords, keywords, keywords

Keywords are the cornerstone of web searching. Making sure that you devise the best combination of them can make a huge difference, like the difference between trying to hit a target with buckshot or with a laser.

In order to achieve more laser-like precision with your keywords, here are some tips from Google itself:

- Every word matters, so it is best to keep it simple.
- Use the words that will probably be used on the pages you seek.
- Use descriptive words, and as few as possible.

Phrases

Sometimes you are looking for a group of words together. To limit your search results, it is helpful to create a phrase (also known as a string) of the words you are looking for. A phrase is a series of word enclosed in quotes, and the search engine will generate results of the phrase with the words in the exact order given. For example, if you are looking specifically for pages with the phrase *web design resources*, then your search phrase would be "web design resources," and the results would be pages with only that full phrase in the content.

Hello? Operator?

To further limit your search results, it also helps to use operators that will give your search certain helpful parameters.

- Terms exactly the way you state them: +. Use the plus (+) sign directly in front of a word when you want that exact term to be used as the search parameter and not that word plus synonyms. Example: `+css ie hacks`.
- Exclude terms: –. Use the minus sign (–) to exclude some terms from the search results. Example: `web conference -california`.
- Wildcard/Fill in the blank: *. Use an asterisk (*) to find your term plus any other term that is associated with it. Example: `illustrator tutorial *`.
- Either one term or the other: OR. Using OR is for finding results for one of your terms or the other one. Example: `web design OR webdesign`.

CHAPTER 3

Site-specific

Do you already know the site that the content is on, but just don't know how to find it? Then you can specify this in your search parameters as well, by putting the search terms and then specifying `site:` in front of the name of the site you want to limit your search to. For example, to find articles with the words *design trends* on smashingmagazine.com, you would enter: `design trends site:smashingmagazine.com` as your search phrase.

Culling through your results

Once you generate some promising links, here are some recommendations for choosing which ones to follow:

1. **Read the short description:** This will be text taken directly from the page, and will give you an idea whether the content will be relevant.

2. **Check the URL of the page:** Looking at the page URL before you even see the page will give you a lot of information about the source website. You can do a cursory glance to see if it is from a recognizable or authoritative-sounding source, and save yourself from going to a site that doesn't provide the information you seek.

3. **Check the "cached" version of the page:** The description looks good, the URL seems legitimate, but you want to cut to the chase. With the cached page, you can easily scan for your keywords, which will be highlighted in different colors. It is a great way to find out quickly if the page is worth reading in earnest.

OK, so you have decided to follow a link and you are on the page. Here are some ways to check that the content will be valuable to you:

1. **Check the author and her or his credentials:** If the article has a section about the author, read it and see if his or her background lends them authority. If the site is by a single author, read the about page if there is one for the same reason.

2. **Check the date of the content:** Sometimes you go to an article that looks great, but then you find that it was written ten years ago. Sometimes information is ageless, but when you are looking to have the most current, you may want to dismiss older sources. Beware of content that has no date at all, for you have no idea of how relevant or current it is.

3. **Don't be shallow:** While it is important to check the date of the content, don't completely dismiss pages that may be poorly designed, don't have the latest graphics, or lack the most current look-and-feel. The content may still be relevant and well worth reading.

Types of sources

The type of source that will be the best for you will depend on what information you are looking for and, again, how you best assimilate information. Almost everything on the Web counts as a legitimate information source as long as you document its origin: articles, pdfs, slideshows, videos, podcasts and images. So, if you are visual learner, articles will be fine for you, whereas if you are more auditory, then a podcast or recorded book might be better. If you are more kinesthetic, then watching a video or a screencast tutorial might be the best way for you to absorb the information.

Tip: http://Easybib.com is a great online tool for citing sources.

Taking notes

All of the resources in the world won't do you much good if you don't make a note of what parts of them are actually useful for you. In the time-honored spirit of learning, taking notes is critical to being able to access and utilize all of the information that you gather. Let's take a look at some the ways you can organize and save important pieces of information for future use.

Saving to "the cloud"

I'm sure you have heard the term **the cloud** when it comes to the Web. In this instance I am using *the cloud* to refer to information stored on web servers (not your computer's hard drive) and accessed through web browsers and various devices, making it virtually infinitely scalable (**Figure 3.1**).

Saving to the cloud is very powerful as it frees you from being tied to a single machine to access your content, whatever it may be. Any

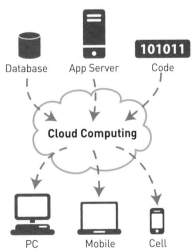

Figure 3.1: All of the components of "the cloud." Courtesy of Boston Interactive at http://www.bostoninteractive.com.

device that can access the Internet can give you access to the information that you have saved and, correspondingly, the ability to alter and add to that information. You can see how powerful that can be for managing and annotating your information.

Blogs

A blog is a great way to take notes, to save references to further resources, categorize the information and have it all accessible to you no matter where you are, and can be device-independent as well. Because blogs are so easy to set up and have so many features that help you organize your posts, they are a natural option for note-taking and saving information in a reliable location that is not the hard drive of your computer.

Wordpress, Blogger and TypePad are all great, free online blogging platforms.

Tip: http://www.scribefire.com/ is a great Firefox plug-in that enables you to make quick updates to your blog without having to log in.

Bookmarking sites

Bookmarking sites is a great way to access and manage your bookmarks without being tied to your computer. Some even have browser extensions that allow you to save to the bookmarking site at the same time you save to your browser's bookmarks on your computer.

Many of the sites that manage bookmarking are in fact social bookmarking sites intended to build community and common interests around bookmarked pages. With the rise of microblogging sites that also have a social bookmarking component like Twitter and Facebook, this feature of these sites is dropping in popularity. However, they are still great for what they do best: saving and tagging bookmarks for later use. With many of these sites, you can also set up a feed that will post your saved bookmarks to your other social media accounts.

The top bookmarking sites are http://Delicious.com and http://Gnolia.com (formerly Ma.gnolia).

Online notebooks

In addition to blogging to save your notes, you could also use an online notebook. Online notebooks work much the way sticky notes and scraps of paper work in the physical world: you can save and organize snippets of information of whatever length for later use. However, with online notebooks, you can save notes in multiple formats: text, screenshots, snippets of web pages and even photos from your cell phone. Once your notes are in the app, you can search for them by keywords, titles, and tags. How cool is that?

Some of the most popular online notebooks with the technorati are Evernote (which has the advantage of having web, desktop and mobile phone apps that can all be synced), Google Notebook, `http://google.com/notebook` (however, Google has ceased its development of the Notebook code), and Zoho, `http://notebook.zoho.com`.

You can often connect these tools to other online apps to import the information. For example, Evernote, `http://evernote.com`, can import bookmarked pages from Delicious.

Analog notes—the old-fashioned way

There are countless resources for taking notes, so I don't think it is necessary to rehash them here. What I do want to talk about is ways of capturing your thoughts so that they are easily accessible and usable for you in the future.

Hand-written notes

There is a vast variety of items to write your ideas in and on. The trick is in finding the one that fits you. While many designers are devotees of Moleskine notebooks, some folks like artist sketchbooks, some like lined notebook paper and others like graph paper. If you are eco-conscious, you could repurpose the blank backs of photocopied paper and use them for notes.

Organizing information is also a question of personal style. Notes usually comprise one or all of these techniques mixed together: outlining, using keywords and shorthand, capturing the main concepts, highlighting and underlining the key ideas. Mind-mapping—a visual and conceptual method of collecting ones thoughts—marries images and words to convey rich meaning and immediate impact (**Figure 3.2**):

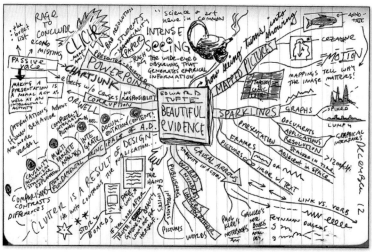

Figure 3.2: A great example of mind-mapping from Austin Kleon at http://www.AustinKleon.com

Another version of taking notes with strong visual impact is to do so with both words and pictures, also called "note-sketching" (**Figure 3.3**).

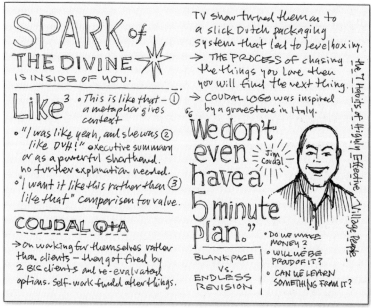

Figure 3.3: Mike Rohde of http://www.Rohdesign.com *creates clear and inspiring sketch notes.*

You don't have to put a lot of time and effort into your notes to make them beautiful—that's not the point. The goal is to accurately put down and mentally catalogue the information that you want to absorb in a format that will enable you to easily access it again when you need it.

Text documents

Maybe you would rather have your notes in electronic text form and want to have a copy on your hard drive as well. There is no shame in using a simple text editor, Word, or any other word processing application to save and manage your notes. If you want to be sure you can access them later from the Web, you can save them on Google docs (or any other document saving repository) for later use.

Staying up to date

Resources and information on the Web are generated in dizzying quantities that increase exponentially every moment. How can you stay up to date with all the new, relevant information being produced? Keep this in mind: you can't keep up with everything—it just isn't possible or necessary. To manage the amount of information you take in, choose the 3-5 most important areas and then only take in information related to those, at least for a while. RSS feeds, podcasts and email subscriptions are all great tools to enable you to keep up with information from your favorite sites.

RSS feeds

As you may be well aware, RSS stands for Really Simple Syndication, and is one of the best tools for keeping track of the new articles being posted on your favorite websites and blogs. While a lot of people know what RSS is, they don't capitalize upon its usefulness as a way to keep up with information.

If you already have a Google account, then the Google Reader is a natural option for you as your RSS feed reader. If you are not married to Google, then some alternatives are http://Bloglines.com and the Live Bookmarks Firefox extension.

Podcasts

If you are an auditory learner, then podcasts are the ideal means for you to get new information and to have it really stick with you. There are several ways to access podcasts, which are actually RSS-based. The most common way is to get them through iTunes. You can also access podcasts through podcast clients like gPodder, http://gpodder.org/.

There are podcasts on every subject. If you are a kinesthetic learner, then podcasts are great because you can listen to them while engaging in an activity like exercising at the gym.

Email subscriptions

Most websites have an area where you can submit your email address to get on their list to receive newsletters and updates via email. If you are more email-oriented and don't feel glutted by your current email load, this may be a good method for you, as the updates will be delivered right into your inbox.

One issue with email subscriptions is that they are less reliable than RSS notification, as they rely upon the author of the site to take the initiative to put together and send out the newsletter. Another issue is the opposite: sometimes a website author is way too prolific, and your email updates end up feeling instead like a constant barrage of spammy marketing.

Staying on task

Learning new skills is not just about acquiring information, but also about putting it to use. As your knowledge grows, several things happen: while you start to gain mastery over some subjects, you also see the areas in which you need to gain further material and know-how. How do you keep track of the moving parts of everything that you have on your "To Do" list to learn in order to advance to the next steps?

Have no fear. Instituting a system of prioritizing and ways of managing your tasks can greatly facilitate the process.

Productivity systems

Most of us can manage to accomplish tasks fairly successfully. However, you may have fallen prey to times when old habits of procrastination or paralysis from not knowing the next step prevented you from reaching your ultimate goals. When you have a lot that you are working towards achieving either within a given period of time or long-term, putting a productivity system in place (that you actually practice) will help you to reach your goals.

It may surprise you, but productivity is a skill—a mix of approaches and habits for dealing with time, attention and tasks. Like any skill, productivity needs to be learned, developed and honed in order to be performed well.

Productivity systems are useful as a way to learn and instill new habits and break old tendencies that thwart productivity. There are many productivity systems out there, but some of the ones that people in the web community swear by are as follows:

- Getting Things Done (usually referred to in the abbreviated form GTD)
  http://en.wikipedia.org/wiki/Getting_Things_Done

- 43Folders
  http://www.43folders.com/

- Zen to Done, a simplified version of GTD
  http://zenhabits.net/2007/04/zen-to-done-ztd-the-ultimate-simple-productivity-system/

In the absence of a set productivity system, here are some tips for increasing your productivity:

- Know your working habits.

- Know your natural cycles.

- Understand the basics of how most productivity systems work and make an effort to incorporate some of those habits into your life.

- Most of the systems have a process that resembles these steps: Dump everything in your head, organize your ideas, break ideas down into actions with action verbs, prioritize actions, make realistic lists of the actions, executive the lists but stay flexible to the unexpected.

- Aim for simplicity.

CHAPTER 3

Task managers and calendars

Once you have decided on your system, you need a way to keep track of your tasks. Much like the option of saving any notes you take to the cloud or staying with writing them down on paper, you have the option of using an online task manager or keeping track of them in a written format.

http://Mashable.com has an excellent (if not a little overwhelming) list of some of the best task managers available online to help you get things done. The link is listed in the Chapter 3 Recommended readings at http://interactwithwebstandards.com. Some popular applications include Things (Mac only), Google Tasks, and Remember the Milk, but there are many, many others that you may find more useful.

Where the first part of productivity is about learning new habits to be better able to manage your tasks, another part is about better managing your time. You can best get a handle on accurately controlling the slots of time in your days with a good calendar. Google Calendar is one of the best, and most easily accessible options. You can even customize it and share with others. As with everything, some people—even web folk—prefer a printed calendar or days and times written in their notebooks as their low-tech calendar.

Finding the answers from other people

It is easy to feel that you are an island, working away towards your goal of becoming a web professional or at least gaining a certain level of proficiency. But of course, you are not alone; you are virtually a click away from untold numbers of people. This is where your learning moves from solo to being community-based.

Crowd-sourcing

Web searches aren't the only way to find information. Crowd-sourcing is a research method that has gained popularity due to its speed and effectiveness. Crowd-sourcing is harnessing the knowledge of a large community of people to generate ideas, problem-solve and create solutions.

The rise of crowd-sourcing has been concurrent with the boom of social media. Indeed, there is practically no better way to access untold numbers of people who share similar interests. The main channels of crowd-sourcing are anyplace there is a critical mass of people reading the information and able to interact with you, such as through social media channels like Twitter and Facebook, blogs, forums, wikis, and mailing lists.

How do you do it? Start by simply asking for answers, resources, opinions, or the sharing of experience. You can provide incentives, but usually people will respond without them. If you've ever asked a question on Twitter and received a number of responses within minutes or have written a blog post with a question and had it answered, then you have experienced crowd-sourcing.

When crowd-sourcing remember this: the answer is only as good as the source. The more people who respond to your request, the better, because then, either you will be able to sift through the responses to find those that are the most appropriate for the situation, or the crowd will vet the responses and give you the best solution.

CHAPTER 3

Providing answers

Being active on the Web is not just about what information you can glean from it and get from other people. In order to be a healthy part of the web ecosystem, it is important to attempt to replenish the Web with as much assistance and resources as you have taken.

Be a good online citizen

There is such a thing as web "karma"—what you say and do (or don't do) can have much farther-reaching ramifications than you know, and will mostly likely come back to you in some way, shape or form. Therefore, it is a good idea to remember several key points about being an active citizen on the Web:

- What happens on the Web, stays on the Web—indefinitely (or a close approximation thereof). Comments that you make on a blog, forum, wiki, and now, Twitter, Facebook and other social network sites are public, searchable and archived.

- Despite what seems to be the incredible vastness of the Web, much like the person-to-person world, once you start frequenting certain places based on common interests, it is in fact a very small world. Thus, you can't truly be anonymous. In certain communities, people know each other, and once you join in and make yourself visible, they will start to know you too. Hopefully, you will endeavor to be seen in a positive light.

- Also similar to the offline world, on the Web you have a visible identity that is based upon your words and actions, and increasingly, your web identity even supplants your in-person identity, as the Web may be someone's first introduction to you—without you even knowing. This is important to be aware of before you start making off-color or negative comments on a blog or website (if not done anonymously). Any of these could easily come up in a search for your name.

Resource // Building and managing your web identity

I'm sure you have gotten the message by now: you have a web identity and it grows and expands with your activity on the Web. To start the process of building your "brand," it is helpful to have an idea of what you want to be known for and then to start making contributions that support it.

For example, if you want to be known for your Illustrator expertise, then many of your blog posts should be about Illustrator tips and techniques, your social media posts can offer Illustrator resources, you can write Illustrator tutorials for websites, and participate on forums and lists about design and creating vectors.

Use good web etiquette

Anytime you deal with people, there are always going to be some guidelines for how the interaction should go, and on the Web it is no different. What are some of the hallmarks of playing well with others on the Web? Here are some good pieces of netiquette advice to keep in mind:

- Spend some time observing before you jump in.

- When you do offer something, know what you are talking about and make sense when talking about it.

- Share your knowledge and expertise openly.

- Link to supplemental information.

- Give credit to the sources of your information—ideas, stories, images.

- Leave insightful and helpful comments, and read over your wording to make sure the message is clear.

> **Tip:** When making comments, especially ones that are less than favorable, while telling the truth, be sure to temper the tone of your message. Being rude or unnecessarily harsh doesn't do anyone any good—and it ends up reflecting poorly on you. Think of how you would feel if that same comment was made to you.

- Limit gratuitous self-promotion and ceaseless self-chatter. People are overwhelmed by information and don't care about what you are doing every second of the day.

- Be forgiving of others' mistakes.

Give back

Now that you have some of the rules of the road for behaving well online, it's time to infuse the Web with your own contributions. Let's look at some of the ways you can do so.

Through blog comments

Adding a comment to a blog post is a great way to do several things simultaneously: to give back by providing additional information and resources, to increase your visibility and people's awareness of who you are and what you know, and finally to direct people to your own website and potentially having the opportunity of both giving back and growing your online persona. While "me too" comments are harmless, they won't really advance your reputation as much as a thoughtful, information-rich response would. Instead, practice good netiquette and observe before you jump in by reading the other comments, share your information and make sense while doing it, and finally, offer relevant information and link to it.

Through forums and lists

Differently from blog posts, on forums and lists people are actively asking for answers and sharing resources. Similar to blog posts, these venues are both great opportunities for you to solve problems, offer solutions, and share your expertise, knowledge and resources—and positively build your reputation while doing so.

CHAPTER 3

Through social media

You probably already have a number of social media accounts such as Twitter and Facebook, but how many of your messages have to do with providing content that will be helpful for other people?

One of the biggest recommendations that social media professionals give to those starting out is to "lend value." What does that mean? That means that while posts about your cats may be amusing for some of your followers, for most of your followers they are just more pieces of the unending useless chatter that constitutes their social media stream. In order for your stream to be valued, provide posts that are informative and useful for your followers. Resources, tips and links to articles are all great ways to lend value.

Through your own blog or website

Through your own website, you can control one hundred percent of what information you present to the world, follow your inspirations to create content, and share your expertise as it grows.

Collaborating

Opportunities for learning and growing your skills increase dramatically when you work with other people. Working in a collaborative environment with an active exchange of ideas has been shown to enhance critical thinking and promote higher levels of performance and better retention of information. In addition, working with other people can be great fun and create an environment in which you can explore and develop your learning, work and communication styles.

Learning and inspiration

Ironically, some of the most important learning that you will do won't be from actively pursuing knowledge, but rather from the downtime in-between reading, studying and practicing new skills. As mentioned before, the mind takes in information best when it is relaxed. Given that, it is really important to schedule breaks for yourself and have moments where it may not look like you are doing much on the exterior.

This is the time when your brain is busy making connections between all of the things you have recently assimilated, and starts firing new flashes of insight for future ideas.

Your mind also takes in information best when you are inspired, so make it a regular practice to seek inspiration. Be open and aware of all of the sources of inspiration around you, whether it is visual design, music, food, topics of conversation, comedy routines, movies, fabrics, or other people. Inspiration can come at any time and in any form, so the best thing is to be ready to capture it when it shows up.

Another, more structured method of generating inspiration is to create a "swipe" file. Swipe files have been used in the copywriting industry for years, where the practice is to save clever pieces of copy, great headlines and powerful phrases to use later as sources of ideas. You can do the same, but of course, you aren't limited to copy—anything that you can save that captures and stimulates your imagination is worthy of going into your swipe file.

One of the online note-taking programs would be a perfect tool for storing your swipe file: screenshots, pictures, pieces of text, scanned sketches, etc. Later on, when you base a design on an item from your swipe file, you will probably be very happy that you saved all of those items that inspired you at one time.

Summary

Much like anything, learning effectively on the Web requires a skill set that goes beyond constructing a solid keyword search in Google (although that is a great start). Knowing your learning style lays the foundation for not only the types of information that you should seek out, but also for how you capture and record it for future use.

There are myriad wonderful online tools for note-taking, bookmarking, keeping up with information and organizing tasks and time. Which you choose depends on how well they fit the way you think and your work style.

CHAPTER 3

Being on the Web is about being part of a larger community that stretches throughout the world. Take advantage of the huge resource that is the people on the Web by connecting with them as your peers, mentors, and reflections of your future self. However, remember as well to give something of yourself—be it advice, techniques, or a website of your own.

Finally, actively feed your brain with inspiration away from the Web. Give yourself the opportunity to take magical pieces of the world around you and weave them into your own unique vision.

Resource // Recommended readings

The following recommended readings for this chapter can be found at http://interactwithwebstandards.com.

- 25 Free Online Resources and Web Apps for Lifelong Learners
  http://www.missiontolearn.com/2009/06/lifelong-learner-free-resources/
- GoogleGuide's Advanced Search Operators
  http://www.googleguide.com/advanced_operators.html
- Netiquette Home Page
  http://www.albion.com/netiquette/
- What happens on the Internet, stays on the Internet. Forever.
  http://www.isound.com/artist_blog/what_happens_on_the_internet_stays_on_the_int

Online Notebooks

- 17 Noteworthy Alternatives to Google Notebook
  http://mashable.com/2009/01/25/notetaking-alternatives/
- Comparison of notetaking software
  http://en.wikipedia.org/wiki/Comparison_of_notetaking_software
- Instapaper: A simple tool to save web pages for reading later
  http://www.instapaper.com/
- VizThink: visual thinkers practicing visual communication
  http://vizthink.com/

(continues)

Resource // Recommended readings

(continued)

Getting Things Done and Task Managers

- GTD Toolbox: 100+ Resources for Getting Things Done
  http://mashable.com/2009/01/29/getting-things-done/

- To-Do Lists: 12 Online Tools for Organizing Your Tasks
  http://www.sitepoint.com/blogs/2009/08/06/online-to-do-list-tools/

- 15 Free Tools for Web-based Collaboration
  http://sixrevisions.com/tools/15-free-tools-for-web-based-collaboration/

- Inspiration on Demand: Create a Swipe File
  http://writetodone.com/2008/11/17/inspiration-on-demand-create-a-swipe-file/

CHAPTER 3

Trollhättan, Sweden

Lars Gunther is a web developer, computer science teacher and pastor who lives in Trollhättan, Sweden. He is the lead editor of several courses for WaSP InterACT and invited expert to develop web technology related courses for Skolverket, the national agency for education in Sweden. When relaxing from theology or teaching, he usually likes to read about history. He is married to Penilla and is bonus dad to two young adults, Alexander and Oliver.

http://keryx.se/
http://twitter.com/itpastorn/
http://itpastorn.blogspot.com/

CHAPTER 4
Internet Fundamentals

by Lars Gunther

When you develop for the Web it is imperative to know a bit about its history and how it works. Too many designers still think that web design is exactly like print design or that the Web is only viewed on a desktop or laptop computer. This chapter will provide some historical context and an educated guess about the near future of the Web and the technology it is built on. (What is this thing called the Internet anyway?)

It will also look at the terminology about web servers, web services, and the devices we use to participate. But the Web is more than technology. It is shaping our society, culture and daily lives. Indeed, it is already interwoven into our lives in more ways than we might realize. We must take a good look at the sociological and ethical challenges we face as developers, as well as the possibilities.

A short history of computers, user interfaces, and computer communications

The first computers were large, heavy and really expensive. Back in the 1950s and '60s, and even into the late '70s, people had a hard time imagining that computers small enough to fit on a desk—or in a pocket—one day would be the dominant type. Not to mention the idea that all these computers would be connected in a network aptly described as a World Wide Web. So how did we get here, where are we and where might we be heading?

Mark Weiser, chief computer scientist at the famous computer lab Xerox PARC from 1988 to 1999, has described three eras of computing:

1. The one computer to many users era (1:n).
2. The one computer per user era (1:1).
3. The **ubiquitous computing** era, where there are many computers for each user (n:1).

This is not simply a math exercise. What Weiser told us is that we would be surrounded by computers everywhere, but since they would be intuitive and invisible, we would not think of them as "computers." Our computing experience would be seamless and transparent.

From the '40s to the '70s computers were "big iron," and only a small fraction of the population actually used them. Those who did use them sat in front of "dumb" **terminals** in a setup where hundreds or even a few thousand users would share a single **CPU** (central processing unit).

The development of the **integrated circuit** made it possible to fit a whole CPU on a single chip. These computers had **command line interfaces** (CLI), paired with the **text user interface** (TUI). The DOS-prompt in Windows, and terminals in Linux and Mac OS X are examples of CLI. Such interfaces are often used by "power users." Meanwhile, the idea developed at Xerox PARC that a user interface should be graphic and involve the use of windows, icons, menus and a pointer (WIMP). Apple made that idea mainstream with the Macintosh computer. **Graphical**

user interfaces (GUI) are now the norm and are user friendly enough to make the *desktop* or *laptop* computer something most people dare to use.

The dawning of the age of ubiquitous computing is happening right now as *mobile phones* have gotten "smart." It is not unreasonable to expect that in a few years' time more people will surf the Web from their phone than from their PC. Smart phones are a first step towards an always-connected experience. Computers are also more and more *embedded* into all sorts of devices.

"Now I sit in front of the computer and now I don't" is probably not the way to think in the future. Everything and everywhere there will be computers to interact with. It's just that we will not see them as "computers." They will perhaps not even be seen as gadgets. They will be walls, they will be furniture, they will be bandages, they will be the glasses you wear or even implants in your body.

> **Tip:** "The most profound technologies are those that disappear. They weave themselves into the fabric of everyday life until they are indistinguishable from it." (Quote from Mark Weiser's seminal work, "The Computer for the 21st Century," which is available at (http://www.ubiq.com/hypertext/weiser/ SciAmDraft3.html).

It's a safe bet that the Web will be the main facilitator, making all these computers work together to provide one seamless user experience. Another way of looking at this is to describe the Web as going through three stages, where aspects are added to the previous ones:

- The web of computers, where machines connect to each other.
- The web of people, where we humans connect to each other. This is the phase we are exploring right now.
- The web of machines, where everything will be connected and every bit of computerized information will be on the Web in some form.

It is for this kind of environment that the web developer of the future must be prepared. And the best way to be prepared is to get the foundations right!

CHAPTER 4

Internet core technology

UUCP and Usenet were invented 1979. Fidonet started in 1984. Perhaps in the 80s, before we had the technologies we use today, Unix users at many universities connected using **Unix-to-Unix-copy** (UUCP). Discussions could take place in **Usenet** groups, also called **newsgroups**.

Users of personal computers in the late '70s found ways to connect to each other using modems and after a while the **bulletin board system** (BBS) was born. BBS's found ways to share information using the daily data exchange system **Fidonet**. Some BBSs, like CompuServe, America Online, or Prodigy, grew to have millions of users. (When MSN was started it originally was intended to be a BBS.) The model was still one of separate networks, though.

If a node on a network shall be able to contact another node, each must have an **address**, and they must have an agreed way to format data, send commands and control the transmissions. That is, they must adhere to **protocols**. A group of protocols that work together is called a **protocol stack**.

The U.S. military, government, and universities decided that they should develop a common protocol stack, now known as the **Internet Protocol Suite**, or sometimes the **TCP/IP stack**. Other solutions have gradually disappeared. Today virtually all networks use IP.

In universities where the fledgling Internet started to take off, the dominant **operating system** (OS) was Unix. It is therefore no surprise that when Tim Berners-Lee—the creator of the World Wide Web— started discussing an information exchange system using hyperlinks, the first implementations were done on Unix systems. (And the discussion took place on Usenet.)

Hyperlinks have been around since the '60s, when Ted Nelson and Douglas Engelbart invented them. However, the World Wide Web raised the usage of hypertext to a whole new dimension. The navigation was not only within a system, but also between systems. Today we call it **external links** and take it for granted, but in 1989 it was truly a revolution.

CHAPTER 4

Characters, character sets, and encodings

Character encoding is a problematic area in computer communication. Computers work in binary, ones and zeroes, but what exact sequence of ones and zeroes should represent an A (uppercase Latin alphabet A), a percentage sign, or a space? In the early days of the Web, characters were encoded in **US-ASCII**, which only uses 7 bits and thus has only 127 characters, 30 of which are unprintable control characters. This means that there was no space left for pesky nordic characters like åäö, German ü, French ô and absolutely no chance to put the myriad of characters for CJK-languages (Chinese, Japanese and Korean) in there.

> **Tip:** English-speaking people are often completely unaware of encoding problems, but they are noticeable from day one for everybody else.

One solution was to use the **ISO-8859** family of encodings. It will provide an encoding for all of the most common languages. Some of those encodings use one byte per character, some use more. ISO-8859-1, also called Latin-1, contains all alphabetic characters used in Western Europe. However, when Microsoft launched Windows it implemented its own version of ISO-8859-1, both extending and breaking its functionality. Because of Windows' dominant position, browsers adapted and made **Windows-1252** their default encoding. This de facto standard has become formalized in HTML5—the newest version of the primary language behind most web pages. Indeed even if you explicitly specify ISO-8859-1, browsers will—and shall according to HTML5—treat it as Win-1252.

As long as we are using an encoding for our websites that does not allow us to specify a character from any given language, some characters must be specified using **entities** instead (see Chapter 10, "HTML Intro"). This is not an optimal solution, and to fix this problem language experts have partnered with computer scientists to create **Unicode**. Unicode has identified and categorized almost every single glyph known to mankind, including the CJK languages, Thai, various Indian languages, cuneiform script, Klingon and the languages from *The Lord of the Rings*!

UTF-8 is an encoding that uses a variable number of bytes to represent one character, and that is able to encode the entire Unicode character set.

For any new project, one should use UTF-8. UTF-8 (like windows-1252) is ASCII-compatible. That means that the first 127 characters use exactly the same sequence of ones and zeroes.

UTF-8 is an **encoding** (or actually **character encoding scheme**). However, in HTML and HTTP it is called a **character set** (**charset**), which in Unicode has a different meaning. It is unfortunate that web technologies and Unicode do not share a common glossary, but that is a problem we have to live with.

Web technologies

The Web was (and is) made up of three core technologies:

1. **HTTP**, which is the protocol used for communication between clients (usually a web browser) and servers.

2. **HTML**, the language used to mark up contents of a page.

3. The **Universal Resource Locator (URL)**, the addresses of pages on the Web.

The meaning of URL has since been altered to mean **Uniform Resource Locator**, which in turn technically is a subset of **Uniform Resource Identifiers (URI)**.

The exact definitions of URL, URI, and URN is one of the great mysteries of computer science.

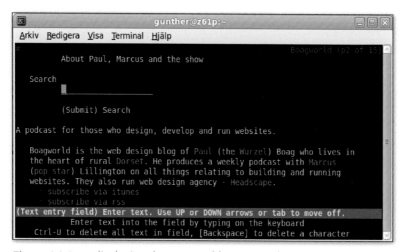

Figure 4:1: Lynx displaying the Boagworld site; note the TUI interface.

The earliest web browsers had text user interfaces. One of them, Lynx (**Figure 4.1**), is still around and can easily be installed on Unix, Linux, and even Mac computers. Ports to Windows are somewhat shaky.

Browsers and their wars

In 1993, one of the first GUI web browsers, NCSA Mosaic, was launched. It originally ran on the X Window System on Unix machines, but was ported to Windows and Mac OS as well. Mosaic was developed by a team led by Marc Andreessen.

Mosaic was the browser that started the web revolution. However, in 1994 Andreessen had joined a new company called Netscape. They launched a browser called Netscape Navigator in that same year. It soon became the most popular browser, even while still in beta, but also started a trend of pushing proprietary extensions to HTML. During the years 1995 to 1999 it was not uncommon to see badges on websites saying "Best viewed in Netscape Navigator."

Microsoft eventually won "the browser wars" of the late '90s. Using the power of pre-installing its browser, Internet Explorer, and, by version 5, also by arguably having the better product. Microsoft also pushed proprietary technologies to HTML and the browser. This made it very difficult to make web sites that worked for all browsers.

It was in this situation, in many ways both the realization of and a mockery of Tim Berners-Lee's vision of an open web, accessible to all, that The Web Standards Project arose, calling for vendors to adopt and authors to use standards. This battle cry was greatly helped when Netscape open sourced its browser. It was decided not to use the old code base, but do a rewrite from scratch and follow standards instead of vendor-specific deviations or additions—even if that meant not supporting Netscape's own stuff!

The rewrite took a long time, so long that Netscape did not survive. From its ashes rose the Mozilla Foundation, but it was not until the launch of Firefox in 2004 that the browser project turned into a success. Firefox pioneered extensions to the browser, many of which are built for developers (See examples on the book's companion website: http://interactwithwebstandards.com).

CHAPTER 4

Tip: Mozilla launched a browser called Phoenix in 2004. It has since changed names twice, first to Firebird and then to Firefox.

The breakthrough for standards-based web development also means that we today can build websites and have great confidence that they will work in all modern browsers, on all operating systems, and on all platforms. Other notable browsers not yet mentioned are Opera, Konqueror, Google Chrome and Apple Safari.

Internet and web architecture

A device on the Internet that shares, receives, or transmits data packets is called a **host**. Every host has an **IP address**. When packets are sent on the Internet they have a header that, among other things, tells what address is their destination and what address is their source. The latter is necessary to enable replies. Today we use the fourth edition of the Internet Protocol, **IPv4**, that uses four bytes for each address, for a grand total of about 4 billion addresses. As the Internet keeps expanding outside North America and Western Europe and as it is increasingly being accessed from mobile devices—and in the future by every conceivable device—we are going to need more. We are slowly seeing a transition to **IPv6**, which uses 16 bytes for addressing, equalling 2^{128} or 3.4×10^{27} possible addresses, more than there are grains of sand in the Sahara desert or molecules in your body.

IPv4 addresses are written using a **decimal** notation, e.g., 114.32.197.18. IPv6 addresses are written using a **hexadecimal** notation, e.g., 00C2:00 00:0000:0000:0123:ABCD:0011:F34B which in turn can be shortened by omitting leading zeros, to C2::123:ABCD:11:F34B.

The Domain Name System

IP addresses are hard to remember and are not very descriptive about the host. Therefore hosts also have names and the names are grouped by **domains**. To keep track of what domain maps to what IP address we have the **Domain Name System (DNS)**.

If you want a domain of your own, the first step is generally to check if it is available. You may use the tool called "whois" to perform such a check. If you think it's too nerdy to run the CLI version, there are many websites available that can provide this information.

The second step is to contact an appropriate **registrar** authorized to register the domain for you. They usually also provide DNS hosting services. All domains must have at least two **authoritative name servers** where the records are kept. Those name servers in turn are registered with the **top level domain (TLD)** name servers.

Every country has a TLD, e.g., Sweden has **se**, Norway has **no**, and Pitcairn has **pn**. In addition to these there are generic top level domains, like **com**, **org**, **net**, **edu**, and **museum**.

Resource // Domains

The official list of top-level domains is at `http://data.iana.org/TLD/tlds-alpha-by-domain.txt`

When a client, such as a web browser, accesses a host, it first queries the nearest **caching name server** for the host's IP address. Caching name servers only keep records for a short time, specified by the **Time To Live (TTL)** setting for a domain record, and must if the cache is stale (= too old) or there is no record in memory "run to daddy," i.e., query their nearest name server which might query yet another one, etc., until the query reaches the TLD server, which tells what name servers are authoritative and thus have persistent domain to IP mapping—unless something has gone horribly wrong!

CHAPTER 4

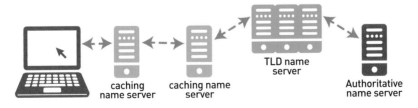

Figure 4.2: How DNS lookups work (`http://www.istockphoto.com/user_view.php?id=1997052`).

This system enables a domain owner to change his records without having to inform every single DNS server in the world about the change. However, it also means that it may take a while for changes to take effect, especially for popular sites since their records are cached everywhere.

The most important types of DNS records are:

- A: maps a host name to an IPv4 address.
- AAAA: maps a host name to an IPv6 address.
- MX (Mail eXchange): if mail should be handled by a specific server, it uses this type of record.
- CNAME: "Canonical name" is an alias, an alternative name for a domain.

Try it yourself!

Imagine yourself launching a site for a small company you know. Try to find a suitable domain for the site.

The IP protocol suite

Having established what IP address the other host has, a connection is set up. The connection is usually handled by the **Transmission Control Protocol (TCP)** or the **User Datagram Protocol (UDP)**. The former is more capable and ensures safe delivery, reassembly of all data packets in correct order (they do not always arrive exactly in the order they were sent out), and flow control. The latter is easier and better suited for things like real-time gaming, web radio and telephony—also called **Voice over IP (VoIP)**.

Actual requests and replies for web resources, such as pages, style sheets, scripts, fragments of data used with Ajax, images, sound clips, video, etc., are handled using the HTTP protocol.

Client/server and peer-to-peer

At the application layer there are two main ways of interacting between hosts. The most common, and the one used on the Web, is **client/server**, where one host serves content to the others. When traffic increases, the server might not be able to serve all requests. In fact a server can be made totally inaccessible if it is subject to a denial of service (DOS) attack, i.e., it is being overburdened with requests. A system where the sharing of data is evenly distributed across all hosts is called **peer-to-peer**. The main advantage of peer-to-peer is that capacity grows when more hosts participate, making them perfectly **scalable**. Examples of peer-to-peer applications are Bittorrent, most VoIP systems, including Skype, and the music service Spotify.

Internet access

A company that offers access to the Internet is called an **Internet Service Provider (ISP)**. A good connection offers high bandwidth and low latency. **Bandwidth** is the measure of how much data arrives per second, and it is measured in bits per second (bps). **Latency** is the time from when a request has been sent out until the first bit arrives. It is measured in milliseconds (hopefully).

The web server

In the early days of the Web it was easy to describe a web server. It mostly served files from their file systems to the clients.

Today much content is dynamically generated, i.e., it is being fetched from databases and other means of storage and assembled as it is being requested. But there is still a place for static files: CSS, JavaScript, images, animations, audio, and video are usually static. Static files are much faster to serve than dynamic content, which means that especially high traffic sites should strive to keep content that seldom changes static. Some sites even offload static content to special servers on separate sub-domains just to avoid speed bottlenecks.

Caching is another technology that speeds up static content. When a browser queries the server for a resource, it often explicitly asks if it has been modified since the last time it was accessed. If not, the server can just return a "not modified" **HTTP-header**, a "304." Dynamically generated content is not cached by default, and building a caching mechanism for such content is not an easy task!

Web services

Traditionally a full web page is loaded into the browser whenever the user has clicked a link, but today web pages are often partially updated with fresh content from the server. Small snippets of information are sent and the browser will put them into the existing page using JavaScript. This model of client/server interaction is called Ajax.

Today information is not only consumed by end users using browsers, but also by other servers. One server could, for example, provide sports results in real time and other sites could in turn fetch the data and display it on their pages. A simpler example is news readers fetching RSS or Atom feeds and showing an aggregated view of the stories.

Yet another example that one usually does not think of as using web technologies is calendar and contact sync between different devices.

All these are examples of **web services**, machine-to-machine interaction over the Web. A web service is defined by the fact that there is an **API (Application Program Interface)** available for client software to use. Such APIs also allow for sites to have dedicated clients on the desktop or on mobile phones. It is APIs that allow me to take an image in my smart phone and with the push of just a few buttons have it uploaded to Facebook, Flickr, or Evernote.

The web experience

So far the Web has been described mostly from a technical perspective. But we must also ask: What does this all mean for you and me, the users? How does the Web affect learning, working, socializing, living, and "ultimately dying" (who will take care of your online identity when you are gone?).

The original vision of the Web was one of community and sharing. The HTTP protocol was designed to facilitate a read/write web. For a few years, the writing aspect required so much technical proficiency that ordinary people rarely did anything but read. Except for contact forms (that all sites should have even today!) there was hardly any communication from the user to the site owner. Then we got guest books, which provided a way to say hi in general. Guest books did not imply commenting upon the subject matter of individual pages, nor did they imply discussion.

Guest books did however quickly attract spammers. Yes, they have been around since the very beginning of the Web, and there still is no 100 percent solution to this plague.

> **Tip: Spam**, by the way, is a form of canned ham, immortalized in a Monty Python sketch, from which the term was taken to describe this particular form of unwanted "advertising."

Taking a hint from the BBSs, Usenet forums also quickly appeared. Indeed, much forum software still has the letters BB in its name. Examples are phpBB, probably the most popular of all, bbPress, OvBB, PunBB, WBB. A forum basically is a place for discussions. A flowing conversation is called a thread. To a web designer or developer, forums are a gold mine. If you can't find the solution to your problem, you can ask in a forum like SitePoint's (http://www.sitepoint.com/forums/). Other places to ask questions are mailing lists and dedicated channels on Internet Relay Chat (IRC). (See the companion web site for suggested forums, lists and channels.)

Try it yourself!

Find five forums dedicated to web development. Investigate how lively the community is on each and whether you can get qualified and authoritative answers from it.

The democratic web

Putting up content on the Web got a lot easier when **content management systems (CMS)** appeared. The first beneficiaries were big organizations, media, and government. The Web soon made the **democratization** of information a reality, when small CMSs appeared, enabling people to have **blogs (web logs)**. Although much information on blogs is false, mundane, or even vicious, there are lots of examples of the opposite. Especially in the field of web design and development, there are lots of blogs worth following.

Today, more than ever, the Internet experience is shaped by the people who participate. However, the perceived anonymity and lack of social control can also bring out the worst in people.

 If you maintain a site—any kind of site—you must lead by example and enforce the values with which you wish to be associated.

One way in which blogs interact is through **linkbacks** (refbacks, trackbacks, and pingbacks). These are means of noticing when someone has referenced your blog post on a blog of their own. It's a handy feature built into many blogs, but it has a pitfall—spam.

Other solutions exist, like using dedicated blog search services, such as Technorati. These often use tagging mechanisms; you tag your posts with keywords and display a link to other blogs that use the same keyword. As soon as a blog is updated, these search services can be pinged and be updated in close to real time. If your blogging software does not include automatic pinging, there are many ping services that can be of help. These will also alert the most common blog aggregation sites, where your content will be available as well.

Blogging highlights a shift in how we use the Web. Running a blog is not only a matter of getting people to come to your own site, it is also a matter of getting your words out onto other sites. Today we are sharing our information as such, not "pages." Site owners better beware of one downside: if you are relying on a revenue model where you need people to visit your pages, you must give visitors something of value that they will not get through reading your content only via third party services.

Before we leave the subject of blogs, another important aspect should be noted. Blogs can serve as a form of citizen journalism that scrutinizes the media. Indeed, one of the battlegrounds of the Web is between traditional media struggling to come to terms with the democratization of information and blog authors seeing themselves as the opposition to the politically correct establishment. It should be noted that this is not the pattern everywhere. In Sweden, media and blogs mostly have found a way to live in symbiosis. An example of this is the leading local blog search service, Twingly, that allows newspapers to include links to blogs in their articles, driving traffic both ways.

Collective wisdom

Social bookmarking services, discussed in Chapter 3, "Learning on the Web", are an example of how users may help each other find good content. As pages are tagged, an information **folksonomy** (folk + taxonomy) gets created. Earlier collections of links on the Web, like the original Yahoo! directory in the '90s made by paid staff, or the Open Directory Project (DMOZ), by volunteers, used **ontologies** for the information; links were sorted in hierarchical structures, a less flexible way. Directories also have scale issues. As the Web grows in size and information speed, it is almost impossible for a staff to keep up, add, change, and delete the information.

Some sites take the concept of link recommendation a step further. Users may submit links, and staff will moderate their submissions and recommend them to others. This is the concept behind Fark (http://fark.com) and Slashdot (http://slashdot.org). These sites provide a forum-style comments section as well. Sites like Digg (http://digg.com) and Reddit (http://reddit.com) do not have a staff of moderators. Instead they rely on the community to "digg" or vote links up and down.

Social bookmarks and social news services rely the collective wisdom of the crowd to find and vet information. This can be considered a form of **crowdsourcing**. Using large crowds to produce quality information, or to carry out very large tasks, is another phenomenon of the social web. reCaptcha is another example of using the crowd to solve a big task. To the user it seems like a CAPTCHA, a way to keep spambots away from logging in or submitting a comment, but it is doing more. It will show two words from a book that has been scanned and put into text format by Optical Character Recognition (OCR). The first word is known, but OCR failed on the second one. The known word acts as the spam block, the second word is used to produce the complete text (**Figure 4.3**).

Figure 4.3: A test from reCAPTCHA.

In this example users perhaps unknowingly are contributing information. Other ways to tap into the collective knowledge is by observing behavior. On a leading shopping site, users are presented with information like "users who bought this book also bought" or "What do customers ultimately buy after viewing this item." Amazon (http://amazon.com) also lets users contribute knowingly by posting user reviews, recommendation lists, and ratings. Another site that lets users contribute in a similar fashion is the Internet Movie Database (IMDB).

Wikipedia is perhaps the most clear example of **citizen science**. Before the Web, the main view of encyclopedias was of a few select and very knowledgeable authors who wrote for the rest of us. Wikis instead let all users contribute, not by comments or votes, but by letting them actually edit the articles. Articles that have been collectively written by hundreds of enthusiasts and have thousands of individual edits often reach a very high quality. On the other hand, readers must beware that not every article has reached that level. Wikipedia is useful as a starting point for research, but in areas where expertise is required, like medicine, it is best to verify one's findings with trusted sources.

Communities on the Web and the Web as community

Long before there was a Web, computers enabled social interaction. In the late '70s and early '80s a Unix computer serving hundreds of users could let them present themselves and what they were working on through the .plan file, send real-time messages through the talk command, and of course send email. Compared to the leading community today, Facebook, few concepts are new, yet everything is different.

Facebook (http://www.facebook.com/) passed 300 million registered
users in September 2009. It is available to anyone who has access to
the (uncensored) Internet, and interaction is at least easy enough to
accommodate usage by otherwise not computer savvy people. On top
of Facebook developers put games, quizzes, and all kinds of useful and
bizarre apps (See http://www.facebook.com/apps/directory.php).
Indeed, providing APIs to facilitate these is one of the main reasons
Facebook is so successful.

> **Tip:** Developing an app to be used on Facebook or on top of another site, rather
> than on an individual website, might be your first job as a web developer.

A **community** can be general purpose (or grow to become general
purpose). But a community can also be about a specific kind of media,
like YouTube (http://youtube.com/) and Flickr (http://www.flickr.com/),
or about a special interest or topic. LinkedIn (http://www.linkedin.com/)
is a site where you can manage your professional network. Ning is an
example of a website where users can create their own special interest
communities. It hosts support communities for a wide variety of topics.

Communities, especially the larger ones, can be seen as almost complete
ecosystems. Users have profile pages, they can discuss in forums, share
links, images, videos, and of course thoughts. They can message each
other, perhaps also in real time. But bear in mind: the content of the
messages being shared very often emanates from the outside. Thus, even
Facebook illustrates that the power of the Web is not that you can have a
community on it, but that it is community in its very essence.

The real-time Web

By 2010 the Web has become a venue for real-time interaction as well
as a place where one can read the classics. It is home to both Project
Gutenberg (http://www.gutenberg.org/) and Twitter (http://twitter.
com/), the **microblogging** service that lets users speak their mind or
share a link, as long as the messages contain less than 140 characters—
enough to put in an SMS. Besides Twitter there are other examples of
microblogging, like Jaiku (http://www.jaiku.com/) or Identi.ca (http://

CHAPTER 4

identi.ca/). These are often used on mobile phones, enabling quick reactions. Specialized client software often also integrates status updates from Facebook or other communities.

Phones also enable people to instantly share pictures and video, with just a few clicks. Events can be **live blogged** and video can be streamed. Things are put on the Net as they happen, and news has never spread so fast as today. Of course, false rumours and outright lies also can travel fast. Unfortunately, investigating the truth behind a rumour is often a time-consuming process.

Issues of trust and integrity come to the forefront even more when there is no time to investigate or apply critical thinking. Users, who now are the content providers of the Net, had better understand that longterm trust is more important than being the "fastest draw," the one who says everything first.

Today our lives are happening on the Internet. What we do and don't do online is part of how we define ourselves.

The downside of the social web and crowdsourcing is that it is not necessarily used for good purposes. After the 2009 demonstrations in Iran demanding a fair election, the reactionary leaders crowdsourced their supporters to identify protesters, enabling their arrest and punishment. Ultimately the Web will reveal, rather than change, human nature. It is thus neither the saviour of mankind nor its doom. It is becoming an extension of us, who we are, in our glory and in our misery.

Summary

The Internet, and particularly the Web, has grown to become a fundamental part of the way in which we learn, do business, entertain ourselves, and socialize. We are seeing an increased use of mobile phones to access the Web, but this may very well only be a step into a future where the Web is an integral part of every possible (and impossible) appliance.

All this relies on some core technologies, which in turn must work according to solid standards. Without these, there will be no data interchange and accordingly no human interaction either.

CHAPTER 4

The key standards are: the IP-protocol suite, DNS, UTF-8 and other character encodings, HTTP, URLs, HTML, CSS, and the DOM + ECMAScript (JavaScript).

Although not as heavily standardized, which is not needed since they run in controlled environments, languages for server-side scripting complement the client-side technologies, allowing websites to be dynamic and web services to be consumed by all sorts of user agents. Even a front-end developer or a designer should be aware that these technologies exist and have a basic grasp of their role.

Resource // Recommended reading

- Video: "World Wide Web in plain English" http://commoncraft.com/world-wide-web
- Video: Douglas Crockford—*Crockford on JavaScript, Volume 1: The Early Years* (This video is an introduction to JavaScript, but really is about computer history per se) http://developer.yahoo.com/yui/theater/video.php?v=crockonjs-1
- What is a browser? http://googlesystem.blogspot.com/2009/10/google-explains-what-browser-is.html
- What is Unicode? http://www.unicode.org/sta

CHAPTER 4

Minneapolis,
Minnesota
USA

Erin Anderson is the Director of Creative Services at Brain Traffic, a nationally renowned content strategy agency. Since joining the company in 2005, she's led the charge on literally hundreds of web content projects for companies all over the world, including Medtronic, MSD, and UnitedHealth Group.

Erin is a recognized expert in web writing best practices, and regularly conducts workshops and presentations around the country. She lives on the mighty Mississippi in Minneapolis, Minnesota.

http://braintraffic.com
http://twitter.com/erinarie

CHAPTER 5
Writing for the Web

by Erin Anderson

No matter what gets you there in the first place, there's one thing every website, mobile application, widget, and web-based video game has in common: words.

Think about it. Even if you're flipping through an online photo gallery, you still rely on textual cues about how to view the pics, upload new files, share stuff with friends, print images, create a profile, tag or post comments, and so on.

In the end, every website must help its visitors (aka web users) complete some kind of task. Maybe that task is to gather data. Or complete a transaction. Or send a message. Regardless, it's the words on these sites—the instructions, the cues, the information—that affect how quickly (or not) users are able to accomplish their goals.

Well. With all those words online, we're going to need smart, savvy people who know how to get the job done.

Writing for print vs. web: what's the difference?

Before I started writing for the Web I was a magazine editor, a freelance journalist, and a print copywriter. So I knew how to write. But it took me a long time to wrap my head around some of the things that make writing for the Web more than just an exercise in lining up the right words on the page.

In my experience, web writers aren't just expected to write well. We're expected to understand the nuts and bolts of web design and development, as well as the user experience.

So even if we're never asked to design a web page, create a site taxonomy, or write HTML code, we need at least a basic grasp of the principles involved in tying all these elements together. And we have to make that knowledge pay off with the words we write.

Web writing goes beyond the copy you see on your screen

No matter what kind of copywriting you do, success depends on your ability to solve content problems, organize information, and follow the rules of good composition. You must create copy that suits your client's brand, voice, tone, style, business objectives, and customer goals.

Web writers must also have the ability to communicate dense, technical concepts in a clear and concise way every user can understand. We must work closely with graphic designers, information architects, content strategists, and web developers. We must know how to interpret wireframes and sitemaps. Finally, we must consider publishing schedules, regulatory requirements, and usability practices.

As you can see, before we write a single word for the Web (or for any other interactive digital media like email, mobile, widgets, or web-based applications), we've got some serious strategizing to do.

Web writing presents a unique set of challenges

The kinds of projects web writers tackle can be downright beastly. Picture an 800-page website with scales and fangs, much of its rotting content more than 10 years old. And a client team too busy with the day-to-day demands of running a business to stop and worry about where to swing the axe first.

In other words, web writing can be grueling. It's about tackling difficult problems in creative ways to make life easier for the people who use the sites you write.

Here are some of the biggest obstacles to that goal:

There's a lot to keep track of

As web writers, it's our job to organize and craft copy that creates sensible, intuitive, desirable paths through the content of a website. We must make it easy for people to do things online. But with so many elements on every page, that can get tricky.

Anatomy of a web page

Web content may include any—or all—of the following content types (**Figure 5.1**):

Figure 5.1: Most web pages feature a wide variety of text-based content types that need to work well together.

- Article abstracts / teaser copy ("Looking for local skilled and hourly candidates?")
- Global navigation labels ("Resource Center," "Post & Manage Jobs")
- Headlines ("Let's Keep America Working")
- Subheads ("Not Sure Where to Start?")
- Hyperlinks ("Find the right hiring solutions," "Job posting tutorial—3 easy steps")
- Action buttons ("Post a Job," "Search Resumes")
- Task instructions ("Log in to access your account")
- Login fields ("Enter ZIP Code")

And that's just the stuff you see on the page itself (there's more).

Behind the scenes: metadata

Written into HTML code and/or displayed in the properties information of a web page are various text descriptions of the pages, documents, images, and files you see online (**Figure 5.2**).

Figure 5.2: The metadata a web writer provides for a web page appears in the HTML source information.

This **metadata** (data about data) lets search engines accurately index and "query" (search for) those elements.

Web writers are often asked to provide metadata for each web page in a content document that includes:

- **Meta description:** A one-line summary of the content for a particular web page. The meta description appears in search engine results.

- **Meta keywords:** These are terms and phrases relevant to the topics on a page (more on keywords in a bit).

- **Page title:** This is the title of the content page, which appears in the Properties information about that page and at the top of the browser window.

- **Alt text:** Every image or graphic element on a website should also have a descriptive text equivalent that gets included in the markup of the page (more to come on alt text, too).

There's rarely someone "in charge" of the content

When "content" refers to print copy (e.g., a catalog, shareholder report, brochure, or direct mail postcard), the person or team with editorial say-so comes from whichever business department happens to be paying for the print piece.

CHAPTER 5

But when "content" refers to a website, everyone (at least in a mid- to large size organization)—and therefore no one in particular—is paying for it. Too often, that decentralization creates a vacuum of editorial oversight. Which means web writers are left without clear leadership.

The danger in this scenario is that the web writer is suddenly answering to several parties with competing agendas, all vying for valuable site real estate. If not empowered to defend our craft, we can quickly become copy order-takers trying to satisfy multiple content owners.

It's not sexy, like ad copywriting, where the *Big Idea* is king

Think about your favorite TV commercial or magazine ad. Is it clever? Funny? Inspiring? It may be all three of these things, and it likely began as an all-day brainstorm between a copywriter and an art director.

For the most part, that's not how web copy comes together. Marketing web content isn't usually focused on a single campaign, idea, or slogan. A lot of it is instructional, informational, or technical in nature.

Instead of brainstorming with a designer or art director, web writers may meet with, say, information architects and user experience design experts to determine the best way to present the content that appears on the page.

For instance, a web writer might create navigational labels for an insurance website, so a policyholder can more easily update his account information. Or he might write to explain the difference between various types of financial aid options so a college-bound kid knows which scholarships she's eligible for.

What makes web writing so awesome?

Web writing at its best can do some pretty amazing things. For example:

It can facilitate a conversation

Websites that balance user needs (what's the user looking for?) with business goals (how can a company grow and thrive long-term?) remove communication barriers between organizations and their customers.

It can create solid, long-lasting relationships between a company and the people it serves

If a user finds reliable, well-written content on a particular site, she's more likely to perceive the organization behind that content worthy of her trust … and therefore her business.

It can help an organization deliver on its brand promises

Well-written websites give businesses dedicated to great customer service another valuable opportunity to make life a little easier for their customers.

It can even solve business problems

If a user is able to find what he's looking for on a website, he may not need to call a company's service center. He saves time and money, and so does the company.

Web writing brings together many different disciplines and skill sets

The web writer may wear several different hats throughout the content creation process. Here are just a few skill sets web writing brings together in any given project:

- **Publishing:** Like a managing editor, the web writer must make sure the content throughout an entire site is consistent in terms of theme, structure, and style.

- **Journalism:** The web writer writes to inform and educate his audience in a clear, concise, and respectful way.

- **Creative writing:** The web writer must tell a compelling, well-crafted story about a particular company, product, or service.

- **Technical writing:** The web writer must often communicate difficult or complex concepts and information in terms a majority of web users can understand.

- **Marketing:** Good web writing builds trust and strengthens relationships between a company and the people it serves by balancing user needs and business goals.

- **Advertising/sales:** Good web writing persuades and motivates web users to take some kind of action (e.g., buy a product, sign up for a newsletter).

- **Public relations:** Good web writing can help a company project a professional, approachable image.

- **Project management:** Good web writing follows a precise and rigorous process involving lots of people, lots of documents, and lots of deadlines.

- **User experience:** Good web writing organizes and presents information on every web page such that users can find exactly what they're looking for as quickly as possible.

- **Information science:** The web writer must understand hierarchies and relationships between content categories, as well as appropriate labeling systems.

Who makes a good web writer?

Why, you! That is, if you happen to have:

- Solid organizational skills and a knack for understanding information taxonomy (classification) techniques.

- An ability to adjust the voice and tone of your writing on a dime to suit different audiences.

- An interest in making the Web more usable for everyone.

- A desire to work with a team of really smart people.

- A thick skin.

- An ability to spin client feedback into web content gold.

- A sense of humor.

- A sense of adventure.

Understanding the online user experience

Maybe you're wondering just how unique writing for websites can actually be. After all, good writing is always clear, concise, and cohesive, no matter what the medium. Right?

Right. But the goals and expectations of online readers differ from those of offline readers in some fairly remarkable ways. Web writers need to craft content based on those differences.

Here's what I mean:

People read differently online

It's not that nobody ever reads online for enjoyment. Or that nobody ever approaches print materials with a goal in mind. But in general, the interactive component of the Web tends to affect user attitudes and behaviors toward marketing copy.

Offline readers are relaxed and passive readers

People read printed materials to soak up information, not to immediately act on it. So offline readers are often more absorbed and engaged in the text than their online counterparts. Maybe they're enjoying a little down time. Or waiting to be called for an appointment. In short, they read passively by just taking in the data as it's presented to them.

Online readers are impatient and task-oriented readers

Online readers often want only information about how to complete a specific task. They're distracted. They're multitasking. They're wondering, "Where do I click?" They're trying to get in, get something done, and then get out. They read actively, because they're ready to take some kind of action.

Try it yourself!

Notice how your own content expectations change depending on whether you're reading: a website, a billboard, a magazine, a brochure, to sign up for a newsletter, to check today's headlines or to buy something on a retail site.

Keep notes about your discoveries. Where were you when you encountered the material? What time of day was it? Which season? Are there certain expectations that don't change, no matter what or why you're reading?

Finally, summarize your findings in a blog post.

Web users don't read. They scan.

In 2006, the Poynter Institute school of journalism conducted a study exploring the differences between reading news in print and online.

CHAPTER 5

The Poynter EyeTrack07 project (http://eyetrack.poynter.org/) monitored the eye movements of nearly 600 individuals as they read both print and online versions of various publications.

The study showed that about 50 percent of the subjects tested didn't read information online word for word, or from the top to the bottom of the page (the way you do with a book or magazine).

Instead, they skipped around, skimming the horizon for something interesting or useful.

For instance, if a user has come to check the balance of his bank account, he doesn't want to waste valuable on-screen time fumbling through an elaborate message like "Welcome to Big Bank. We're so happy you chose us, etc."

He just wants a word or two about how to access his accounts, an idea about how many steps are involved, and a hint about how long the whole process might take. Anything else is going to get in his way. Which is going to make him want to take his business elsewhere.

Resource // Steve Krug

Steve Krug has a lot to say about putting yourself in your user's shoes. His book, *Don't Make Me Think: A Common Sense Approach to Web Usability* (New Riders, 2006), is a heavyweight in the user experience canon.

Websites aren't linear

Most books have a definable beginning, middle, and end. Websites, on the other hand, do not. A user may enter a website through the home page. Or she may link in from another site or arrive via search engine results. But no matter where on the site she happens to end up initially, she must be able to quickly orient herself.

It's up to the web writer to make sure the user understands where she's landed, and leave clues about how to get around. Those clues may come in the form of hyperlinks to other relevant topic pages. Or in the global navigation menu.

And all these clues must be mapped out and presented with careful consideration for and in relation to all the other pages in that content universe.

For example, a web writer must think about which pages are the most important to link to from the page the user is currently on. (That's a question you can only answer if you truly understand what the users of the site are going to need, and when they're going to need it most.)

Websites are harder to read than print materials

Staring at a screen for long periods of time (as so many of us do every day) is hard on our eyes.

That's why the web writer must help ensure the way information gets presented on-screen is as visually forgiving as possible. Online, that means minimizing eye fatigue by breaking up text into smaller, more scannable chunks than those you might find in a book.

For instance, paragraphs on a web page shouldn't exceed 60 words. Headlines should clock in at eight words or fewer. Each topic or new idea should receive a subhead that alerts the user to what she'll find in that section if she decides to read further.

(You'll find more specific guidelines like these in the "Top 10 web writing tips" section.)

Websites must be accessible for users with impaired vision

Most of us think of the Web as a visual medium. We don't consider how users with no vision or low vision navigate websites.

These users often get assistance from screen reader devices that electronically scan web pages, then provide simulated speech output or print Braille sheets. A person who uses a screen reader can program his device to "read" only headings, subheadings, and links ... or to read all information on the page.

Visually impaired web users scan information, too. They just do it with their ears. Or their fingertips.

According to a study by Mary Frances Theofanos and Ginny Redish (http://www.redish.net/content/papers/interactions.html), there were 180 million blind or visually impaired people worldwide in 2001. In the U.S. alone, there were 7.7 million. That's a pretty major segment of the population.

The study states that users with impaired vision "scan" information in much the same way visual web users do: by listening to just enough of each headline, subhead, or page to decide whether they want to read on or skip to another item. (They also frequently increase the reading speed in order to "skim" a paragraph.)

So where a visual web user may happen upon a word of interest by "accident" as she scans an entire page, a user experiencing that same page via screen reader might miss the phrase if a web writer hasn't strategically placed it at the beginning of a link or line of text.

So web writers need to lead with relevant information

Users aided by screen readers can't take in the whole screen at once, or jump quickly from page to page the way visual users can. So web writers must always put the most relevant words and phrases first in headings, links, and paragraphs.

(We should do that anyway. It just makes for better reading.)

Web writers must also learn how to write alt text

Screen readers only scan text. They can't interpret graphic elements like charts, photos, or color-coding. So web writers must provide a text alternative ("alt text") to these images. Every image or graphic element on a website should have a descriptive text equivalent that gets included in the markup for that page.

The developer of the website will use the alt text information to write HTML code that screen readers (and search engines, and users who have elected to disable graphics in their browser) can decipher using your description.

Web users talk back

The Web is a place where stuff gets done: users fill out forms, download PDFs, and click links to submit personal information. They also chat with customer service representatives in real time. They blog about what they like (and what they dislike) as soon as it happens. They share reviews with friends, and generally leave their mark wherever they go.

Websites should be tools for facilitating customer feedback

Websites enable a two-way conversation between a company and its customers. That forum empowers the company to interact in a meaningful way with those customers. It also exposes the company to highly accessible (and infinitely repeatable) scrutiny.

So the risk of exposure inherent in web content is also an amazing opportunity. With our clients in such a vulnerable (yet potentially rewarding) position, web writers must turn these websites into accessible, approachable forums for customer input and feedback.

I'm not necessarily talking about a dedicated user comment area. I just mean that for every piece of content we write we need to anticipate customer needs (so customers feel heard and understood from the get-go). We also need to post customer service information in prominent locations on the site.

Websites should strike a balance between user goals and business objectives

Another task of the web writer is to consider those user needs alongside or in context with business objectives.

To satisfy the needs of the user, the web writer must:

- Think about their concerns, hopes, and expectations.
- Consider their desired tasks.
- Provide information to support decision making.
- Write easy-to-understand task instructions.

To satisfy business goals, the web writer must consider:

CHAPTER 5

- What the company wants its customers to know and understand.
- What it wants its customers to do.
- How the company will keep those customers happy for a long time to come.

Web writing that works (or doesn't)

There's a lot of crappy writing out there, both off- and online. Sometimes identifying the bad and the ugly can help us define what works well.

So let's start with what doesn't.

What does bad web writing look like?

Bad web writing (and bad writing in general) is:

- Overwritten. It's full of long, rambling sentences and nonessential information.
- Lazy about spelling and grammar. It shows the site owners aren't paying attention to the details.
- Scattered. It lacks focus, and doesn't seem to have a driving purpose or main point.
- Hard to act upon. It leaves a user uncertain about what his next steps should be.
- Full of marketing jargon and unnecessarily complicated terminology. It forces a user to search for context, and can make her feel excluded or talked down to.
- All about the company and not enough about the user. It overwhelms a user with information without considering his needs.

What does good web writing look like?

Four things are true about all good web writing. It's **useful**, **usable**, **engaging** and **findable**.

Let's break that down.

Good web writing is useful

Writing useful copy means you will:

- **Know what information the user wants (and how she wants it presented).** Then give it to her without a lot of fuss.

- **Help the user accomplish something.** Even if it's a simple task, like signing up for weekly airfare alerts to favorite travel spots—useful copy always offers clear cues, instructions, and descriptions.

- **Be consistent.** Don't write a subheading about applying for student loans if you're talking about college scholarships.

- **Answer the user's questions before she has them.** Understand where she'll want to go as soon as she gets to the site, and respect her time by making it obvious what she should do to get there quickly.

Good web writing is usable

Writing usable copy means you will:

- **Write clear navigation cues.** Check that labels, menu items, page titles, and links make sense in the context of the site goals.

- **Avoid unnecessary (repetitive, redundant, excess) copy.** Enough said.

- **Write descriptive headings.** Users are willing to stick with longer copy if it's punctuated with well-written headings that clue them in to what they're about to spend time reading.

Good web writing is engaging

Writing engaging copy means you will:

- **Write to make your user feel smart (not to make yourself look smart).** That doesn't mean "dumbing down" your copy. It just means serving up the information in a direct and no-nonsense way.

- **Be personable.** Imagine yourself sitting across the table from someone and speaking the words you've written out loud. Would you feel awkward? Would your audience take you seriously? Would you sound natural?

- **Be authentic, not overly authoritative.** You'll show you're an expert by finding a way to communicate even complicated concepts in a simple and straightforward way that doesn't talk down to the user.

- **Avoid "marketing speak."** Remember whom you're talking to, and their level of experience with the subject you're presenting. Be welcoming. Be approachable. Be reassuring and positive, not cute or clever. Be professional and personable.

Good web writing is findable

Writing findable copy means you will:

- **Place relevant keywords first.** Do so in titles, links, subheads, and opening sentences (they're worth more to search rankings here).

- **Use synonyms for the keywords throughout the page or website.** For example, if one keyword is "vintage" you might interchange it with "retro" to break up the monotony of repeated words and to capture yet another word that a user might search for. Just make sure the use of synonyms feels natural as part of the flow of the copy, and doesn't interfere with its consistency.

- **Never sacrifice readability for searchability.** Make sure your copy doesn't end up sounding artificial once the keywords are in place.

What does *findability* mean?

Findability refers to how easily web users can locate the information they came looking for on a particular web page (i.e., how scannable is the content? How well organized?). Findability also refers to how high the site rates in search engine rankings.

Here's a quick refresher on search engine optimization (SEO):

How does a search engine work?

Search engines (like Google, Bing, or Yahoo!) are programs that respond to user queries (terms or phrases you type into your browser). Enter the phrase "Art Deco" and a search engine might return results that include links to antiques brokers, architectural history overviews, and furniture blogs.

Search engines create these databases by periodically using indexing programs called "spiders" or "bots" to "crawl" the Internet. Early search engines often required pages to be submitted to them before they could be crawled. These days, most searchable information gets indexed by spiders and bots following links from other pages.

How do search engines rank search results?

How does a search engine like Google decide in which order the indexed websites should appear? The results are based on a combination of the following factors:

- **Site age:** As long it meets other criteria as well, an older site is likely to rank higher than a newer one.

- **Amount of content:** Sites for large corporations or internationally recognized organizations like the BBC are likely to rate higher in search rankings because of the sheer volume of content they contain.

- **Number/quality of inbound links:** Websites that get linked to frequently by high-rated sites will move up in search rankings.

- **Popularity/trends:** If a certain site suddenly gets an overwhelming number of clicks from users, it will move up in search rankings (at least temporarily).

- **Search engine optimization (SEO):** Websites that feature frequently entered search terms in headings, links, domain names, titles, and page content tend to perform well in search rankings.

Web writers can affect a website's findability through SEO (search engine optimization)

One of the challenges of writing for the Web involves making sure a website's content will perform well in search rankings so users find it before they find a competitor's site.

To ensure good rankings, a web writer must first obtain a list of keywords from the client. Keywords are terms and phrases proven through testing or user research to represent the kinds of products and services offered by the organization. Often, each page of the website has its own set of keywords, though some keywords may apply to more than just one page.

For instance, the list of keywords for an antiques dealer may include terms like "high quality," "vintage," "mid-century modern," "collectibles," "estate sale," and "auction."

It all starts with the keywords

A web writer's goal is to use as many of these keywords as many times as possible throughout the page or site. Keywords have more impact on search results if they're used in page titles, headings, subheadings, links, and image captions. That's because spiders and bots assign greater value to keywords appearing in these highly visible locations. (So do your readers, incidentally.)

Beware: SEO and user experience (UX) aren't always compatible

You've probably been wondering, "Doesn't using the same words over and over for the sake of good search rankings make it less readable to the person actually trying to use the website?"

It's certainly a fine line to walk. Even SEO experts disagree about the best way to balance readability with usability. But that's why yet another goal of the web writer is to make sure the readability of a web page doesn't get sacrificed for its findability/searchability. The ultimate objective isn't to write for search engines. It's to write for the people who use them.

Before you write, you need some tools. And a process. And a team.

Unfortunately, web writers often get brought into the content creation process after the information architecture (site structure) and design (site aesthetics) processes are already well underway. Even web veterans sometimes make the mistake of assuming a writer can "just add words" to a nearly finished site...

Tools/documentation

Whether you're given a seat at the table early on in the process or in the 11th hour, there are some handy tools and documents the web writer can use to make the content creation process run as smoothly and efficiently as possible.

Copy deck

The copy deck is the web writer's bible. Typically an MS Word document, it contains all the text elements a web writer has written, edited, or otherwise influenced. It's this document that gets passed back and forth between the writer and the team of web designers, web developers, and client reviewers for discussion.

Of course, all that input from different parties makes clear labeling of these copy deck files (and their iterations) absolutely critical.

Content audit/inventory

A content audit or "inventory" is a spreadsheet that documents the current state of a website in terms of page titles, corresponding URLS, and anything else that's important for the organization to keep track of (**Table 5.1**).

Page ID	Page name	Url	Notes
0.0	Home	http://www.braintraffic.com/	
1.0	Services	http://www.braintraffic.com/ services/	
1.1	Audit and Assessment	http://www.braintraffic.com/ services/audit-assessment/	
1.2	Strategy and Integration	http://www.braintraffic.com/ services/strategy-integration/	
1.3	Governance and Guidelines	http://www.braintraffic.com/ services/governance-guidelines/	
1.4	Editorial Services and Support	http://www.braintraffic.com/services/ editorial-services-support/	
2.0	Company	http://www.braintraffic.com/company/	
3.0	Clients	http://www.braintraffic.com/clients/	List of clients; may add case study links
4.0	Blog	http://blog.braintraffic.com/	Lists posts chronologically by most recent; includes links to topic categories and posts by author; page also includes links to speaking engagements
5.0	Contact Us	http://www.braintraffic.com/contact/	Links to email addresses and twitter address
6.0	Privacy Policy	http://www.braintraffic.com/privacy/	
7.0	Sitemap	http://www.braintraffic.com/sitemap/	
8.0	RSS	http://blog.braintraffic.com/feed/	

Table 5.1: A content audit/inventory is a spreadsheet showing the current state of all the pages on a website. It may include information about page titles, source documents, downloadable files, and writers' notes.

The type of audit you see here is called a **quantitative audit**. And it answers some pretty important questions. For instance:

- What content does your client have?

- Who creates that content? (An editorial team? A business unit? A marketing group? Regional branches? Users?)

- Where does it live? (In brochures? On a server? In the collective memory of staff members?)

CHAPTER 5

- If there's an existing website, how is that content organized?
- What types of files are included (e.g., pdfs, videos, forms)?

If it's helpful, you can add information fields to the spreadsheet to make it a **qualitative audit**. In other words, you can provide analysis for some of that data and answer questions like:

- What does the content say?
- Is it accurate and useful?
- Is it well-written? User-friendly?
- How's the meta data working out? Is it written in such a way that search engines and content management systems can organize and deliver it when and where users need it most?

And so on. Each page on the inventory corresponds to a specific wireframe (we'll get to those in a minute).

Style guide

It's also helpful to obtain an editorial style guide from the client for keeping track of word usage preferences, voice and tone guidelines, and so on. You don't want to be constantly second-guessing your instincts as you write or having to track down answers about whether subheads should appear in title case or sentence case... That's just a waste of valuable writing time.

The more explicit the style guide, and the more descriptive, the easier creating content will be. The style guide might contain language that describes generally the way all the copy should go.

Or it might get more detailed with examples showing which words suit the voice and tone of a particular site, and contrasting those with words that don't. For instance, maybe the word *skip* would be appropriate for a particular site where *eliminate* would not.

Wireframes

Wireframes sketch out a web page's layout more or less the way it will appear in the browser, but without all the final design elements

(**Figure 5.3**). Some wireframes also describe relationships between the content elements (text, images, links, etc.).

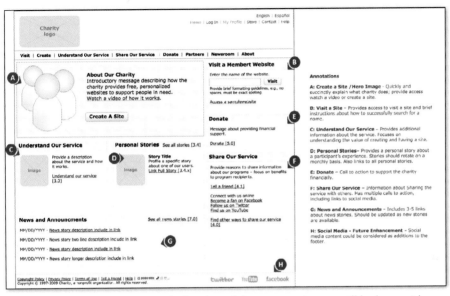

Figure 5.3: Wireframes are rough sketches of the way a web page will look once it's been designed and built. These sketches help writers visualize their copy in its final form on the website.

Web writers often receive wireframes (as opposed to completed designs) as the primary template for figuring out approximately how much copy to write, and for which areas of the page.

Ideally, the person who has created the wireframes has a deep understanding of the way the information will need to appear for the best possible user experience. He or she will provide context for why particular elements or topics have been included and how they're related.

Sitemap

A sitemap shows the hierarchy of the site. It lets a writer, designer, or developer see the relationship among all the pages of the site at a glance (**Figure 5.4**):

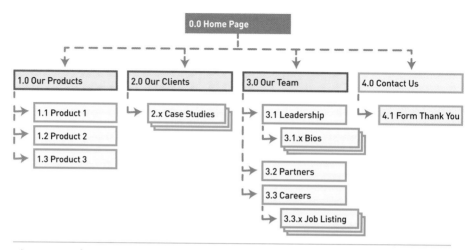

Figure 5.4: This site map shows a site with four global/top navigation items, and topic subsets.

Where does web content come from?

When a client says, "We'd like you to rewrite our 200-page website," your line (right after "I can't wait to get started!") should be, "So where does all my source content live?"

Odds are, they'll tell you it lives on the current website, in brochures, shareholder reports, user personas, usability reports, video files, audio files, pdfs … etc., etc.

Or maybe they've never published a website before, so there's no existing source content to speak of. In this case, you may get your information by interviewing the founders of the company. Or by scouring competitor websites and then learning exactly how your client goes above and beyond to crush the competition.

Who's on your content creation team?

Regardless of the size or scope of the website, it's best if there's someone who fills each of the following roles, even if some of those roles overlap. You (yes, you) might end up taking on a few, depending on your unique skills and experience.

- **Content reviewers:** These folks may be members of the client's editorial team. They may also be subject matter experts or part of the legal department. They read your copy in the copy deck to check for accuracy, editorial excellence, and fidelity to brand standards.

- **Content strategist:** This person is your partner in content-creating crime. He or she works with clients to define actionable, useful strategies for web content processes. The strategist also works with web writers and the client team to make sure these strategies get implemented effectively.

- **Designer (aka "web designer"):** Designers determine the look and feel of a website. They may build the pages or may let a developer handle the actual coding. Many (but not all) designers focus more on the aesthetic of a website than its functionality.

- **Developer (aka "web developer"):** Web developers make the content come to life online using various types of code.

- **Executive editor:** The executive web editor sets standards for content creation, assigns projects and deadlines, and generally keeps all the content owners accountable for their portion of the website.

- **Information architect (IA):** IAs work with the structure of information on a website and/or define that structure. They may also affect elements of organization, labeling, visual design, and writing.

- **Subject matter expert (SME):** The SME is a client contact intimately familiar with the subject matter being published.

- **Web writer:** A web writer uses creativity and strategy to write websites that are useful, usable, findable, and engaging. (See also: You!)

Resource // Kristina Halvorson

Kristina Halvorson's *Content Strategy for the Web* talks about how to integrate the people, processes, and plans that go into creating better web content (New Riders, 2009).

Top 10 web writing tips

OK. We've covered a bit about the user experience, what good web writing looks like, and how to wrangle your content in preparation for writing.

That means it's time to dig in to some serious web writing tips. Ready? Here we go:

CHAPTER 5

1. Love the inverted pyramid

- First, start with your conclusion.
- Then provide supporting information.
- Finally, give background and technical details.

The inverted pyramid should be familiar to most of you. It's the way news stories are written (and many research papers, too). Your thesis comes first, as does the Who-What-When-Where-Why-How type of information. As you move through the piece, the content builds on and supports that main thesis statement.

2. Believe less is (almost always) more

- Don't overwhelm the user.
- Cut all unnecessary words. (Then cut more.)
- Get out of the user's way.

One of a web writer's most valuable skills is being able to communicate an idea using as few words as possible. Remember: The user probably hasn't come here to read for fun. She's come to gather information and complete a task.

3. Avoid sounding like an infomercial

- Keep it simple. Write to inform, not to impress.
- Don't be afraid to use contractions and first-person construction.
- Speak plainly, but do be specific.
- Avoid exclamation points (most of the time).
- Limit use of bold and italicized copy.

Websites are conversations between an organization and its site users. The best way for web writers to help facilitate that conversation is by writing the way we would speak to someone we know and respect. In other words, we should be authentic and engaging.

4. Make your copy easy to scan

One of the easiest ways to make your content easy to scan is by dividing information into nice bite-sized chunks.

Here are a few rules of thumb:

- **Paragraphs should be 60 words or fewer.** It's important to give users a chance to "come up for air" as they're reading longer sections of content.

- **Headlines should be eight words or fewer.** That's both a design consideration (the larger text simply won't fit on the page if there are too many words), and also a contextual consideration. Headlines are really just there to let the reader know he's in the right place.

- **Subheads should be 12–14 words or fewer.** Like headlines, subheads exist to summarize the information that follows. So they should be brief and hard-hitting.

- **Page length depends on a number of factors.** Ultimately, it's about creating a consistent experience for the user. For example, if most of your pages about different heart conditions on a medical website have roughly 300 words, but one page has only 50 words worth of useful information, ask your client why that's the case. (Is there not enough information on that topic? Should it be combined with another page? Should the structure for the way the topics are presented be reconsidered?)

- **Bulleted lists are a great way to chop up long paragraphs that list lots of information.** Just remember: a list doesn't make the content relevant, it just makes it easier to read. If you can cut unnecessary copy, do so before you put it into a list.

- **Numbered lists should be used sparingly.** A numbered list is a specialized type of bulleted list. Use numbered lists only for "sequential" tasks, like describing steps in a process, ranking items, or presenting information where total number is important (for instance, a top 10 list).

- **Use headings strategically to help guide the user through the page.** Headings show hierarchy and communicate relative importance of topics on a page. They draw a user's eye to the main ideas and provide clues about where to go next.

5. Write killer headings

- Remember: Task-focused readers don't read. They scan.
- Just tell them what they'll find—be clear, not clever.
- Use keywords.

Most of the time, the user isn't reading your copy. She's scanning it. So write attention-grabbing headings that faithfully represent the copy that follows. And remember to pump them full of SEO keywords (as long as doing so isn't disruptive to the content flow) for maximum findability.

Resource // Ginny Redish

Ginny Redish describes why users don't read every word on the Web in *Letting Go of the Words* (Morgan Kaufmann Publishers, 2007). This book is a must-read for any writer serious about writing the kind of links, headings, and long copy that attract positive user attention.

6. Lead with active words

- Start headlines, links, and phrases with verbs when possible.
- Use active constructions (avoid "to be" verbs wherever you can).
- Start with the point. Don't waste valuable real estate leading up to it.

Take a look at this faux promo ad:

> *You know you're getting a great deal every time you log on to SweetDealsNow.com. We have everyday low prices, fabulous money-saving offers and all your favorite products, right here online, 24 hours a day.*

There's some good stuff, here: great deals, low prices, money-saving offers, favorite products, etc. But what about the way it's presented? How could we make it more active?

If we strip out filler phrases like "you know you are," "we have," and "every time you log on" we're left with something that might look like:

> *For fabulous savings and everyday low prices, shop online 24 hours a day at SweetDealsNow.com*

Now "fabulous savings" and "everyday low prices" stand out a little bit more. The message is streamlined, and we don't lose anything important from the first example. We still get the same information, just in a more compelling, active way.

Can we simplify and liven things up further? What about:

> *Save more money. Shop SweetDealsNow.com*

The main message ("save money") remains intact. Plus, we've created a much more active, engaging message for the user. And all we did in this case was lead with verbs and cut unnecessary copy. Voila.

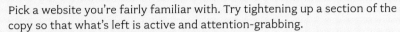

Try it yourself!

Pick a website you're fairly familiar with. Try tightening up a section of the copy so that what's left is active and attention-grabbing.

7. Use simple sentences

- Make verbs and nouns your best friends.

- Use adjectives and adverbs sparingly.

- Avoid semicolons at all cost. Use a comma instead. Or better yet: dare to use a full stop.

- Notice when too many commas signal copy that's too complicated for the Web.

Some people assume lengthy, complex sentences and big words equal profound content. Not necessarily. If your writing is clear and concise, the message will come through much more effectively without fancy words or complicated structure. And it will be easier for the user to scan quickly.

8. Keep your promises

- Make sure links and labels match section/page titles. (Don't reference something in a link or headline that doesn't appear in the text that follows.)

- Don't leave your reader hanging with nothing to do.

There's nothing worse than clicking on a link that says "Ways to Invest," and arriving at a page titled (for example) "Mutual Funds." How does that make you feel? Didn't the "Ways to Invest" link give you the impression you were getting an overview of multiple ways to invest, not just information about one kind of investment?

You'd be surprised how often this sort of oversight occurs on otherwise well-written websites. Many of these inconsistencies are the result of site updates in which some (but not all) pages get refreshed, revamped, and added to. Other times it's just carelessness. The moral of the story is to always double check your work.

CHAPTER 5

And remember: Web users are often task-oriented and looking for somewhere to click. So make sure you give it to them—at least one or two actions per page.

9. Set up a review process

- Don't be your own editor. Get other writers or client team members on board.

- Schedule enough time to have every set of documents you deliver reviewed.

As with any kind of writing or publishing, it's important to have a review process in place that gets followed religiously. You'll want someone involved who understands the subject matter inside and out, and someone who knows the rules of good web writing. (Sometimes one person can play both roles.)

10. Steal from good websites (sort of)

- Start critiquing the websites you visit.

- Keep a list of sites that work well, and sites that don't. Talk with friends or colleagues about the differences between those sites.

Try it yourself!

Search for a website that's especially well-written, think about why you like it. What makes it good, in your opinion? Is it concise? Is it easy to navigate? Does it make you feel smart? Included? Like part of a community?

Now find a website that feels particularly unwelcoming. Why does it feel that way? How does the writing contribute to this vibe? What would make it better? How would you write it differently?

Resource // Gerry McGovern

Gerry McGovern is a recognized expert in writing web copy that gets people to respond. Check out *Killer Web Content* (A & C Black, 2006).

Keep web content fresh with routine updates

Like laundry, a website is never truly finished. You have to run it through the rinse cycle now and then to keep it from smelling like dirty sweat socks. That means routine checks to make sure the content is still relevant and links are still functioning.

It's ultimately up to the client to make sure this maintenance happens, but a web writer often gets involved. Also, it never hurts to be the smart one in the room raising your hand to suggest this important—yet often overlooked—process.

Perform regular content audits

Keep the content audit/inventory spreadsheet up to date (**Table 5.1**) during the writing phase—and beyond—as a "living" document you can add to or remove items from. So you'll always have an accurate snapshot of what's out there on the site.

Use an editorial calendar

An editorial calendar is a schedule in spreadsheet form showing events, holidays, industry trends, brand campaigns, company changes, etc. that have the potential to trigger website content updates.

When these triggers have been plotted out, it's easier to proactively plan content updates far enough in advance to make them useful, usable, engaging, and findable.

Make a content owner list

It's always wise to have a list indicating which people within an organization are responsible for each page or piece of content. That way if there's ever a problem with a particular page, the "owner" of that page can weigh in on the value or the risk of making changes.

You may want to make a spreadsheet to track this information. Include columns for update frequency, writer, reviewer, approver, and publisher.

Play executive web editor (or find out who does)

It's critical to choose someone who can be the final word on what goes on the website (or doesn't). For this person, content quality is priority number one. He or she sets standards for content creation, assigns projects and deadlines, and generally holds all the content owners accountable for their respective sections of content.

Summary

One of the great things about writing for the Web is that as web users ourselves, we all understand the consequences of bad web copy: the story always ends with a frustrated user leaving the site, cursing the screen, or telling all his friends what a bad experience he had. (None of these outcomes are good for business, by the way.)

When it comes right down to it, every web writer is simply a web user trying to make the Web a more pleasant, convenient, useful place for other web users. The rules for making that happen evolve along with the Web itself, which is always growing and changing in ways print materials never will.

And you thought I was exaggerating when I said web writers need a sense of adventure, didn't you?

Hey, I'm a web writer. I meant every word.

Resource // Recommended readings

- Words that Zing
  http://www.alistapart.com/articles/words-that-zing/

- Grammar Girl
  http://grammar.quickanddirtytips.com/

- Your About Page is a Robot
  http://www.alistapart.com/articles/aboutpagerobot/

- Communicate Clearly with Online Customers
  http://blog.braintraffic.com/2009/11/communicate-clearly-
  with-online-customers/

- Writing for the Web
  http://www.useit.com/papers/webwriting/

- 10 Tips on Writing the Living Web
  http://www.alistapart.com/articles/writeliving

CHAPTER 5

Part II:
Planning a Website

With your preparation done, it is now time to start planning and scoping out your website. But hold on there a second—at this point you shouldn't just open up your editor and start coding away! Every good website has had a great deal of work put into its planning, before the implementation begins—working out the target audience for the site and their needs, what structure the site should have, how users should interact with the site, and more. And this is what this part will cover.

We will start by looking at the role of **information architecture**, which basically means planning the structure of a web site. We move on to defining the web site project including: primary business goals, target audience and the project time line of tasks (also known as a work breakdown structure). The next section on content analysis covers another vital part of this process—analyzing what features your target audience needs, determining what content you already have and looking at what your competition has. In the last part, we will learn how to develop a content strategy for the web site that will help keep the project team focused on the business goals and the audience needs. The content strategy includes the approved content outline and the information architecture diagrams that are the blueprints for the overall workflow and structure of the site.

In brief, this part covers:

- Information architecture introduction
- Information architecture defined
- The roles and tools of an information architect
- Site Planning
- Defining the site's primary goals and target audience
- Drafting the technical requirements and maintenance plan
- Defining the project time line (work breakdown structure)
- Content Analysis
- Conducting competitive analysis
- Using web analytics
- Content Strategy
- Developing page description diagrams, wireframes and storyboards

Austin, Texas
USA

Glenda Sims is an accessibility consultant and trainer for Knowbility, a non-profit whose mission is "barrier free IT." She is also the Web Standards and Accessibility Evangelist for the University of Texas.

She gives back to the Web by volunteering on the Web Standards InterACT Project and the W3C Open Web Education Alliance Incubator Group. Glenda, also known as the goodwitch, is delighted to call Austin, Texas, her home.

http://www.glendathegood.com/blog
http://interact.webstandards.org
http://www.knowbility.org
http://www.utexas.edu
http://twitter.com/goodwitch

CHAPTER 6
Information Architecture Intro

by Glenda Sims

Attempting to build a website without a plan is like trying to construct a house without an architectural blueprint. To consistently design and build quality websites you need a website planning process. This chapter begins with an overview of the website planning process and then explains how the information architect contributes to a balanced design with the strong foundation of content analysis and strategy.

Planning process

Ask any successful web professional the path they take from "I need a website" to "The site you built for me is great!" (**Figure 6.1**) and you will discover a planning process that has the basic steps of any successful project:

1. Define project requirements
2. Conduct research and analysis
3. Develop design
4. Build
5. Test
6. Deploy
7. Maintain

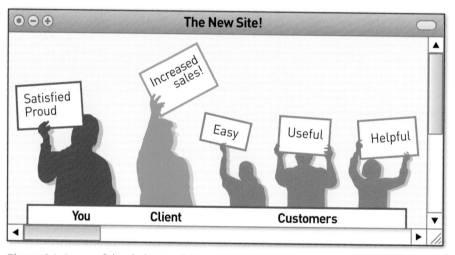

Figure 6.1: Successful web design. (http://www.istockphoto.com/user_view.php?id=564978)

While there are many approaches to project management—such as traditional (**Figure 6.2**), iterative, or agile—all projects generally include the following major stages: **start**, **plan**, **build**, **test** and **close**.

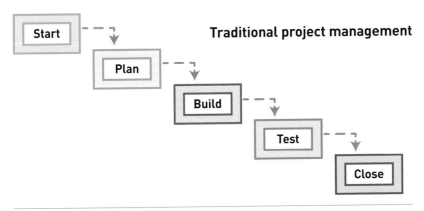

Figure 6.2: *Traditional project management.*

In the traditional approach to project management, the steps occur one after another in a linear fashion. This can be successful on small, well-defined projects.

Phased project management (**Figure 6.3**) is more flexible, with multiple feedback loops and shorter deliverable timeframes. Agile and extreme project management are phased approaches.

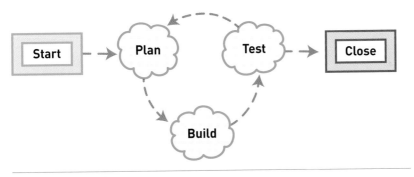

Figure 6.3: *Phased project management.*

Dangers of "seat of the pants" design

What happens when you don't spend time to plan a new website? You may experience the following problems:

Designing the site just for you

When the project definition is not clearly defined, you can end up making a number of assumptions based on your own preferences. Remember that you are unique and very few people think exactly like you. If you don't clarify expectations, you are at high risk of disappointing your client. Dilemma:

- Client does not like new site.

- Customers do not use the site.

Designing the site just for the client

A more subtle danger can occur even when you take the time to listen closely to your client's wants and needs. You document all the project requirements and have full support from your client. But you did not consider the goals and expectations of your client's customers. Dilemma:

- Client loves the new site.

- Customers do not use the site.

Designing the site just for the customers

The customer is always right, right? You spend hours researching your client's customers and you build the site to make the customers deliriously happy. But the customer's goals and your client's business goals are in conflict. Dilemma:

- Client is not satisfied.

- Customers are using the site and love it.

Balanced design

If you can't design just to please yourself, or your client, or the customers, do you have to settle for everyone being less than fully satisfied? On the contrary, the challenge is to gather all the wants, needs and requirements from each of these distinct viewpoints and find a mutually beneficial solution.

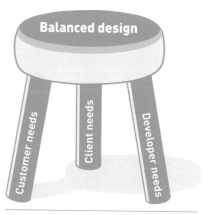

Figure 6.4: Balanced design.

If you place all three perspectives on a flat surface, an endless tug-of-war will occur. But, if you move the problem into the third dimension, then each perspective can serve as a support leg to the solution (**Figure 6.4**).

Project roles

The website planning process requires a set of professional roles. Think of these roles as different hats. You can wear multiple hats.

1. **Project manager**

   The project manager serves as point of contact for the client. Responsibilities include: lead the team, help the team be successful, develop a project definition, manage the task list and timeline, help keep the team on focus and facilitate communication.

2. **Information architect**

   The information architect analyzes, organizes and labels information on the Web to be intuitive and usable.

3. **Usability analyst**

   The usability analyst creates a usability testing plan, conducts tests and prioritizes and communicates usability issues to the team.

4. **Writer/content manager**

   The writer/content manager writes and adapts content specifically for the Web.

5. **Visual designer**

   The visual designer develops design options that meet project goals based on knowledge of design principles (balance, rhythm, proportion, dominance); design elements (point, line, shape, color, typography); and user-centered design (usability).

6. **Developer**

   The developer builds the front-end (HTML, CSS, JavaScript) and the back-end (server-side scripting, database) of the website.

7. **Quality tester**

   The quality tester creates a realistic testing plan, conducts tests and prioritizes and communicates quality issues to the team.

Resource // Too many hats?

Question from a New Web Designer: I'm trying to design and develop websites as a consultant. I didn't realize I would need to wear so many hats. I'm worried that I can't do a good job all by myself.

It is challenging to wear all of these hats, but with a little help from your friends, the web pros, you can successfully wear many hats. We do suggest that you don't try to wear all of them by yourself.

- Project Manager and Information Architect—*Web ReDesign 2.0: Workflow that Works* by Emily Cotler and Kelly Goto. Peachpit Press.
- Information Architect—*Information Architecture: Blueprints for the Web* by Austin Govella and Christina Wodtke. New Riders Press.
- Usability—*Don't Make Me Think: A Common Sense Approach to Web Usability* by Steve Krug. New Riders Press.
- Writer/Content Manager—*Letting Go of the Words: Writing Web Content that Works* by Janice (Ginny) Redish. Morgan Kaufmann.
- Visual Designer—*Universal Principles of Design* by Jill Butler, Kritina Holden, and William Lidwell. Rockport Publishers.
- Developer—*Developing with Web Standards* by John Allsopp. New Riders Press.
- Quality Tester—*The Software Test Engineer's Handbook* by Graham Bath and Judy McKay. Rocky Nook.

What is an information architect?

Out of all these roles and responsibilities, the newest one is the information architect. The Information Architecture Institute defines **information architecture** as:

- The structural design of shared information environments.
- The art and science of organizing and labeling websites, intranets, online communities and software to support usability and findability.
- An emerging community of practice focused on bringing principles of design and architecture to the digital landscape.

So, what does an information architect do? Analyze, organize and label information on websites so regular people (not involved in the design of the site) can actually find what they are looking for.

Listen to how users describe sites built on solid information architecture versus haphazard information architecture:

- **Solid information architecture**—well organized, good navigation, intuitive, logical, easy to find answers and complete my task.

- **Haphazard information architecture**—confusing, frustrating, cryptic, inconsistent, hard to use.

The term *information architecture* was first coined by Richard Saul Wurman in 1975. Richard recognized the common problem of information overload caused by a deluge of content. He realized that a new discipline was required to help make information understandable (http://www.interaction-design.org/encyclopedia/information_architecture.html).

Today, degrees in information architecture are offered in a wide variety of schools (http://iainstitute.org/en/learn/education/schools_teaching_ia.php), under a variety of disciplines including:

- Computer science
- Graphics and information design
- Human-computer interaction (HCI) design
- Library science
- Technical writing
- Usability engineering

Information architecture bridges all of these to help make websites findable and usable.

Try it yourself!

Add Information Architecture to your brain 140 characters at a time by following @boxesandarrows on twitter. Boxes and Arrows is one of the leading online journals focused on IA.

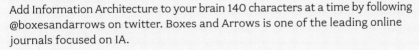

Information architecture boundaries

Information architecture is the foundation of good web design and development. However, it is no more important than the content, visual design, code, usability and quality testing of the site.

Information architecture is NOT:

- Project management
- Copywriting
- Usability testing
- Visual design
- Web development
- Quality testing

Information architecture responsibilities

So, exactly how does an information architect contribute to the website planning process? **Table 6.1**, at the end of this chapter, illustrates the ten major roles across the five major stages of a project.

Information architecture deliverables

When an information architect is involved in the website planning process, she or he will develop the following documentation: primary audience goals, persona(s), current content inventory, competitive analysis, content strategy statement, content outline, content gap analysis, site diagram, page description diagrams and wireframes.

Primary audience goals

Defining the primary audience for the website is critical to success. In user-centered design, the needs of the primary audience (and the business goals) will help guide the project. Questions to ask:

- Who is the primary target audience for this site?
- How does (will) this audience use this site?
- What are their goals?

Persona(s)

Because your primary audience won't be sitting with your team during the design process, you need to bring them to life with a persona. A **persona** is a fictional character created to represent an important audience.

Current content inventory

What content is already available? Conduct a thorough content review including text, images and media.

Competitive analysis

The website you are building won't exist in a vacuum. It is important to understand the competition so you can compare functionality, use common vocabulary, identify best practices, and identify opportunities for a competitive advantage.

Content strategy statement

How will the content writers and editors stay focused on the audience's needs? What writing style should be used to complement the branding and strategic goals of the site? Prepare a high-level summary of the purpose of the content, including key themes, major topics, tone and search engine optimization goals.

Content outline

What content will be available on the site at launch? Create a detailed list of all the content needed for the new site.

Content gap analysis

What content will need to be created or revised? Develop a list of all available content, content that needs to be edited to match the content strategy and content gaps that need to be filled.

Site diagram

A high-level architectural blueprint of the site. Maps out the organization and labeling of major areas of the site. **Figure 6.5** shows a simple site diagram for a university website.

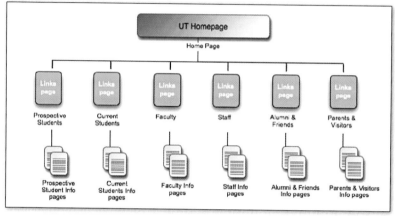

Figure 6.5: Site diagram.

Page description diagrams (PDD)

A written description of top-level pages that specifies what content/functionality belongs on the page and the priority of each content/functionality chunk. **Figure 6.6** illustrates the most common layout for a page description diagram.

Highest Priority Items		Lowest Priority Items
Restaurant Logo	**Branding Message** Supreme Cuisine	**Address**
Main Navigation Links • About • Menus • Photos • Reservations	**Inviting Description** Brief home page copy that compliments branding	**Phone Number** **Hours** **Copyright** This is the lowest priority item on the page.
Feature Dish Photo		

Figure 6.6: Page description diagram.

Wireframes

A simple layout of a web page that is free of any visual design elements. It is a tool for the information architect to try to lay out all the elements listed in the PDD on the page. **Figure 6.7** is an example of a hand-drawn wireframe.

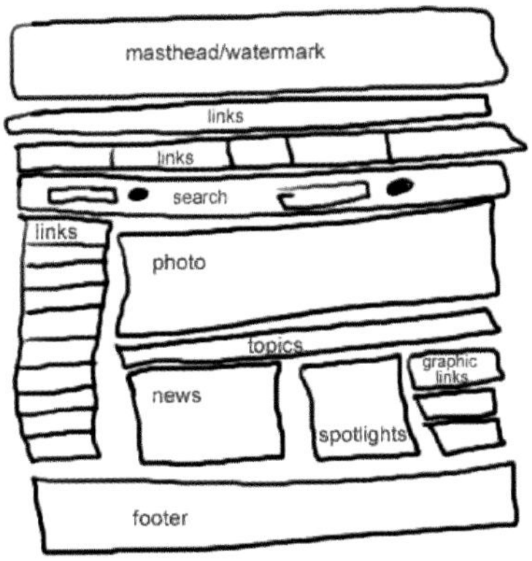

Figure 6.7: Hand-drawn wireframe.

masthead/watermark
links
links
search
links
photo
topics
graphic links
news
spotlights
footer

Summary

Designing websites is a complex process filled with ambiguity. You can greatly increase your chances of success by using the website planning process. Producing a website is similar to producing any project with the key stages of start, plan, build, test and close. A number of skills are necessary to produce a quality website, including project management, information architecture, usability testing, writing, editing, visual design, development and quality testing.

Information architecture is an emerging professional field in web design. IA provides the blueprint for building a successful site via personas, content inventories, competitive analysis, content strategy, content outline, content gap analysis, site diagrams, page description diagrams and wireframes.

In the next few chapters we will look at examples of each IA deliverable and give you a chance to try creating your own website blueprints.

Resource // Recommended reading

Want to see how information architects contribute to the website planning process in the real world? Check out the following articles:

- Web Design Process: http://www.utexas.edu/learn/designprocess/

- Information Architecture—Planning Out a Website: http://dev.opera.com/articles/view/6-information-architecture-planning-o/

- Am I an Information Architect?: http://iainstitute.org/documents/learn/Am_I_an_IA.pdf

Ten major roles of an information architect

	Start	Plan	Build	Test	Close
Steps	Define project requirements.	1. Conduct research. 2. Draft design options and select design.	Produce the design.	QA testing	1. Deploy 2. Maintain
Project management	Define project goals, expectations, deliverables, timeline and resources.	Facilitate communication, keep team on focus, document progress, keep client informed.			
Information architect	1. Primary audience goals	2. Personas 3. Current content inventory 4. Competitve analysis 5. Content strategy 6. Content outline 7. Content gap analysis 8. Site diagram 9. Page description diagrams 10. Wireframes	Advocate for usability and findability.		
Usability tester	Primary audience goals	Personas	Advocate for usability and findability.	1. Conduct usability testing. 2. Prioritze and report issues to team.	

Table 6.1: Website planning process detailing information architecture responsibilities.

	Start	Plan	Build	Test	Close
Steps	Define project requirements.	1. Conduct research. 2. Draft design options and select design.	Produce the design.	QA testing	1. Deploy 2. Maintain
Content manger	Determine voice and style guide.	1. Provide access to current content. 2. Write and adapt content for the Web. 3. Provide content requested by visual designer.	Pour content into site.	Review content for accuracy and grammar.	Keep content current.
Visual designer	Identify branding and perception goals.	1. Conduct creative research. 2. Develop visual designs.	Code HTML and CSS templates (Developer).	Resolve design issues discovered during testing.	Put site into production.
Developer	Identify functional and technical specs.	Research options to meet functional and technical specs.	1. Code HTML and CSS templates (Designer). 2. Develop backend scripts and databases.	Resolve code and functionality issues discovered during testing.	Put site into production.
Quality tester	Identify QA metrics and communicate them to the team.			1. Conduct technical, functional, security testing. 2. Prioritze and report issues to team.	

Table 6.1: *Website planning process detailing information architecture responsibilities.*

CHAPTER 7
Site Planning

by Glenda Sims

I keep six honest serving-men
(They taught me all I knew);
Their names are What and Why and When
And How and Where and Who.
—Rudyard Kipling

The most critical step in the website planning process is defining the project. You haven't completely defined a project until you have discovered the answers to the five Ws and one H: Where, When, Why, Who, What, and How.

- **Where** will the site live? (URL)
- **When** does the site need to be available? (timeline)
- **Why** is the website needed? (business goals)
- **Who** is the primary audience for the site? (audience)
- **What** information/functionality needs to be available on the site? (content/technology)
- **How** will the site be discovered and kept up to date? (marketing and maintenance)

In this chapter, you will learn how to interview the client and gather the information necessary to clearly define the project goals and the primary audience needs. You will also see how to design a detailed project plan, including a work breakdown structure, functional and technical specifications, and a maintenance strategy.

Discover the project definition

Imagine a musician has just come to you and said, "I need a website to promote my music. Can you make a website for me?" You say "Sure! I would love to do that." Then you think to yourself, "Where do I start?"

Remember, the seven steps of any successful project are:

1. Define project requirements
2. Conduct research and analysis
3. Develop design
4. Build
5. Test
6. Deploy
7. Maintain

So, let's focus on how to create the project definition.

1. **Interview the client** to discover the purpose of the project, the target audience, branding/perception goals, content sources, technical specs, and communication strategy.

2. Write a one-page **project brief** based on the information gathered in the client survey. The project brief clearly states the purpose, goals, primary audience, and key deliverables.

3. Document **technical specifications** to clearly establish requirements like screen resolution, browser compatibility, download time, web standards, accessibility, server-side languages, and databases.

4. Develop a **maintenance plan** that documents how the site will be updated and reviewed regularly.

5. Develop the **work breakdown structure**. Establish the timeline for deliverables and tasks for each phase of the project. Assign due dates and resources.

Interview the client

The best way to conduct a client interview is to have a prepared set of interview questions. Whenever possible, share these questions with the client in advance so they have a chance to think about them. Conducting the interview in person will give you the opportunity to adjust the questions based on the client's answers. Let's look at a set of client interview questions based on the five Ws and one H model (Where, When, Why, Who, What, and How).

Client interview—website planning

Project Name:

Contacts for this project: (name, email, phone)

1. **Where?**
   I.   Preferred/existing domain name (URL):
   II. Domain name already registered: Yes/No
   III. Preferred/existing web server:

2. **When?**
   I.   Preferred target date for launching the new site:
   II. Any external factors that influence/affect the schedule:

3. **Why?**
   I.   Business problem(s) you hope to solve with this site:
   II. Primary business objectives/goals for this site:
        (objectives should be measurable)

4. **Who?**
   I.   Primary customer/target audience:
   II. Target audience description (age, gender, education, occupation, income, preferred browser, computer device, Internet skill level...)

5. **What?**
   I.   Function
        A. Why do your customers need you? What is the most important benefit you offer (from your customers' perspective)?
        B. Who are your direct competitors? (include URLs)
        C. What do you offer that is different from your competition?
        D. How do (will) customers use your site? What are their goals?
   II. Perception
        A. Adjectives describing how you want visitors to perceive the new site.

B. Is this different than their current perception?

C. URLs of sites you like. What do you like about these sites?

III. Content

A. Do you have existing content for the site or will you create new content? Who will write the new content?

B. Any visuals or content you want to use from your current site or marketing materials (logo, color scheme, navigation, naming conventions, etc.)?

IV. Technology

A. Do you already have a content management system?

B. Do you already have content in a database? Database Type (Access, MySQL, Oracle...)?

C. List special features you would like to have on the site. For each intermediate or advanced technology, explain how this feature will solve the primary business objectives and benefit the target audience and their goals.

   a. Basic: Search engine

   b. Intermediate:

       1. Blog

       2. Bulletin board

       3. Login (for restricted areas)

       4. Surveys/polls

       5. Wikis

   c. Advanced:

       1. Customization/personalization for users

       2. Database/dynamic content

       3. Ecommerce

       4. Rich Internet apps (AJAX, Flash, Java, Silverlight)

       5. Security

D. Any additional programming/feature requirements?

CHAPTER 7

6. How will you use resources to pay for, market, and maintain the site?

   I. Budget

      A. Pick Two: Low Cost, Fast Timeline, Full Featured

  II. Marketing

      A. Do you have a marketing strategy in mind to promote this project? If yes, could you describe it?

 III. Maintenance

      A. How do you plan to keep the content on the site current?

      B. How often should content change on your site?

      C. Who is responsible for providing and updating content?

As you look at these questions, you might feel comfortable asking the client about where and when. You might also feel confident asking the questions about technology in the "what" section. Don't just ask the easy questions. To help yourself feel more comfortable, feel free to change the wording of these questions to suit your style and your needs. Ask a friend to let you practice interviewing them for an imaginary website.

And whatever you do, *do not answer the questions yourself!* These are client interview questions to be answered by the client. Do not assume you know how the client will answer these questions. Ask them for the purpose of clarity.

But what if the client asks you for advice? You can brainstorm ideas with the client and give them your opinion. Helping them think about the questions and possible answers is helpful. Assuming you know the answers and never asking the questions to the client is a recipe for trouble.

Red Flags

What should you do if your client is unwilling to think about and answer your questions on where, when, why, who, what, and how? Perhaps they think this is a waste of time and you should be able to quickly develop a demo and stop asking so many questions. Well, unless you are psychic, I advise you to let the client know that the foundation of a successful website is a clear-cut project definition. Building a site on ambiguity and assumptions is equivalent to building a house on quicksand.

Project brief—10,000-foot view

Now it is time to take what you have learned during the client interview and boil it down to a one-page project brief. The purpose of the project brief is twofold. First, you will use it to confirm that you understood what the client said they wanted/needed. Second, you will use it to share the big picture with anyone who works on the project. The project brief reduces ambiguity and helps keep the project team focused on the big picture.

Here are the elements of a project brief:

1. **Project name:**

2. **Big picture:**

3. **Project summary:** description of the project in a sentence or two. Imagine you have to explain your project quickly to a colleague in the elevator.

4. **Business objectives/goals:** concise list of measurable objectives and goals discovered in the client interview.

5. **Preferred date for launch by client:** ability to meet this target date is still subject to final agreement on budget and features.

6. **Target audience:**

   I. Audience description: age, gender, education, occupation, income, preferred operating system, browser, computer device, Internet skill level...

   II. Audience objectives/goals: what does the audience want and/or need?

7. **Perception strategy:**

   I. Current perception: list three adjectives describing current audience perception.

   II. Desired perception: list three adjectives describing desired audience perception.

   III. Strategy: briefly describe how the new site will produce the desired perception.

8. **Message Strategy:**

   I. Primary message: what is the primary message you want to convey to the target audience (in a short sentence or phrase)?

   II. Strategy: briefly describe how the new site will convey the primary message.

9. **Competitive Advantages:** Short list of key business strengths that give an advantage over the competition.

Remember, a project brief isn't brief if it is longer than one page! If you struggle writing the brief, don't hesitate to contact the client and ask additional questions. Sharing a draft of the brief with the client is also a good way to elicit additional information and make sure you are on target.

Let's get technical: tech specs

Next we need to discover and document any known technical requirements of the project. At this point in the project, the answer to any of the following questions may be "to be determined." It is better to ask these questions now to avoid any unnecessary surprises.

Preliminary technical survey

1. **Domain Name & Host/Web Server**

   I. Preferred domain name:

   II. Need to register domain name? Yes/No

   III. Preferred host/web server:

   IV. Need to establish new account? Yes/No

2. **Required software/systems:** List any software or system (cms, blog, bulletin board, survey poll, wiki, shopping cart...) that is a pre-determined requirement for this project.

3. **Server requirements:** Need for large disk space: Will initial site content be big, like hundreds of hours of online videos?

   I. Need for high bandwidth: Is initial site traffic expected to be very high, like the first day of online enrollment at a major university?

   II. Database(s): Determined by required software. Can also be influenced by web developer's experience, preference, and considerations for long-term maintenance.

   III. Programming language(s)/framework(s): Determined by required software. Can also be influenced by web developer's experience, preference, and considerations for long-term maintenance.

   IV. Multimedia streaming: List any types of multimedia expected to be served from the site, such as Flash, QuickTime, Real Media, Windows Media...

   V. Security: List pre-determined need for security features like SFTP, SSL Secure Certificates, and VPN access.

   VI. Preference for one-click install/auto upgrade features: List of software for required features like a content management system, blog, bulletin board, survey/poll, wiki, shopping cart…

4. Web code requirements:

   I. Accessibility: Indicate web accessibility laws/guidelines that code will be validated against, such as W3C WCAG 2.0 or U.S. Federal 508.

   II. CSS version: Indicate version of CSS that code will be validated against.

   III. Style sheet types: Indicate whether multiple versions of CSS will be required to support features like high contrast, mobile, or printing.

   IV. HTML version: Indicate version of HTML that code will be validated against.

5. End-user platforms supported: Review current statistics to determine an appropriate list of operating systems, screen resolutions, and browsers to support. If you don't have current stats to work from, use reports from services such as Market Share http://marketshare.hitslink.com as a guide.

   I. Desktop

      A. Operating systems

      B. Screen resolutions

      C. Browser versions

      D. Connection speed

   II. Mobile

      A. Operating systems

      B. Screen resolutions

      C. Browser versions

      D. Connection speed

CHAPTER 7

By specifying the list of browsers that the site will be optimized for, you help the project focus resources effectively. However, browsers that are not on your supported list should not be left out in the cold. Adopt a graceful degradation or progressive enhancement development approach to ensure that the site is available to the widest audience. This will also help the site stay functional in the future as new browsers and browser versions are released. Read more about these web development approaches in Opera's Web Standards Curriculum article on "Graceful degradation versus progressive enhancement" (http://dev.opera.com/articles/view/graceful-degradation-progressive-enhance/).

Remember, it is perfectly acceptable to indicate "to be determined" on any of these questions at this early stage of the project. By reviewing the technical specifications early, you will avoid missing assumptions made by the client.

Maintenance plan

When a client comes to you wanting a redesigned or a new site, it is tempting to just focus on the plan for producing a perfect site by the target date. But few sites maintain appeal if their content is not kept complete, current, and accurate. It is important to clarify how the site will be maintained and who will be responsible. Will the client maintain the site? Do they expect you to maintain it for them?

1. **Website maintenance plan—keepin' it fresh**

2. **Content schedule:** What areas of the site will be updated and how often?

3. **Content contributors:** Who are the content contributors? (list name, title, hours per week/month, web page/section responsibilities)

4. **Contribution/update method**

    I.   How will the site be updated? (HTML editor, WYSIWYG editor CMS...)

    II. Will the content contributors require training and/or software?

    III. Is there an automated process for changing content on any pages on the site? (list page, process and name of technical contact)

    IV. Who will maintain and tune the search engine?

5. **Quality review**

    I.   Who will conduct a quality review on at least an annual basis for:

        A. Accessibility

        B. Broken links

        C. HTML/CSS validation

        D. Security

        E. Site guidelines (templates, branding...)

    II. Who is responsible for approving look and feel changes (as the site expands) to ensure quality of site is maintained?

    III. How often do you anticipate new sections will be added to the site?

IV. Will new sections use the same template or will additional design templates be needed?

6. **Technical support:** Who will be responsible for future

I.   HTML/CSS changes

II. Graphic changes

III. Software/system upgrades and patching

The purpose of asking questions about ongoing maintenance now is to determine if the client wants you to provide these services or if they will be able to handle this with internal resources. This also serves as an opportunity to make the client aware of the importance of (and resources required for) keeping any site fresh.

Work Breakdown Structure (WBS)

The Work Breakdown Structure (WBS) is a detailed list of tasks and milestones that need to be accomplished to meet the project objectives. The WBS breaks the project down into manageable tasks. Each task includes a short description of the work to be completed, the resources assigned, the estimated time to complete the task, and due dates.

Table 8.1 shows a basic high-level WBS for building a website.

CHAPTER 7

Task ID	Task	Hour estimate	Resource	Due date	Done!
1	**Define project**		**Project manager**		
1.1	Client interview		Client and project manager		
1.2	Project brief		Project manager		
1.3	Preliminary tech specs		Project manager		
1.4	Maintenance plan		Project manager		
1.5	Project timeline (work breakdown structure)		Project manager		
1.6	Budget/cost estimate		Project manager		
1.7	Contract/scope of work		Project manager		
1.8	Sign contract		Client		
2	**Information architecture**		**Information architect**		
2.1	Research/benchmarking		Info architect		
2.2	Personas & scenarios		Info architect		
2.3	Proposed content outline		Info architect		
2.4	Proposed site diagram		Info architect		
2.5	Direct user input—interview, surveys, Card Sorts		Info architect		
2.6	Content model & IA strategy		Info architect		
2.7	Page description diagrams		Info architect		
2.8	Content development		Content manager		
2.9	Wire frames		Info architect		
3.0	**Visual design**		**Visual designer**		
3.1	Design round 1		Visual designer		
3.2	Feedback		Client & project manager		
3.3	Design round 2		Visual designer		
3.4	Feedback		Client & project manager		
3.5	Finalize design		Visual designer		

Table 8.1: Work Breakdown Structure.

Task ID	Task	Hour estimate	Resource	Due date	Done!
3.6	Approve design		Client & project manager		
4.0	**Development**		**Developer**		
4.1	Review/adjust technical specs and functional requirements		Developer & project manager		
4.2	Update project plan/timeline and further define any additional coding & integration tasks. Review time estimates and resources.		Developer & project manager		
4.3	Approval for any additions to scope of work.		Client		
4.4	Build & integrate Site		Developer		
4.5	Insert specific coding tasks here including backend programming, software installation, integration, search...		Developer		
4.6	Build templates using web standards.		Developer		
4.7	Enter content into templates		Content team		
5.0	**Testing**		**Quality tester**		
5.1	Content review		Write/editor/ content manager		
5.2	Functionality review		Quality tester		
5.3	Code validation		Quality tester		
5.4	Accessibility review		Quality tester		
5.5	Browser/OS resolution testing		Quality tester		
5.6	Connection speed & load testing		Quality tester		
5.7	Usability testing		Quality tester		
5.8	Search engine optimization		Quality tester		
5.9	Security review		Quality tester		
6.0	**Production plus**		**Team**		
6.1	Style guide		Team		
6.2	Site goes production		Team		
6.3	Initial troubleshooting		Team		
6.4	Celebrate		Team		
6.5	Maintenance		Client		

Table 8.1: Work Breakdown Structure.

CHAPTER 7

Ideally, each task should be clearly defined as a deliverable or planned outcome. The more granular and discrete the task, the easier it will be to estimate the amount of time to accomplish it. Small tasks are also easier for individuals to focus on and complete.

Accurately estimating time for tasks can seem daunting at first. But you will get better every time you do it. To improve your ability to estimate, you should:

- Break tasks down into small pieces.
- Ask the person assigned to the task how many work hours they think it will take to complete.
- If you don't have any idea how long the task might take, take a guess and just write something down.
- Track the time it actually took to complete the task.
- Be aware of your estimation tendencies and attempt to adjust. Are you always underestimating? Then increase your estimates.
- Review your estimates with another person who has project management experience for a reality check.
- Remember ... estimates aren't exact!

Note that there is not a "percent complete" column, but rather a "Done!" column. It is not as useful to track the percent complete because often tasks can get to 60–80 percent complete in a short amount of time, but can take seemingly forever to reach completion. I recommend that you just give credit for completed tasks and not waste time tracking percent complete.

Developing the work breakdown structure, estimating time, and managing a web project are important professional skills that merit their own book. Kelly Goto and Emily Cotler's book *Web Redesign 2.0: Workflow that Works* is a must-read for anyone managing web projects (http://www.web-redesign.com/).

Summary

You may be thinking that the work breakdown structure and all of these tasks, like project definitions, information architecture, testing, and launch are standing in the way of you diving into the real work of visual design and web development.

Be warned! If you skip any of these major steps you are very likely to end up with one or more of the following problems:

CHAPTER 7

- Unexpected requirements that have you pulling all-nighters.

- A server that won't support the software you need to use.

- A beautiful CSS template in the best CMS, but no content because your client won't provide the pictures, copy, and multimedia.

- A site that works fine for you but fails on the primary target audience's browser.

- An angry client who won't pay you because the site doesn't meet web accessibility laws.

- A client phoning you in the middle of the night to "just update the pages" and sending you lots of small change requests after you completed the site for them months ago.

You can avoid pain and actually save time by using the website planning process.

Resource // Recommended readings

- Interview with Kelly Goto http://www.wise-women.org/features/kelly_goto/
- *Web Redesign 2.0: Workflow that Works* http://www.web-redesign.com
- Real Web Project Management: Case Studies and Best Practices from the Trenches http://www.realwebprojects.com/projectbook/

CHAPTER 8
Content Analysis

by Glenda Sims

In the early stages of a web project, you rarely have access to all the content for the site. It is a common practice to use filler text as a placeholder until the actual content is available. The default standard for filler text is known as *Lorem Ipsum*. There is even a handy Lorem Ipsum generator available at http://www.lipsum.com/ to make your life easy. But don't be lulled into thinking that you can design a site without understanding the nature, size, and source of the content that will fill it. In this chapter, we will focus on getting to know your audience and their content needs well and conducting a content analysis. At the end of this chapter, you will know how to find the answers to these important questions using specific information architecture tools (**Table 8.1**).

Questions	Information architecture tools
Exactly who is the content for and what do they want/need?	1. User surveys and interviews 2. Personas and task-based scenarios
What content do we already have?	Content analysis: content inventory
What is the source of each piece of content?	
What content are people using?	Content analysis: web analytics
What do the "other guys" have?	Content analysis: competitive review
What content would we like to have at launch?	Proposed content outline
How would users organize and label our proposed content?	Card sort

Table 8.1: Content questions and information architecture tools.

Focus on the users

Who should the website be designed for? The target audience should be at the center of all design decisions balanced by the client's business goals and the web designer/developer needs. During the process of defining, designing, and building the site, the developers and the clients are physically present as decisions are made. But the target audience rarely gets to voice opinions until the site is already in production. How do we make sure the design focuses on the needs of the end users? We listen closely to what the users are saying in **interviews** and **surveys**, then we develop key **personas** and **task-based scenarios** to clearly define audience tasks.

- Conduct **user interviews and/or surveys**. Find out exactly what users want by asking them in interviews or online surveys.

- Develop key audience **persona(s)**. A **persona** (**Figure 8.1**) is a fictitious character created to represent the primary audience. The persona is developed based on data discovered through user interviews and/or surveys. The persona helps keep the project focused on the needs of the user by bringing an imaginary audience member to life.

- Write **task-based scenarios**. Identify the top 10 to 20 most common situations that bring the target audience to your site to accomplish a specific task. These scenarios will guide the design of the site and are also used as the basis for usability testing.

Figure 8.1: *Persona for a high school student applying to a university.*

Interviews and surveys

Unless you are designing a website for an audience of one (and that audience is you), you need to take some time getting to know the target audience better. Do not assume you know what users need or think. Conducting interviews and/or surveys with members of the target audience will provide valuable data and insight necessary to build effective personas.

Whether you are conducting a face-to-face interview or running an online survey, the information you are trying to discover is:

- What do you **think** about the company? (current perception)

- What is your **experience** with the company's product/services? (history)

- How much do you **know** about this type of product/service? (knowledge level)

- What do you **want** when you use the company's site now? (goals)

- What do you **do** when you are on the company's site now? (tasks)

- What do you **like best/like least** about the company's site now? (satisfaction level)

- How would you **rank** the following new features that are proposed for the site? (priorities)

- What do you **suggest** to improve the site? (opportunities for improvement)

If your client does not have a current site, you can focus the questions on a similar site (for instance, that of your major competitor).

How long should the interview/survey be? Keep interviews to an hour or less and ideally conduct them in the users' environment, giving you the opportunity to observe them in their natural habitat. Try to keep online surveys to 10 minutes or less. Users are more likely to complete an online survey that is short and sweet.

How many people should you interview/survey? Interviews are more time-consuming and also allow for deeper information gathering. Interviewing five people (for each target audience) will often provide enough qualitative data to construct the persona. The number of responses you will want for online surveys is much higher. A rule of thumb is to have at least 100 survey responses for each target audience type. Keep in mind that response rates to surveys are 2 percent to 3 percent on average, unless you have an extremely loyal and engaged audience.

Both interviews and surveys are valuable methods for learning more about the users. Tools like SurveyMonkey and Zoomerang provide free software options for collecting and analyzing the data. For in-depth information on designing and conducting user interviews and surveys, refer to Steve Mulder's book *The User is Always Right*.

Personas

A **persona** is a fictitious character you will create to represent the primary target audience. A persona should include the following basic elements:

1. **Basic demographics**
   I.   Age
   II. Occupation
   III. Education
   IV. Income
2. **Personal**
   I.   Name
   II. Picture
   III. Description

3. Technical profile

I.   Preferred operating system

II. Preferred browser

III. Internet skill level

IV. Favorite sites

4. **Audience goals:** What does the user want to do? Top three to ten tasks this user wants to accomplish on the site.

5. **Business goals:** What does the client want the user to do? Top three business objectives for this audience.

The basic demographic information is usually gathered during the initial client interview. Ask the client if they already have personas for current branding or marketing initiatives. If they do, start from their established persona and add any additional details for this specific project (like technical profile, task-based scenarios, and specific business goals).

Select a name and a photo to represent this persona based on the description the client gave you for this target audience. The name and photo should be appropriate for the stated age of this persona. You can use a tool like the Baby Name Voyager to help you find common names for that age range http://www.babynamewizard.com/voyager. Consider selecting photos from a stock photo service or more casual shots from Flickr. Respect intellectual property and copyright law by obtaining permission to use photos when required. Don't use names or photos of people your project team knows.

Resource // Personas are priceless

Question: Seriously? Why do I need to create a fake person and give them a name and a face (picture)? Can't I just define the primary audience and be done?

Answer: During the design and development stage, without a detailed persona, you will have a tendency to assume that the audience needs are the same as yours. By creating a persona with a name and a picture as well as a detailed description, you bring the target audience into your design process.

For the "Audience Goals" section, use the data you gathered from user interviews/surveys to determine the most important tasks that the target audience will perform on the site. Base the task importance on the user's perspective. Be realistic about what the user wants to do. For example, on a musician's website, a user might want to locate specific information about the artist or a specific song; the musician's business goals might be to have this persona visit the site often (increased traffic on site), friend them on Facebook (increased marketing opportunities), buy/download a song (sales). The client's goals for the user should be realistic and mutually beneficial.

Task-based scenarios

A **scenario** is just a short description of a realistic situation that brings a user to a website with a specific goal or task in mind. Scenarios help you focus the design process on what the target audience really needs and wants.

> **Example:** I heard the singer John Pointer at SXSW this year and I want to know when I can hear him in person again. When and where is his next gig in Central Texas?

> **Example:** I need to find a place for my study group to meet. I want to reserve a room at the library. How do I reserve a study room?

More detailed scenarios can be created to help developers have a deeper understanding of the users. A detailed scenario is a one or two paragraph story that includes the users' task goals as well as their thoughts, concerns, previous experiences, and tendencies.

> **Example:** Jeremy is considering applying to University X. He is very tech savvy. He has built a few personal websites using HTML, CSS, and JavaScript. He has an iPhone and can't imagine life before Facebook. His dad went to University X and is really pushing Jeremy to go too. His mom is encouraging him daily to apply to University X, Y, and Z, but he keeps procrastinating. He expects the online application process to be boring and clunky. He thinks he could design a better site. He wants to get through the application process fast so he can get back to his favorite multi-player online game. He is worried whether he will be happy and fit in at University X.

Task-based scenarios are used during the design stage, before development begins, as well as during the usability testing phase, to measure target audience satisfaction in achieving the primary goals on the site.

Content—the body of the site

"Redesigning a website is like remodeling a kitchen: You must figure out what features and capabilities you need and how you will use them before you design your layout, place appliances and plugs, and select tiles, curtains, and countertops."—Kelly Goto in Web Redesign 2.0

You may be itching to get started on the back-end code or the visual design, but the wise web developer insists on first knowing what content will be available when the site launches. Clients often have a misconception that all they need is a pretty website and that will magically solve all their problems. However, creating the content can often take as much time as designing and developing the site. So, it is important to take the time to plan out the content and functionality requirements using the following tools:

- **Content inventory/audit**—What do we already have?
- **Web analytics**—What do people really use?
- **Competitive review**—What do the others have?
- **Proposed content outline**—What content do we plan to have?
- **Card sort**—How would users organize and label content?

Content inventory—what do we have?

Discovering what content your client already has is the goal of the content inventory. This task is best done by the client, because they know their content best. If the client suggests that a content inventory is not necessary, emphasize that content is the core of the site. Without a strong understanding of the current content and a strategy for creating new content, they risk dooming the site to be incomplete, outdated, and inaccurate.

Let's look at a mock content inventory for a university's old mobile website (**Table 8.2**).

ID	Link name	Current source	Content owner	Keep, upgrade, remove
1.0	**Courses**	`https://utdirect.utexas.edu/diia/hub/`	DIIA	keep
1.1	Mobile blackboard	`http://m.courses.utexas.edu/`	DIIA	keep
1.2	eGradebook	`https://utdirect.utexas.edu/diia/egb/`	DIIA	keep
2.0	**Libraries**	`http://lib.utexas.edu/m/`	Library	keep
2.1	Hours	`http://lib.utexas.edu/m/hours/`	Library	keep
2.2	Catalog search	`http://lib.utexas.edu/m/catalog/`	Library	keep
3.0	**Maps**	`http://www.utexas.mobi/maps/`	ITS	upgrade
3.1	Building list	`http://mobile.utexas.edu/maps/index.html`	ITS	upgrade
3.2	Map beginning at UT Tower	`http://mobile.utexas.edu/maps/coord_search.php?area=3b`	ITS	upgrade
3.3	Garage list	`http://mobile.utexas.edu/maps/garages.html`	ITS	upgrade
4.0	**Sports**	`http://mobile.utexas.edu/sports/`	Athletics	upgrade
4.1	Football	`http://mobile.utexas.edu/sports/schedule.php?sport=football`	Athletics	upgrade
4.2	Baseball	`http://mobile.utexas.edu/sports/schedule.php?sport=base-m`	Athletics	upgrade
5.0	**Austin/world**	`http://mobile.utexas.edu/austin_world/`	ITS	remove
5.1	Austin weather	`http://mobile.weather.gov/port_mp_ns.php?CityName=Austin&site=EWX&State=TX&warnzone=TXZ192`	external	remove
5.2	BBC mobile	`http://www.bbc.co.uk/mobile/web/`	external	remove

Table 8.2: A sample content inventory.

As you see in the previous example, a simple content inventory includes:

- **Content ID**—useful for referencing and locating content in the outline. Choose whatever identification scheme you like, as long as it's unambiguous.

- **Link name**—the current or proposed link name for this content. Don't worry about getting the link name perfect at this time. For now, just make sure it is unique and descriptive.

- **Current source**—indicate where the content is currently located. List the URL if the content is already available online.

- **Content owner**—the person or group responsible for writing and maintaining this content.

- **Keep/upgrade/remove**—indicate if this content is perfect as is (keep), needs to be improved (upgrade), or is not needed on the new site because it is redundant, outdated, or trivial (remove).

Creating the content inventory is not glamorous but it is a necessary step in good information design. For a humorous and insightful look at this process see Jeff Veen's article "Doing a Content Inventory (Or, A Mind-Numbingly Detailed Odyssey Through Your Web Site)" at http://www.adaptivepath.com/ideas/essays/archives/000040.php.

Web analytics—what are visitors doing?

What pages are viewed most? Where do people enter and leave the site? Which keywords are frequently used to search the site? Web analytics tools can provide answers to these questions and help you better understand the effectiveness of a site.

Many web hosting companies offer statistics packages as part of their services. For example, MediaTemple offers free Urchin Analytics and Dreamhost offers free Analog statistics on their basic accounts. If your server does not already have analytics or you want more than they offer, you could consider using Google Analytics, which is free up to 5 million page views per month. If you outgrow the free options, for a fee you can have the most powerful analytic services, which include ClickTracks, WebSideStory, and WebTrends.

Once you have access to the statistics for a website, where do you start to look? Web analytics is a bit like archeology: You are not actually observing people and their behaviors. You are sifting through the tracks they left behind. Let's look at six basic web statistics and what insights they can provide for content analysis:

1. **Hits**—number of requests for files from the server. This statistic is not very useful for content analysis because not only does it include hits for pages, it also includes hits for images, JavaScript, CSS, and any other files that are embedded in a web page.

2. **Page views**—number of requests for web pages from the server. This is a very useful statistic that shows you which pages are viewed most.

3. **Entry pages**—a listing of the page where each visitor entered the site. Are the key entry pages what you expected? Do not assume users are only entering the site via the home page. Are these entry pages designed in such a way that they help users accomplish their goal?

4. **Exit pages**—the last page viewed by each visitor. Are visitors leaving in unexpected places? Are visitors abandoning processes at a critical step? Statistics will not tell you why they left, but they encourage you to investigate what is causing problems.

5. **Bounce rate**—percentage of visitors who enter on one page and exit from that same page without visiting any other pages in the site. Avinash Kaushik shares his thoughts in "Bounce Rate: Sexiest Web Metric Ever?" at http:// www.mpdailyfix.com/bounce-rate-sexiest-web-metric-ever/.

6. **Keywords**—terms and phrases people used in external search engines to find your site. These keyword statistics help you understand your visitors' vocabulary in relationship to your site.

Resource // Web analytics warning

Web analytics are only half of the picture. These web statistics show you what happened, but they do not tell you why it happened (or what steps to take based on this data). For example, a page may have very low page views for any of the following reasons:

- Users do not need this information (delete page).

- Users need this information, but cannot find it due to usability problems (keep page and improve findability).

- A few users need this information and find it very useful (keep page).

Returning to the content inventory, let's add two new columns for page views and bounce rate. Then review your decisions to keep, upgrade, or

CHAPTER 8

CHAPTER 8

remove each page. Check to make sure you are not planning to remove pages that have very high page views (without providing an easy transition path for your users).

You may need to consider upgrading pages that show up unexpectedly high in your exit page statistics and or have a high bounce rate (over 35 percent). Consider carefully reviewing pages (and their content) that are listed as high entry pages to make sure they are helpful and user friendly. Check to see if the keywords visitors used to find your site through external search engines are reflected in how you name your links (**Table 8.3**).

ID	Link name	Current source	Content owner	Keep, upgrade remove	Page views 12/2008-11/2009	Bounce rate
0.0	**UT mobile**	http://mobile.utexas. edu	ITS	upgrade	39,643	**30%**
<---- rest of table data here ---->						
4.0	**Sports**	http://mobile.utexas. edu/sports/	Athletics	upgrade	64,689	**24%**
5.0	**Austin/ world**	http://mobile.utexas. edu/austin_world/	ITS	remove	6,864	**82.32%**

Table 8.3: Content inventory with web analytics data.

The web analytic measures we have focused on here are just a few of the most obvious statistics to consider when monitoring activity on a site. If you want to dive deeper into this area, I recommend reading Avinash Kaushik's book *Web Analytics: An Hour a Day*. Keep in mind that web statistics are just a report of what happened. They can help you verify certain activities and spot potential problem areas once you know how to analyze and interpret the data based on customer behavior and business outcomes.

Competitive review—what are the others doing?

A high level analysis of major competitors is vital to a website's success. It is better to know the competition's strengths and weaknesses before you finalize your website strategy. Here are the basic steps for conducting a competitive review:

1. **Identify the competition**—Ask the client who their major competitors are. Use services like Alexa to discover competitors you client may not be aware of (http://www.alexa.com/siteinfo). When possible, identify seven to 10 main competitors to review. At the very least, review three competitors.

2. **Decide what to analyze**—Reviewing the competition has many benefits, including increased understanding of this business sector, common vocabulary, best practices, as well as the obvious strengths and weakness of the competition. Types of information you might gather include:

   I.   High level inventory of features/functionality

   II. Visual design characteristics

   III. Labels and organization schemes

   IV. Usability heuristics

3. **Develop a competition survey**—Develop a list of objective questions. The more consistent you are when you review each competitor, the more you will gain from this analysis. For a practical example of data to collect, see Jason Withrow's article "Competitive Analysis: Understanding the Market Context" at http://www.boxesandarrows.com/view/competitive_analysis_understanding_the_market_context and Thomas Myer's article "How to conduct a Web site competitive analysis" at http://www.ibm.com/developerworks/webservices/library/us-analysis.html.

4. **Answer survey for each competitor**

5. **Analyze survey data**

6. **Write a report of the findings and recommendations**

The experience of surveying the competition is a priceless reality check that, when done well, increases the probability of designing a successful website.

CHAPTER 8

Proposed content outline

Now the fun begins. Taking everything you have learned from the user survey/interviews, personas, task-based scenarios, content inventory, web analytics, and competitive analysis, draft a proposed list of content and functionality for the new site. Begin to group and categorize the list in a way that you think will make sense to the target audience. Don't be overly concerned about getting it perfect, just take your best shot based on everything you have learned up to this point from your research and analysis. Review the proposed content outline with your project team and client. Let them know you are trying to make sure you have a complete outline of proposed content with a reasonable organization structure. Make adjustments to the proposed content outline based on this internal feedback. Remind everyone that the outline is just a draft, because the next step is to get direct feedback from the target audience(s).

Card sorting

It has been a while since we have invited real users into this design process. As useful as personas and task-based scenarios can be, nothing is better than feedback from actual users. Card sorting is an inexpensive way to let the target audience tell us exactly how they would label and organize the content being proposed for the site.

Card sorts are either open or closed. Both types begin with a set of cards, where each card represents a content item listed in the proposed content outline.

- **Open card sort**—Participants are asked to sort the site content cards into groupings that make sense to them. Participants are not given pre-defined groupings or categories.

- **Closed card sort**—Participants are asked to sort the site content cards into predefined categories.

- **When is it most valuable to do a card sort?** Card sorts are extremely useful when designing a new site or redesigning an old site.

- **How many cards should I have?** Try to have at least 20 cards and no more than 50. Fewer than 20 cards and there isn't enough to sort. More than 50 cards and sorting can be time-consuming and/or frustrating.

- **How many people should I test?** Jakob Nielsen recommends testing 15 people. See his article "Card Sorting: How Many Users to Test" (http://www.useit.com/alertbox/20040719.html).

- **Should I use an open or a closed sort?** Start with an open sort to generate ideas for how content should be organized or labeled. Consider using a closed sort to evaluate the effectiveness of predetermined categories. But be careful of relying too much on a closed sort. Categorizing information is not the same activity as finding information. Read Donna Spencer's article "Closed Card Sorting—I finally found a use for it" (http://maadmob.net/donna/blog/2005/closed-card-sorting-i-finally-found-a-use-for-it).

You can conduct card sorts in person, using index cards, or you can use software to help you conduct a remote card sort. Services like OptimalSort and WebSort offer free plans as well as pay-as-you-go options.

> **Tip:** See detailed instructions on how to plan, conduct, and analyze a card sort at http://www.usability.gov/methods/design_site/cardsort.html.

Summary

You can distinguish yourself as an effective web professional by taking the time to analyze the proposed site content before developing a content strategy (See Chapter 9, "Content Strategy"). When a client says to you, "We have most of the content," ask them to show it to you. If they suggest, "We can focus on content after we have visual designs," respond that the site needs to be designed to fit the content. When they say, "Our communications team will write the content," ask to invite them to the next meeting. When they say "Creating content will be easy," let them know that websites are often launched late because the content is not ready.

Useful, usable content doesn't just happen.

Resource // Recommended reading

- Contextual interviews http://www.usability.gov/methods/analyze_current/learn/contextual.html
- User surveys http://www.usability.gov/methods/analyze_current/learn/surveys.html
- Developing personas http://www.usability.gov/methods/analyze_current/personas.html
- Task-based scenarios http://www.usability.gov/methods/analyze_current/scenarios.html
- "Content analysis: a practical approach" by Colleen Jones http://www.uxmatters.com/mt/archives/2009/08/content-analysis-a-practical-approach.php
- Content inventory http://www.usability.gov/methods/design_site/inventory.html

(continues)

CHAPTER 8

Resource // Recommended reading

(continued)

- "A few good web analytic tools: measuring your website's success " by Laura Quinn http://www.techsoup.org/learningcenter/internet/page6760.cfm

- "How to conduct a website competitive analysis" by Thomas Myer http://www.ibm.com/developerworks/webservices/library/us-analysis.html

- "Card sorting: a definitive guide" by Donna Spencer and Todd Warfel http://www.boxesandarrows.com/view/card_sorting_a_definitive_guide

- *Card sorting: designing usable categories* by Donna Spencer http://rosenfeldmedia.com/books/cardsorting/blog/card_sort_analysis_spreadsheet/

- *Content Strategy for the Web* by Kristina Halvorson

CHAPTER 9
Content Strategy

by Glenda Sims

In this chapter you will learn how to finalize the information architecture plan for the site. Based on the project definition (Chapter 7, "Site Planning") and the content analysis (Chapter 8, "Content Analysis") you will see how to develop a content strategy that serves as the blueprint for the developers, designers and writers to begin constructing the site. The content strategy will include:

- Content strategy statement
- Approved content outline
- Gap analysis
- Content map
- Page description diagrams
- Wireframes
- Storyboards for interactive design

Chez Sous le Vent: the client

Imagine that you have recently started the Smart Web Design firm with two of your friends, Steph and George. A brilliant chef by the name of Aarron Walter has asked you to create a website for a new restaurant he is opening in a few months. The name of the restaurant will be Chez Sous le Vent.

Steph and George interviewed the client and took great notes. They have also created the project brief, a persona (**Figure 9.1**) for the primary target audience, and a proposed content outline (**Table 9.1**). Let's look at these documents to get a sense of what this project is about.

Project brief for Chez Sous le Vent

Project name: Chez Sous le Vent website

1. **Big picture:**

    I. **Project summary**: establish a web presence for Chez Sous le Vent, a new French restaurant in Austin, Texas.

    II. **Business objectives/goals:**

        A. Website that matches brand/message of Chez Sous le Vent.

        B. High ranking in Google for phrase "Austin French restaurant."

        C. Ability to take reservations online.

    III. **Preferred date for launch by client**: April 15, 2015.

2. **Target audience:**

    I. **Audience description:** Urban professionals. 30-40 years old, college degree, middle to high income, tech savvy mobile web user.

    II. **Audience objectives/goals:** see menus, pricing, location, hours, and contact information. Able to make reservations online.

3. **Perception strategy:**

    I. **Current perception:** unaware.

    II. **Desired perception:** sophisticated, laid-back, French with a Texas twist.

    III. **Strategy:** Working with Lion Advertising, we will select imagery, typography, and a color palette that reveal the personality of Chez Sous le Vent.

4. **Message strategy:**

    I. **Primary message:** Supreme Cuisine—French Austin Fusion, Contemporary French Cuisine with a Texas Twist.

II. **Strategy:** We will work with Lion Advertising to develop the writing style guide. Lion will providing the copy and images.

5. **Competitive Advantages:**

I.   **Brilliant chef** (see press file).

II. **Relaxed, intimate, romantic atmosphere.**

III. **Extraordinary wine list.**

IV. **Strong emphasis on local ingredients—Austin fresh.**

Figure 9.1: *Primary persona for Chez Sous le Vent.*

ID	Link name	Current source	Content owner
0.0	**Home**	Copy/images will be provided by Lion Advertising	Mike (manager)
1.0	**About**	Philosophy section in business plan	Mike (manager)
1.1	Bios	Copy/images will be provided by Lion Advertising	Mike (manager)
2.0	**Menus**		Chef Aarron
2.1	Dinner	Word doc on Aarron's laptop	Chef Aarron
2.2	Wine list	Word doc on Aarron's laptop	Chef Aarron
3.0	**Reservations**	http://www.opentable.com	Mike (manager)
4.0	**Contact**	Mike will send info via email	Mike (manager)

Table 9.1: *Proposed content inventory for Chez Sous le Vent.*

CHAPTER 9

Content strategy statement

A content strategy statement is the guideline for anyone who will be creating or editing content for the site. It is a high-level summary of what was learned during the content analysis (Chapter 8) and a set of guidelines that clarify to the writers and editors:

- Content for whom and why?—primary audience(s) and their goals.
- What content?—high level content topics.
- What style?—general branding, messaging, and tone.
- Findable content?—search engine optimization considerations.

The content strategy statement can be a simple one-page document. Leen Jones shares some content strategy statement examples at http://www.leenjones.com/2008/08/what-is-content-strategy-part-ii-examples/. Based on what we've discovered, here is an example content strategy for Chez Sous.

Content strategy for Chez Sous le Vent

1. **Content for whom and why?**

    I.   Who: Sophisticated urban professional (Michaela persona)

    II. Why: Audience and business goals

        A. Michaela wants to be able to:

            a. See menu/pricing.

            b. Get a sense of the restaurant's vibe.

            c. Decide if Chez Sous is worth visiting.

            d. Get directions.

            e. Make reservations.

        B. We want Michaela to:

            a. Perceive Chez Sous as sophisticated, laid-back French cuisine with a Texas twist.

            b. Make reservations online.

            c. Recommend Chez Sous to others.

CHAPTER 9

2. **Core Content**

3. **Menus**

4. **Hours/Locations**

5. **Contact**

6. **Reservations**

7. **Restaurant philosophy and chef bio**

8. **Style**

9. **Brand:** Contemporary French cuisine with a Texas twist.

10. **Message:** Supreme cuisine—French-Austin fusion.

11. **Tone:** Sophisticated yet laid-back, welcoming, unpretentious, engaging, conversational.

12. **Findability/search engine optimization:** Content reviewed for SEO on terms: "French Fusion," "Chez Sous," "Austin French restaurant."

Approved content outline

The time has come to finalize the content outline for Chez Sous le Vent. Adjust the topics and link names based on the research and findings of the content analysis (Chapter 8). A discovery during the competitive review was the value of adding a photo tour of Chez Sous, similar to what is found at Olivia's, http://olivia-austin.com/pictures/. The photo tour supports the business goal of helping Michaela get a sense of the restaurant's vibe. So, the content outline is adjusted to include a new section for the tour with a link name of "Photos."

The client also originally requested that the main navigation links be icons instead of words. You were concerned about this request and decided to gather feedback from the target audience. Using a closed card sort activity with these icons you learned that busy urban professionals did not find the icon navigation intuitive to use. The test subjects repeatedly said things like, "I don't have time to figure out what these pictures mean (on the navigation bar). I'm just looking for the menu and how to make reservations." The research you gathered in the card sort helped the client understand that their personal preference for icons would not make a pleasant user experience for site visitors (**Table 9.2**).

CHAPTER 9

ID	Link name	Current source	Content owner
0.0	**Home**	Copy/images will be provided by Lion Advertising	Mike (manager)
1.0	**About**	Philosophy section in business plan	Mike (manager)
1.1	Bios	Copy/images will be provided by Lion Advertising	Mike (manager)
2.0	**Menus**		Chef Aarron
2.1	Dinner	Word doc on Aarron's laptop	Chef Aarron
2.2	Wine List	Word doc on Aarron's laptop	Chef Aarron
3.0	**Photos**	See if Lion Advertising will do this	
4.0	**Reservations**	http://www.opentable.com	Mike (manager)
5.0	**Contact**	Mike will send info via email	Mike (manager)

Table 9.2: Approved content outline for Chez Sous le Vent.

To formally finalize the content outline, set up a meeting with the client for review and approval. Ask the client to determine who is best suited in his organization to provided new or edited content. Document these assignments in the content outline. Additions to the content outline after it has been approved should be made with care to avoid project bloat.

Tip: Project bloat, also known as scope creep or featuritis, is an increase in project deliverables without accounting for the required increase in cost/resources and often without regard for user needs. Don't be a victim of the creep!

Gap analysis and the content creation plan

Before we take time to craft information architecture diagrams for the site, we need to make sure that the content the client wants on the site will actually be ready before the site needs to launch. Good content is not created without good planning.

The first step in developing a content creation plan is to identify what content is missing by doing a gap analysis. To conduct a gap analysis, simply take the approved content outline and add a new column labeled "Gap." Working with the client, determine which items in the outline need to be created or edited.

You may be thinking, "Why am I doing the content gap analysis? Isn't this the client's responsibility?" In an ideal world, the answer is, yes, the client should be in charge of the gap analysis and the content creation plan. Part of your role as an information architect is to help the client understand the importance of developing and maintaining quality content. Give your clients the best opportunity to succeed by helping them realize what content needs to be created or edited, and assigning those tasks early in the project.

Good content doesn't just happen

When a client says to you "We have most of the content," ask them to show it to you. If they suggest "We can focus on content after we have visual designs," repond that the site needs to be designed to fit the content. When they say "Our communications team will write the content," ask to invite those team members to the next meeting. When they say "Creating content will be easy," let them know that websites are often launched late because the content is not ready.

Good content is the core of a good site. Don't wait until the end of the project to discover that the quality content needed is nowhere to be found. Be smart. Insist on a content strategy that includes a plan for content development, creation, editing, tuning, and maintenance.

Ask the client to assign one of their employees as a content manager, whose responsibility it is to create and manage the project plan for all content creation and editing. If the client resists claiming this responsibility, you can absorb the content creation and editing tasks into the overall web project plan, but let the client know that content creation and management is a permanent client responsibility that prevents the site from quickly becoming inaccurate, incomplete, and ineffective. Involving client's employees who will keep the site fresh at the beginning of the process is a best practice and a wise investment (**Table 9.3**).

ID	Link name	Current source	Content owner	Gap
0.0	Home	Copy/images will be provided by Lion Advertising	Mike (manager)	gap
1.0	About	Philosophy section in business plan	Mike (manager)	
1.1	Bios	Copy/images will be provided by Lion Advertising	Mike (manager)	gap
2.0	Menus		Chef Aarron	
2.1	Dinner	Word doc on Aarron's laptop	Chef Aarron	
2.2	Wine List	Word doc on Aarron's laptop	Chef Aarron	
3.0	Photos	See if Lion Advertising will do this		gap
4.0	Reservations	http://www.opentable.com	Mike (manager)	gap
5.0	Contact	Mike will send info via email	Mike (manager)	

Table 9.3: Gap analysis for Chez Sous le Vent.

Blueprints: information architecture diagrams

The content of the site is starting to take shape. Up until now, we have been using words to define the purpose, audience, high-level content topics, and recommendations. In this section, we turn to the tools information architects use to diagram the site structure—boxes and arrows. The four types of diagrams we will cover are:

1. **Content map**—a graphic representation of the approved content outline.

2. **Page description diagram**—a lightweight representation of the chunks of content required on a page and their priority.

3. **Wireframe**—bare-bones layout of the required content and functionality on a page. By definition, wireframes exclude any reference to color, typography, or visual imagery.

4. **Storyboard**—diagram of a primary user scenario to visualize the user experience.

Content map

The approved content outline we have for Chez Sous le Vent is short and easy to visualize. However, you may have projects where the content outline is hundreds of rows. When you are dealing with large amounts of content it is very enlightening to look at the data from different angles.

Software like OmniGraffle (Mac) and Visio (PC) make it very simple to convert your content outline into a **content map**. OmniGraffle's outline view (**Figure 9.2**) is an easy way to enter your hierarchical text-only outline and have the software automatically draw the content map diagram. Stephen Turbek gives step-by-step instructions on how to use Excel and Visio in his article "The Lazy IA's Guide to Making Sitemaps" over at Boxes and Arrows http://www.boxesandarrows.com/view/ the_lazy_ia_s_guide_to_making_sitemaps.

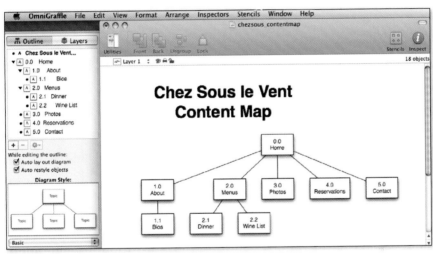

Figure 9.2: Content map for Chez Sous le Vent.

Include the content ID numbers in the diagram for easy reference back to the approved content outline. These ID numbers will also come in handy as we move on to the page description diagrams, wireframes, and storyboards. Whether your content outline is small or large, take the time to create a content map to help the project team visualize the structure of the site.

Page description diagrams

A brilliant tool in the information architect's tool belt is the **page description diagram (PDD)**. Dan Brown developed the first PDD in 1999 to clearly communicate strategic content priorities for a page, without stepping into the visual designer's territory of effective layout. A page description diagram:

1. Lists all content chunks that belong on a specific page.

2. Prioritizes each chunk of content.

3. Removes visual design (color, font, layout) from this stage of the conversation.

A common layout for the PDD is to use the horizontal axis for priority. For example, a PDD for any given page might have three columns. The first column would list the high priority content. The second column would list the medium priority content. The third column would list the lowest priority content.

Figure 9.3 shows an example of a page description diagram for Chez Sous le Vent's home page.

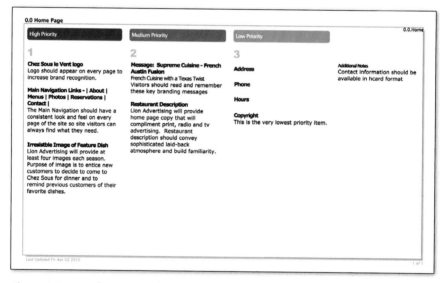

Figure 9.3: Page description diagram for Chez Sous le Vent's home page.

Try it yourself!

Imagine you are the web designer for "An Event Apart". Write a simple page description diagram for the home page at http://www.aneventapart.com/.

Develop a page description diagram for each of the key pages of the site. Review the PDDs with the client and confirm that all content listed is included in the content strategy plan (with a person assigned to write it as well as a target date for content delivery).

Why are PDDs so valuable? Dan Brown sums it up nicely when he says "The page description diagram is a tool to allow designers and information architects to stay comfortably within their own realms without compromising communication."

Resource // Dan Brown

I encourage you to read Dan Brown's article on page description diagrams entitled "Where the Wireframes Are," http://www.boxesandarrows.com/view/where_the_wireframes_are_special_deliverable_3.

Wireframe

A **wireframe** is a bare-bones layout of a web page. It is a simple drawing of the chunks of information and functionality for key pages in the site. You will want to create a wireframe for the home page, each unique second level page, and any other significantly different pages on the site. Wireframes include the containers for all the major elements of the page. Elements include navigation, placeholders for images, content and functional elements (like search), and footer. Wireframes do not include any reference to color, typography, or visual imagery.

Tip: GraffleTopia.com is a great resource for OmniGraffle stencils that make drawing wireframes like the one shown in **Figure 9.4** easy. You'll find a host of other valuable wireframing tools including stencils and gridded sketchpads at http://konigi.com/tools/overview.

CHAPTER 9

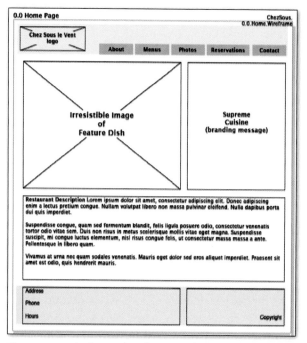

Figure 9.4: *Wireframe for Chez Sous le Vent home page.*

Wireframe warnings

The moment you begin to draw a wireframe you have entered the zone of the visual designer. One could argue that you should not be drawing wireframes unless you are formally trained in the visual design principles of balance, rhythm, proportion, and dominance. Three possible solutions to the natural tension that occurs between information architects and visual designers over wireframes is to:

1. Put a large disclaimer at the bottom of every wireframe stating: "Disclaimer: Wireframes are NOT visual design (typography, colors, images, final layout, etc.). Wireframes are a rough draft of required content only."

2. Have the visual designer develop the wireframes based on the page description diagrams.

3. Skip the wireframe deliverable all together. Warning: Skipping both wireframes and page description diagrams is severely dangerous to the health of a website.

Wireframes and page description diagrams focus on required elements and their relative importance without the added complexity of visual design.

CHAPTER 9

Wireframes are an inexpensive way to test structural design ideas. Making major changes to a wireframe is simple compared to making major changes to a visual design.

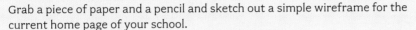

Try it yourself!

Grab a piece of paper and a pencil and sketch out a simple wireframe for the current home page of your school.

Storyboards for interactive design

Before we complete the content strategy for the site, we need to identify any interactive elements or web applications. Interaction design is about functionality, the path users take to accomplish a task, and their real world surroundings. Creating a **storyboard** for key interactive elements in the site is useful in helping the project team understand what brought the user to the site, the situational context, and what they are trying to do. Questions to consider when constructing the storyboard include:

- What are the thoughts that trigger the user to come to your site?
- How does the user get to the site? (search, link from an email, URL from an ad or a friend)
- What is the user specifically wanting to accomplish?
- What path does the user take to get what they need?
- What is going on around the user while they are trying to accomplish their task? Are other people present? Is anyone helping them? Are they focused or distracted?
- What happens when the user finishes the task? Are they satisfied? Did you give them a helpful confirmation? Is this a good time to tempt them with similar services or information?

A storyboard is a high-level illustration of a key user scenario. Detailed task or process flows would be developed at a later stage by the interaction designer.

You can create your storyboard using paper and pencil, OmniGraffle, Visio, or your favorite drawing tool. You can even get creative and use a free comic strip generator like http://www.stripgenerator.com/strip/create/.

Figure 9.5 shows a simple storyboard for online reservations at Chez Sous le Vent created using `http://www.stripgenerator.com/strip/create/`.

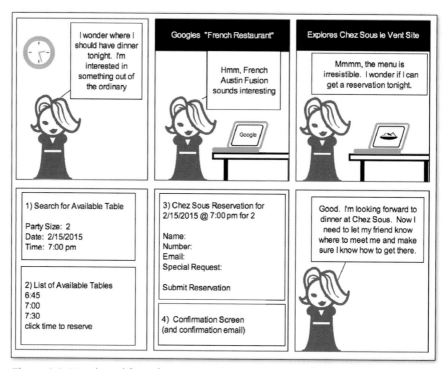

Figure 9.5: Storyboard for online reservations at Chez Sous le Vent.

Summary

You can distinguish yourself as an effective web professional by taking the time to analyze the proposed site content and developing a content strategy. You've heard carpenters advise us to "measure twice and cut once." In the web design world we measure for a site by defining the project, bringing the target audience into the process through personas, analyzing the content, and mapping out a clear content strategy. A formal content strategy will include a content strategy statement, an approved content outline with a gap analysis, a content map, page description diagrams, and wireframes. Storyboards should be included for any key interactive elements on the site. The content strategy is a powerful tool that keeps the web design process focused on the user's needs and the business goals.

Well-designed websites filled with useful, usable content don't just happen. The content strategy is the architectural design underneath the code and visual design.

Resource // Recommended readings

- The Content Strategist as Digital Curator
  http://www.alistapart.com/articles/content-strategist-as-digital-curator/
- The Discipline of Content Strategy
  http://www.alistapart.com/articles/thedisciplineof contentstrategy/
- The Case for Content Strategy-Motown Style
  http://www.alistapart.com/articles/the-case-for-content-strategy-motown-style/

Part III:
Implementation— HTML and CSS Fundamentals, and Accessibility

By this point in the book, you already know what tools you need to design and develop web pages, how to use the Web effectively as a learning resource, the fundamentals of how the Web works, and how to plan your site's structure. In this section we will delve into the practicalities of implementing your site design using HTML and CSS. HTML stands for Hypertext Markup Language; this is the language you use to structure your site content, and give it meaning. CSS stands for Cascading Style Sheets; this is the language you use to style your content and position it on the page.

We will also spend several pages discussing accessibility—the practice of implementing websites so that their content can be accessed by anyone, regardless of any disability they may have (for example, blindness or mobility impairments), or what platform or browser they are using. A wide variety of devices are being used to browse the Web these days, from desktop and laptop computers to mobile phones, televisions and game consoles. Because accessibility is so important to good web design, all examples in this book are written with it firmly in mind, and there are also some chapters near the end of this part that deal with specific accessibility topics. This part concludes with suggestions for a real website project that will put your skills into action and bring it all together.

To summarize, we will be looking at the following topics in this part:

- **CSS and HTML background and syntax basics**
- **HTML DOCTYPEs**
- **The HTML <head> element, and its contents**
- **Using whitespace effectively**
- **Images**
- **HTML text, links, lists, tables, forms, and generic containers**
- **Styling specific HTML features with CSS**
- **CSS layouts with floats and positioning**
- **Accessibility and assistive technologies overview**
- **Accessibility testing**
- **How to bring these concepts together to create a website**

Oldham, Lancashire
United Kingdom

Chris Mills works for Opera Software (the Viking web browser vendor),
evangelising open web standards and Opera technologies, and heading up
Opera's education activities. He publishes regular design and development
articles on http://dev.opera.com, and is the creator of the Opera Web
Standards Curriculum.

Outside of work, Chris is a metal warrior, playing really fast drums in the
mighty Conquest of Steel. He lives in Oldham in the Northwest of England,
with Kirsty, Gabriel and Elva.

http://www.opera.com
http://dev.opera.com
http://www.opera.com/wsc
http://twitter.com/chrisdavidmills

CHAPTER 10
HTML Intro

by Chris Mills

In this chapter I will start to take you through probably the most important web technology used when building websites: Hypertext Markup Language, or HTML. HTML is the technology that you use to contain all of the data—or content—that is to appear on your website. It gives your content structure, and allows you to ascribe meaning to different parts of it. For example, is that part a paragraph, or a list, or a data table, or a form for site visitors to enter feedback into? Are those words more important than the others; are they a quote?

There are many different parts to HTML, and we will look at all the details in forthcoming chapters. Here we will look at the basics, to get you acquainted with the technology.

At the end of the chapter we will also have a brief look at the upcoming new version of HTML, HTML5, seeing how the code differs, and what the new version might mean for your work.

*In this chapter you have the opportunity to **Try it yourself!** with the convenient sample code downloads found on the book's companion website—http://interactwithwebstandards.com.*

The history of HTML

When Tim Berners-Lee invented the World Wide Web, he created the first web server and web browser and the first version of HTML. HTML has changed considerably since its early days, but more than half of the original features of the language are still used today, and the original spirit of HTML lives on. The idea is to provide a simple technology that anyone can use to publish content that is viewable by anyone else. Web content should be accessible regardless of the device being used to browse the Web, or the user's personal circumstances (such as where they live, or if they have any disabilities).

As more people started writing web pages and more web browsers became available, more features were added to HTML. Many were adopted universally (e.g., the `<img>` element used to insert an image into a document was first implemented in the NCSA Mosaic browser, and is now supported by very nearly all browsers), whereas some were more proprietary and really only used in one or two browsers. There was a growing need for standardisation—so that authors of web browsing software had a guide that definitively described to them what HTML looked like to help them judge whether they were missing out on implementing some features. The IETF (Internet Engineering Task Force—a standards body concerned with interoperability across the Internet) published a draft proposal of HTML in 1993. This expired without becoming a standard in 1994, but prompted the IETF to create a working group to look at HTML standardisation.

In 1995, HTML 2.0 was written, taking ideas from the original HTML draft. An alternate proposal called HTML+ was written by Dave Raggett; it was used as a basis for many of the new elements implemented by browsers (such as the method for inserting images into documents, pioneered by NCSA Mosaic). A draft of HTML 3.0 followed later that year, but work on that version was discontinued because of a lack of support for the direction by browser makers. HTML 3.2 dropped many of the new features of 3.0, and instead adopted many creations of the then-popular browsers Mosaic and Netscape Navigator. In 1997, the World Wide Web Consortium (W3C) published HTML 4.0 as a recommendation that adopted more browser-specific extensions but also attempted to rationalise and clean up HTML. This was done by marking various elements as **deprecated**—this means the elements are obsolete and, whilst they still exist in this version, they will be removed in a later revision. This was to encourage better and more meaningful use of HTML in documents (described later in "The importance of good semantics").

HTML 4.01 was published in 1999, with some errata noted in 2001. In 2000, the W3C also published the XHTML 1.0 specification, which was HTML re-structured as valid XML.

In 2005, a splinter working group called the Web Hypertext Application Technology Working Group (WHATWG) started work on HTML5, a new version of the specification that aims to address the shortcomings of HTML 4.01. You will learn more about this version in the last section of this chapter, entitled "HTML5."

What HTML is

Web browsers read HTML, a type of file that usually has an extension of `.html`, just like common desktop applications such as Microsoft Word and Open Office read `.doc` files, and Photoshop and Fireworks read common image formats like `.psd`, `.gif`, `.png`, and `.bmp`. When you look at an HTML page on the Web, the `.html` file is sent to your computer and interpreted and displayed by the web browser you are using to surf the Web.

HTML consists of content—the words, references that pull in images to be displayed, and other data found on a web page—wrapped in special syntax markers that indicate what the different pieces of content are (paragraphs, lists, images, etc.) These special markers are called **elements**, which are further subdivided into opening and closing **tags**. Web browsers (sometimes known as **user agents**) take this content and the elements it is wrapped in, and display it as intended. For example, a simple paragraph and heading is marked up in HTML like so:

```
<h1>A simple HTML example</h1>
<p>This is a simple paragraph of text, marked up in
HTML. Above it there is a heading, or title, which tells
you instantly what this HTML page is all about.</p>
```

When interpreted in a web browser, this will appear as shown in **Figure 10.1**.

Figure 10.1: A simple HTML example, rendered in a web browser.

In most browsers there is a **Source** or **View Source** option, commonly under the **context menu** (the menu that comes up when you right-click on a PC or Cmd + click on a Mac while viewing the HTML page). Viewing source and looking at other people's code is how many people have learned HTML for years, and this is indeed one of the beauties of the Web; it is an open, sharing environment.

Resource // User agent

The term **user agent** refers to more than just web browsers—it means any software that is used to access web pages on behalf of users. There is an important distinction to be made here: All types of desktop browser software (Internet Explorer, Opera, Firefox, Safari, etc.) and alternative browsers for other devices (such as the Wii Internet channel, and mobile phone browsers such as Opera Mini and WebKit on the iPhone) are web browsers. But there are other types of user agents. There are automated programs that Google and Yahoo! use to index the Web to be displayed as search engine results. These are also user agents, although no web user is controlling them directly.

One of the great things about HTML is that it is free to create. All you need to write or edit HTML is a text editor such as Notepad++ on Windows, Text Wrangler on Mac, or Gedit or KATE on Linux. All of these are free.

You could choose a more feature-rich alternative such as Dreamweaver, Coda, Quanta or Eclipse if you like, but the choice is yours. Some people like a really basic, stripped-down text editor, and some people like a more visual approach to web design involving dragging boxes around the screen and filling in forms.

You should have chosen a text editor by this point. Just make sure it supports both UTF and ISO encodings (see Chapter 4, "Internet Fundamentals"); ideally it should also have syntax highlighting and line numbering.

When you are editing an HTML file, it is a good idea to have it open in your text editor, while at the same time having it open in a web browser. This way you can make edits to the code, save the file, and then jump over to your browser and refresh the page to check that your changes have given the desired results (some more advanced code editors have a "preview" feature, which allows you to check your web page output without leaving the editor application—look out for those).

Try it yourself!

It's your turn to start having a play with some HTML:

1. Look at some of your favorite web pages. Use the View Source feature to have a look at the underlying HTML code that makes up the page. Bear in mind that not all of the code you will see will necessarily constitute best practices HTML.

2. Find some simple content to mark up—it could be anything, from your favorite poem, or a recipe in a cookbook, to your life story! Research what elements are needed to mark it up.

3. In the code download for this chapter, find the file named `simple_html_example.html`, open it in your text editor, and replace the content (the stuff in between the `<body>` and `</body>` tags) with your content. Add elements as necessary to mark up your content.

4. Once you've finished, save your file and then load it in a web browser to see what it looks like when rendered. If it doesn't look quite like you were hoping, feel free to make more edits.

5. Take some time to discuss the code with your teacher/tutor/other students: whether it is correct, whether it could be done better, etc.

The structure of an HTML document

The smallest possible valid HTML document would be something like **Figure 10.2**.

```
❶ ┌─ <!DOCTYPE HTML PUBLIC "-//W3C//DTD HTML 4.01//EN"
   └─ "http://www.w3.org/TR/html4/strict.dtd">
   ┌─ <html>
   │   ┌─ <head>
❸ ─┤   │     <title>Example page</title> ─ ❹
   │   └─ </head>
❷ ─┤     ┌─ <body>
   │  ❺ ─┤     <h1>An even simpler HTML example!!</h1>─ ❻
   │     └─ </body>
   └─ </html>
```

Figure 10.2: *Valid HTML document.*

Let's go through each of the features in order:

❶ The document starts with a **document type definition** or **DOCTYPE** (described in more detail in Chapter 12, "<head>"). This points to a set of rules that the HTML in the document should follow to be regarded as correct.

❷ After this, we have the <html> element, which is a wrapper around the entire document. The closing </html> tag is the last thing in any HTML document.

❸ Inside the <html> element, we first find the <head> element. This contains information about the document (also known as metadata), which is generally not displayed in the browser (again, see Chapter 12 for more information).

❹ Inside the <head> is the <title> element, which defines the "Example page" heading you can see in the title bar at the top of the browser window in **Figure 10.3**.

❺ After the <head> element there is a <body> element, which contains the actual content of the page.

❻ In this case the entire page content is a single header element—<h1>—that contains the text "An even simpler HTML example!!"

And that's our document in full. Rendered in a browser, it looks like **Figure 10.3**.

Figure 10.3: An even simpler HTML example.

As you can see, elements often contain other elements. The <body> of the document will invariably end up involving many elements placed inside one another (also known as **nested elements**). It might help you to think of HTML elements as boxes that can contain other smaller boxes.

The syntax of HTML elements

As you have already seen, a basic element in HTML consists of two tags wrapped around a block of text. There are some elements that don't wrap around text, and in almost every case elements can contain sub-elements (such as <html> containing <head> and <body> in the previous example). Elements can also have **attributes**, which can modify the behavior of the element and introduce extra meaning. **Figure 10.4a** and **Figure 10.4b** show the anatomy of a basic HTML element.

```
       <h1>The Basics of
❶ ─ ❷ ──<abbr title="Hypertext Markup Language">HTML</abbr>
       </h1>
```

Figure 10.4a: The anatomy of a basic HTML element.

❶ Parent element

❷ Child element

CHAPTER 10

Figure 10.4b: The anatomy of a basic HTML element.

③ Opening tags

④ Attribute

⑤ Closing tags

In this example we have an <h1> element with an <abbr> element inside it. abbr is short for **abbreviation**, so that element's job is to specify that HTML is an abbreviation. The title attribute of <abbr> specifies an expansion of the abbreviation, and most browsers will display title attributes as a **tooltip** when the element is moused over (**Figure 10.5**).

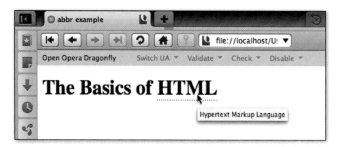

Figure 10.5: How browsers display the title *attribute.*

There are many types of HTML elements available, and you will learn about most of them over the remaining chapters. In brief, the most important HTML content elements are as follows:

- Elements for emphasising pieces of text inside paragraphs, such as quotes, cited quote sources, strong/important text, variables, code excerpts, deleted or inserted text, etc.

- Elements for marking up numbered or bulleted lists.

- Elements for marking up data contained in tables (**tabular data**).

- Form elements that allow website visitors to enter information into the page.

- Image elements—allowing us to insert images into a web page.

- Elements that allow us to link from our document to other people's documents.

- Elements that allow us to specify custom semantics and divisions in content.

Tip: The Web is case sensitive—be very mindful of this. For example, if you are trying to display an image file and you've written `cats.jpg`, but the file has actually been named `Cats.JPG`, your web page won't display it. This is often a problem for beginners working on local Windows environments, which are not case sensitive. The casing of your file names is one of the first things to check if something inexplicably fails to appear.

Try it yourself!

Do some research! Have a look through the recommended resources available on the InterACT website (`http://interact.webstandards.org/curriculum/`) and find out some information about three to five HTML elements not already covered in this chapter. Write a blog post about what they do, with code examples.

The Document Object Model

The previous example contained a heading element with an abbreviation element inside it. When a browser renders this code to display it for you, it converts the HTML into a **Document Object Model** (DOM), which can be thought of as a tree-like structure, or hierarchy. So the following HTML:

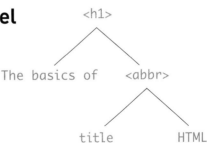

Figure 10.6: A basic Document Object Model diagram.

```
<h1>The basics of
    <abbr title="Hypertext Markup Language">HTML</abbr>
</h1>
```

can be represented by the DOM seen in **Figure 10.6**.

In DOM-speak, `<h1>` is the **parent** element **node** of both the `<abbr>` element node and the text node "The basics of." The `<abbr>` element is referred to as a **child** element node of the <h1> element, and contains two children of its own: an attribute node of `title`, and another text node containing the text "HTML."

> **Tip:** Every element, attribute, and chunk of text is represented by a node, which is a generic container for a piece of content inside the DOM. When an element contains another element, the contained element can be referred to as a child, and the container can be referred to as a parent. If you have two elements inside another element, those elements are at the same level in the DOM, and are referred to as siblings. These terms are standard computer science terms used when talking about datamodels.

Now, you may be wondering what the point of this DOM representation is. Simply put, a well-formed DOM is essential to make sure that browsers interpret your web page structure correctly and consistently. When you start working with CSS and JavaScript, you'll see that you need to travel up and down the different levels of the DOM hierarchy to select elements you want to manipulate. The only way to ensure that this will work correctly is to make sure that the DOM is well-formed—see the "HTML best practices" section later in the chapter.

Block level and inline elements

There are two general categories of elements in HTML, which correspond to the types of content and structure those elements represent: block level elements and inline elements. **Block level** means a higher-level element, normally informing the structure of the document. It may help to think of block level elements being those that start on a new line, breaking away from what went before. Some common block level elements include paragraphs, list items, headings and tables.

Inline elements are those that are contained within block level structural elements and surround only small parts of the document's content, not entire paragraphs and groupings of content. An inline element will not cause a new line to appear in the document; it is the kind of element that would appear in a paragraph of text. Some common inline elements include hypertext links, emphasized words and abbreviations, and short quotations.

The importance of good semantics

Semantics means the meaning of a word, phrase, sentence, etc. In HTML terms, having good semantics means that your HTML should be self-describing—the elements wrapping the content should match the function or purpose of the content itself. Let's look at an example. If we wanted to mark up a top-level heading followed by two lower-level headings, with content in between them, we *could* do it like this:

```
<font size="5">Information about cats</font>
<font size="2">This document contains information
about cats.</font>
<font size="4">Feeding cats</font>
<font size="2">Cats eat cat food.</font>
<font size="4">Cat games</font>
<font size="2">Cats like to play with balls of wool,
and chase mice.</font>
```

But this is bad—<font> elements are bad, bad old practice, and you should never use them in your work. In the bad old days of the Web this sort of markup was common, and it can still be found on many sites today.

Visually this results in the desired look, but in the end it's just a bunch of text blocks that have no meaning. In addition, you should never specify how your HTML looks inside the HTML—all styling information should go in the CSS.

This is not good at all. Instead you should use the right elements to convey the right meaning:

```
<h1>Information about cats</h1>
<p>This document contains information about cats.</p>
<h2>Feeding cats</h2>
<p>Cats eat cat food.</p>
<h2>Cat games</h2>
<p>Cats like to play with balls of wool, and
chase mice.</p>
```

That's much better. This example uses heading elements to mark up headings, and paragraph elements to mark up paragraphs. And it doesn't rely just on how it looks for meaning, so it's unambiguous and machine-readable.

As a side note, you could also mark up the content like this:

```
<div id="top-heading">Information about cats</div>
<div class="paragraph">This document contains
information about cats.</div>
<div class="second-level-heading">Feeding cats</div>
<div class="paragraph">Cats eat cat food.</div>
<div class="second-level-heading">Cat games</div>
<div class="paragraph">Cats like to play with balls
of wool, and chase mice.</div>
```

And then use different CSS rules to style the different types of content how you want them to look. This is fine, surely? <div> elements with id and class attributes are perfectly allowed in modern HTML, and now we are putting all the styling information in CSS, to satisfy best practices.

But this is still bad! <div> elements are generic container elements and have no intrinsic meaning, and there are much better elements available to use for marking up headings and paragraphs.

You can style it to look like a top-level heading and two second-level headings with paragraphs in between, but the HTML elements used *do not* describe the content as being so. The content is currently described as "six pieces of text, all of the same weight and function."

So why is a lack of semantics so bad? There are many reasons, but the two main ones are as follows:

- First of all, people with impaired vision use an assistive technology called a screen reader to read web pages out to them. These use semantics in many ways—for example, they use headings to navigate the different pieces of content, so the users can find what they want on a page. If there are no heading elements present, it is impossible for these users to effectively navigate the content.

- Second, search engines such as Google and Yahoo! use keywords they find on pages to index and rank content, and they give more weight to keywords in headings. If your content contains no headings, it will be less likely to come up in search results, so fewer users will find it.

Generic containers: <div> and <span>

One question you might be thinking at this point is "What do I use if there are no suitable elements available to mark up my content?" Fortunately, the HTML spec contains two elements that serve as generic containers you can use to identify custom pieces of content—<div> and <span>:

- <div> is used to wrap block-level elements. For example, if you wanted to identify three paragraphs as the main content of the page, and a list and two paragraphs as the navigation menu of the page, you would wrap them in <div>s with suitable classes, such as class="content" or class="menu".

- <span> is used to wrap inline elements/content. For example, if you wanted to identify a few words of text inside a paragraph as an editor's note or warning note with a special style, you'd wrap them in <span>s.

You'll see a lot of examples of these elements in action throughout this book, so all will become clear. The most common use you will see for these elements is as common page elements that you'll see on many sites, such as headers, footers or content sections.

As you'll see later in this chapter, HTML5 includes specific elements to mark up many of these common sections, as it was thought that they were *de facto* standards that should be officially recognised.

Try it yourself!
Research other reasons why bad semantics in your HTML causes problems, and write a blog post about them.

HTML best practices

There are certain best practices that you should follow when writing your HTML. Browsers are resilient with built-in error handling, so if you make mistakes (for example, a stray quote mark, or not closing an element, which leads to a poorly formed DOM), it doesn't cause problems up front, as browsers compensate for it. They fill in the blanks and guess what you intended.

However, different browsers interpret your broken markup in different ways. This can lead to inconsistencies and weird behaviour later on when you want to style things with CSS, add behaviour with JavaScript, etc. Therefore it's best to follow consistent proper syntax rules and best practices. It is analogous to dotting your i's and crossing your t's.

In general, wherever possible, you should try to follow these best practices when writing HTML:

Best Practice	Correct	Incorrect
Always include quotes around attribute values.	`title="Hypertext Markup Language"`	`title=Hypertext Markup Language`
Always close elements properly after they have been opened.	`<h1>This is a heading</h1>`	`<h1>This is a heading`
Always nest elements properly.	`<p><em>This text is emphasised <strong>strongly </strong> in parts </em></p>`	`<p><em>This text is emphasised <strong>strongly in parts</em> </strong></p>`

Table 10.1: HTML best practices.

Tip: The Web is a very forgiving programming environment compared to, say, Java or C++. This is a blessing and a curse—it lowers the barrier of entry so that more people can create web pages, but it has led to some really bad code being put up there on the Web. This is what we are hoping to eventually stamp out!

The trouble in the last example is that the `<strong>` element is no longer cleanly inside the `<em>` element, and they overlap, so the logical DOM parent-child structure no longer works, and you get uncertainties: is the text "strongly in parts" made stronger by the `<strong>` element or not?

In addition, there are some best practices that are not directly related to making markup valid:

- Always separate content from presentation—you should keep all content inside the HTML, but separate all styling information into CSS. This means not using presentational elements like `<font>`.

- Make sure your text is always well-worded and easily readable. Read Chapter 5, "Writing for the Web," for more information on this.

- Make sure your content is as usable and accessible as possible: see Chapters 22-24 for more information on accessibility.

Character references

One last item to mention in an HTML document is how to include special characters. In HTML the characters <, >, and & are special. They start and end parts of the HTML syntax, rather than representing the characters less-than, greater-than, and ampersand. One of the earliest mistakes you might make when dealing with character references is including an ampersand in your HTML content and then having something unexpected appear. For example, writing "Imperial units measure weight in stones&pounds" could end up appearing as "...stones£s" in some browsers because they get confused and interpret special characters as markup rather than simply text. The literal string £ is a character reference in HTML.

A **character reference** is a way of including a character in a document that is difficult or impossible to enter using a keyboard, or in a particular document encoding. The ampersand (&) introduces the reference and the semi-colon (;) ends it.

References can either be numbers (numeric references) or shorthand words (entity references). An actual ampersand has to be entered into a document as &, which is the character entity reference, or as & which is the numeric reference. A full chart of character references can be found on http://evolt.org/entities.

HTML5

In 2005, a group of professional web developers decided to write a new version of the HTML specification—HTML5—under the mantle of the WHATWG. This was officially adopted by the W3C as a draft in 2008, and is still in progress. Why do we need a new HTML? Well, the current version works very well for the original purpose of HTML—which was to create collections of static documents connected together by links—but it doesn't do so well for the purpose HTML has been adopted for in modern times.

These days, web developers often use HTML and associated technologies to create applications that behave more like desktop software, with more dynamic user interaction and features. So far developers have been doing this with HTML 4.01, but it has involved a lot of hacking and complicated scripting. HTML5 removes a lot of this by providing things like built-in form validation, offline storage, video rendering and more. Different browsers already have support for some HTML5 features, although some parts of the technology are still at an early experimental stage.

So how does this affect you? Don't fret: you are not suddenly going to have to ditch the teachings in this book and learn a new version! HTML5 does not replace HTML 4. It simply adds powerful new elements and other features, while also clarifying (and in many cases simplifying) the syntax that makes a document valid.

Resource // HTML5 tutorials

You can find a lot of good articles showing how to use HTML5 features on http://dev.opera.com. Another great resource for HTML5 tips, tutorials, and news is http://html5doctor.com. The article "Designing a blog with HTML5" is a particularly good guide to basic HTML5 syntax—see http://html5doctor.com/designing-a-blog-with-html5/.

HTML5 elements, although a bit different, are logical and well thought out—a sample HTML5 document looks like so:

```
<!DOCTYPE HTML>
<html>
    <head>
        <title>A sample HTML5 document</title>
    </head>
    <body>
        <header>
            <h>Sample document</h>
        </header>
        <section>
            <article>
                <h>Subheading</h>
                This is some of the content of the document.
            </article>
```

```
    <article>
        <h>Subheading 2</h>
        This is some more content, in a different
        section of the document.
    </article>
</section>
<footer>
    <a href="mailto:me@opera.com">Chris Mills</a>
    &copy; 2009
</footer>
</body>
</html>
```

Nothing has changed that radically—the elements are a bit different, but they reflect common semantics that you find on many websites that developers tend to create using <div> elements, for example <div id="header">, which is replaced with <header> in HTML5. You'll also notice that the DOCTYPE is much simpler than the ones you saw earlier.

Try it yourself!

You can start experimenting with these new elements already, even though browsers don't yet officially support them. All you have to do is write a rule in your CSS to make them all display as block elements. Try this out!

Summary

By this point, you have taken your first steps towards understanding how HTML works. In the following chapters we will look at HTML features in much more detail, as well as Cascading Style Sheets, the technology that styles HTML content.

CHAPTER 11
CSS Intro

by Chris Mills

In the last chapter we looked at HTML, the language used on the Web to give your web page content structure and meaning. In this chapter we will look at the basics of another technology: **Cascading Style Sheets**, or **CSS**. If HTML is the most widely used important technology on the Web, CSS is the second-most important and widely used.

CSS is a rule-based language that applies styling to your HTML elements— you write rules in CSS that select various groups of elements, and modify **properties** of those elements such as text color, background color, width, border thickness, font size, etc.

In this chapter we will briefly look at the history of CSS, learn what CSS rules look like, and how to apply them to an HTML document. We'll look at some techniques to keep CSS short and easy to read, and discover some exciting new features in CSS3.

*In this chapter you have the opportunity to **Try it yourself!** with the convenient sample code downloads found on the book's companion website—*http://interactwithwebstandards.com.

CSS—a brief history

CSS is not as old as HTML, but it is not far behind. It was first proposed as a technology by Håkon Wium Lie circa 1994, and standardised in 1996 by Håkon and Bert Bos. There were other web styling language proposals around at this time, such as **Style sheets for HTML** and **JSSS**, but CSS won through.

CSS2 became a W3C recommendation in 1998, and a revised spec— CSS 2.1—was agreed upon in 2001. Funnily enough, work on the next version—CSS3—also started in 1998, but work on this spec has been slow, and in fact is still ongoing as of the time of writing of this book, although some parts are now complete, with reasonable support across modern browsers.

The anatomy of a CSS rule

Without further ado, let's have a look at some CSS code, and dissect it to highlight all the important bits. First, some pseudo-code for a CSS **rule set** (often just called a **rule**):

```
selector {
    property1: value;
    property2: value;
    property3: value;
}
```

The pertinent parts are as follows:

1. The **selector** identifies the HTML elements that the rule will be applied to, identified by the actual element name, e.g., <body>, or by other means such as class attribute values.

2. The curly braces contain the properties of the element you want to manipulate, and the values that you want to change them to. The curly braces plus their contents is called a **declaration block**.

3. The **property/value** pairs are separated from each other by semicolons; the properties are separated from their respective values by colons. Each one of these lines is called a **declaration**.

Now let's look at a specific example:

```
p {
    font-size: 2em;
    font-family: Arial;
    color: red;
    border: 2px solid blue;
}
```

This rule set selects every single <p> element in the HTML document(s) the CSS is applied to, and:

- Makes the font size double the default size
- Changes the font of the paragraphs to the Arial font
- Changes the colour of all the text to red
- Adds a two pixel thick solid blue border around the paragraphs

So, without the CSS applied to it, our HTML will look something like **Figure 11.1**.

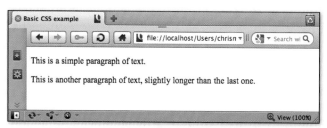

Figure 11.1: A default HTML example with no CSS applied.

With the CSS applied to our HTML, it will look like **Figure 11.2**.

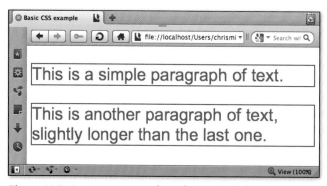

Figure 11.2: Our HTML example with our CSS rule applied to it.

Resource // CSS reset

The CSS rules you apply to your HTML add styling to your elements *on top of* the existing styles the browser applies to your HTML. These default styles are called the **user agent style sheet** and they tend to differ slightly between browsers. Some designers get rid of these default styles to make their styling more consistent across browsers using what is called a **CSS reset**. Read `http://meyerweb.com/eric/tools/css/reset/` for more details on CSS resets.

Try it yourself!

Now it's your turn. At this point I'd like you to open up the two example files that make up the example seen in **Figure 11.2** (check out `basic_css_example.html` and `basic_css_example.css` in the Chapter 11 code examples):

1. Start playing with the HTML and CSS.

2. Try adding some more elements, and CSS rules to style them (this may require some research on the Web).

3. After you have spent some time doing this, spend some time discussing your work with your teacher, tutor, colleagues, or fellow students.

How CSS is applied to HTML

There are three methods of applying CSS to HTML: **inline CSS**, **internal style sheets** (officially termed **header style information** by the HTML spec), and **external style sheets**. In this section I will go through each one briefly and discuss its advantages and disadvantages. In each of the examples featured in this section, the output will look the same (the paragraphs are colored red)—see **Figure 11.3**—but the method of applying the CSS to the HTML will be different.

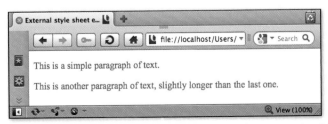

Figure 11.3: Internal, external, or inline CSS? The output should be the same.

Inline CSS

Inline CSS involves applying styles directly to elements by adding declarations into `style` attributes on those elements (you don't put selectors or curly braces inside `style` attributes). For example, if you check out the file `inline_css.html`, you'll see the following:

```
<p style="color: red;">This is a simple paragraph of
text.</p>
<p style="color: red;">This is another paragraph of text,
slightly longer than the last one.</p>
```

The property/value pairs inside the `style` attributes are applied directly to the paragraphs.

Internal style sheet

An internal style sheet is applied to HTML by placing the CSS rules inside a `<style>` element inside the document `<head>`. Check out `internal_stylesheet.html` and you'll see this code:

```
<head>
    <title>Internal style sheet example</title>
    <style type="text/css">
      p {
          color: red;
      }
    </style>
</head>
<body>
    <p>This is a simple paragraph of text.</p>
    <p>This is another paragraph of text, slightly longer
    than the last one.</p>
</body>
```

External style sheet

The CSS rules for an external style sheet are placed inside a separate file with a `.css` extension, and that file is then referenced from inside the `<head>` element by a `<link>` element. If you check out the `external_stylesheet.html` file, you'll see the following code:

```
<head>
    <title>External style sheet example</title>
    <link rel="style sheet" type="text/css"
    href="external_stylesheet.css">
</head>
<body>
    <p>This is a simple paragraph of text.</p>
    <p>This is another paragraph of text, slightly longer
    than the last one.</p>
</body>
```

You can check out the CSS applied to the HTML by the `<link>` element by opening the `external_stylesheet.css` file in your text editor.

CHAPTER 11

Resource // Applying styles with `@import`

There is a class of CSS constructs called **@rules**, or **at-rules**. These simply encapsulate a group of CSS rules and apply them in a specific way. We won't cover these in depth in this book, as they are an advanced CSS feature that you won't use very often. We will however look at a couple over the course of this part of the book.

You can find out more details about at-rules by reading Patrick Griffiths' At-Rules article—http://htmldog.com/guides/cssadvanced/atrules/. Also good is Sitepoint's reference on `@import`: http://reference.site point.com/css/at-import.

The `@import` rule allows you to import a style sheet into another set of styles. The `import_example.html` file inside the code download uses an `@import` rule inside the `<head>` element, like so (you can use them inside external style sheets too, if you like):

(continues)

Resource // Applying styles with @import

(continued)

```
<head>
    <title>@import example</title>
    <style type="text/css">
        @import url("external_stylesheet.css") screen;
        /*...other import statements or CSS styles could
        go here...*/
    </style>
</head>
```

You'll sometimes see import statements without the parentheses, although it doesn't really make any difference—either syntax is equally valid. Another thing to be aware of is that @import should always be first in a style sheet. Finally, you can specify that the imported style sheet be applied only to certain types of media by including the media type at the end of the import statement: screen, print, tv, etc.

So why use the <link> element instead? That is considered better practice because some older browsers, e.g., Internet Explorer 4 and Netscape 4 (Internet Explorer 6 does not support putting the media type at the end of the statement), do not support @import. Saying that, some web designers have deliberately used @import to hide styles from these browsers.

A better strategy for Internet Explorer is to use conditional comments to serve specific styles to it. http://dev.opera.com/articles/view/supporting-ie-with-conditional-comments/ by Bruce Lawson is a good write-up of how to use conditional comments to serve specific content to Internet Explorer.

Which one to use?

To be honest, you will very rarely use inline CSS, unless you want to override (see the "Resolving conflicts—inheritance and the cascade" section, later on) CSS contained in an internal or external style sheet. It goes against the best practice of separating content from presentation, and is not very efficient—you have to add a separate style declaration to every element you want to style.

Internal style sheets are better—you can style multiple elements with one rule and take advantage of the cascade as well (see later). You also only have to update styling information in one place within your document. But it is still inside the HTML!

External style sheets are best—they allow you to remove the styling information from the HTML completely, and you can style many HTML documents using a single style sheet, allowing control over a whole site's styles from one place!

CHAPTER 11

Tip: Bear in mind that you will not always be in control of all of a website's styling information, for example if you are tasked with adding content to a site that uses a third party content management system. In cases like this you might well have to use inline styles to beat your pages into shape, which is not ideal. In imperfect situations, you just have to do the best you can.

Try it yourself!

1. Create your own example HTML, and apply styles to it using external, internal and inline styles.
2. Use an `@import` rule to add more styles to your document.
3. Research the different types of at-rules, and write a blog post about them.

CSS comments

One thing to learn early on is how to comment in CSS. You add comments by enclosing them in /* and */. Comments can span several lines, and the browser will ignore these lines:

```
/* These are basic element selectors */
selector {
    property1: value;
    property2: value;
    property3: value;
}
```

You can add comments either between rules, or inside declaration blocks—for example in the following CSS the second and third properties are enclosed inside comment delimiters, so they will be ignored by the browser. This is useful when you are checking out what effect certain parts of your CSS are having on your web page; just comment them out, save your CSS, and reload the HTML.

```
selector {
    property1: value;
    /* property2: value;
    property3: value; */
}
```

Unlike other languages, CSS only has block level comments—single line comments do not exist. You can of course constrain the comment to a single line if you wish, but you still need to include the opening and closing comment delimiters.

CSS shorthand

There are several different CSS properties that can be combined into single declarations, allowing you to cut down on the amount of code you need to write—this is referred to as CSS **shorthand**. For example, we have already seen an example of shorthand in an above example:

```
border: 2px solid blue;
```

This is actually the shorthand equivalent of the following lines:

```
border-width: 2px;
border-style: solid;
border-color: blue;
```

In fact, each of these lines styles the border on all four sides of an element, and are themselves shorthand. For example, the line:

```
border-color: blue;
```

could be further broken down into:

```
border-bottom-color:
border-top-color:
border-left-color:
border-right-color:
```

to manipulate borders on different sides individually. You can also apply different values to the four different borders on a single line by specifying the different values one after the other, like so:

```
border-color: blue red green yellow;
```

The order that the sides are specified in such rules is top, right, bottom, then left (it might help you to remember it by thinking of *clockwise, starting from the top*). Also note that you can use a two-value declaration, like so:

```
border-color: blue red;
```

The first value specifies top and bottom, and the second value specifies left and right.

There are many different types of CSS shorthand that you will meet in your journey through CSS, and we'll cover them as we explore different aspects of web design in more detail in coming chapters. For now, it is important just to know that CSS shorthand exists, and to have a healthy appetite for experimenting with it!

Try it yourself!

1. Take `external_stylesheet.html` and `external_stylesheet.css` as a basis, save a copy of them, and prepare to get your hands dirty.

2. Apply a different colored border to each side of the paragraphs.

3. Why doesn't the border appear when you just use a `border-color` declaration? What else do you have to do?

4. Research the `padding` property, and its syntax. Experiment with its longhand and shorthand, and give one side a different `padding` value to the others.

5. `background` is another feature of block-level elements that shorthand is used with a lot. Research `background` properties, and try to apply a background image that repeats horizontally to the paragraphs.

CSS measurement units

When specifying the size of any dimension in CSS—e.g., `width`, `font-size`, `margin`, etc.—you have many options available to you for the units you specify the measurements in. You've already seen two in this chapter: pixels (px) and typographic ems (em). **Table 11.1** shows the units that you will be most likely to use in your day-to-day work, along with descriptions and examples.

Unit	Description	Example
Pixel (px)	A pixel is one dot on a computer monitor.	`width: 200px;`
Em (em)	An em is equal to the default font size of the page. So if that is 16px, then 1em = 16px.	`font-size: 2em;`
Point (pt)	A point is equal to 1/72 of an inch, although this is not completely reliable across platforms.	`line-height: 36pt;`
Percent (%)	The measurement you specify will be equal to the percentage of the space available in the containing element.	`width: 50%; /* The element's width will always be equal to 50% of its parent element's width */`
Inch (in), centimeter (cm), millimeter (mm)	Equal to the measurement units you'd expect from real life. Physical sizes like these tend to be reliable only for styling printed matter.	`height: 12in;`

Table 11.1: Commonly Used CSS Units

 Tip: There are other units, but you'll very rarely find cause to use them. I'll leave it as an exercise for you to look the others up!

In subsequent chapters we'll go much more deeply into the best practices of what units to use at appropriate points. For now, be aware that different units are appropriate for different situations. For example:

- It is usually best to size text using ems, as then the text will resize proportionally to its surroundings when browser resize controls are used, even in older browsers such as Internet Explorer 6.

- If you want a column of content to always remain the same size, then pixels will usually suffice.

- If you want a column of content to resize proportionally to browser width, percentages are ideal.

Colors in CSS

Throughout the course of this chapter you have seen a few examples of CSS properties that set colors, e.g., on borders or text. It may not surprise you to learn that, like many things in CSS, there are many different ways to set colors in CSS. In the following subsections I will go through each one.

Keywords

The most human-readable way of specifying colors in CSS is by use of **keywords**. You can specify common colors by name, for example:

```
p { color: red; }
h1 { color: fuchsia; }
h2 { color: black; }
```

There are 17 of these color keywords that you can use; a full list is available at http://reference.sitepoint.com/css/colorvalues. You will be likely to use the more common ones, such as black and white. However for more detailed designs you will want more precise control over the colors you display, and more color choices. After all, modern computers are capable of displaying approximately 16.7 million colors!

Hex values

Hex values are the most common way of specifying colors for professional web designers. Hex is short for **hexadecimal**, and the idea is that you specify six hexadecimal values, two each for the red, green, and blue channels that make up each color, preceded by a hash or pound sign. For example:

```
p { color: #ff0000; }
/* This is equivalent to the keyword red */
```

This system allows you to precisely set a color. Each hex value has 16 possible values (0 to 9, then a to f). Each of the three color channels (R, G, and B) has a possible 256 values (16 x 16). So the total number of possible colors you can choose from is 256 x 256 x 256 = 16,777,216: the 16.7 million color value first mentioned above.

> **Tip:** You can find a good color scheme picker at http://colorscheme designer.com/, and a hex to RGB converter at http://www.321webmaster .com/hex-to-rgb.

RGB(a)

RGB stands for simply **Red Green Blue**; this color system is very similar to the above hex value system, except that you specify the values for R, G, and B in either whole decimal numbers or percentages. This makes it a bit easier than hex values, and more logical to designers. For example:

```
p { color: rgb(255,0,0); } /* This color is equivalent
to #ff0000 */
p { color: rgb(100%,0,0); } /* And so is this one */
```

The whole number value for full red is 255—you use numbers ranging from 0 to 255 to cover the range of 256 possible values.

In addition to defining colors, CSS3 also provides a way to define the **transparency** of a color, or *how see-through it is*. This is what the (a) at the end of RGB(a) means—(a) stands for **alpha**, which is another way of saying transparency. Another term you'll meet is **opacity**, which is the opposite of transparency. It is a measure of how solid a color is—a completely **opaque** color is completely solid, whereas a completely **transparent** color can't be seen at all!

So, to specify a color that includes transparency, you specify a value for the red, green, and blue channels, plus a value between 0 and 1 for the alpha channel. 0 is completely transparent while 1 is completely opaque. For example:

```
p { color: rgba(255,0,0,0.25); } /* This color is very
transparent… */
p { color: rgba(255,0,0,0.7); } /* …this one less so… */
p { color: rgba(255,0,0,0.95); } /* …while this one is
almost completely opaque */
```

In **Figure 11.4** I have added a patterned background to the page, and included our paragraphs with varying degrees of transparency set on their background colors, to show you what effect you can get by manipulating the alpha channel.

Figure 11.4: RGB(a) colors, and the effect of manipulating the alpha channel.

You can create some nice design features via subtle use of transparency.

HSL(a)

HSL(a) works in a very similar way to RGB(a), except that the way of calculating the colors is different. HSL stands for **Hue Saturation Lightness**—some argue that this is an even more logical color system for designers to work with, as you can choose variations on a color by simply increasing the saturation or lightness values. For example:

```
#p1 { background-color: hsl(0,100%,50%); }
#p2 { background-color: hsl(0,100%,60%); }
#p3 { background-color: hsl(0,100%,70%); }
#p4 { background-color: hsl(0,100%,80%); }
```

The hue accepts a whole number between 0 and 360 as the value, while the saturation and lightness values accept a percentage—0–100%. Applying these color values to successive paragraphs gives you the result shown in **Figure 11.5**.

Figure 11.5: Easily selecting different variations of the same HSL color by varying the percentage of lightness.

The alpha channel works in exactly the same way as before, for example:

```
p { color: hsla(100,50%,20%,0.5); }
```

Tip: RGB(a) and HSL(a) colors are supported in most modern browsers, with the exception of Internet Explorer. You can find a much more detailed analysis of RGB(a) and HSL(a) in http://dev.opera.com/articles/view/color-in-opera-10-hsl-rgb-and-alpha-transparency/ by Molly Holzschlag.

CSS selectors guide

So far in this chapter you have only seen the most basic of CSS selectors—the humble *element* selector, which matches the element specified by the selector, for example:

```
p { color: red; }
```

But there are many other selectors available to use, to allow you to select more specific groups of elements. **Table 11.3** details the different types of selectors.

Selector type	Example	Description

Element selector	`p { color: red; }`
	
	`<p>A paragraph.</p>`
		Selects the element specified in the selector.

Class selector	`.summary { color: red; }`
	
	`<p class="summary">A paragraph.</p>`
		Selects any element that has a `class` attribute equal to the value specified in the selector.

ID selector	`#author-bio { color: red; }`
	
	`<p id="author-bio">A paragraph.</p>`
		Selects the element (you can only have one of each ID on each HTML page) on the page that has an `id` attribute equal to the value specified in the selector.

Universal selector	`* { color: red; }`	Selects every single element on the page.

Attribute selector	`img[alt] { border-color: red; }`
	
	`img[src="image.png"] { border-color: red; }`
	
	`<img alt="An image" src="image.png">`
		Selects any element with the attribute specified within the square brackets. You can select just the attribute type, or an attribute with a specific value.

Child selector	`li > p { color: red; }`
	
	`<li><p>A paragraph.</p></li>`
	
	But not
	
	`<p>A paragraph.</p>`
		Selects the right-hand element in the selector only if it is a direct child of the left-hand element.
		
		WARNING: These selectors are not supported in Internet Explorer 6 or earlier.

Descendant selector	`li p { color: red; }`
	
	`<li><p>A paragraph.</p></li>`
	
	and
	
	`<li><div><p>A paragraph.</p></div></li>`
	
	But not
	
	`<p>A paragraph.</p>`
		Similar to the child selector, except that the right-hand element does not have to be a direct child of the left-hand element—it selects elements further down the DOM hierarchy too.

Table 11.3: CSS selector types

CHAPTER 11

Selector type	Example	Description

Adjacent sibling selector	`h2 + p { color: red; }`
	
	`<h2>Heading</h2>`
	
	`<p>A paragraph.</p>`
	
	But not
	
	`<p>A paragraph.</p>`
	
	or
	
	`<h1>Heading</h1>`
	
	`<p>A paragraph.</p>`
		Logic prevails here: **Parent** means an element one level higher up in the DOM hierarchy; **child** means an element one level further down; so **sibling** means an element on the same level in the DOM hierarchy.
		
		This selector selects the element on the right-hand side of the selector, only if it has an instance of the element on the left-hand side next to it, on the same level of the DOM hierarchy.
		
		WARNING: These selectors are not supported in Internet Explorer 6 or below.

Pseudo-classes	`a:hover { color: red; }`
	
	Applies the rule to all `<a>` elements, but only when they are moused over.
	
	`a:focus { color: red; }`
	
	Applies the rule to all `<a>` elements, but only when they are focused, e.g., by keyboard navigation.
	
	`a:visited { color: red; }`
	
	Applies the rule to all `<a>` elements that have previously been visited in the current browser history.
		These allow you to style elements based not on what the elements are, but on more esoteric factors such as the states of links (e.g., if they are being hovered over, or have been visited already).

Pseudo-elements	`p:first-letter { font-size: 300% }`
	
	Triples the size of the first letter of every paragraph on the page.
	
	`p:first-line { font-weight: bold; }`
	
	Bolds the first line of every paragraph on the page.
		These allow you to style specific parts of elements, rather than the whole element (e.g., the first letter within that element); they also allow you to insert content before or after specific elements.

Table 11.3: CSS selector types

You will see examples of more complicated selectors as you progress through this book, but don't worry if you don't understand them all immediately—you will get there as you gain more experience in styling web pages! It is best to start off easy in your own work with the first three selectors at the start of the table, and then move on to the others as you gain more confidence.

Resource // Grouping selectors

You can also group different selectors. Say you want to apply the same style to `<h1>` and `<p>`—you could write the following CSS:

```
h1 { color: red; }
p { color: red; }
```

This however is rather repetitious and therefore not ideal, but there is a way around it—you can shorten the CSS by grouping the selectors together with a comma (or multiple commas if you are grouping more than two) on a single rule that will be applied to all the selectors:

```
h1, p { color: red; }
```

Also be aware that you can join some selectors to define even more specific rules. For example:

```
p.warning { color: red; }
```

matches all paragraphs with a `class` of `warning`, and:

```
div#example { color: red; }
```

matches the element with an `id` attribute of example, but only if it is a `<div>` element.

Joining both techniques discussed in this sidebar is possible. The following is a single rule that matches paragraphs with a `class` of `info` *and* list items with a `class` of `highlight`, turning their text red:

```
p.info, li.highlight { color: red; }
```

Try it yourself!

In this exercise you will start off with some ready-made HTML, and write some CSS to solve the problems set out in the following questions. You can find the ready-made HTML in the file `selectors_challenge.html`. Get a copy of this file from the code download.

(continues)

Try it yourself!

(continued)

1. Write a rule that will apply the Georgia font to every element on the web page. Apply this rule to the HTML using whatever method you think is best.

2. Give all the `<div>` elements a light-colored background (your choice), and apply 10 pixels of padding between the content and the edge of the `<div>`s.

3. Make the content 500 pixels in width.

4. Apply a dark-colored border (your choice of color and style) to the `<div>` elements.

5. Override the previous font setting just for the headings—make every heading use the Helvetica font (or another sans-serif font of your choice).

6. Write a test using attribute selectors that will highlight links without `title` attributes in red.

7. (advanced) Apply pseudo-classes to the links so that they are a different color to the rest of the text, and when you mouse over them, the underline disappears.

8. (advanced) Use CSS3 selectors to give the `<div>` elements rounded corners and a subtle drop shadow. The relevant properties may not work in older browsers.

Resolving conflicts—inheritance and the cascade

Another question that often trips people up when learning about CSS is "How is it decided what style ends up being applied when there is a conflict, and two or more conflicting styles are applied to the same element?" To understand this, you have to understand **inheritance** and **the cascade**:

- **Inheritance** is the mechanism by which certain properties are passed from a parent element on to its children. It's quite similar to inheritance in genetics: if the parents have blue eyes, their children will probably have blue eyes, too.

- **The cascade** is a very important concept—it's where CSS gets a large chunk of its name from. It's the mechanism that controls the end result when multiple conflicting and overlapping CSS declarations apply to the same element.

Inheritance

Inheritance makes a lot of sense. If it didn't exist, you'd have to specify every property for every HTML element, every time you wrote a web page. In reality a lot is done for you behind the scenes! It makes things a lot easier to be able to, for example, set a default font on the <body> element and know that it will be inherited by all <body>'s children. You can then override this declaration for specific elements later on, if desired:

```
body { font-family: georgia; }
h1, h2, h3 { font-family: helvetica; } /* This overrides
  the first rule, because it appears later in the code */
```

Note the comment above—bear this in mind! You'll find more about overriding later in this chapter.

Every element in an HTML document except the root element (<html>), which doesn't have a parent, will inherit all inheritable properties from its parent. Not all CSS properties are inherited, because that wouldn't make sense. For instance, margins are not inherited, since it's unlikely that a child element should need the same margins as its parent. In most cases common sense will tell you which properties are inherited and which aren't.

Tip: You can look up which CSS properties are inherited in the CSS 2.1 specification property summary table at http://www.w3.org/TR/CSS21/propidx.html.

The cascade

The cascade is made up of three main concepts, which control the order in which CSS declarations are applied:

- Importance
- Specificity
- Source order

Importance is most … er … important. If two declarations have the same importance, the specificity of the rules decides which one will apply. If the rules have the same specificity, then source order controls which rule will win.

I will look into these concepts below, one by one.

Importance

The **importance** of a CSS declaration depends on *where* it is specified. The conflicting declarations will be applied in the following order; later ones will override earlier ones:

1. User agent style sheets
2. Normal declarations in author style sheets
3. Normal declarations in user style sheets
4. Important declarations in author style sheets
5. Important declarations in user style sheets

A **user agent style sheet** is the built-in style sheet of the browser, as mentioned earlier on in the chapter. For instance, unvisited links are blue and underlined by default.

A **user style sheet** is a style sheet that the *user* has specified. Not all browsers support user style sheets, but they can be very useful, especially for users with certain types of disabilities. For instance, a dyslexic person can have a user style sheet that specifies certain fonts and colours that help reading.

An **author style sheet** is what we normally refer to when we say "style sheet." It's the style sheet that the author of the document (or, more likely, the site's designer) has written and linked the site's HTML to.

Normal declarations are just that: normal declarations. The opposite is **important declarations**, which are declarations followed by an !important directive (* selects all elements):

```
* { font-family: "Helvetica" !important; }
```

In this case, no matter what is specified elsewhere in the CSS, everything will be displayed in Helvetica. Users might add this rule to their user style sheet if they find this font easier to read.

The default browser rendering will only apply if those declarations aren't overridden by any rules in a user style sheet or an author style sheet, since the user agent style sheet has the lowest precedence.

> **Tip:** To be honest, most designers don't have to think too much about importance, since there's nothing we can do about it. There is no way we could know if a user has a user style sheet defined that will override our CSS. If they do, they probably have a very good reason for doing so, anyway. Still, it's good to know what importance is and how it may affect the presentation of our documents.

Specificity

Specificity is something every CSS author needs to understand and think about. It can be thought of as a measure of how specific a rule's selector is. A selector with low specificity may match many elements (like p, which matches every paragraph in the document), while a selector with high specificity might only match a single element on a page (like #nav, which only matches the element with an id of nav).

The specificity of a selector can easily be calculated. If two or more rules are conflicting, and they all have the same importance, then the rule with the most specific selector will win.

Specificity has four components; let's call them a, b, c, and d. Component "a" is the most distinguishing, "d" the least.

- Component "a" is quite simple: It's 1 for a declaration in a style attribute, otherwise it's 0.
- Component "b" is the number of id selectors in the selector (those that begin with a #).
- Component "c" is the number of attribute selectors, class selectors, and pseudo-classes.
- Component "d" is the number of element selectors and pseudo-elements in the selector.

You can string these four components together to calculate the specificity of any rule. CSS declarations in a `style` attribute don't have a selector, so their specificity is always 1,0,0,0.

Table 11.2 shows a few examples—after this it should be quite clear how this works.

Selector	A	B	C	D	Specificity
h1	0	0	0	1	0,0,0,1
.foo	0	0	1	0	0,0,1,0
#bar	0	1	0	0	0,1,0,0
ul#nav a:link	0	1	1	2	0,1,1,2

Table 11.2: Examples of calculating specificity on CSS selectors

It's worth noting that combinators (like >, +, and the white space) do not affect a selector's specificity. The universal selector (*) has no impact on specificity, either.

Also worth noting is that there is a difference in specificity between an `id` selector and an attribute selector that happens to refer to an `id` attribute. Although they match the same element, they have very different specificities. The specificity of #nav is 0,1,0,0 while the specificity of [id="nav"] is only 0,0,1,0.

Source order

If two declarations affect the same element and have the same importance and the same specificity, the final distinguishing mark is the **source order**. The declaration that appears later in the style sheet will win.

If you have a single, external style sheet, then the declarations at the end of the file will override those that occur earlier in the file if there's a conflict. The conflicting declarations could also occur in different style sheets. In that case, the order in which the style sheets are linked, included, or imported controls which declaration will be applied, so if you have two linked style sheets in a document <head>, the one linked to last will override the one linked to first.

> **Tip:** You can find much more detail on all the concepts in this section in the article http://dev.opera.com/articles/view/28-inheritance-and-cascade/ by Tommy Olsson. Also very useful (and fun) is Andy Clarke's Star Wars specificity selector—http://www.stuffandnonsense.co.uk/archives/css_specificity_wars.html.

One more thing to mention before we move on is that longform values can be used to override specific parts of shorthand values. For example, you can specify border width, color, and style using the following declaration:

```
border: 1px black solid;
```

Then later on in the style sheet you can specify the following to only override border-width:

```
border-width: 2px;
```

Browser support for CSS

A decade ago, support for web standards in browsers was patchy to say the least. Firefox didn't exist, neither did Safari or Chrome, Opera's standard support was imperfect-but-improving, and the main browser superpowers on the Web—Internet Explorer and Netscape (RIP)—were in the midst of a battle for supremacy in which both browsers were trying to win users by implementing exciting-sounding new features that the other one didn't have, or implementing the same features in incompatible ways. The result was a nightmare for web developers, who often had the choice of writing websites that would only work in a single browser, or maintaining two separate versions of the site for the two major browsers, which was obviously going to be a maintenance nightmare.

These days things are a lot easier. You'll find the odd web standards support idiosyncrasy or two in any browser, but support—at least for HTML 4.01, CSS 2.1, and JavaScript—is pretty decent across the last couple of versions of Internet Explorer, Firefox, Opera, Safari, and Chrome.

The main problem comes with having to support older versions of browsers, particularly Internet Explorer. You can't guarantee that web users will all upgrade to the latest version. Some aren't as web-savvy as us, and might not understand how to; others are forced to stick with older browser versions due to company policy (e.g., compatibility requirements of essential software, or fear of security vulnerability).

Internet Explorer 6 still has a large user base, yet its support for CSS is really problematic (HTML support is not so much of a problem)—it would be nice to ignore it, but you can't afford to turn your back on that many users. It's not their fault that their browser can't interpret your CSS properly, and they won't understand what the problem is, nor should they be expected to. If a visitor to your site encounters a problem, they will be much more likely to blame your website than the browser they are using.

We won't discuss browser support quirks in great detail here, but we will bring them up at pertinent points throughout the other chapters.

The future of CSS—CSS3

CSS3 is a new spec that adds new features to CSS to provide solutions to problems and implementations of common design patterns that previously were only available via hacks or scripting.

As mentioned earlier, work started on the CSS3 specification in 1998, yet only in the last couple of years have any of the parts of CSS3 been brought close to completion, or seen support in browsers. However, many parts of CSS3 now work across most of the modern set of browsers.

CSS3 is modular, meaning that the different parts of the specification are organised into modules of related functionality, so that they are easier to work on and learn. The modules that have a reasonable amount of support in modern browsers at the time of writing of this book are detailed in **Table 11.4**.

CSS3 module	Description
Backgrounds and borders	Controls new features to do with backgrounds and borders.
Media queries	Media queries are a way to apply CSS selectively, depending on the evaluation of different conditions, such as maximum or minimum browser window width or height, aspect ratio, resolution, etc.
Web fonts	Defines a way of allowing you to apply custom fonts to your web pages.
Multi-column layout	Provides an official way to create multi-column layouts in CSS.
2D transformations	Allows modification of elements using only CSS, for example scaling or rotation.
Transitions	Enables us to create animations using only CSS.

Table 11.4: CSS3 Modules with Reasonable Browser Support

Tip: I'd recommend that you start looking into and experimenting with CSS3 functionality in your work, and keeping up with the latest happenings. http://css3.info and http://dev.opera.com are good resources for CSS3 tutorials and news.

Summary

We have covered a lot in this chapter, in a very short space, so it may seem like a lot to take in, but don't worry if you didn't get it all the first time round. In fact, I'd recommend that you read this chapter through a couple more times straight away, and keep referring back to it as you go through the other chapters, as it contains many of the fundamental base concepts vital to understanding CSS.

In the rest of the chapters in Part III, we will look in detail at specific HTML and CSS constructs that go together to make up a typical website.

CHAPTER 11

CHAPTER 12
<head>

by Chris Mills

This chapter does not show you how to add content to your HTML documents. Instead, it is concerned with the different features found inside the <head> element, at the top of the document. These features do not show up as visible content on your HTML page (perhaps with the exception of the <title> element)—they are metadata, which means "data that describes data." They provide useful data about your HTML document, or which can be used by your HTML document.

Below we will look at DOCTYPES, and the difference between HTML and XHTML, adding titles to your browser window, specifying what character set and language your document will use, providing descriptions and keywords to describe your document to user agents such as search engine indexers, applying style and script to your HTML, and using a custom favicon with your site.

*In this chapter you have the opportunity to **Try it yourself!** with the convenient sample code downloads found on the book's companion website—http://interactwithwebstandards.com.*

DOCTYPES

Every single HTML page should have a DOCTYPE to be valid HTML (or XHTML)—this is the line that appears at the top of every HTML file in the code download for this book (OK, so it's not actually inside the <head> element—so sue me), for example:

```
<!DOCTYPE HTML PUBLIC "-//W3C//DTD HTML 4.01//EN" "http://
www.w3.org/TR/html4/strict.dtd">
```

This line points to a set of rules that the HTML document should follow to be correct (i.e. what version of HTML the author is using), and tells web browsers what rendering mode to use when rendering each HTML document. You can test whether your HTML is correctly following the rules outlined in the DOCTYPE by getting it checked by the W3C HTML validator at http://validator.w3.org/.

> **Tip:** You can find a lot more detail out about what the different parts of the DOCTYPE mean in Brian Wilson's article at http://www.blooberry.com/indexdot/html/tagpages/d/doctype.htm.

DOCTYPE is short for *Document Type Definition*, sometimes abbreviated *DTD*. These all mean the same thing.

DOCTYPE switching and rendering modes

If you do not provide a DOCTYPE, browsers will handle and render the document anyway—they need to make an attempt to render all the strange things that they come across on the Web. But without a DOCTYPE, the results may not look like you intended, because of something called **DOCTYPE sniffing** or **DOCTYPE switching**.

Most web browsers released in the 21st century look at the DOCTYPE of any HTML document they encounter and use that to decide whether the author of that document took care to write their HTML and CSS properly according to web standards.

If they find a DOCTYPE that indicates that the document is coded well, they use something called **Standards mode** when they layout the page. In Standards mode, browsers generally try to render the page according to the HTML and CSS specifications—they trust that the person who created the document knew what they were doing.

On the other hand, if they find an outdated or incomplete DOCTYPE, they use **Quirks mode**, which is more backwards-compatible with bad old practices that we aren't teaching you about in this book, and old browsers. Quirks mode assumes that the document is old or that it has not been created with web standards in mind—it means that the web page will still render, but it will be error-prone and more likely to look different across different browsers.

The differences are mostly related to how CSS is rendered, and only in a few cases about how the actual HTML is treated. As a web designer or developer, you will get the most consistent results by making sure that all browsers use their Standards rendering mode, hence you should stick to web standards, and use a proper DOCTYPE!

Try it yourself!

1. There is another mode called **Almost Standards mode** that exists across browsers. Research this mode, and write a blog post about what it is and how it differs from Standards mode.

2. (optional) The account I have given above is fairly simplistic, and covers all you really need to know for now. If you want to know more, feel free to do some research and write a blog post about all of the different rendering modes.

Choosing a DOCTYPE

So which DOCTYPE should you choose? The four main DOCTYPEs you'll be likely to use in your work are described in the following section.

I personally stick with HTML 4.01 strict in my documents unless specifically tasked with using something else, for reasons explained in types 1 and 2 below. But I use many XHTML conventions in my markup—for example, writing all element and attribute names in lower case, making sure I put quotes around attribute values, and closing elements properly. I don't think it is worth using the XHTML DOCTYPE, especially not when you are actually serving it as HTML. See the "XHTML versus HTML" section for more details.

CHAPTER 12

There are also frameset DOCTYPEs available, which specifically allow use of framesets in your HTML. But they are a really bad old practice, so we won't be teaching you how to use them in this book! Don't use frameset DOCTYPEs.

1. HTML 4.01 strict

If your content is HTML, then you should really use this DOCTYPE. It doesn't allow deprecated HTML, so is a good match for HTML written to standards and best practices.

```
<!DOCTYPE html PUBLIC "-//W3C//DTD HTML 4.01//EN"
"http://www.w3.org/TR/html4/strict.dtd">
```

2. HTML 4.01 transitional

This DOCTYPE is a bit less strict than the first one, and does allow some deprecated HTML. It is sometimes worth using this DOCTYPE if you really want your page to validate, but it is a page that will have content inserted into it by users or other content contributors, so you can't guarantee content quality. Validation isn't, however, the be-all and end-all of everything—there are other factors that are important to a web page being usable and accessible, and while validation is a useful debugging tool and a well-formed DOM is important, a couple of small validation errors often won't matter a great deal.

```
<!DOCTYPE HTML PUBLIC "-//W3C//DTD HTML 4.01
Transitional//EN" "http://www.w3.org/TR/html4/loose.dtd">
```

3. XHTML 1.0 strict

This is the XHTML version of the strict DOCTYPE, so the same strictness applies, as well as not allowing deprecated elements. See the next section for more on how XHTML differs from HTML.

```
<!DOCTYPE html PUBLIC "-//W3C//DTD XHTML 1.0 Strict//EN"
"http://www.w3.org/TR/xhtml1/DTD/xhtml1-strict.dtd">
```

4. XHTML 1.0 transitional

This is the XHTML version of the transitional DOCTYPE, so the same strictness applies—deprecated elements are allowed. See the next section for more on how XHTML differs from HTML.

```
<!DOCTYPE html PUBLIC "-//W3C//DTD XHTML 1.0
Transitional//EN" "http://www.w3.org/TR/xhtml1/DTD/
xhtml1-transitional.dtd">
```

Try it yourself!

Open up the file doctypes_example.html from the code download and check it out. It currently has the HTML 4.01 transitional DOCTYPE at the top of it.

1. Enter the code into the W3C HTML validator (http://validator. w3.org/), click Validate, and see what output you get.

2. Replace the current DOCTYPE with the HTML 4.01 strict DOCTYPE and see what output the HTML validator gives you now.

3. Now give the example file the XHTML strict DOCTYPE and see what output you get from the HTML validator.

4. Finally, remove the DOCTYPE altogether and see what output the validator gives you.

XHTML versus HTML

In Chapter 10, "HTML Intro," we discussed the history of HTML, and where it came from. Where does XHTML fit into the puzzle, and what is it? HTML (Hypertext Markup Language) is a separate technology in its own right, whereas **XHTML** (eXtensible Hypertext Markup Language) is really XML (Extensible Markup Language). XML is a technology that allows you to create your own custom markup languages, called **vocabularies**. XHTML is a reformulation of HTML as an XML vocabulary (as is SVG, and MathML— look them up!), and hence it is a lot stricter than HTML. You have to use lower case elements and attributes, make sure all elements are closed properly and attributes have quotes round their values, and properly encode all entities, otherwise the XHTML page will not even display.

This highlights the problem with XHTML—some people argue that the Web is a bit of a lawless place, with lots of bad-quality code around, and that more strictness is better. But this is what made the Web so great in the first place—it is forgiving enough to allow pretty much anyone to write a page and have it display in some form. XHTML (XML) is not really in keeping with the spirit of the Web. You wouldn't like if your blog fell over and refused to display anything every time a small markup error made it into a post.

In addition, most so-called XHTML is really just HTML served with XHTML rules applied to it. To really serve content as XHTML, you need to:

- Put an **XML declaration** at the start of your document, *before* your DOCTYPE. Every XML document requires this, and XHTML is XML:

  `<?xml version="1.0" encoding="UTF-8"?>`

- Set the content-type of your document to application+xhtml+xml (the default is text/html).

But there are problems here—first of all Internet Explorer 6 switches into Quirks mode when you include an XML declaration in your document. More seriously though, if you create markup with the correct mime type for XHTML—application+xhtml+xml—Internet Explorer doesn't display your content; it prompts your site visitors to download it. You really don't want that!

You could just omit the XML declaration and use the text/html mimetype, *but in the spirit of doing things properly™, I think it is better to stick to HTML.*

Setting the document's primary language

The lang attribute of the <html> element allows you to set the human language of the document—French, Thai, Russian, English, etc. This first of all helps screen readers—for example the word *six* is pronounced "sicks" in English, and "seece" in French, even though it is spelt the same in both languages. The lang attribute also helps search engines when they are trying to appropriately index content written in different languages.

It's a good idea to define the primary language of a document, especially when you are writing pages for an international audience, although you don't tend to see it that often on the Web of today. The HTML looks like so:

```
<html lang="en-GB">

    ...

</html>
```

The first part of the attribute value is the major language—en means "English." The second—optional—part is the language subclassification. In this case it is GB—British English, but it could be set as US or CA, for American or Canadian English. For a reference list of HTML language codes, check out the Sitepoint HTML reference (http://reference. sitepoint.com/html/lang-codes). There are also many useful resources at the W3C Internationalization (I18n) Activity homepage—see http:// www.w3.org/International/.

Note that you can also set the language of subsections of your document by using the lang attribute on other elements, for example: <span lang="fr">Bonjour</span>. Also note that the attributes you use to set the language depend on the DOCTYPE of your document. For HTML you use the lang attribute only; for XHTML 1.0 served as text/html use the lang and xml:lang attributes, and for XHTML served as XML use the xml:lang attribute only. Also see the W3C language tags reference at http://www.w3.org/International/articles/language-tags/ for more information and references.

Giving your document a <title>

One of the most important elements in the <head> is the <title>. The text contained within the <title> is displayed by pretty much all user agents/browsers in the browser application title bar (the bar bordering the top of the browser window in **Figure 12.1**).

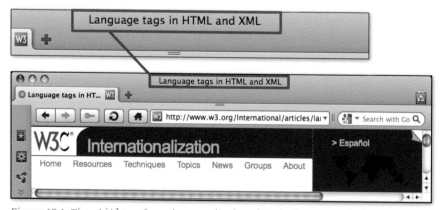

Figure 12.1: The <title> of a web page, displayed in the browser title bar.

The <title> is the first piece of content that web users will see when they visit your site, and therefore it is very important. Assistive technologies like screen readers (software that reads out web pages to users with visual impairments) give this as a first hint of what visitors can expect from the document. Bear in mind that search engines take search terms to categorize your page from the <title>, so your chances of being found on the Web increase drastically when you use a good title that is human readable and contains the right keywords. And when you bookmark a page, the browser uses the title attribute as a text label for that bookmark.

There are many tutorials on the Web about how to write good document titles, most of which are related to Search Engine Optimization (SEO). Don't go overboard and try to trick search engines into showing up an inflated number of search results with loads of keywords—you should still write a concise, human-readable title piece about what the document is. "Breeding Dogs—Tips About Alsatians" is a lot more human readable than "Dogs, Alsatian, Breeding, Dog, Tips, Free, Pet."

Adding keywords and a description

The next thing you could consider adding to your HTML document is a description and keywords. Both of these get added to the <head> inside <meta> elements. The following example is taken from the Yahoo! Eurosport site.

```
<!DOCTYPE HTML PUBLIC "-//W3C//DTD HTML 4.01//EN" "http://
www.w3.org/TR/html4/strict.dtd">
<html>
    <head>
        <title>Yahoo! UK & Ireland Eurosport-Sports News |
        Live Scores | Sport</title>
        <meta name="description" content="Latest sports
        news and live scores from Yahoo! Eurosport UK.
        Complete sport coverage with Football results,
        Cricket scores, F1, Golf, Rugby, Tennis and more.">
        <meta name="keywords" content="eurosport,sports,
```

```
        sport,sports news,live scores,football,cricket,f1,
        golf,rugby,tennis,uk,yahoo">
    </head>
    <body>
        ...
    </body>
</html>
```

> **Tip:** Note that the `name` attribute specifies the type of meta information the `<meta>` element contains. See `http://en.wikipedia.org/wiki/Meta_element` for more information on other uses of the `<meta>` element.

When the previous example was put online, the meta information was indexed by search engines and is now utilised (**Figure 12.2**).

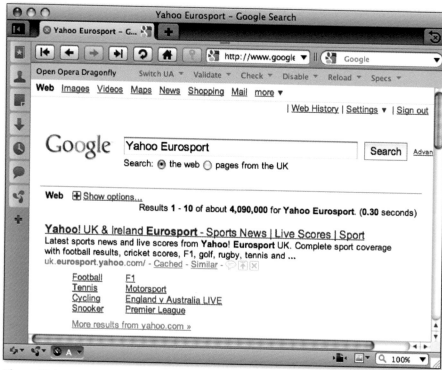

Figure 12.2: Descriptions show up in search engine result pages.

CHAPTER 12

This could be the crucial bit of information a web user was looking for and the reason for him or her to click through to your site. Descriptions have another use too: some browsers show the description as extra information when you add the document to your favourites/bookmarks (**Figure 12.3**).

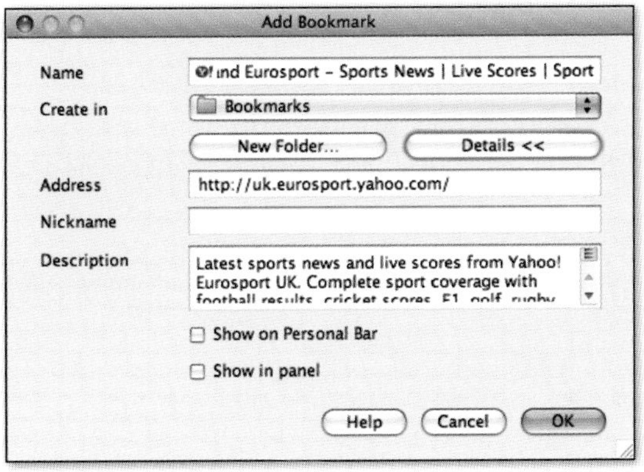

Figure 12.3: Descriptions show up in some browsers when you add the document as a favourite/bookmark.

Tip: Years of abuse by spammers has resulted in search engines not taking keywords as seriously anymore, therefore keywords and descriptions are not as essential as they once were.

Adding styles and script

Probably the most important features that you'll find in the `<head>` from a web design and development point of view allow you to apply CSS styles and JavaScript to your HTML, to style your web page and add dynamic features. You already saw how to apply CSS to your document in Chapter 11, "CSS Intro," but let's review it for completeness. First of all, an internal style sheet:

```
<style type="text/css" media="screen">
    p {
        color: red;
    }
</style>
```

Next, a link to an external style sheet:

```
<link rel="stylesheet" type="text/css" href="external_
stylesheet.css" media="all">
```

Media types

Note the previous `media` attribute—this is one feature we haven't talked about much before. This is known as a **media type**, and it allows you to specify what type of media this CSS will be applied to. The most common values are:

- `all`: The CSS is to be used by all media types; this is the default behaviour if the `media` attribute is not provided.

- `screen`: On screen only, i.e., when your browser is displaying the page on your desktop computer.

- `print`: Styles only applied when the document is being printed out.

- `handheld`: Some web-capable handheld device browsers use `handheld` media by default if it is found, however, most of the newer devices don't, as many mobile browsers are now capable of displaying the same websites as desktop computers. Also, `handheld` media started to be abused by developers to provide a dumbed-down set of styles for mobile browsers with the hope of easy support for mobile devices, which is not fair to those browsing whilst on the move.

- `projection`: The original intention of this option was to provide specific styling for HTML slide presentations, although this is very rarely used. Check out Opera's Opera Show feature for a very good use of `projection` (see http://dev.opera.com/articles/view/html-css-slideshows/).

Try it yourself!

1. If you have a web page with a navigation sidebar and a main content column, how do you use media types to hide the navigation menu when the page is printed?

2. Create an example page that does this.

We won't be covering JavaScript in this book in any detail, but I need to mention the `<script>` element in this section—you use this to add JavaScript to your HTML document. When a browser encounters a `<script>` element, it'll drop everything else and pause parsing of the rest of the document while it tries to execute the code inside it. For example:

```
<head>
    ...
    <script>
        function leave() {
            return confirm("This will take you to another
            site,\n are you sure you want to go?")
        }
    </script>
    ...
</head>
```

> **Tip:** You don't actually have to put your `<script>` elements in the `<head>` of your document, although they are most commonly found there. In some cases it actually makes more sense to put scripts after the `</body>` tag. Read the discussion at `http://stackoverflow.com/questions/855077/does-putting-scripts-on-the-bottom-of-a-web-page-speed-up-page-load` to learn more about the subject.

In the same manner as external CSS, you can load external JavaScript into a page. The syntax looks like so:

```
<script src="example.js" type="text/javascript"></script>
```

Link elements

`<link>` elements can be used to define relationships between the current document and other documents or files. We've already seen it used to point to an external style sheet, however there are many other uses for `<link>`, a couple of which we'll review in this section.

Feeds

A **feed** is a document containing condensed information detailing the new additions to your site in chronological order. Users can subscribe to it and get to know what has changed on your site recently without having to visit it. They do this using feed readers such as Google Reader, Netvibes, or Bloglines. Some modern browsers (such as Opera) and e-mail clients (such as Mac Mail, or Outlook on Windows) can also process and display feeds. You can recognise that a website offers a feed by the RSS icon next to the URL (**Figure 12.4**).

Feed pages are structured using HTML, or an XML format like RSS or Atom, and they are hardly ever created by hand. Most of the time personal publishing systems (such as WordPress) will do that work for you and all you need to do to offer the world a feed of your site is link to the XML document with the correct <link> element in the <head> of your document. The following is an excerpt from the http://dev.opera.com <head>; these two lines provide an RSS and an Atom version of the latest articles feed:

```
<link rel="alternate" type="application/rss+xml" title="New
articles - RSS 2.0 Feed" href="/feeds/rss/articles" />

<link rel="alternate" type="application/atom+xml" title="New
articles - Atom 1.0 Feed" href="/feeds/atom/articles" />
```

Supplying a feed makes sense for content-heavy websites that change very often (like blogs or photo sites)—readers can keep up with those changes more quickly and easily by using a feed reading tool.

If you don't update your site that often but you have a lot of content and want people to have a visual reminder of your website, then you might want to consider using a shortcut icon to stand out in people's bookmark lists. This is what I'll cover in the next section.

Making bookmarking more fun—using favicons

One last subject we'll cover here is shortcut icons, or **favicons**. These are small images, generally with a file format of .ico, because Internet Explorer doesn't support other formats (other browsers can also use .pngs and other formats for favicons). If you place one on your web server and add the relevant <link> element to your document <head>, the icon will be displayed in the browser's address bar to the left of the URL and in the tab that site is open in when someone accesses the page (and next to the site in the browser's bookmark list) (**Figure 12.4**).

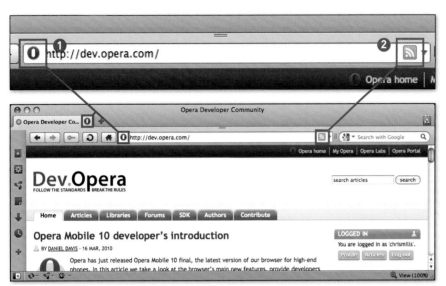

Figure 12.4: Favicons make it easier to remember a site, and give it a little more personality. Opera shows an orange RSS icon next to the location of websites that offer a feed.

① Favicon

② RSS icon

You can add a favicon to your site by using a `<link>` element with a `rel="Shortcut Icon"` attribute to reference it, as seen in the following example. The `href` attribute should point to the location of the favicon on your server.

```
<head>

    ...
    <link rel="Shortcut Icon" href="favicon.ico"
    type="image/x-icon">

    ...
</head>
```

The biggest obstacle to adding your icon is creating it in the right format, as not many graphics packages support the `.ico` format. One option is to use the free online tool genfavicon (`http://www.genfavicon.com/`). Also note that you need to call it `favicon.ico`, because Internet Explorer always looks for this specific filename.

Try it yourself!

Now it is time to add your own favicon to a page.

1. Find yourself a sample page to add the favicon to. Anything will do—an example from one of the previous chapters, perhaps?

2. Think about what you want your favicon to be. It should be a fairly simple graphic, not too busy; after all, you only have an image 16 x 16 pixels to play with. Your initials, or a really simple little shape, might work well. An architectural blueprint of the Death Star won't. You don't have to work inside a 16 x 16 pixel file necessarily, but this is what it will be converted into in the end.

3. Once you have made your graphic, convert it into the `.ico` format.

4. Save the favicon in the same directory as your sample HTML file.

5. Reference your favicon using the appropriate `<link>` element.

6. Save all files, and try it out.

If you have done this sucessfully, your browser should show your icon next to the URL in the address toolbar and the tab the page is open in. If you bookmark it, the same icon will appear next to the bookmark.

Summary

This simple chapter has taken you through all of the most important things you can add to the `<head>` of your HTML documents. This information doesn't appear on your website, but it is vital to get right, to make sure your site has the best chance of being found by your target audience, has the right CSS and JavaScript applied to it, and more besides. In the next chapter we will step inside the `<body>` element, and look at the basics of styling text.

CHAPTER 13
Headings and Paragraphs

by Chris Mills

Now that we have covered some general essentials of using HTML and CSS to structure and style web pages, we will give you some detailed treatments of implementing specific web page features. And what better place to start than basic plain ol' text? After all, text is central to most web pages, so learning how to deal with it is of great importance.

In this chapter we will look at the proper usage of the most important elements you'll need to mark up text, from paragraphs and headings to slightly more specialised features such as quotations, subscript and superscript, and emphasis. We will also look at the most important CSS properties for styling basic text.

We *won't* be looking at any CSS that deals with adding margins, padding, etc. to these elements. These will be discussed in Chapter 14, "Whitespace."

In this chapter you have the opportunity to **Try it yourself!** *with the convenient sample code downloads found on the book's companion website*—http://interactwithwebstandards.com.

Recap! Headings and paragraphs

As mentioned in previous chapters, the most important thing about an HTML document is a concisely written, logical structure of headings and other content, much of which will be paragraphs.

> **Tip:** There are six levels of headings you can use in HTML—<h1> through to <h6>—but you shouldn't really need more than three to four for most documents.

Something like this is ideal:

```
<h1>Pets</h1>
<p>This page provides information on different animals
that are suitable for keeping as pets.</p>
<h2>Cats</h2>
<p>Cats are very independent creatures, and tend to
have servants rather than owners. They becoming loving
and loyal if treated with respect.</p>
<h2>Guinea Pigs</h2>
<p>A type of rodent, guinea pigs come in many different
colorful varieties, and are cute and cuddly, if a little
jumpy. They make ideal pets for young children, and
breeding them is fun, as long as you don't let it get
out of hand!</p>
<h2>Parrots</h2>
<p>Parrots are colorful birds that typically come from
hot climates. Some of them can learn human words, so
they provide great company. They can also live for
a long period of time, typically 30 years or more.
Varieties of parrot are as follows.</p>
<h3>African Gray</h3>
<p>One of the most common species to be domesticated,
African Grays are good natured and learn words
easily.</p>
```

```
<h3>Norwegian Blue</h3>
<p>A rare and very exotic species. Beautiful
plumage.</p>
```

Tip: This example will be used throughout this chapter to demonstrate different elements. We will add to it as we go along, but the original can be found in headings_paragraphs1.html at http://interactwithwebstandards.com.

The importance of good content and document structure

We have covered this before, so as a quick recap—your content absolutely needs to be concise and well structured for it to be

- Generally usable and enjoyable for all users.
- Accessible for users with disabilities using assistive technologies to browse the Web.
- Easily manipulable using CSS and JavaScript.
- Indexable by search engines and therefore easy to find on the Web.

General styles for text

At the moment, our content looks like **Figure 13.1**, which is all well and good, but actually reading it leaves a lot to be desired.

The lines of text are too long to read and uneven, the heading levels are not that easy to differentiate between, plus the default typeface makes it look very like the Web of the 90s. In short, it's a bit of a mess.

The way the page looks by default is determined by the default browser styles that are being applied. These will differ somewhat across browsers, but the effect is always pretty much the same. We can make things better with some simple CSS styles. Let's look at the styling now.

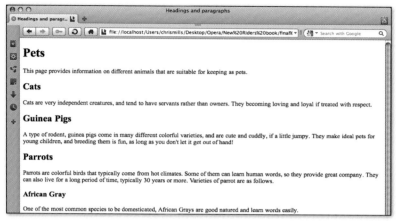

Figure 13.1: Our default text is not really that legible.

Line lengths

One easy thing you can do to make things more legible is to make the content narrower. A general guideline is to make your text columns about 60—70 characters in length for easier reading. This can be easily achieved using the `width` property. You will most commonly use pixels and percentage—the first one if you want your content column to be a fixed width (also known as "static"), and percentage (%) if you want the content column to always take up the same proportion of the browser window width, and resize as the window is resized (also known as "fluid"). There is also a third option termed "elastic," which relies on using ems to size content width. Since ems are related to the size of your text, these measurements will get bigger as the text size increases. These are not as commonly used as the other two.

Examples of `width` usage are as follows:

```
width: 500px;
width: 60%;
```

In our site example, I have put a `<div>` with an `id` of `main_content` round the main content (everything excluding the `<h1>`, which is the heading of the page) so I can control the width of the whole content column as one entity. Then I have given the `<div>` a `width` of 50%, so the line length is more legible and it scales with the browser width.

```
main_content {
    width: 50%;
}
```

The content now looks like **Figure 13.2** (`headings_paragraphs2.html`).

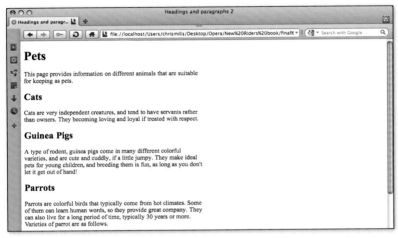

Figure 13.2: This is immediately more readable.

You can also use the `max-width` and `min-width` properties to set a maximum or minimum width that you want an element to be. It can be effective to use a percentage width in combination with a fixed pixel `min-width` and/or `max-width`. For example:

```
main_content {
    width: 50%;
    min-width: 300px;
    max-width: 600px;
}
```

This stops the content becoming too long or too short to be easily readable. The problem with this is that these properties are not supported by Internet Explorer 6 or below. Luckily IE6 is much less popular these days. Check your site's stats to see if your audience is still using it.

CHAPTER 13

Resource // General site layout

In many sites you will have one or more columns of content, and a column that contains the navigation menu, sandwiched between a header at the top of the site (containing pretty graphics, corporate logos, site title, etc.) and a footer at the bottom of the site (usually contains site-wide supplementary information such as copyright notice, legal information, accessibility statement, contact details, etc.). Most sites stick to this kind of general layout, although some will be slightly more left field.

The header and footer and navigation menu will usually be the same across each page of your site, whereas the content will change on each page as you navigate to different areas of the site. In the example in this chapter, we will just be looking at a single content column—we will get onto implementing layouts in the chapters near the end of this book (see Chapters 20-21).

Setting fonts

You can set fonts in web pages using the `font-family` property. When someone surfs to your site, the browser finds the font file on the user's computer and applies it as directed by the CSS. You can specify a single font to apply to a given element selection:

```
p {
    font-family: Helvetica;
}
```

Or you can specify a comma-delimited list of fonts:

```
p {
    font-family: "Trebuchet MS", "Times New Roman",
    Georgia, serif;
}
```

In this case the browser will try to find the first font, then the next one, then the next, until it finds one from the list to use. If it can't find any, the last font declaration tells the browser to apply the system's generic serif font, whatever that may be (you can also use `sans-serif` at the end of a list of sans-serif fonts). Note how fonts with more than one word in the title need to be enclosed in single quote marks.

Bear in mind that whatever font you specify needs to be available on the user's machine, which is why it is best to stick to the fonts seen in

Figure 13.3—these "web safe" fonts are fonts that you can guarantee will be installed across Windows, Mac and Linux.

Andale Mono	Verdana	Trebuchet MS
Times New Roman	Arial	Comic Sans
Georgia	Courier New	Impact

Figure 13.3: The classic list of "web safe" fonts.

Traditional best practice tends to recommend that you use a sans-serif font for headings, and a serif font for body text, for improved legibility. However, serifs can still get lost and muddled at a small body copy size, and equally they can really show their full beauty when used in large headlines. It is really up to you what kind of look and feel and target audience you are going for. Times New Roman might work better for serious news copy, whereas Verdana might work better for text on a music or video game site. Just do me a favour and be careful with any usage of Comic Sans—this is good for a children's site or if you have a paragraph that you want to look like it has been chalked on a blackboard. But many uses of it on the Web are *horrible*.

Try it yourself!

1. Take a copy of our example file, `headings_paragraphs2.html`.
2. Have a play around with setting fonts on the different elements.
3. As a final move, use two rules that will set a sans-serif font on all paragraphs, and a serif font on all headings (**Figure 13.4**).

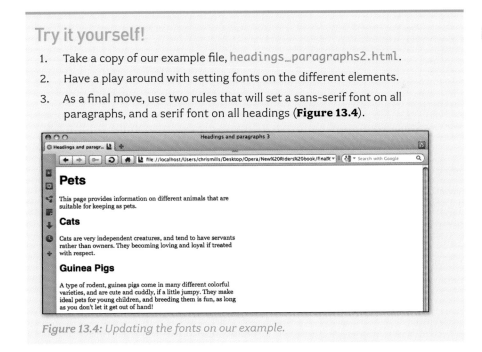

Figure 13.4: Updating the fonts on our example.

Resource // Web fonts

One rather exciting module in the CSS3 spec is web fonts. This gets around the problem of having only a limited font set available across platforms by allowing you to specify font files on your machine to be downloaded along with your web page and then used on it. For example, **Figure 13.5** shows a web page that makes use of web Fonts (you can see an example implementation and find out more information in Chapter 20, "Floats").

Figure 13.5: Web fonts allow you to spice up your web typography!

You can find more great examples and information at http://dev.opera. com/articles/view/seven-web-fonts-showcases/.

Text sizing

The next step we'll take is to do some resizing of our text; this is done using the font-size property, and you can use pretty much any CSS units you want, although it is recommended that you use percentages or ems, and not pixels. The two former options will size the text relative to the default text size, whereas the latter will give the text an absolute size irrespective of any other settings. This often causes problems because if the designer wants to increase the general size of the whole page, individual elements sized using pixels will stay the same size, and start to look out of proportion.

Also, some users will want to resize the text on your site using browser functionality to read it more easily. Some older browsers do not resize the whole page when the browser's zoom function is used, and instead just resize the text—these browsers will not be able to resize text sized using pixels. This is not so much of a problem any more, as all modern browsers resize the whole page, irrespective of pixel sizes, but you should not rely on all of your target audience using a modern browser.

Let's move on to the practicalities. Sometimes you will want to change the overall relative text size of the whole site, to make it bigger or smaller than the browser default, depending on the look you are going for. This is done using something like the following:

```
body {
    font-size: 0.8em;
}
```

You will then probably want to adjust your heading sizes. This can be done effectively using either ems or percentage, but sticking to ems is more consistent:

```
h1 {
    font-size: 3em;
}
h2 {
    font-size: 2em;
}
h3 {
    font-size: 1.3em;
}
```

An em is a scalable web measurement unit that is always equal to the current font size of the document, so for example if a default font size of 16px is currently being used for paragraphs, 16px is equal to 1em. Setting a font size of 2ems will always make the font double the default size. There is another equivalence to note here too—since 2ems doubles the font size, 2ems is equal to setting the size as 200%, while 80% will equal 0.8ems and 100% equals 1em, etc.

Tip: A fantastic article to check out for more in-depth information on using ems is "How to size text using ems" by Rich Rutter—check out `http://www.clagnut.com/blog/348/`.

Resource // Computed values vs. specified values

The `<body>` element's font size in our example is set to 0.8ems, or 80%—but 80% of what? And shouldn't the font size of the heading and the paragraph be 80% of that of the `<body>`? The value that is inherited is not the **specified value**—the value we write in our style sheet—but something called the **computed value**. *If the specified value was inherited, each successive child element would have smaller and smaller text—80% x 80% x 80%… etc.!*

The computed value is, in the case of font size, an absolute value measured in pixels. The percentage value for font size relates to the default font size set in the browser. Most contemporary browsers have a default font size setting of 16px. Because 80% of 16 is 12.8, the computed value for the font size of the `<body>` element will probably be 13px. And that is the value inherited by the paragraphs. The font size of the headings, even before we apply our custom size settings, is larger because the browser applies some built-in styling of its own.

Relative font sizing can make your head hurt. Richard Rutter explores this issue in more detail on A List Apart `http://www.alistapart.com/articles/howtosizetextincss/`.

Other text properties

Other text properties available in CSS that you probably won't use as often are as follows:

- `font-weight` specifies how heavy/bold the text is, and can take values of 100, 200, 300, 400, 500, 600, 700, 800, or 900 (each one is progressively bolder), or it can take simpler human-readable values of `lighter`, `normal` (the default), `bold`, `bolder`. Bear in mind that not all fonts will accept all of these values, so you may need to do a little experimentation.

- `font-style` specifies what variant of the font should be used, and takes values of `italic`, `oblique`, or `normal` (the default). This is likely to be used only if you absolutely need to style something to look italic but don't want the associated semantic emphasis. `oblique` is similar to `italic`, the difference being that `italic` uses any available italic font of the font family being used, whereas `oblique` just takes the normal font and adds a slant to it.

- `font-variant` specifies usage of a small-caps variant of the applied font, in which upper case letters are rendered normally, and lower case letters are rendered as smaller versions of their upper case equivalents. To set this on an element, use the declaration `font-variant: small-caps;`.

- `line-height` specifies the height of each text line (just the line the text sits on; not the text itself), in whatever unit you choose. You can see this in use in the next chapter.

- `text-transform` transforms the textual content of an element. Possible values are `capitalize` (capitalises all words), `lowercase` (makes all letters lowercase) and `uppercase` (makes all letters uppercase).

- `text-decoration` specifies different types of decoration on the textual content of an element. Possible values are `blink` (makes the text blink on and off), `underline` (draws a line under the text), `overline` (draws a line above the text), and `line-through` (draws a line through the text).

Resource // font shorthand

You can actually combine several font-related properties into a single font declaration in your CSS. For example, the following CSS:

```
p {
    font: 2em/1.3em bold italic Georgia, serif;
}
```

Is equivalent to

```
p {
    font-size: 2em;
    line-height: 1.3em;
    font-weight: bold;
    font-style: italic;
    font-family: Georgia, serif;
}
```

This shorthand won't work unless you specify the `font-size` and the `font-family`—if either is missing the CSS rule will be ignored completely.

CHAPTER 13

Try it yourself!

Applying the earlier font-size rules to our example will result in a display like the one shown in **Figure 13.6** (headings_paragraphs4.html).

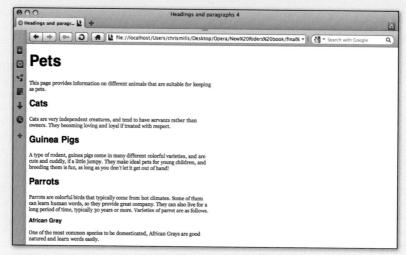

Figure 13.6: Our text has been resized. The paragraphs are a bit less weighty, and the difference between the heading levels is now a lot more distinct.

1. Have a good play with resizing text on the example I've provided, to get used to different units and how they work together.

2. Experiment with the CSS properties covered in the "Other text properties" section to see what effects they have on the text in our example.

Other HTML elements for giving text meaning

In this section I'll look at the most common of the other elements you are likely to use at least fairly often to improve your HTML's semantics. Note that the examples in this section can all be found in the code example file headings_paragraphs5.html (see **Figure 13.7** for the finished example). You can, of course, choose to style any of these elements in any way you want, but often the browser default styles are good enough.

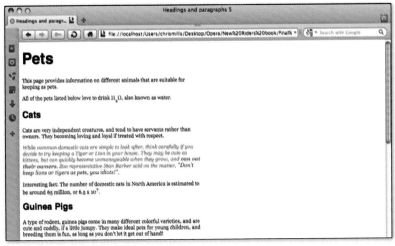

Figure 13.7: The finished example has many semantic elements added to it. Note that not all of these will, by default, result in much of a visual change.

Emphasis—<em> and <strong>

HTML contains two elements for indicating that the text within needs to be emphasised to the user, as it is more important or just different. For visual browsers this normally means applying a different colour, font, or making the text bolder or italic. For users of screen readers this can result in a different voice or other auditory effect.

For text that needs to be emphasised, you can use the <em> element, like so:

```
<p><em>While common domestic cats are simple to look
after, think carefully if you decide to try keeping
a tiger or lion in your house. They may be cute as
kittens, but can quickly become unmanageable when
they grow</em>.</p>
```

If an entire sentence was to be emphasised, but there was still a point within that sentence to be emphasised further, you could use the <strong> element to indicate stronger emphasis than normal, like so:

```
<p><em>While common domestic cats are simple to look
after, think carefully if you decide to try keeping
a tiger or lion in your house. They may be cute as
```

```
kittens, but can quickly become unmanageable when they
grow, and <strong>can eat their owners</strong>
</em>.</p>
```

Quoting other sources—<blockquote>, <q>, and <cite>

Very often articles, blog posts, and reference documents will quote other documents. In HTML, there are two elements that handle quotes.

The first, <blockquote>, is used for lengthy quotations such as entire sentences, paragraphs, lists, etc. It looks something like this:

```
<blockquote><p>Just be careful to keep an eye on the
gender of your guinea pigs, and the rate at which they
breed. We didn't want to breed ours, so we set out to
buy two males. Unfortunately, the pet store owner got
it wrong, and our guinea pig family trebled in size in
a matter of months!</p></blockquote>
```

A <blockquote> must contain other block elements directly inside it. You should use the same block level element(s) as used in the original document, e.g., if you are quoting a paragraph of text, use a paragraph.

You can use a <cite> element to name the person/source being quoted, for example:

```
<blockquote><p>Just be careful to keep an eye on the
gender of your guinea pigs, and the rate at which they
breed. We didn't want to breed ours, so we set out to
buy two males. Unfortunately, the pet store owner got
it wrong, and our guinea pig family trebled in size in
a matter of months!<cite>-- Mrs. W, Pinetree, Kentucky
</cite></p></blockquote>
```

Short quotes that are used within a normal sentence or paragraph are contained within the <q> element:

```
<p><em>While common domestic cats are simple to look
after, think carefully if you decide to try keeping
a tiger or lion in your house. They may be cute as
kittens, but can quickly become unmanageable when they
grow, and <strong>can eat their owners.</strong> Zoo
```

```
representative <cite>Stan Barber</cite>said on the
matter, <q>Don't keep lions or tigers as pets, you
idiots!</q></em>.</p>
```

Supplying contact information for the page author—<address>

The <address> element is probably the most badly named and misunderstood element in HTML. At first glance, with a name like "address" it would appear that it is used to encapsulate addresses: email, postal, or otherwise. This is only partially the case.

The actual meaning of <address> is to supply contact information *for the author or authors* of the page, or the major section of the page, that it appears within. This can take the form of a name, an email address, a postal address or a link to another page with more contact information. For example:

```
<address>This page is maintained by the <strong>We Love
Pets Foundation</strong>. If you have questions or want
more information, contact us at contact@example.com or
phone us on 555-666-7777.</address>
```

Resource // Microformats

For any general address, you can use something called a **microformat** to indicate that a paragraph contains an address. Check out the microformats home page at http://microformats.org/ for a lot more information. There is a good microformats introductory article at http://en.wikipedia.org/wiki/Microformat.

Linebreaks

Because of the way HTML defines white space, it is not possible to control where lines of text break by simply pressing the Return key whilst writing the text (you'll read a lot more about this in the next chapter).

A line break can be introduced into the document using the <br> element. However, this should only be used to force line breaks where they are required, and never to apply more vertical spacing between paragraphs or other elements in a document—that is more appropriately done with CSS.

A common error is to use double line breaks—

—to define beginnings and ends of paragraphs:

```
<br><br>
First paragraph.
<br><br>
Second paragraph.
<br><br>
```

Please, please don't do this. Just use <p> like you are supposed to!

So, for example, you could add a contact address into our contact details like so:

```
<p>This page is maintained by the <strong>We Love Pets
Foundation</strong>. If you have questions or want more
information, contact us on email at contact@example.com,
phone us on 555-666-7777, or write to us at:</p>
<address>We Love Pets<br>
       400 Kitty Street<br>
       Los Angeles, CA 23456</address>
```

Tip: If you are writing XHTML rather than HTML, the element should be self-closing, like so: <br />. This goes for all elements that don't require closing tags—
, <hr>, <link>, <meta>, <img>, etc.

Horizontal rules—<hr>

A horizontal rule is created in HTML with the <hr> element. It inserts a horizontal line into the document, which represents a boundary between different sections of a document.

While some argue that this is inherently non-semantic and purely a visual, presentational effect, there is actually some precedent in literature for such an element to exist. Within a chapter (which could be described as a section within a book), a horizontal rule may appear between scenes that occur in different times and/or places. Also, poetry can use decorative breaks to separate different stanzas of the poem.

Neither use would justify the existence of a new heading element, which is the accepted way of marking the boundaries between document sections. The <hr> element has no uncommon attributes and should be styled using CSS if the default appearance in unsatisfactory.

> **Tip:** As with the line break, if you are writing XHTML and not HTML, use the self-closing form—<hr />.

Abbreviations

The <abbr> and <acronym> elements are used to indicate where abbreviations occur, and provide a method for expanding upon them without unnecessarily interrupting the flow of the document. The abbreviation text gets wrapped in the <abbr>/<acronym> element, and the full version is placed in a title attribute, like so:

```
...Parrots can range in weight from 10
<acronym title="Grams">g</acronym> to 4<acronym
title="Kilograms">kg</acronym>, and they live for
<abbr title="approximately">approx.</abbr> 50 years...
```

Resource // <acronym>

Whilst the HTML 4.01 specification allows for both <abbr> and <acronym> elements, often some confusion exists about which to use where.

An acronym is a type of abbreviation in the form of a word created by the initials of the full expansion, and spoken as a single word, not spelt out (for example, scuba—an acronym for "self-contained underwater breathing apparatus"). Acronyms are a subset of abbreviations, and strictly speaking, it is incorrect to mark up something like "HTML" using the <acronym> element (that's an initialism!)..

Internet Explorer (before version 7, and 7 doesn't provide the dotted underline underneath abbreviations that other browsers do) doesn't support the <acronym> element, but does recognise <abbr>.

Also, in the draft of HTML5, the <acronym> element has been dropped in favour of standardising on <abbr> for both, as any acronym is also a valid abbreviation. The best thing to do is to avoid using <acronym> and just stick to using <abbr> throughout your code.

Superscript and subscript

To mark up a part of some text as being super- or sub-scripted (slightly raised or lowered compared to the rest of the text) you use the <sup> and <sub> elements. Some languages require these elements for correct usage of abbreviations and it can be used when a small amount of mathematical or chemistry-related content is being marked up, for example:

```
<p>All of the pets listed below love to drink
H<sub>2</sub>O, also known as water.</p>
<p>Interesting fact: The number of domestic cats in
North America is estimated to be around 65 million, or
6.5 x 10<sup>7</sup>.</p>
```

You should not use <sup> and <sub> simply for visual effects.

Changes to documents (inserting and deleting)

If a document has been changed since the first time it was available, you can mark these changes so that return visitors or automated processes can tell what has changed, and when.

New text (insertions) should be marked up with the <ins> element. Text that has been removed (deletions) should be marked up with the <del> element. If a deletion and insertion have been made at the same point in the document, good form suggests having the deleted text first, followed by the insertion.

Both elements can take two attributes that give more meaning to the edits:

- cite: If the reason for the change is stated in the page or elsewhere on the Web, you should reference to that document or fragment in the cite attribute. This effectively says "This change happened because of this reason."

- datetime: You can also indicate the time at which the change was made by using a datetime attribute. The value should be an ISO-standard timestamp, which is generally of the form YYYY-MM-DD HH:MM:SS ±HH:MM (see http://en.wikipedia.org/wiki/ISO_8601 for more information).

Here is an example that uses both attributes:

```
<p><del cite="edit_log.html" datetime="2010-01-04
00:26:55 Z">The most common species of parrot to be
domesticated, African Grays are of good nature and
they can learn many human words</del>
<ins datetime="2010-01-04 00:41:36 Z">One of the most
common species to be domesticated, African Grays are
good natured and learn words easily</ins>.</p>
```

Tip: Browsers don't currently do anything with the cite and datetime attributes, but you can use them in conjunction with JavaScript or CSS to do useful things, and support may well improve in the future.

Code and variables

The <code> element is used to indicate computer code on a page—you simply wrap the element around the code snippet, like so:

```
<p>I am starting to write notes here on how to maintain
this page. Surround each separate paragraph with the tags
<code>&lt;p&gt;</code> and <code>&lt;/p&gt;</code>.</p>
```

The <var> element is used to indicate variables in textual content. This can be used in algebraic mathematical expressions or within programming code. For example:

```
<p>The value of <var>x</var> in 3<var>x</var>
+2=14 is 4.</p>
```

Remember that you need to escape special characters that appear in code if you want to use them in your textual content, otherwise the browser will try to render them as code and you'll get errors. The most commonly escaped characters are:

- <—escaped using <
- &—escaped using &
- >—escaped using >

Presentational elements—never use these

The HTML specification includes several elements that are widely described as "presentational" because they only specify what the content within them should look like, and not what it means.

Some of these have been labeled as deprecated in the specification. This means that they have been superseded by a newer method of achieving the same result. I will describe them briefly here, but note that this is mostly for historic interest—these elements should never be used in any modern web page.

<font face="…" size="…">

The text within is rendered by the browser using a font different from the default—instead, fonts and font sizes should be set using CSS.

<b>

The text within is bold—this almost always means the text has been emphasised, so you should use <em> or <strong> as shown earlier.

The visual results of <b> and <strong> (and <i> and <em>) are pretty much the same in most visual browsers, but screen readers will not communicate any difference between the two in each case. Bold and italic are purely visual effects, whereas strong and emphasis indicate that the text should be emphasised in some way. Therefore stick with <strong> and <em>.

<s> and <strike>

The text within has been struck-through with a line—if this is merely a presentational effect, this should be achieved with CSS. Alternatively, if the text is actually being marked as having been deleted it should be marked up with the <del> element described earlier in the chapter.

<u>

The text within is underlined—this is almost always a visual effect, and so should be achieved with CSS. Also note that underlined text generally indicates a link you can click on, so it may confuse web users.

<tt>

The text within is presented in a "teletype" or monospaced font—this should be achieved with CSS or a more appropriate semantic element such as <pre>, which is discussed in the next chapter.

<big> and <small>

The size of the text within is made bigger or smaller—this should be achieved with CSS.

Summary

This chapter has looked at the ins and outs of marking up and styling standard text. In the next chapter we will move on to how white space is handled in HTML, and how to control the spacing between your content using CSS.

CHAPTER 13

CHAPTER 14
Whitespace

by Chris Mills

Now you have a good understanding of how to mark up and add meaning and style to your headings and paragraphs, let's look at how to control the space between your different pieces of content. This might sound trivial, but when designing a page this is just as important as the content itself. Obviously you need to think carefully about your site's content—so, your navigation menu, heading structure, and writing style, etc. create a usable, comfortable user experience—but even the best content in the world will be horrible to sift through if it is all jammed together and crammed into a small space!

In this chapter we will look at how to use CSS to control your **whitespace**. I will give you a solid understanding of the **CSS box model**, which controls how spacing of content in CSS works; then look at padding, margins, line height, letter spacing, and other related topics.

*In this chapter you have the opportunity to **Try it yourself!** with the convenient sample code downloads found on the book's companion website—http://interactwithwebstandards.com.*

Reiterating the importance of whitespace

A lot of the theory behind the topics introduced in this chapter and the last one has its roots in traditional print design, to which web design owes a great deal. Think about a newspaper layout—the different stories and other bits of content are organized into thin columns to make it easier to digest them (**Figure 14.1**).

Figure 14.1: A typical newspaper layout is effective for scanning to find what you want, and reading the content quickly and easily.

If all the content was placed in a single wide column, without whitespace separation, it would be much harder to read. Another good example to look at is classic Swiss graphic design, which is known for using lots of whitespace and minimalist design sensibilities for a great impact. Visit http://www.flickr.com/groups/swisslegacy/pool/ for great examples of Swiss design.

Taking this to the web medium, you can easily see how a cluttered, content-heavy website (**Figure 14.2**) makes things very hard on the reader.

Figure 14.2: Cluttered sites with little whitespace are hard to scan to find what you want.

Especially when you compare it to a nice roomy design such as Dan Cederholm's website (**Figure 14.3**).

Figure 14.3: A good bit of space goes a long, long way.

Of course, I am using extreme disparity here to prove my point. Some would argue that the content types on these sites are very different and it is like comparing apples to oranges and thus not fair. But it does illustrate the point: if your pages are starting to look like **Figure 14.2**, you should really think about reorganizing your content.

> **Tip:** For more information on organizing web content sensibly, Steve Krug's awesome book *Don't Make Me Think* is a must-have. Check out `http://www.sensible.com/dmmt.html` for more information.

Try it yourself!

Find three good and three bad examples of content layout in print publications (any kind will do). Take pictures with a digital camera or other imaging device and write a blog post including these pictures to discuss what is good or bad about the layouts.

Do the same thing for websites—three good and three bad.

How browsers render whitespace in HTML

As you may have guessed, the term *whitespace* is pretty self-explanatory—it refers to any unoccupied space between content, rather than the content itself. An actual space character, as you would get when you hit the spacebar on the keyboard, is the most common, but there are others such as the tab character and the marker between two separate lines in a document (called a carriage return or new line).

In HTML, multiple occurrences of these characters are (almost) always treated by browsers as a single space character, except when `<pre>` is used, as we'll see later in the chapter. For example, the code download file `white_space_example.html` contains the following content in the `<body>`:

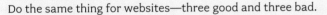

```
<p>There            is          only one
thing         in life                worse
than being              talked
about, and              that is              not
being          talked              about.</p>
```

Despite having lots of excess whitespace in it, it is interpreted by a web browser and displayed as shown in **Figure 14.4**.

Figure 14.4: Excess whitespace in HTML content is condensed down to single spaces when displayed by a browser.

Overriding the rules with <pre>

There is one exception to the above rule, and that is when you mark up text using the <pre> element (*pre* is short for *preformatted*). This element is useful if you deliberately want to show the whitespace in the source in the final output in the browser. Being a tech writer, I mainly tend to use it when I want to show code examples inside HTML documents, but it has other uses, e.g., displaying short-lined poetry. The first part of the <body> content of preformatted_example.html is as follows—it is an HTML code sample:

```
<pre><code>&lt;body&gt;
    &lt;div id="actor_profile"&gt;
        &lt;h1&gt;Hugo Weaving&lt;/h1&gt;
        &lt;p&gt;Hugo Weaving is a really cool actor,
        known for very varied roles including Agent Smith
        in The Matrix, Lord Elrond in Lord of the Rings,
        and Mitzi in The Adventures of Priscilla, Queen of
        the Desert!&lt;/p&gt;
        &lt;p&gt;He was born in Nigeria, but now lives
        in Australia.&lt;/p&gt;
    &lt;/div&gt;
&lt;/body&gt;</code></pre>
```

The second part of the <body> content is identical to the first, except that the <code> element is wrapped in a <p> element, not <pre> and <code>. This content is displayed in the browser as shown in **Figure 14.5**—note the difference the <pre> makes!

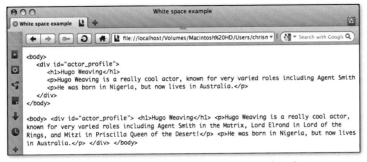

Figure 14.5: The <pre> *element in action, compared to the same content inside a paragraph element.*

I have used < and > to escape the HTML angle brackets, < and >, because if I didn't the browser would try to interpret these elements as code rather than just displaying them on the page.

> **Tip:** Why have I wrapped this content inside <code> as well as <pre>? Because <pre> doesn't describe the meaning of the content—it just preserves whitespace. The <code> element adds semantics to the content. And bear in mind that <code> needs to go inside <pre> (or another block level element). <code> is an inline element, and <pre> is block level. Block cannot go inside inline.

The box model

Since we are talking about layout here, it is time to introduce another fundamental concept that you should understand when working with HTML and CSS: the **box model**. This is the model browsers use to work out how much space HTML elements take up on the page, and how much space to put between them.

By default, block elements in your HTML appear one after another in the same order you placed them in the document (also known as *source order*), with some default margins separating them, and other default styles applied (see **Figure 14.6** for a demonstration).

Inline elements are placed one after the other inside block elements, kind of like placing some smaller boxes inside a larger box.

CHAPTER 14

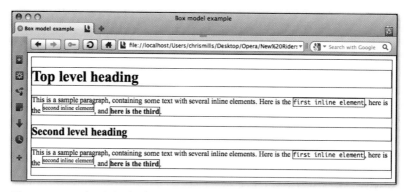

Figure 14.6: *The default placement of block and inline elements (check out* box_model1.html*). I have placed a border around each of the elements to give you an idea of the area the box model boxes take up.*

Tip: Block level elements can be placed inside other block elements, and inline elements can be placed inside other inline elements as well as block elements, but you can never place a block element inside an inline element, as we mentioned earlier.

As you can see, the headings and paragraphs have some default margins above and below them. The outermost box is the <body> element. You can alter the whitespace around the elements using CSS, as we shall see later.

The space around a block element

Now let's concentrate on a single block element. There are three layers that go around the element's content, rather like the layers of an onion. **Figure 14.7** illustrates them.

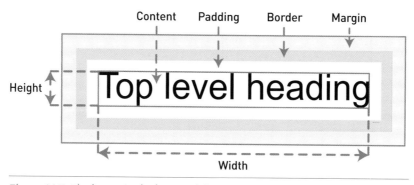

Figure 14.7: *The layers in the box model.*

So the layers in the box model are content, padding, border, and margin. Also note the inclusion of height and width on this diagram. When you set the `width` and `height` properties of an element, you are actually just setting the width and height of the content. All the other layers add extra width and height on top of that.

Study this carefully, and remember the order they are in—it will make it easier for you in future when you are solving content placement problems!

When two margins meet

When two vertical margins meet—for example, when a bottom margin is set on an element, and a top margin is set on the element directly below it—the margins collapse into one another, and the resulting margin is the same size as the larger of the two original margins.

Box model problems in older browsers

One problem that has plagued web designers for years is that older browsers incorrectly implement the box model. This problem is lessening in recent times as the market share of older browsers drops to the realm of the insignificant, which as of the time of writing this book definitely includes version 5 browsers and below (Netscape 4 and Internet Explorer 5 had notoriously bad box model implementations).

The only browser we still really have to worry about in this respect is Internet Explorer 6. As **Figure 14.7** illustrates, a correct box model implementation classifies `width` and `height` as *the width and height of the content only*. In Internet Explorer 6, `width` and `height` are *the width and height of the content plus the padding*, so your layouts will differ slightly in Internet Explorer 6, compared to other browsers. You might not care about this, but your site visitors using Internet Explorer 6 will, so you'll have to figure out a way to serve different CSS to fix Internet Explorer 6, for example via JavaScript, CSS hacks, or conditional comments. I personally think conditional comments are the best way to solve this, because they don't require JavaScript and are less, well, *hack-ish*—see `http://dev.opera.com/articles/view/supporting-ie-with-conditional-comments/`.

There are a few other subtle differences in how the box model works between modern browsers and bad old browsers, but I won't go into them here, as they are far from vital to your learning at this stage.

Setting padding, border and margin via CSS

To set the padding, border and margin of an element, you can use the `padding`, `border` and `margin` families of CSS properties.

padding

Only five padding properties exist in CSS: `padding-top`, `padding-right`, `padding-bottom` and `padding-left` rather unsurprisingly set the amount of padding on the four sides of the element in question. The most common units you'll use to set padding are pixels and %. `padding` is a shorthand property that allows you to set the padding for all four sides at once—you can use the shorthand in different ways:

- `padding: 10px 0px 20px 30px`; sets the padding for the four sides separately, starting with top, then right, bottom, and finally left (think *clockwise, starting from the top*).

- `padding: 10px 20px`; sets an equal padding for the top and bottom sides, and then an equal padding for the right and left sides.

- `padding: 10px 20px 5px`; sets a padding for the top (`10px`), an equal padding for the right and left sides (`20px`), and last of all a padding for the bottom (`5px`).

- `padding: 10px`; sets an equal padding for all four sides in one value.

You can also set `padding` (and `margin`) to a value of `auto`, which causes it to take up all the available space inside its parent element, after any other declarations have used up space.

Try it yourself!

To demonstrate the effects of the properties we are discussing here, I will use a modified version of the `box_model1.html`. Check out `box_model2.html` and `box_model2.css` in the code download—it looks like **Figure 14.8** by default.

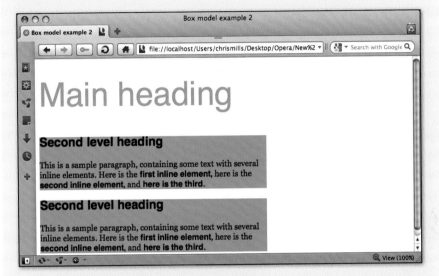

Figure 14.8: The starting point of our example.

The section boxes currently don't look very good with the text coming right up to the edge of the background color. Take a copy of the sample code and add some padding values to the content to improve how it looks. Play around with different combinations of padding on the different sides to see what you think looks best.

border

The `border` family of values set different aspects of an element's border and are explained in this section.

- `border-color`: This is shorthand that sets the colour of the element's border—you can use hex, keywords or whatever other CSS-supported colour value you like. You can also set the colour for individual sides using a single declaration with multiple values, e.g., `border-color: red blue white black`; or `border-color: black white`;, or even more specific declarations—`border-bottom-color`, `border-top-color`, `border-left-color`, and `border-right-color`.

- border-style: This is shorthand that sets the style of the border—dashed, dotted, double, groove, ridge, etc. In the same way as border-color, this can be broken down into properties for individual sides, e.g., border-right-style, or you can set different styles on different sides, for example border-style: dotted dashed;.
- border-width: This is shorthand that sets the width of the border, e.g., 1px. In the same way as border-color, this can be broken down into properties for individual sides, e.g., border-right-width, or you can set different styles on different sides, e.g., border-width: 1px 2px;.
- border: This is a super-shorthand property that allows you to set the width, colour and style of all sides of an element's border in one easy declaration, for example, border: solid 1px black;.

Try it yourself!

Your content boxes should now look something like box_model3.html and box_model3.css (**Figure 14.9**).

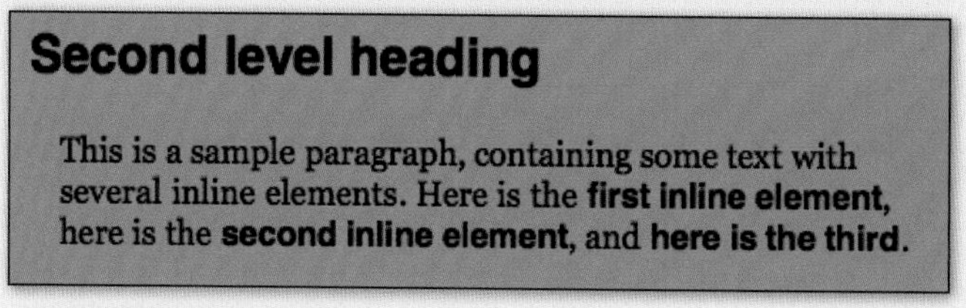

Second level heading

This is a sample paragraph, containing some text with several inline elements. Here is the **first inline element,** here is the **second inline element,** and **here is the third.**

Figure 14.9: An excerpt from the next stage of our example—much neater.

Your next task is to add a border to the content boxes that is in keeping with the design. Experiment with different styles and colour combinations and see what you can create.

margin

Just like padding, there are only five margin properties in existence: margin-top, margin-right, margin-bottom, margin-left and the shorthand property margin. These work in exactly the same way as the padding properties, except of course they set margin values! Refer to the padding section above for guidance, and remember that adjacent margins collapse, as mentioned earlier.

Try it yourself!

Now you need to manipulate the margins in the example to round it off. Take the example files and add margin values as you see fit.

If you want to see what I did in this section and the last, check out **Figure 14.10**.

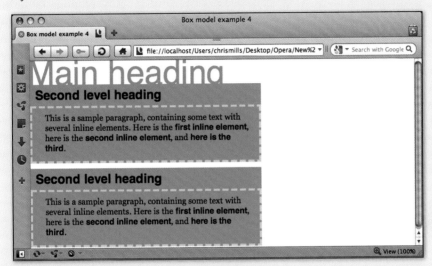

Figure 14.10: *The example finished off (for now), with margins and borders updated (see* box_model4.html*).*

Controlling spacing within paragraphs

There are properties you can use to control spacing within paragraphs—text-align, letter-spacing, word-spacing and line-height. I will cover them all in the subsections below.

text-align

text-align controls how your text is justified. Similar to a word processing application, you can choose left, right, center or justify (makes each line of text exactly the same length by varying the spacing between words on the lines). **Figure 14.11** shows the effect of the different settings.

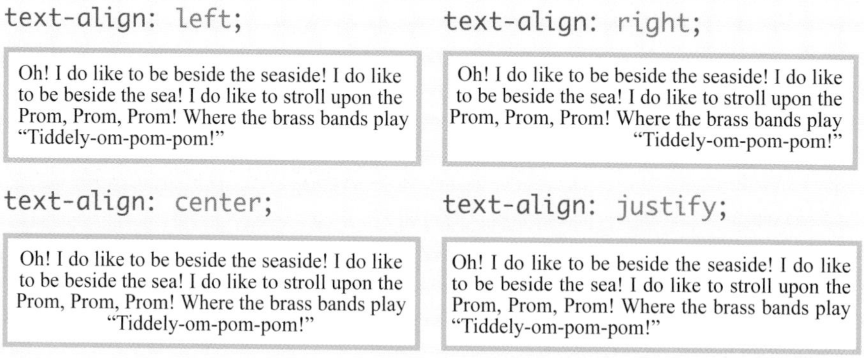

```
text-align: left;
```

> Oh! I do like to be beside the seaside! I do like to be beside the sea! I do like to stroll upon the Prom, Prom, Prom! Where the brass bands play "Tiddely-om-pom-pom!"

```
text-align: right;
```

> Oh! I do like to be beside the seaside! I do like to be beside the sea! I do like to stroll upon the Prom, Prom, Prom! Where the brass bands play "Tiddely-om-pom-pom!"

```
text-align: center;
```

> Oh! I do like to be beside the seaside! I do like to be beside the sea! I do like to stroll upon the Prom, Prom, Prom! Where the brass bands play "Tiddely-om-pom-pom!"

```
text-align: justify;
```

> Oh! I do like to be beside the seaside! I do like to be beside the sea! I do like to stroll upon the Prom, Prom, Prom! Where the brass bands play "Tiddely-om-pom-pom!"

Figure 14.11: The different text-align settings—left (the default), right, center, and justify.

letter-spacing

letter-spacing alters the horizontal spacing between each letter, which is similar to the effect of *kerning* or *tracking* in print design/ typography. **Figure 14.12** shows the effect of applying different amounts of letter spacing to a sample paragraph. Remember that 1em is the size of one character, so you'll probably want to change this setting by a fraction of an em, or a small percentage. The default setting is 0—if you want to make the letters really close and possibly overlap, you can use negative values for letter-spacing.

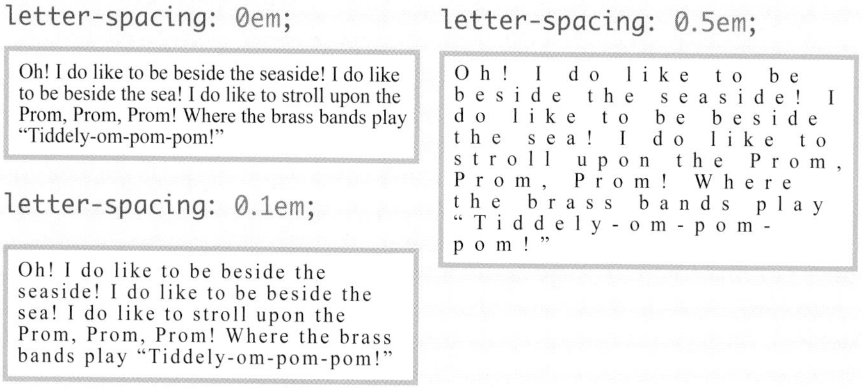

```
letter-spacing: 0em;
```

> Oh! I do like to be beside the seaside! I do like to be beside the sea! I do like to stroll upon the Prom, Prom, Prom! Where the brass bands play "Tiddely-om-pom-pom!"

```
letter-spacing: 0.5em;
```

> Oh! I do like to be beside the seaside! I do like to be beside the sea! I do like to stroll upon the Prom, Prom, Prom! Where the brass bands play "Tiddely-om-pom-pom!"

```
letter-spacing: 0.1em;
```

> Oh! I do like to be beside the seaside! I do like to be beside the sea! I do like to stroll upon the Prom, Prom, Prom! Where the brass bands play "Tiddely-om-pom-pom!"

Figure 14.12: The effects of increasing the letter spacing.

word-spacing

word-spacing works in exactly the same way as letter-spacing, except that it instead alters the horizontal spacing between each word —**Figure 14.13** illustrates its effects. The default setting is 0—if you want to make the words really close and possibly overlap, you can use negative values for word-spacing.

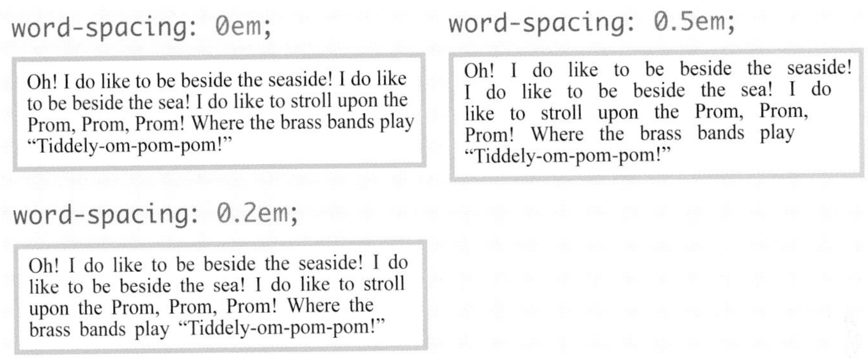

word-spacing: 0em;

Oh! I do like to be beside the seaside! I do like to be beside the sea! I do like to stroll upon the Prom, Prom, Prom! Where the brass bands play "Tiddely-om-pom-pom!"

word-spacing: 0.5em;

Oh! I do like to be beside the seaside! I do like to be beside the sea! I do like to stroll upon the Prom, Prom, Prom! Where the brass bands play "Tiddely-om-pom-pom!"

word-spacing: 0.2em;

Oh! I do like to be beside the seaside! I do like to be beside the sea! I do like to stroll upon the Prom, Prom, Prom! Where the brass bands play "Tiddely-om-pom-pom!"

Figure 14.13: The effects of increasing the word spacing.

line-height

line-height again works in the same way as the previous two properties, except that it alters the vertical spacing between each line; this is usually called *leading* in print design/typography. As with letter spacing, you'll want to use a small value for this. The default setting for line-height is 1em—the absolute height of each text character. If you want to have your lines closer together, you can use values of less than 1em (or less than 100%), but putting it too low will result in a mess; if you set it to 0, then all the lines of text will appear on a single line!

Figure 14.14 shows the effects of this property.

```
line-height: 0.7em;                 line-height: 1.5em;
```

```
line-height: 1em;
```

Figure 14.14: The effects of increasing the line height.

Try it yourself!

1. Find yourself a sample page and experiment with the above properties. These can give you some cool effects, depending on the look your want to find for your page. Increasing letter spacing and word spacing slightly can also improve legibility.

2. Now take `box_model4.html` and `box_model4.css` and make a few modifications:

   - Justify the text in the paragraphs.
   - Increase distance between lines and letters slightly to improve legibility.

I ended up with the result seen in **Figure 14.15** (check out `box_model5.html` in the code download).

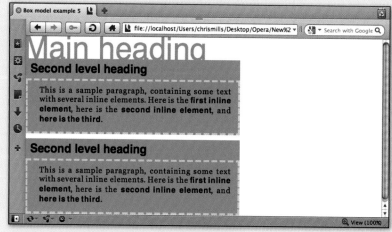

Figure 14.15: Our example with letter spacing, line spacing, and justification added.

Centering content on a page

One very common use of margins is to provide an easy way to center your website horizontally in the browser. To do this, you need to add two things to your code. First of all, you need to add a wrapper <div> around your entire content, like so:

```
<body>
    <div id="wrapper">
        /* Your content */
    </div>
</body>
```

Then you need to style this in your CSS as follows:

```
#wrapper {
    width: 450px;
    /* This can vary according to how wide your want
    your site to be */
    margin: 0 auto;
    /* auto forces the left and right margins to share
    the available space outside the wrapper <div> equally
    between them */
}
```

These additions cause a change in your site as illustrated in **Figure 14.16**.

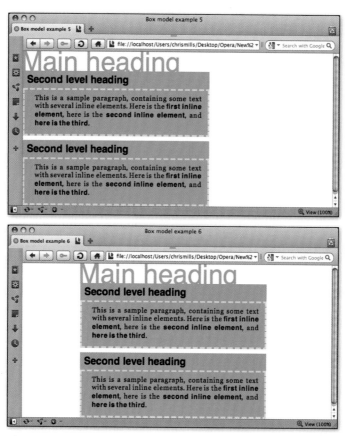

Figure 14.16: Centering your content in the browser.

Summary

After reading this chapter, you will have learned the essentials of how whitespace is dealt with in HTML, how document layout works, and how you can manipulate whitespace using CSS. In the next chapter we will move on to marking up and styling hyperlinks.

CHAPTER 15
Links

by Chris Mills

Links (**hyperlinks**, to give them their full name) are arguably the *most* important elements in HTML—it is links that make the Web a *web*. This is the most significant thing about the Web: it allows us to create pathways between different resources residing on the web servers of the world, resulting in an infinitely extendable communication and information network, accessible to people of different nationalities and with different abilities.

The two types of links used on the Web are:

- Links created with the <link> element in the document <head>, for example the links used to apply external CSS and JavaScript to HTML files. We have covered these in Chapter 11, "CSS Intro," and Chapter 12, "<head>."

- Links that appear in the document <body>, created using the <a> element. These provide links for our site visitors to click through from our HTML documents to other resources on the Web, including other HTML documents, text files, PDFs, images, Word documents, and whatever else people put up on the Web. These are called **anchor links**.

In this chapter we will look at the HTML syntax of different types of anchor links (from here on in we'll just use the word **links**), link best practices and how to use CSS to style links.

*In this chapter you have the opportunity to **Try it yourself!** with the convenient sample code downloads found on the book's companion website—*http://interactwithwebstandards.com.

Link syntax

You can turn any piece of text or inline element in a document into an anchor link by wrapping it an *<a>* element. For example, the following code snippet contains two links that link to other resources related to the topics linked from:

```
<p>Hello and welcome to the UK personal satisfaction and
well-being pages. Be sure to visit our newest feature pages
for more information on <a href="features/bad_weather.
html">coping with bad weather</a> and <a href="features/
losing_at_sport.html">losing at cricket (and every other
sport we invented)</a>.</p>
```

This gives us the HTML output shown in **Figure 15.1**.

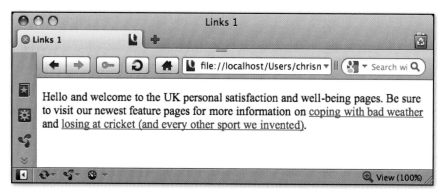

Figure 15.1: Two basic links.

Visitors activating a link—by clicking it with a mouse, selecting it with the keyboard, or in some cases even with the voice—will cause the browser to leave the current page and load the page specified in the *href* attribute.

Link attributes

The attributes that you'll commonly use with links are as follows:

- *href*: As indicated in the above example, *href* contains the path to the file you want the link to point to.

- `title`: If needed, you can put extra information about the external resource into this attribute, such as more description, the authors, or whatever else is needed. This should not be used for essential information, as it may not be exposed to users in certain situations—you shouldn't rely on it. For example, some browsers may not display it as tooltips (see the following material for more information).

- `id` or `class`: As explained in previous chapters, you can use an `id` or a `class` to act as a hook if you want to style specific links inside an HTML document.

Let's have a look at an updated version of the previous example that makes use of all these attributes:

```
<p>Hello and welcome to the UK personal satisfaction and
well-being pages. Be sure to visit our newest feature
pages for more information on <a href="features/bad_
weather.html" title="rain and wind is manageable, but snow
brings the country to a standstill" class="feature">coping
with bad weather</a> and <a href="features/losing_at_
sport.html" title="With coverage of cricket, soccer, and
athletics" class="feature">losing at cricket (and every
other sport we invented)</a>.</p>
```

The `title` attribute gives us links that display tooltips when moused over, as shown in **Figure 15.2** (see `links_example2.html` on the book's website.)

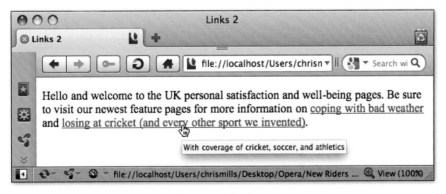

Figure 15.2: Updated links, with classes and titles.

Resource // `title` attribute

The `title` attribute should just contain useful supporting information, which isn't absolutely essential, and isn't the length of *The Lord of the Rings*. Blind people using screen readers can't be expected to perceive this information, as having the screen reader read out `title` attribute contents tends to be turned off by default. In addition, users browsing using only the keyboard won't normally get to see information in `title` attributes, as keyboard navigation doesn't trigger a tooltip. Some people describe exactly what the resource is inside the `title` attribute, but this is unnecessary if the text of the link is descriptive enough. See the link best practices section later on for more information on writing good link text.

Different kinds of link target

An *<a>* element can link to resources in different ways, depending on the kind of value found inside the `href` attribute. We'll explain the different ways in this section.

Absolute links

To start with we have **absolute links**. These links will take you to a resource from any starting point. You can use an absolute path to link to a file on another server, or even to a file on the same server. To get to one of these, you have to point to its full URL. Some examples:

- http://www.amazon.com/
- http://interact.webstandards.org/curriculum/front-end-development/
- http://mywebsite.co.uk/resources/form1.pdf

Relative links

There are also **relative links**, links that exist on the same server as the current page, and identify a required starting point to reach the final destination. It's a bit like giving directions to someone by saying, "It's down one block and over two blocks." Those directions only work if you start in the right place. You don't need to specify the full URL to these pages—instead, you specify a **file path** to the file you want to link to. Consider the directory structure shown in **Figure 15.3**.

Figure 15.3: A sample directory structure.

We will assume that the file `file_to_link_from.html` is the file you are linking from. So for example:

- If you want to link to the `link.html` file—in the same directory as the current one—you just need the file name: `link.html`.

- If you want to link to `link2.html`, which is inside a folder in the same directory as the current file, you need `folder/link2.html`. This tells the browser "go into the *folder* directory, then you will find the file you are looking for."

- If you need to go up into the parent directory of the folder the current file is in to find the file to link to—for example `link3.html` is in a directory above the *current directory* folder that `file_to_link_from.html` resides in—you use two dots to signify "go up one level," like this: `../link3.html`.

- If the file you want to link to is in the very top directory (the **root**) of the website, you can get there simply by putting a slash at the beginning of the file path. For example we could instead link to `link3.html` using `/link3.html`. File paths starting with a / will always be relative to the root of the server.

Tip: If you are linking to a file on the same server, you can still use an absolute link if you really want to, but it will be less efficient than using the equivalent relative link, as you are telling the browser to go and find the server before then going to find the file. The first part of this in unnecessary if you are on the correct server already.

Fragment identifier

The third type of link to mention is a **fragment identifier**. You use this to link to another part of the *same* document. To make an element in your document linkable to, you simply need to give it an `id`. For example:

```
<h2 id="cats-and-dogs">Raining cats and dogs</h2>
```

Then to link to this heading, you use the `id` preceded by a hash:

```
<p>Find more out later about <a href="#cats-and-
dogs">Raining cats and dogs</a>.</p>
```

Mixing link types

The last thing to mention in this section is that you can use a mix of absolute links with fragments, and relative links with fragments:

- `http://example.com/features/bad_weather.html/#cats-and-dogs`
- `../features/bad_weather.html/#cats-and-dogs`

Try it yourself!

So let's look at a few examples that show these different kinds of links in action. Open `links_example3.html` and have a play. I'd like you to create new examples of:

- A working absolute link to an external site.
- A working absolute link to a document fragment on an external site (have a bit of a look around).
- A working relative link to a file that is one directory level up, then three directory levels down (following a different directory path than before). You will need to create some directories and a new HTML file.
- An absolute or relative link to a resource that is not an HTML file.

Link best practices

There are a number of best practices you should follow when putting links on your HTML pages. These are not hard to follow, and once you have created a few web pages, they should start to become second nature. Above all, you want to give your site visitors a user experience they will find easy to use and can trust, otherwise you will lose credibility and they will surf elsewhere.

Link text should be concise and describe what you're linking to

Make sure you write your content so that you can link to further resources from a piece of text that is easy to understand, unique to the page, and effectively describes what is being linked to. For example, this is *REALLY* bad:

```
<p>For more information on Whales, <a  href="info_pages/
info1.html">click here</a>.</p>
<p>For more information on Tigers, <a href="info_pages/
info2.html">click here</a>.</p>
<p>For more information on Dugongs, <a href="info_pages/
info3.html">click here</a>.</p>
```

First of all, users using assistive technologies like screen readers to browse your website will often find the link they are looking for by just browsing a list of all the links on the page, so for them, the links need to make sense out of context. With these links, all they get is:

"click here"
"click here"
"click here"

which is obviously confusing and unhelpful.

Second, search engines indexing your site will often use link text for significant keywords as well as headings, so by including such bad link text, you are making your site harder for users to find in the first place too.

Third, this text is harder for all users to use, regardless of (dis)ability. Remember that users won't read every bit of your web page; they will quickly scan it, looking for the information they want. Pretty much every little thing you can do to make your web page easier to use is worth it.

These links would be better written like so:

```
<p><a href="info_pages/whales.html">More information on
Whales</a>.</p>
<p><a href="info_pages/tigers.html">More information on
Tigers</a>.</p>
<p><a href="info_pages/dugongs.html">More information on
Dugongs</a>.</p>
```

Or even like this:

```
<p>We have more information available on
<a href="info_pages/whales.html">Whales</a>,
<a href="info_pages/tigers.html">Tigers</a>, and
<a href="info_pages/dugongs.html">Dugongs</a>.</p>
```

Alert users to large or unexpected files

When users click on a link, they expect to be taken to another HTML page quickly, unless told otherwise. It is therefore a good idea to provide extra information in the document to alert users to anything unusual. Here are some good examples (see `links_example4.html`):

```
<p>Download our fact files on <a href="info_pages/whales.
pdf">Whales (PDF document, 4.3mb)</a>, <a href="info_
pages/tigers.pdf">Tigers (PDF document, 6.1mb)</a>, and
<a href="info_pages/dugongs.pdf">Dugongs (PDF document,
5mb)</a>.</p>

<p>Want to work here? <a href="application_form.
doc">Download our job application form (Word document)
</a>.</p>

<p>To find more locations, <a href="interactive_locator.
html">use our interactive map (2.5mb, contains
Flash)</a>. To use it, you may need to <a href="http://
get.adobe.com/flashplayer/">install the Flash plugin</a>
if you have not already got it. Or you could use
our <a href="address_list.html">non-interactive address
list</a> (good for users on mobile, or on a slow
Internet connection).</p>
```

This looks like **Figure 15.4** in a browser.

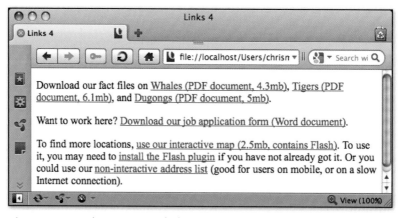

Figure 15.4: Our best practices links example.

Don't surprise users with unexpected behaviour

If you want your users to know that your links are to be clicked on, make sure they look like links! Because of browser default styles, users generally expect pieces of underlined text to be clickable links, although of course, users will also expect things such as an obvious set of navigation buttons to be clickable links, so it depends a bit on context. Just don't style them so that they look too wildly different from these accepted conventions. And conversely, don't underline things that aren't links.

Web developers often use JavaScript to hijack the functionality of links, making them open or close different parts of the interface, act as navigation menus, change the styles applied to the page, or display different panels in a tabbed interface (see **Figure 15.5** for a drop-down menu example). If you are using links to do different things, don't make them look the same as your "normal" links. You'll find more out about styling links later in this chapter.

Figure 15.5: A drop-down menu example, involving many links.

Frames, new windows and pop-ups—just say no

The fear of losing visitors to other sites while still wanting to link to them gave us some inventions in web development that have been a thorn in the side of usable sites for years: frames and pop-ups.

Using HTML frames means you separate the page shown in the browser into several different documents, shown at the same time in different panes. The benefit is that you can bring different pages together from different servers and display them at the same time as a single page. This is where the usefulness ends, however—frames are a terrible user experience and actually harmful:

- Search engines can never index a whole page of frames, and instead might show up parts of a page in search results that don't make sense out of context.

- Visitors cannot bookmark the page—the next time they open their bookmark they'll get the initial state of the frameset and not the page as they left it.

- Visitors who depend on assistive technology have a very hard time navigating around framesets.

- Third party sites might not like to be shown inside a frameset and use "framebreaker" scripts that replace framesets with the real URL when you try to embed them. This is to stop criminals from luring Internet users into entering, for example, credit card information into a website that appears to be a bank website but *isn't* (so-called "phishing").

Links inside a frameset use the `target` attribute of the <a> element to target the correct frame. Each frame in a frameset gets a certain name, and activating the link opens the document defined in the `href` attribute in that frame. If the frameset is not available (for example, when a visitor finds the document with the links via a search engine), each link opens in a new browser instance.

Opening a new browser instance is another common way to link to third party sites—either with a scripted pop-up window or via a `target` attribute with a value of `_blank`. The fact that every modern browser comes with a pop-up blocker should give you an indication of how much people enjoy being greeted by pop-up windows—they *don't!*

Frames and `target="blank"` attributes are also invalid HTML unless you use the frameset doctype.

Link styling

We'll get on to styling other, more complicated uses of links such as navigation menus and later in this book (and in other books in the series), but for now we'll look at styling plain old links to other places! In general, it is a good idea to be fairly conservative with your link styling—they don't need to look that different from the normal text beside them in the paragraphs of your site, as long they feature enough clues that they are clickable/focusable and therefore links. Remember what I said before about making links look the way users expect them to look.

Certainly don't go crazy and have them styled in 400 percent flashing rainbow text with dancing unicorn graphics. Otherwise I'll hunt you down, personally.

The most important thing to understand here is that links have several different **states** to be aware of:

- link: The default state—it defines what links should look like by default, when you first get to them. By default, unvisited links are coloured blue.

- visited: The style of a link that has already been visited (clicked on, or followed). By default, already visited links are coloured purple.

- hover: The style of a link whilst the mouse cursor is hovering over it.

- focus: The style of a link when it has been *given focus* by means other than the mouse, for example, if the user has used the keyboard to navigate to it. Note that old versions of Internet Explorer do not support the focus state, and just use active in place of focus.

- active: The style of the link while it is activated, i.e., as the mouse button is held down while the pointer is over the link (when the mouse button is released the state changes to :focus); it is also the style of the last activated link when you arrive back at the original document by going back in your browser history.

Tip: You may come across a code construct along the lines of <a name=""> as you view different sources around the Web. This is an old-school style of link, used in the early days of the Web, which is now deprecated.

Figure 15.6 shows default link styles for link, visited, and focus. The default styles for hover and active are basically the same as link/visited.

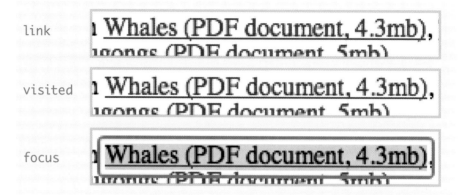

link

visited

focus

Figure 15.6: Default styles for link *(top),* visited *(middle), and* focus *(bottom).*

Try it yourself!

Go to some of your favourite websites and try following some of the links, going back to the original page, and then using keyboard navigation to select the links. Pay close attention to how the links look at each stage.

Tip: Most browsers have a built-in mechanism for navigating between links and form elements using the keyboard. For example Firefox allows you to do it by pressing the Tab key, Safari's equivalent is Alt + Tab, and Opera has spatial navigation, which allows you to navigate these elements by holding down Shift and using the arrow keys.

Link CSS

The CSS to style the different link states uses the pseudo-classes we first mentioned in Chapter 11, appended onto the selectors you are using to select the links, for example:

```
a:link { color: red; }
a.resources:visited { color: green; }
a.resources:hover { background-color: yellow; }
```

You should ideally specify CSS for every one of these states. Each one conveys information to the user about the fact they are interacting with a link.

If in doubt about focus, hover and active, you can simply style focus and hover in the same way, as their functions are pretty similar. You can then add some simple variation for active, for example, setting the text to italics, or even just styling active the same as hover and focus. (I find this usually satisfies most website needs—see below for an example.)

link and visited should probably be given exclusive styles, however, as they serve important and distinct roles.

These states are not all mutually exclusive. Although it is not possible for a link to be unvisited and visited at the same time, it is perfectly possible for a link to be hovered, active, and visited at the same time.

Let's look at an example. I have taken our previous example and added some basic styling plus a few choice CSS3 properties to make it look a bit juicier—see **Figure 15.7** (check out links_example5.html and links_example5.css to see the finished files).

Figure 15.7: Some basic styling added to our last example.

In terms of the link state, I've kept the underline and only altered the colour slightly, so that they will be familiar to users as links. The link CSS is as follows:

```
a:link {
    color: #00A6B9;
    text-decoration: underline;
}
```

The visited state is shown in **Figure 15.8**—note the "Tigers" link.

Figure 15.8: The link visited state for our example.

The CSS for this simply sets a darker text colour:

```
a:visited {
    color: #177380;
}
```

The interesting bit is when you get to the rule that sets the styling for links in the hover, focus, and active states:

```
a:hover,a:focus,a:active {
    text-shadow: 1px 1px 2px #00A6B9;
    text-decoration: none;
}
```

Here I've removed the underline using text-decoration: none; and set a subtle CSS3 text-shadow to make the link look nice and responsive when interacted with using mouse or keyboard (**Figure 15.9**).

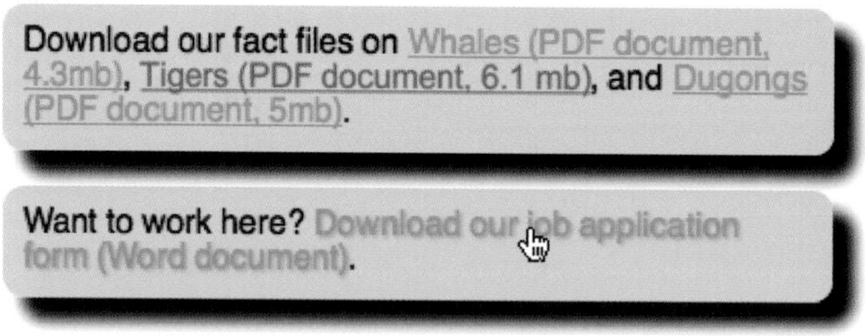

Figure 15.9: *The* hover/focus/active *state for our links.*

A love/hate relationship

Before we move on, there is one more thing to mention—you need to specify `link`, `visited`, `hover` (and `focus`), and `active` in *that* order. Note the order in which I've put the rules in the CSS file.

Why?

Because of inheritance, and because of the order in which the browser triggers the different states.

First of all, you want the `link` state to have basic styling, and the other states to build on it in various ways. You don't want `link` to inherit styles from `hover`, for example, as that would make the links look all wrong, and not what you intended.

Second, think about state triggering order. You hover over the link to show your intention to click, you click the link to put focus on it, and while holding the mouse button down it's active. Styling it in a different order may not work for this reason as well.

Luckily there is a way to remember the order in which you have to put them—the **Lo**V**e** **HA**te mnemonic (`link … visited … hover/focus … active`). Just remember that `:focus` always goes next to `:hover`.

Try it yourself!

Take the example file from this section and create your own system of link styles—have fun and play around!

Resource // Use colour carefully

When you are styling links, be careful not to rely entirely on colour to distinguish between link states. Not everyone can see colour the same (e.g., people with colour blindness), so you should use colour along with properties such as `text-decoration`, `outline`, `border`, etc.

You should also check that your colour choices have enough contrast—this is really easy using tools like the Colour Contrast Analyser (`http://www.paciellogroup.com/resources/contrast-analyser.html`)

Adding icons to links

Another good technique you can use to further distinguish different links is to attach icons to them depending on their type. For example, check out `links_example6.html/links_example6.css`, which produces the result shown in **Figure 15.10**.

Figure 15.10: My last example for this chapter uses an icon to highlight the external links on the page—an arrow (often coming out of a box) is the accepted convention for an external link on the Web.

This is pretty simple to achieve. All you need is an icon, a little CSS, and an extra class in your HTML. The class is added to each external link, i.e., the links you want to add the icon to:

```
<a href="http://animals.nationalgeographic.co.uk/"
class="external">National Geographic animals home
page</a>
```

The icon should be saved in a suitable place near your HTML and CSS files; the CSS to add it to the page is as follows:

```
.external {
    background: #94D7E3 url("arrow.png") center right
    no-repeat;
    padding-right: 17px;
}
```

The first declaration is a shorthand property we first saw in Chapter 11. It sets a background colour that is the same as the paragraph background colour, attaches the icon to each .external link, then specifies that it should be placed on the center-right of the elements and should not be repeated.

The second declaration creates some blank space on the right of each link. The visual effect is that it pushes each link over to the left a bit to make some space for the icon; otherwise the icon would sit over the top of the link. Make sure that your icon is not too tall, otherwise it might overlap text lines and get cut off.

Tip: You can find several royalty-free icons on the Web, if you don't want to spend the time making your own.

Try it yourself!

1. First of all, create or find icons that will represent the different animals, and attach them to the links for the different creatures in the first set of links.

2. Next, think of another good real-world use for attaching icons to elements as background images.

Summary

In this chapter you have learned the ins and outs of adding links into your web pages, including best practices and styling them with CSS. You will see links come up again and again in the remainder of the book—they are arguably the most important tool that we use. So get out there, and make a web!

CHAPTER 16
Images

by Chris Mills

In the beginning, there was only text, and lo, the Web was quite boring. But then images came along, and they said "This place is drab, fellas, let's have a party—whoo hoo!"

To put it in other words, the Web began life as text and not much else. Its main purpose was to provide a method to share government and academic documents. Images were first seen on the Web in the early '90s when the Mosaic browser introduced the <img> element. All of a sudden web pages incorporated pictures, artwork, decoration! The ability to add background images on elements using CSS followed around the turn of the century.

Nowadays images are used in abundance on the Web, for many purposes—icons as we saw in Chapter 15, "Links," custom bullet points, decorative backgrounds, headers and footers, custom titles, and more.

In this chapter we will take you through all aspects of what it takes to put images on the Web, including HTML and CSS image syntax, different image formats, image best practices, and specific techniques such as image replacement of headings, CSS sprites, background tiles, and gradients.

*In this chapter you have the opportunity to **Try it yourself!** with the convenient sample code downloads found on the book's companion website—*http://interactwithwebstandards.com.

HTML <img> syntax

Images are inserted into a document via HTML using the <img> element. This is an inline element that at the very minimum has to contain a src attribute, which holds the path to the image you want to insert:

```
<img src="elva.jpg">
```

> **Tip:** This is an empty element—it doesn't have any textual content, and you don't include a closing </img> tag, although if you were writing XHTML, you would make the element self-closing by writing <img src="kittens.jpg" />.

As long as the relevant image is contained in the same folder as the HTML, this will render as seen in **Figure 16.1** (check out images_example1.html).

Figure 16.1: It's an image. Move along, nothing to see here.

> **Tip:** The image paths contained in the src attribute work in exactly the same way as the paths used in the href attribute of links—see Chapter 15 for more details.

Providing a textual description with `alt`

Images are wonderful, but they do raise issues:

- Users with visual impairments using screen readers to access your content can't see them!

- Search engines such as Google and Yahoo! cannot index any textual content in images, as they can't see text that is inside an image, so it impacts negatively on your site's findability.

- Some users who have really slow web connections may have images turned off to reduce the amount of data they need to download.

- The image might be unavailable for some reason, for example, if the path to the image has been misspelled or if the file has been corrupted.

The evils of having too much content in images

I really need to reiterate that having too much content contained in images is naughty. Very naughty. From an accessibility perspective, it is terrible, unless you provide text alternatives, and it is also very bad for search engine indexing. I've seen a page that did not appear on search engines because all of the text content was stored inside a huge image! Please never do this, or if you do, never admit that it was this book that put the idea in your head…

The above points are not too much of an issue if your images are not part of the content and are merely being used as decoration. But if they contain content (whether they are showing people or places you are writing about, or data such as pie charts or bar charts), then this presents a problem.

But help is at hand. The `alt` attribute allows you to include a text description of your image that will be read out by screen readers, indexed by search engines, and displayed if the image is unavailable. For example:

```
<img src="elva.jpg" alt="A picture of Elva Mills,
the author's daughter">
```

Figure 16.2 shows the output when the image is not available.

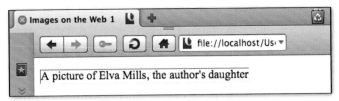

Figure 16.2: The alt *attribute in action.*

You should never refer to this alternative text as an alt tag, as some people do—there is no such tag. It is an alt attribute, or "alt text".

The content of the alt attribute should only be displayed when the image is unavailable, and not as supporting extra information alongside the image (some versions of Internet Explorer wrongly display alt text as a tool tip when the image is moused over). Supplying extra information along with the image is the job of the title attribute, which we'll look at next.

Resource // The limits of alt and longdesc

One thing to note is that you shouldn't put a large amount of content into an alt attribute—multiple paragraphs and suchlike. You can't structure it inside the alt attribute, so it will just come out as a long stream of pure text. And depending on the browser or assistive technology (e.g. screen reader) accessing the content, it may be truncated or not fully read out, limiting its usefulness.

One solution is to include a longdesc attribute on your image, the value of which should be a path to a page containing a textual representation of the same data.

For example, if you have an image containing a pie chart showing percentages of families with no children, one child, two children, three children, and four children or more, you could use a longdesc attribute to link to a page containing the same information represented in an HTML table (see Chapter 18), or even in a paragraph. The image code would look like this:

```
<img src="piechart.png" alt="Pie chart showing
percentages of families in the area with different
numbers of children" longdesc="percentages_table.html">
```

Assistive technology will then let a user know that the image has this alternative representation of the information available, and give them the option of accessing it.

(continues)

Resource // The limits of `alt` and `longdesc`

(continued)

This however brings up the limitation of `longdesc`—users not using assistive technologies won't be given access to the alternative data representation, or even be told that it exists. This is a shortcoming, as the table may be useful for any user, for example if someone wants to copy and paste the data, or if someone just finds the alternative version easier to understand.

It therefore makes more sense to not use the `longdesc` attribute, and instead just put alternative data representations on the same page as the image (or linked from the page using a normal `<a>` element). `longdesc` is not used very much, and may be deprecated in HTML5.

The title attribute for supporting information

The `title` attribute is certainly not new to us—we have seen in previous chapters that other elements are also able to have a `title` attribute, and it does the same thing for all elements—provide extra supporting information alongside it, which may be of use. As you've seen before, it is simple to use:

```
<img src="elva.jpg" alt="A picture of Elva Mills, the
author's daughter" title="Elva's favourite toys are her
In the Night Garden dolls">
```

It also gives us a tooltip, as shown in **Figure 16.3**, and most browsers will also display the `title` text at the bottom of the browser window.

Figure 16.3: The `title` *attribute in action.*

Defining image dimensions using width and height

When the browser finds an `<img>` element in the HTML, it starts loading the image the `src` attribute points to. By default, it doesn't know the image's dimensions, so it'll just display all the text lumped together, then shift the document layout around to make way for the images when they finally load and appear. This can slow down page loading and looks a bit confusing to your site visitors, as the layout can suddenly "jump" and rearrange itself. To stop this happening you can tell the browser to allocate the right amount of space for the images before they are loaded using the `width` and `height` attributes:

```
<img src="elva.jpg" alt="A picture of Elva Mills, the
author's daughter" title="Elva's favourite toys are her
In the Night Garden dolls" width="682" height="562">
```

This results in a placeholder being displayed until the image loads, which takes up the right amount of space, avoiding the unattractive layout shift mentioned earlier.

Resource // Image sizing

You can also resize images using these attributes (try halving the attribute values in `images_example1.html`, saving it, and then reloading the page), but this is not a good idea as image quality often degrades and is certainly not as smooth as if you resized it in an application such as Photoshop, plus the image will still take up the same amount of file size regardless of what it is resized to (you would save a lot of downloading by just making the images the correct size to begin with on the server).

CSS background image syntax

The other way of inserting images into your web page is via the CSS `background-image` property, which contains the path to the image in much the same way as the `<img>` element `src` attribute (bear in mind that this path is relative to the style sheet, not the HTML page). You can use this property to apply a background image to any element:

```
p {
    background-image: url(tile2.png);
}
```

The example this appears in (images_example2.html) looks like **Figure 16.4**.

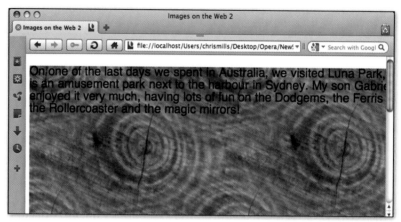

Figure 16.4: A simple CSS background image.

Tip: As you might expect, the background image is totally in the background of the element, so the element's content does not displace the image, and is instead drawn over the top of it. By default, the image starts being drawn from the top left corner of the content (i.e., the area inside the element's border).

Controlling image repeat

As you may have noticed, the image in the last example has repeated itself horizontally and vertically to fill up the background of the paragraph. We can control this using the background-repeat property, which can take one of the following values:

- repeat: The default value, if none is specified—this repeats the image both horizontally and vertically. You'll also hear people say "along the x and y axes" and "in the x and y directions."

- no-repeat: Don't repeat the image at all.

- repeat-x: Repeat only horizontally.

- repeat-y: Repeat only vertically.

Have a look at `images_example3.html` in your browser, which has `background-repeat: no-repeat`; set on the paragraph—you'll see something like **Figure 16.5**.

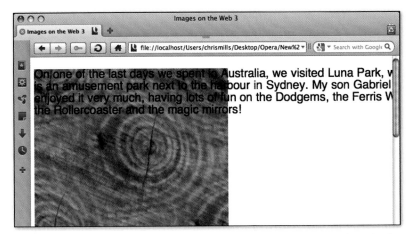

Figure 16.5: Using `background-repeat: no-repeat`; *causes only a single copy of the image to appear in the background of the paragraph.*

Try it yourself!

Take a copy of the `images_example3.html/images3.css` example files and experiment with the possible values to see what effects they have on the image.

Positioning the background image

Now we'll explore another background property—you can position your background image in different places inside the elements with `background-position` (see **Figure 16.6**). The available ways of setting the position values are as follows: try out your own text and background images if you wish.

- Keywords: Rather self-explanatory, the available values are `left top`, `top`, `right top`, `left`, `center`, `right`, `left bottom`, `bottom`, `right bottom`.

- CSS units: You can set the position of the background image using any of the available CSS units, for example, `10% 30%`, `100px 200px`, `5em 7em`. The first value in each instance is the horizontal distance from the top-left corner, and the second is the vertical.

- Mixture: You can also choose to mix units and keywords, for example `200px top`.

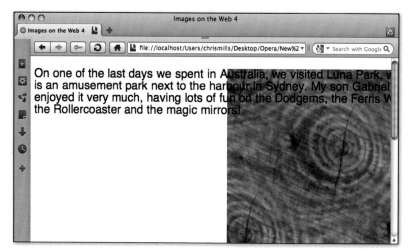

Figure 16.6: The effect of setting background-position: right top; *on our background image.*

Tip: If you only specify one CSS unit value—for example, background-position: 0px;—this will play the part of the horizontal value, and the vertical value will be set at 50%.

Try it yourself!

Take the sample files images_example4.html and images4.css and experiment with setting different values on the background-position property.

1. Bearing in mind that the dimensions of the background image are 400 pixels x 350 pixels, how would you put the image in the same position as right top would achieve, but using pixel values?

2. How about setting the image in the same position as left would achieve, but using % values?

3. What happens when you position a repeated background image in different places? Write a blog post on whether you think the resulting effects are useful.

background-attachment

One final property we will talk about before moving on is background-attachment. This controls whether the background moves when you scroll the content.

The two available values of background-attachment are:

1. scroll: The default value, this causes the background to scroll along with the content.

2. fixed: This value causes the background to be fixed in position, so only the content scrolls. This can result in some quite nice effects.

Try it yourself!

To see this in action, load up scrolling_example.html in your browser. Try changing the background-attachment property value between fixed and scroll, to see what the difference is.

background shorthand

There is a way to combine all of the background properties into one single background property. The separate properties are as follows:

```
background-color: color;
background-image: url(image.png);
background-repeat: repeat;
background-position: x y;
background-attachment: scroll/fixed;
```

All these properties can be combined into one single background property:

```
background: color url(image.png) repeat x y scroll/fixed;
```

background-color

Last but not least, you can set a solid background colour on any element using the background-color property like so:

```
background-color: red;
```

You can use any type of colour value available inside CSS, and even set a value of transparent to make it see through (this is also the default). You'll see background-color used many times in examples throughout the book.

If you leave some of the values out of the background declaration, the browser will assume the following defaults:

```
background-color: transparent;
background-image: none;
background-repeat: repeat;
background-position: top left;
background-attachment: scroll;
```

`<img>` versus CSS: When to use each one?

There is a fairly simple rule to stick to here: if the image is crucial to the content of the document, for example, a photo of the author or a graph showing some data, it should be added as an `<img>` element with proper alternative text made available.

If the image is there as decoration ("eye candy" or "bling"), you should use CSS background images. These images do not need to have alternative text, and in fact they shouldn't—what use is "pretty background gradient" to a blind person? In addition, you have a lot more control over the look of images available in CSS than HTML, and the term *decoration* should give you the clue—these images are part of the style of the page, rather than the content.

A crash course in image formats

There are many different types of image formats—some of them are suitable for use on the Web, and some aren't. When you want a suitable image format for printing, you are looking for something that handles high resolution, retains detail well, and is sharp and clear, such as a .tif. Low file size is not so important, as it will be presented to the consumer of that content in printed form. When you are looking for a suitable web format, size is important—you are looking for a compromise between acceptable quality so that your content doesn't look awful, and low file size, so that your site visitors don't get frustrated waiting for hours (well, they'll likely be frustrated after 10 seconds) for your website to download.

In this section I'll give you a quick summary of all you need to know to get by when choosing image formats for your web graphics. It is beyond the scope of this chapter to actually teach you design techniques to create the graphics!

Tip: For more on designing graphics for use on the Web, consult our InterACT Design courses—see http://interact.webstandards.org/curriculum/design/.

There are a number of good image applications available for creating and saving your web graphics. I'd recommend Adobe Fireworks for web graphics—Adobe Photoshop is more powerful and more of an all-around product not specifically for web graphics, but also more complicated. There are also free alternatives such as the GIMP (http://www.gimp.org/) and Inkscape (http://www.inkscape.org/), which you could check out. The image formats you will likely encounter on the Web are explained below:

.bmp

.bmp (Bitmaps) are a Microsoft Windows file format, but they have seen much usage on the Web probably due to Windows and Internet Explorer's market dominance. They are usually uncompressed and support 16.7 million colours, therefore are fairly good for displaying photos, but they are also quite large, so there are better formats you could use.

.gif

.gif (Graphics Interchange Format) is a popular but fairly limited graphics format. It uses **lossless compression**, meaning than it can be compressed to a smaller file without reduction in quality, and it is good for simple diagrams, shapes and cartoons. However, it only supports an 8-bit colour palette, meaning a maximum of 256 colours per image, so it is no good for images that require many colours, such as photographs. When you save a copy of an image in .gif format, its colours get dithered down to 256, which can result in unsightly loss of detail.

`.gif` supports 1-bit transparency, which means that you can have one colour as a transparent colour in the image. When you use it on your web page, background colours will then shine through the transparent colour. However, this is not that useful in many situations. Many transparent effects require multiple transparent colours to be effective—anti-aliasing, for example, (see **Figure 16.7**), which is the practice of making diagonal edges appear smoother by use of transparent pixels, won't work effectively with `.gif` images.

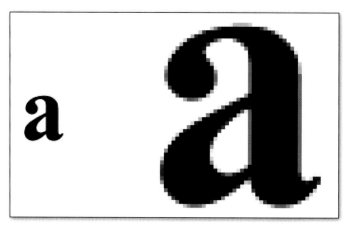

Figure 16.7: When you zoom in on an image containing smooth curved edges, you get an idea of how anti-aliasing works. The edges contain colours with varying degrees of transparency.

Tip: For more on anti-aliasing, read `http://www.lunaloca.com/tutorials/antialiasing/`.

`.gif` also supports animation—you can use certain graphics packages to make a single `.gif` file contain many frames, which then play sequentially when the image is displayed (e.g., in a web browser). These have fallen out of fashion of late, and should only really be used for decorative effects, unless you are representing simple information and can effectively provide details inside an `alt` attribute. Please don't try to present complicated critical information using an animated `.gif`, otherwise the accessibility police will lock you up.

.jpg

JPEG (Joint Photographic Experts Group) is actually not an image format as such, but a compression format—the files are actually stored as a JFIF (JPEG File Interchange Format), even though the files have an extension of .jpg or .jpeg (confusing, I know). .jpg supports 16.7 million colours (24-bit) with a relatively small file size, and is good for photographs, although the quality does suffer if you compress the image too much, or repeatedly edit and save it. Again, it's a compromise between acceptable quality and acceptable file size.

> **Tip:** You can choose varying levels of quality to save a .jpg at (from 0-100), allowing you to fine-tune how much detail is retained.

.png

The .png (Portable Network Graphics), touted as an open-source successor to the .gif, is probably the best all-round graphics format for the Web, although you'd still be advised to use .jpg for photos as the files will be smaller, and older browsers (such as Internet Explorer 6) do not support this fully support .png.

.png is excellent for most uses, though. It supports 16.7 million colours (24-bit), and 8-bit transparency (you can have 256 transparent colours). If your images only need a small number of colours, you can choose to save them with a low colour depth for really small files, e.g., PNG-8 is 8-bit PNG (256 colours in total)—you'll find this option in most image applications.

.svg

You'll sometimes see .svg (Scalable Vector Graphics) files on websites—this is a vector graphics format (the others are all rasters) allowing you to create graphics using markup similar to HTML (although a bit more complicated). For example, the code to create a simple circle is:

```
<circle cx="200" cy="200" r="50" stroke="black" stroke-
width="2" fill="blue"/>
```

This defines a circle 200 pixels across and 200 pixels down from the top-left of the parent element with a radius of 50 pixels, a black border (usually called the outline or stroke in graphics applications) 2 pixels wide, and a blue fill colour. Aside from drawing very small, crisp diagrams, SVG can support animations, text, video and more, and because it is markup it can be styled using CSS and scripted using JavaScript.

It is beyond the scope of this book to discuss SVG in more detail, but you can find more information, tutorials, etc. at:

- http://dev.opera.com/articles/svg/
- https://www.mozilla.org/projects/svg/
- http://www.w3.org/Graphics/SVG/
- http://en.wikipedia.org/wiki/Scalable_Vector_Graphics

There is an open-source vector graphics editor called Inkscape that can produce and edit .svg files—see http://www.inkscape.org/.

Resource // Raster graphics versus vector graphics

Raster graphics formats (e.g., .bmp, .gif, .jpg, .png) store information about every pixel in the image separately. Vector graphics (e.g., .svg), on the other hand, generate the image using mathematical algorithms to create the different shapes in the image. Therefore, vector graphics will work out to a smaller file size than the equivalent raster graphics for geometrical images like logos, etc., and they will also remain crisp when you zoom in on them.

Vector graphics however aren't very good for photos, and aren't supported across all browsers (e.g., Internet Explorer), which is why raster graphics are used more commonly, and .svg hasn't seen wider adoption.

Figure 16.8 shows an example of why you shouldn't use .gifs or other low-colour-depth formats for photographs:

 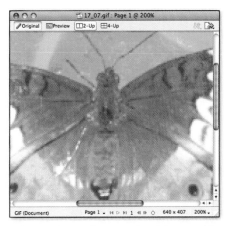

Figure 16.8: On the left, a zoomed in photograph saved as a .jpg. *On the right, a* .gif. *Notice the pixellation and distortion on the* .gif.

Image best practices

It is very tempting to use a lot of imagery on your websites. Images are a great way to set the mood for the visitor and illustrations are a nice way to make complex information easier to take in. There are some best practices to follow, however: every image should be used with careful consideration—there is nothing worse than a cosmic, garish, confusing, overpowering, image-heavy site.

Keep information in images to a minimum!

Keep the amount of information communicated in images to a minimum, because:

- People surfing on mobile devices might have images turned off because of small screens and the slowness and cost of downloading data.

- Visitors to your site might be blind or otherwise visually impaired and not able to see your images properly.

- Search engines only index text—they don't analyse images (yet), which means that information stored in images cannot be found and indexed.

Tip: Having good `alt` text on your images can reduce or nullify the problems discussed here, but you should still keep these points in mind.

Optimise your images

Optimise your images to keep the file size as small as possible—in general, people have faster Internet connections these days, but even so every little bit helps. Also, your web host will either give you a bandwidth limit per month/year, or charge you in some way per amount downloaded. If we are talking about a low-key personal site then we are only concerned with a few users downloading a few Kb each, but think of how many users google.com, yahoo.com, or bbc.co.uk has—a few Kb multiplied by tens or hundreds of millions of users makes a large difference!

Choose appropriate formats

Choose appropriate image formats to suit the images you are dealing with. In general, .jpg is better for photographs, whereas .gif or .png is better for non-photographs.

Always provide fallback content

Always provide a fallback for any images that contain useful content, whether that is an alt attribute, a longer description available on a separate page, etc.

Tiles and gradients

A very common use for background images is creating regular tiled backgrounds for various parts of your site. Such techniques allow you to cover a wide area using one very small image, repeated several times using background-repeat. The example I have created for this section is called tiles_gradients.html/tiles_gradients.css.

The first interesting bit of CSS is that applied to the <body> element:

```
body {
    background-image: url(tile.gif);
    font-family: Verdana;
}
```

A single small tile is repeated horizontally and vertically to create a complete background (**Figure 16.9**).

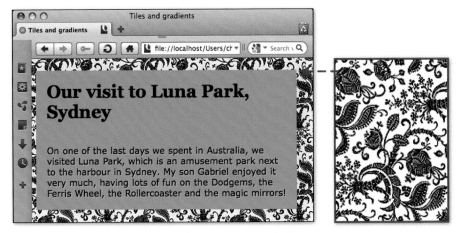

Figure 16.9: A background created using a repeated tile.

For this to work, you need to use an image that joins together seamlessly at all sides. Regular patterns are easy to get to work in this manner, but irregular ones are not so easy.

Next we will add a repeating image to the heading. This time it will be a thin slice that we will repeat only horizontally. The CSS is as follows:

```
h1 {
    font-family: Georgia;
    padding: 20px 20px 0px 20px;
    background-image: url(gradient.png);
    background-repeat: repeat-x;
}
```

This gives us the effect shown in **Figure 16.10**—I've set up the colour gradient to end with exactly the same colour as the background, and start with a fairly similar shade, so that the transition is not too wild, and it fits in with the colour scheme of the <div>.

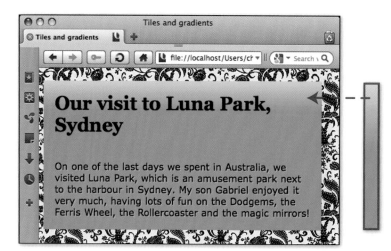

Figure 16.10: A horizontally-repeated gradient slice applied to the header can create a nice illusion of depth.

This creates a really nice effect, and the gradient's file size is only 1Kb!

Tip: You can find many sites on the Web that offer shareware/freeware graphics for you to use. There is also a really good gradient slice generator available at http://www.allcrunchy.com/Web_Stuff/Gradient_Generator/.

Image replacement

In Chapter 13, "Headings and Paragraphs," we talked about the number of fonts commonly available across platforms, and the limitation this presents to designers on the Web. You *could* create your text in a graphics editor with the font you desire and put it on your site as an image, but this presents an accessibility and search engine indexing problem, as previously discussed (the problem can be lessened using good alt text).

One common solution that solves both problems is **Image Replacement (IR)**—the idea is that you put your text in place on your site, attach a background image to that element containing the text displayed exactly as you'd like it, and then use CSS trickery to shunt the HTML text off the edge of the screen. This way your users will see the text just as you want it, without having the HTML in the way of it, but the HTML text will still exist on the page (albeit positioned off-screen) so that it is still readable by screen readers and search engines.

Note that web designers tend to use this method only for short pieces of text such as headings, because to use image replacement for your entire site would be far too fiddly and awkward! Older browsers would not be able to resize any of the text, plus every time you wanted to adjust any of your text, you'd have to open up your image application and change it manually. Nightmare—don't go there, um, girlfriend.

This process will be easier to follow with an example, so let's get to it! First of all, we'll take the gradient/tile example (**Figure 16.10**) and modify that further.

We need to create an image to replace the heading with, which fits in the space the heading takes up—this can simply be the same text in a custom font, or even a company logo. I'll go for text in a custom font (**Figure 16.11**). I've created it to be about the right size to fit in the space occupied by our header, and saved it as a .png with a transparent background to make it flexible, good quality, and a small file size. Check out image_replacement.png in the example files.

OUR VISIT TO LUNA PARK, SYDNEY

Figure 16.11: Our image to replace the text with.

The next step is to apply it to the heading. Now we have a bit of a problem here—we *already* have the gradient background image attached to our heading, and CSS doesn't allow us to have more than one on each element (well, CSS3 allows multiple background images, but this isn't supported across all major browsers as yet).

So what do we do? Well, there is nothing to stop us from attaching another image to the <div> parent element! I've changed things round so that the background gradient is attached to the <div>, and the image replacement heading is attached to the heading. I have also changed around some of the padding, and set some positioning on the heading background image to make it hang in the space better.

The CSS for the `<div>` and heading now looks as follows:

```
#content {
    width: 480px;
    background-color: #00a6b9;
    background-image: url(gradient.png);
    background-repeat: repeat-x;
}

h1 {
    font-family: Georgia;
    background-image: url(image_replacement.png);
    background-repeat: no-repeat;
    background-position: 5px 25px;
}
```

But there is one further problem to overcome, as **Figure 16.12** shows: We now have both headings on display!

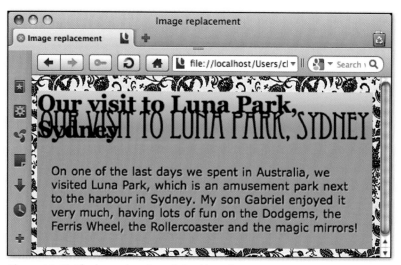

Figure 16.12: The logo plus the original heading text—not pretty.

This doesn't look great, but we can remedy this by adding in a large negative text-indent value to shove the original text off the screen, and fixing the height to stop the heading area from collapsing as a result:

```
h1 {
    font-family: Georgia;
    background-image: url(image_replacement.png);
    background-repeat: no-repeat;
    background-position: 5px 25px;
    height: 80px;
    text-indent: -2000px;
}
```

This gives the final effect shown in **Figure 16.13**.

Figure 16.13: The final effect—that's much better.

So there we have it—it looks cool and it's accessible, although it's still not perfect. Any sighted users that have the CSS turned off won't be able to see the title.

Tip: There are a number of CSS image replacement methods, none of which are perfect. Dave Shea has written a very in-depth article contrasting the different types of IR available—check out http://www.mezzoblue.com/tests/revised-image-replacement/.

Try it yourself!

Now you've gone through this section, have a read of Dave Shea's article cited above, and put together your own image replacement example. Be as creative as you like, and try mixing and matching the different IR techniques to see what works best for you.

Can you think of a way to make a heading (or some alternative text) appear if CSS is turned off?

Resource // Clever alternatives to IR

There are also some image replacement techniques that make use of other technologies. These tend to be a bit more sophisticated and flexible than the simple IR technique shown previously.

sIFR: Scalable Inman Flash Replacement, involves replacing the text with a Flash movie. Some clever JavaScript allows control over some basic text properties such as colour. This is pretty cool, but not so good if you don't want to rely on Flash, plus using multiple sIFR movies can significantly slow down your site. Check out http://dev.opera.com/articles/view/custom-web-fonts-with-sifr/ for more information.

Cufón: Cufón converts the font file information into a JavaScript file containing all the visual data, which is then rendered as SVG (or Vector Markup Language in Internet Explorer) within the browser, and replaces the desired text. JavaScript is used to make the original text still readable. For more details, see http://cufon.shoqolate.com/generate/.

With sIFR, you are using Flash, and your fonts are embedded in the Flash therefore people can't borrow them from your site. With Cufón the fonts are stored in separate files, so they can be easily accessed and downloaded.

CSS "sprites"

Another common technique that has become popular in recent years is **CSS sprites**. The idea is that if you have a lot of images that are the same size on your site, such as several icons, you can put them in a single file (one long strip of icons) so that only one download is required. As well as saving on file size, this cuts down considerably on the number of HTTP requests required—how many round trips to the server are required to download your website. This is great for improving site performance, as it is much more efficient to grab one medium-sized image than 20—30 small ones. Some large sites use a CSS sprite file containing hundreds of icons!

Tip: The name CSS sprites is borrowed from old computer games, which used to have their graphics (e.g. spaceships, explosions, pieces of terrain) stored in one big image. The individual pieces were then cut out and displayed when needed. These were called sprites.

To include the images in your pages, you can use `background` properties as normal. To control which individual icon is displayed, you vary the `background-position` property so that a different portion of the single image is displayed in that part of the page. One more important part of this is that the container the image is attached to (be it a `<div>`, `<p>`, etc.) in the HTML needs to be sized with the correct dimensions to contain the sprites.

To think of it a different way, the container acts like a cookie cutter, and the `background-position` property positions the "cookie cutter" over the correct part of the image to be cut out (**Figure 16.14**).

Figure 16.14: Our "cookie cutter" cuts out the sprites, as directed by the `background-position` *property. Icons by:* `http://www.icondock.com`.

On to an example—I will create a simple page containing some summary descriptions of three animals. I'll not explain the HTML very much, as it is just three paragraphs, each with a separate id. One important thing to note about the paragraphs is that each has been set to have a fixed height of 55 pixels. We will be making the sprites 55 x 55 pixels. Some padding has been added to the left of the paragraphs, to make space for the background images. The example looks like **Figure 16.15** at this stage—check out `css_sprites.html/css_sprites.css` to see what the code looks like.

Figure 16.15: (left) Our example, before the CSS sprites have been added and Figure 16.16: (right) Our CSS sprite image.

CSS is then used to give basic styling, and attach background images to each paragraph. The CSS sprite image looks like **Figure 16.16**. There is a 10-pixel gap between the different icons. The relevance of this will become clear later.

The following CSS rules are then added to attach the CSS sprite image to each paragraph:

```
#butterfly {
    background-image: url(css_sprites.jpg);
    background-repeat: no-repeat;
}
#dugong {
    background-image: url(css_sprites.jpg);
    background-repeat: no-repeat;
}

#wombat {
    background-image: url(css_sprites.jpg);
    background-repeat: no-repeat;
}
```

The image has been attached to the paragraphs at this point, but there is a problem: without any positioning, the image sits in the top-right corner of the paragraph, and only the first icon is displayed in all three cases. In each case, we need to add a different amount of vertical positioning to shunt the image upwards so that the correct icon is displayed (the horizontal positioning stays the same in each case):

```
#butterfly {
    background-image: url(css_sprites.jpg);
    background-repeat: no-repeat;
    background-position: 5px 0px;
}

#dugong {
    background-image: url(css_sprites.jpg);
    background-repeat: no-repeat;
    background-position: 5px -65px;
}

#wombat {
    background-image: url(css_sprites.jpg);
    background-repeat: no-repeat;
    background-position: 5px -130px;
}
```

> **Tip:** Take a closer look at the background-position values. The horizontal values are all 5px, to give a nice 5-pixel gap on all sides of the icons. The first vertical value is 0—because the first icon starts at the top of the image. The top of each icon is 65 pixels away from the next one in the sprite image (10-pixel gap plus 55-pixel-tall icon), so to move to each successive icon you need to shunt it *upwards* by 65 pixels. To do this, you need to use *negative* positioning values.

This gives the effect we are after (**Figure 16.17**).

Figure 16.17: Our CSS sprites are now successfully displayed.

The Chez Sous Le Vent case study

Our Chez Sous Le Vent case study example site (**Figure 16.18**) contains many images used in different ways.

Figure 16.18: *Many images are contained in the Chez Sous Le Vent case study site.*

Try it yourself!

Looking at the case study site, study the images carefully to see what you can learn from them. Find an example of:

1. An image inserted using an `<img>` element
2. An image inserted using `background-image`
3. Image replacement

And write a blog post about the techniques used.

Summary

That just about wraps up the basics of images on the Web. There are a lot more techniques to explore, and things to learn as you gain more experience with creating web pages, but this gives you pretty much everything you need to know to get started.

CHAPTER 17
Lists

by Chris Mills

The purpose of HTML lists is to group related pieces of information together, so they are clearly associated with each other and easy to read—think about shopping lists, or steps in a recipe, or a list of upcoming concerts your favourite band is playing.

In this chapter we will cover the different HTML list types available and when and how you should use them, go through list styling best practices, and then look at some slightly more advanced examples. **Figure 17.1** shows an example of a typical HTML list being used to display some content items.

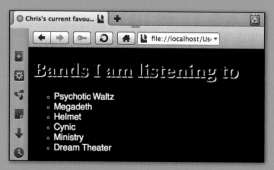

Figure 17.1: A typical HTML list.

In this chapter you have the opportunity to **Try it yourself!** *with the convenient sample code downloads found on the book's companion website—*http://interactwithwebstandards.com.

But their use doesn't end there. In modern web development lists are workhorse elements, frequently used for navigation menus, tabbed content and other website features. **Figure 17.2** shows an example of such a user interface element.

Figure 17.2: An HTML list-based user interface feature.

The three list types

There are three list types in HTML. Each list type has a specific purpose and meaning—they are not interchangeable:

List type	Description
Unordered list	Used to group a set of related items, in no particular order.
Ordered list	Used to group a set of related items, in a specific order.
Definition list	Used to define a set of terms and their associated definitions.

Table 17.1: Three list types.

Let's now look at each one in more detail.

Unordered lists

Unordered lists, or bulleted lists, are used when the items listed can be placed in any order. An example is a shopping list (**Figure 17.3**). Try opening `simple_shopping_list1.html` from the code download in a browser.

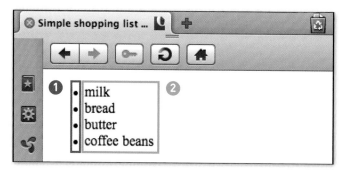

Figure 17.3: A simple shopping list.

1 Bullets—This is the bullet point that keeps things neat and denotes this as an unordered list.

2 List items—These are the different items in the list.

To demonstrate the unordered part of it, you could put the items in any order and the list would still make sense (**Figure 17.4**) (simple_shopping_list2.html):

Figure 17.4: The same shopping list, but with the items reordered—still makes sense.

You can use CSS to change the bullet to one of several default styles, use your own image, or even display the list without bullets—we'll look at how to do that in the "List styling" section later on.

Unordered list markup

Unordered lists use one set of `<ul></ul>` tags, wrapped around many sets of `<li></li>` tags, like so:

```
<ul>
  <li>bread</li>
  <li>coffee beans</li>
  <li>milk</li>
  <li>butter</li>
</ul>
```

Ordered lists

Ordered lists, or numbered lists, are used to display a list of items that need to be placed in a specific order. An example would be cooking instructions, which must be completed in order for the recipe to work— see **Figure 17.5** (recipe1.html).

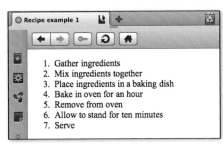 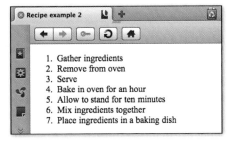

Figure 17.5: (left) A recipe needs to be in the right order to work. **Figure 17.6:** (right) If you reorder it, it no longer makes any sense!

If the list items were moved around into a different order, the information would no longer make sense (**Figure 17.6**) (recipe2.html).

Ordered list markup

Ordered lists use one set of <ol></ol> tags, wrapped around many sets of <li></li> tags:

```
<ol>
  <li>Gather ingredients</li>
  <li>Mix ingredients together</li>
  <li>Place ingredients in a baking dish</li>
  <li>Bake in oven for an hour</li>
```

```
<li>Remove from oven</li>
<li>Allow to stand for ten minutes</li>
<li>Serve</li>
</ol>
```

Beginning ordered lists with numbers other than 1

It is possible to get an ordered list to start with a number other than 1 (or i, or I, etc.). This is done using the `start` attribute, which takes a numeric value. This is useful if you have a single list of items, but you want to break the list up with some kind of note, or some other related information. For example, we could do this with the previous example (see `recipe3.html` in the code download):

```
<ol>
  <li>Gather ingredients</li>
  <li>Mix ingredients together</li>
  <li>Place ingredients in a baking dish</li>
</ol>

<p class="note">Before you place the ingredients in
the baking dish, preheat the oven to 180 degrees
centigrade/350 degrees Fahrenheit in readiness for
the next step</p>
```

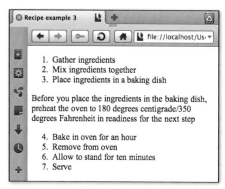

Figure 17.7: A numbered list beginning with a number other than 1.

```
<ol start="4">
  <li>Bake in oven for an
  hour</li>
  <li>Remove from oven</li>
  <li>Allow to stand for ten
  minutes</li>
  <li>Serve</li>
</ol>
```

This gives the result shown in **Figure 17.7** (`recipe3.html`).

Resource // Counting with CSS instead?

The start attribute is actually deprecated in the latest version of the HTML spec, which means that it will cause your pages to not validate when using strict DOCTYPEs. This may seem odd, as the attribute makes sense, and there is no direct CSS equivalent. This shows that validating HTML is an ideal goal to follow, but not always the absolute be all and end all. In addition, the start attribute is no longer deprecated in the HTML5 spec (the "HTML5 differences from HTML 4" document attests to this—see http://www.w3.org/TR/2008/WD-html5-diff-20080122/).

If you want to make use of such functionality in an HTML 4 Strict page, and it absolutely has to validate, you can do it using CSS Counters instead, although this technique is contentious, as some would argue that numbering is content and should therefore go in your HTML. Find out about CSS Counters at http://dev.opera.com/articles/view/automatic-numbering-with-css-counters/.

Definition lists

Definition lists associate specific items and their definitions within the list. For example, if you wanted to give a definition to the items on your shopping list, you could do that like **Figure 17.8** (see definition1.html in the code download).

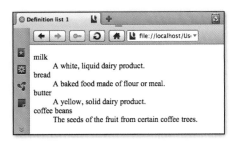

Figure 17.8: A basic definition list.

Each definition and term is a definition group (or name-value group). You can have as many definition groups as you like, but there must be at least one term and at least one definition in each group. You can't have a term with no definition or a definition with no term.

You can associate more than one term with a single definition, or vice versa. For example, the term *coffee* can have several meanings, and you could show them one after the other, as shown in **Figure 17.9** (definition2.html).

Alternatively you can have more than one term with the same definition. This is useful to show variations of a term, all of which have the same meaning, as shown in **Figure 17.10** (definition3.html).

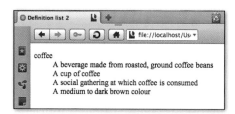

Figure 17.9: (left) One item with many definitions. *Figure 17.10:* (right) Several items with the same definition.

In general, it is unusual to associate multiple terms with a single definition, but it is useful to know it is possible in case the need arises.

Definition list markup

Definition lists are different from the other kinds of list, as they use definition terms and definition descriptions instead of list items.

Definition lists use one set of <dl></dl> tags, wrapped around groups of <dt></dt> and <dd></dd> tags. You must pair at least one <dt></dt> with at least one <dd></dd>; the <dt></dt> should always be first in the source order.

Let's consider the code behind the examples above. The code for the example shown in **Figure 17.8** (see definition1.html) looks like so:

```
<dl>
<dt>milk</dt>
<dd>A white, liquid dairy product.</dd>
<dt>bread</dt>
<dd>A baked food made of flour or meal.</dd>
<dt>butter</dt>
<dd>A yellow, solid dairy product.</dd>
<dt>coffee beans</dt>
<dd>The seeds of the fruit from certain coffee
trees.</dd>
</dl>
```

Try it yourself!

Try out the following sample exercises. Use the example template provided in the code download (`example_template.html`) as a starting point:

1. Using the knowledge presented above, and without looking at the definition list code examples, write the code for the examples shown in **Figure 17.9** and **Figure 17.10**.

2. Think of your own unordered list example, and mark it up appropriately. Look around the room you are in, or think about it as you walk down your street. How about the coloured pencils in your stationery drawer, or the cars parked outside your house?

3. Think of your own ordered list example, and mark it up appropriately. What about the shops in your local mall, listed in the order they appear?

4. Think of your own definition list example, and mark it up appropriately. How about the names of your teachers or colleagues and what roles they have, or the times and titles of your favourite TV shows?

CHAPTER 17

Choosing among list types

When trying to decide what type of list to use, you can usually decide by asking two simple questions:

1. Am I defining terms (or associating other name/value pairs)?
   If yes, use a definition list.
   If no, don't use a definition list—go on to the next question.

2. Is the order of the list items important?
   If yes, use an ordered list.
   If no, use an unordered list.

The difference between HTML lists and text

You may be wondering what the difference is between an HTML list and some text with bullets or numbers typed in by hand. Well, there are several advantages to using an HTML list:

1. If you have to change the order of the list items in an ordered list, you simply move them around in the HTML. If you typed the numbers in manually, you would have to go through and change every single item's number to correct the order—which would be tedious to say the least!

2. Using an HTML list allows you to style the list properly—you can use CSS to style just the list elements. If you just use paragraphs, you will find it more difficult to style the individual items in any useful manner, as the elements used will be the same as those used for every other paragraph.

3. Using an HTML list gives the content the proper semantic structure, as well as a "list-ish" visual effect. This has important benefits such as allowing screen readers to tell users with visual impairments they are reading a list and giving additional information such as the number of items in the list and which item they're currently on, rather than just reading out a confusing jumble of text and numbers.

To put it another way: *text and lists are not the same.* Using text instead of a list makes more work for you and can create problems for your document's readers. So if your document needs a list, you should use the correct HTML list elements.

Nesting lists

A list item can contain another entire list—this is known as **nesting** a list. It is useful for things like tables of contents, such as the one shown in **Figure 17.11** (`nested.html`).

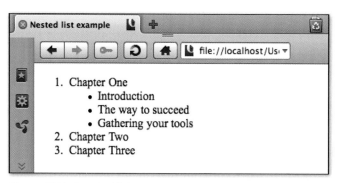

Figure 17.11: A nested list.

The key to nesting lists is to remember that the nested list should relate to one specific list item. To reflect that in the code, the nested list is contained inside that list item. The code for the previous list looks as follows:

```
<ol>
  <li>Chapter One
    <ul>
      <li>Introduction</li>
      <li>The way to succeed</li>
      <li>Gathering your tools</li>
    </ul>
  </li>
  <li>Chapter Two</li>
  <li>Chapter Three</li>
</ol>
```

Note how the nested list starts after the `<li>` and the text of the containing list item ("Chapter One"); then ends before the `</li>` of the containing list item. Nested lists often form the basis for website navigation menus, as they are a good way to model the structure of the website.

Theoretically you can nest as many lists as you like, although in practice it can become confusing to nest lists too deeply. For very large lists, you may be better off splitting the content into several lists with headings, or even splitting it across separate pages.

Try it yourself!

Take the `nested.html` example shown previously and add another level to the hierarchy. Add some sub headings below the "Introduction," "The way to succeed," and "Gathering your tools" headings.

List styling

In this section we will take a basic list example and give it some styling to improve its presentation. There is nothing particularly complicated to worry about when styling lists until you start getting into navigation menus and suchlike, which we'll look at later on. The list we will style is the nested list from the previous section—`nested.html`. At the moment, it looks rather dull when rendered, so we need to give it some care and nurturing.

Tip: One of the best sources of styling inspiration for lists is Russ Weakley's Listamatic, available at http://css.maxdesign.com.au/listamatic/.

Making basic improvements

So, let's start by adding some basics to our list. We have already covered padding, font-size, font-family, and other such CSS basics, so I will just touch on these briefly. I have applied the following CSS to our nested list (nested_style1.css) and added some more text, just to make it look a bit more cheerful.

```
ol {
    background-color: #FF9393;
    width: 20em;
    padding-top: 1em;
    padding-bottom: 1em;
    font-family: Helvetica, Arial, sans-serif;
    border: 2px solid #A60000;
}

ol > li {
    margin: 1em 1em 1em 0.5em;
    font-weight: bold;
}

ul > li {
    margin-top: 0.5em;
    margin-left: -24px;
    font-size: 0.8em;
    color: #A60000;
    font-weight: normal;
}
```

This gives us the output shown in **Figure 17.12** when our list is rendered in a browser (nested_Style1.html).

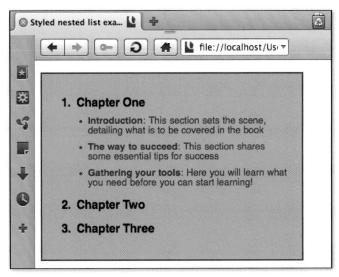

Figure 17.12: Our nested list with some basic styling.

Now let's move on to some list-specific CSS properties.

Changing bullet/numeral types

You can use `list-style-type` on a `<ul>` element to change the style of the bullet used. The options for unordered lists are as follows:

- `square`: Makes the bullets square
- `circle`: The default—circles
- `disc`: Makes the bullets take on the form of hollow circles
- `none`: Removes the bullets altogether

Ordered lists can be displayed with one of several numeric or alphabetic systems—that is, numbers or letters. The default in most browsers is decimal numbers, but there are more options, as shown in the following list.

Letters

- `lower-alpha`: Lowercase ASCII letters (a, b, c...)
- `upper-alpha`: Uppercase ASCII letters (A, B, C...)
- `lower-greek`: Lowercase classical Greek: (έ, ή, ί...)

Numbers

- Default (or use `decimal`): Decimal numbers (1, 2, 3...)
- `decimal-leading-zero`: Decimal numbers with leading zeros (01, 02, 03...)
- `lower-roman`: Lowercase Roman numerals (i, ii, iii...)
- `upper-roman`: Uppercase Roman numerals (I, II, III...)
- `georgian`: Traditional Georgian numbering (an, ban, gan...)
- `armenian`: Traditional Armenian numbering (mek, yerku, yerek...)

Tip: Setting a value of `none` removes the numerals altogether, in the same way as it removes the bullets in unordered lists.

To change your list to use a different number type, apply the `list-style-type` property to your `<ol>` element, for example:

```
list-style-type: upper-roman;
```

With this in mind, I've made some additions to the code, to make my example take on the look shown in **Figure 17.13** (`nested_style2.html`).

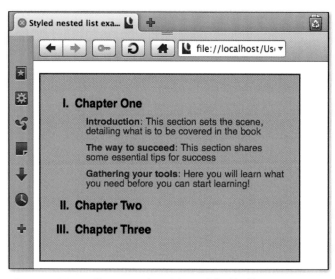

Figure 17.13: Our list example, with modified bullets.

Using your own custom bullet image

Figure 17.13 looks OK, but we are starting to miss having bullet points in the sublist, no? Time to use our own custom bullet point! You can do this using the `list-style-image` property. Applying this to your `<ul>` element will cause it to adopt a custom bullet, the path to the graphic for which is specified as follows:

```
list-style-image: url(bullet.gif);
```

I have applied a custom bullet to the example and the result can be seen in **Figure 17.14** (also check out `nested_style3.html`).

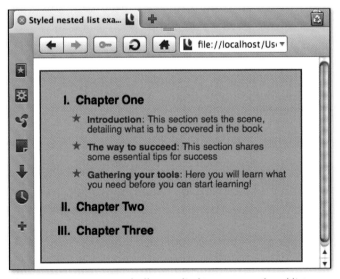

Figure 17.14: *A custom bullet applied to our unordered list.*

CHAPTER 17

You need to make sure that your custom bullet image is not too big, otherwise it will be in danger of getting cut off, or resulting in unsightly overlaps. Also, be careful when using Roman numerals, images, or other special bullet types in your pages. If, for example, you use Roman numerals and then refer to them in your text (e.g., "see section XII"), and your bullets aren't displayed because the browser doesn't support them or the image is corrupt, then your text will not make sense. It is therefore a good idea to refer to the section name rather than the number in these situations.

Try it yourself!

Experiment with custom bullets:

1. Search on the Web to find some sites that offer royalty-free bullet icons. Download some that you like the look of (alternatively, make some of your own, if you feel so inclined).
2. Create your own bulleted list.
3. Apply some of these bullets to your list and see the kind of effects you get with bigger and smaller bullets.

list-style-position

The last list property I'll cover is `list-style-position`, which can take two values, `inside` and `outside`. `outside` is the default value and causes the bullets to sit outside the bullet text. `inside` on the other hand makes the bullets move inside the bullet text:

```
ul {
    list-style-position: inside;
}
```

Figure 17.15 shows the effect of applying the above rule to our list example (see `nested_style4.html`).

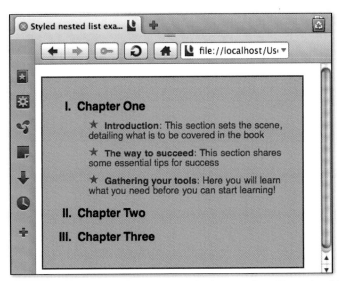

Figure 17.15: Moving the bullets inside the unordered list using `list-style-position`.

list-style shorthand

It may not surprise you too much to discover that you can use the `list-style` shorthand to declare the above properties all on one line:

```
list-style: url(bullet.gif) none inside;
```

This single line is equivalent to:

```
list-style-image: url(bullet.gif);
list-style-type: none;
list-style-position: inside;
```

Using lists for navigation menus

Now we've looked over lists of content items in a fair amount of detail, lets turn our attention to the other main use of lists on web pages—the humble navigation menu. Since navigation menus are generally a list of links, basing them on a list makes semantic sense, plus you'll generally want to style the different list items in a pretty similar fashion.

You can make the navigation menu look pretty much however you want— the different menu choices can be simple text links, or different images

CHAPTER 17

inside the list items that you click on. One thing is for certain—pretty much every navigation menu will start off with a combination of a list and some links, something like this:

```
<ul id="nav">
    <li><a href="#">Home</a></li>
    <li><a href="#">Site map</a></li>
    <li><a href="#">Photos</a></li>
    <li><a href="#">Tour map</a></li>
    <li><a href="#">Contact</a></li>
</ul>
```

If you want the navigation to be a vertical list of links, then it is generally already there, position-wise. However, if you want the menu to be a horizontal list of links over the top of your content, then you need to employ a little trickery:

```
ul#nav li {
    display: inline;
}
```

This will cause the list item contents to display as if they were inline elements, not block-level elements, so the links shunt up next to one another on one line. Then it is just a matter of adding some more styling to get them displaying nicely:

```
ul#nav li {
    font-size: 0.75em;
    font-family: Helvetica, Arial, sans-serif;
    display: inline;
    margin: 0.05em;
}

ul#nav {
    margin-left: -2.45em;
}
```

```
ul#nav li a:link {
  padding: 0.8em;
  text-decoration: none;
  color: #A60000;
  font-weight: bold;
}

ul#nav li a:hover, ul#nav li a:focus, ul#nav li a:active
{
  color: #A66666;
}
```

There is nothing complicated going on here—nothing that you haven't seen before. I have styled the links so they fit in with the look of the rest of the text on the page, positioned them using margins and padding, and used pseudo-classes to make the link change colour when it is hovered over or given focus using the keyboard. This simple menu looks like **Figure 17.16** (see `simple_navigation_menu.html`).

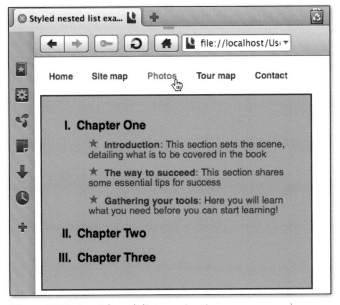

Figure 17.16: A quick and dirty navigation menu example.

Navigating the Chez Sous Le Vent site

Turning again to the Chez Sous Le Vent website case study, you'll see that Christopher Schmitt has implemented a similar navigation menu (**Figure 17.17**).

Figure 17.17: The navigation menu from the Chez Sous Le Vent case study.

The restaurant name on the left (an <h1>) acts as a link back to the home page, and the menu is composed of an unordered list:

```
<h1><a href="index.html">Chez Sous le Vent</a></h1>
<div id="nav">
<ul>
    <li><a href="about/index.html">About</a></li>
    <li><a href="menus/index.html">Menus</a></li>
    <li><a href="reservations/index.html">
Reservations</a></li>
    <li><a href="contact/index.html">Contact</a></li>
</ul>
</div><!-- /end #nav -->
```

The CSS for the menu looks like so:

```
#nav {
   font-size: 1.4em;
   position: absolute;
   right: 160px;
   bottom: 3px;
}

#nav ul {
   list-style-type: none;
}
```

```
#nav ul li {
    float: left;
    font-family: Verdana, Helvetica, Arial, sans-serif;
    text-transform: uppercase;
    font-weight: 700;
    background-image: url(-/img/nav-bkgd.gif);
    background-position: 4px 50%;
    background-repeat: no-repeat;
}

#nav ul li: first-child {
    background-image: none;
}
#nav ul li a {
    display: block;
    color: #656158;
    margin-left: 20px;
    border-radius: 4px;
    -webkit-border-radius: 4px;
    -moz-border-radius: 4px;
    -o-border-radius: 4px;
    -webkit-transition: all .2s ease-in-out;
    -o-transition: all .2s ease-in-out;
    border-top: 1px solid #FFF;
    padding: 4px 6px 5px;
}

#nav ul li a: link:hover {
    background-color: #67645d;
    color: #FFF;
    border-radius: 4px;
    border-top: 1px solid #67645d;
    -webkit-border-radius: 4px;
    -moz-border-radius: 4px;
    -o-border-radius: 4px;
    text-shadow: 0 0 1px #656158;
}
```

CHAPTER 17

Aside from the styling being a bit more complicated than my simple example, the technique is pretty much the same. Highlights include `border-radius` being used to give rounded corners to the focus/hover highlight, transitions being used to make that highlight appear in a smooth animation, and `:first-child` being used to make it so that the custom bullet image doesn't appear before the first menu item.

Try it yourself!

Have a play around with the menu in the case study site—study the CSS carefully to gain a better understanding of how it works, and try experimenting with changing the design.

Rescource // Recommended readings

- A List Apart: Taming Lists: http://www.alistapart.com/articles/taminglists/
- W3C CSS2: list-style-type definition: http://www.w3.org/TR/REC-CSS2/generate.html#lists
- Creating a list-based tabbed interface using jQuery: http://net.tutsplus.com/javascript-ajax/create-a-tabbed-interface-using-jquery/

Summary

By this stage you should have a clear understanding of the three different list types in HTML. Using the step-by-step examples, you should have created all three and learned how to nest lists inside list items.

CHAPTER 18
Tables

by Chris Mills

From travel timetables to the periodic table to the phone book to spreadsheets, if sifting through reams of data arranged in linear rows and columns is what excites you, this is just the chapter for you. Read on, but also take the time out to do another hobby...learn to play guitar or something.

How do we represent data tables in HTML? You might think it is done by some system of carefully sized and positioned paragraphs, which sounds tedious and difficult. But fear not—HTML has a special group of elements just for marking up tabular data.

This chapter will cover the basic table elements, then move on to advanced table elements that add more meaning and improve accessibility. Finally, we will take a careful look at styling tables with CSS to make them look more visually appealing (trust me, default table styling is not pretty).

*In this chapter you have the opportunity to **Try it yourself!** with the convenient sample code downloads found on the book's companion website—http://interactwithwebstandards.com.*

Basic table elements

To create a functional HTML table, you only need three elements:

- `<table>`: Wraps the entire table; defines it as a data table

- `<tr>`: Defines each row of the table

- `<td>`: Contains the content of each single table cell—multiple `<td>`s are found inside each `<tr>`

Let's look at an example to show you how it's done (apologies to all Penguin and Catwoman lovers—I'm really not a fan):

```
<table>
    <tr>
        <td>Villain</td>
        <td>Main weapons/abilities</td>
        <td>Height</td>
        <td>Real name</td>
        <td>First published</td>
    </tr>
    <tr>
        <td>Poison Ivy</td>
        <td>Can control plant life...</td>
        <td>5' 8" (1.73m)</td>
        <td>Pamela Isley</td>
        <td>1966</td>
    </tr>
    <tr>
        <td>The Joker</td>
        <td>Regularly employs Joker Toxin...</td>
        <td>6' (1.83m)</td>
        <td>Unknown</td>
        <td>1940</td>
    </tr>
```

```
<tr>
<td>Killer Croc</td>
    <td>Superhuman strength...</td>
    <td>11' (3.35m)</td>
    <td>Waylon Jones</td>
    <td>1984</td>
</tr>
<tr>
    <td>The Riddler</td>
    <td>Intellect at genius level...</td>
    <td>6' 1" (1.85m)</td>
    <td>Edward Nigma</td>
    <td>1948</td>
</tr>
<tr>
    <td>Scarecrow</td>
    <td>Fear-inducing gas...</td>
    <td>6' (1.83m)</td>
    <td>Dr. Jonathan Crane</td>
    <td>1941</td>
</tr>
<tr>
    <td>Bane</td>
    <td>Venom steroid...</td>
    <td>6' 8" (2.03m)</td>
    <td>Unknown</td>
    <td>1993</td>
</tr>
</table>
```

In a browser, this will look like **Figure 18.1** (see `tables_example1.html`).

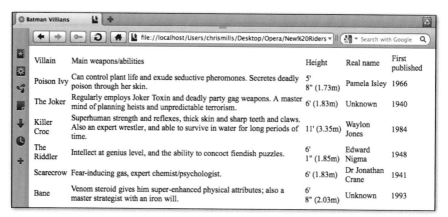

Figure 18.1: Our oh-so-glorious default table layout.

This is not very readable or visually appealing, to say the least, but before we get on to fixing that, let's get our other elements in place first.

Tables for layout? Welcome to hell!

There are many dark secrets littered around the history of the Web and web design, many bad ideas that were thought to be good at the time, many "innovations" that their creators have since tried to sweep under the carpet. Does this sound like your prom night photos? The outfit you wore, and the way it went so well with your acne and braces? If so, you'll know what I'm talking about.

Unfortunately, what is said and done on the Web tends to hang around forever, and you'll still find many bad "old" practices being used today, even by alleged modern web folk. One such <table>-related topic is that of **tables for layout**. Instead of using tables for tabular data and CSS for layouts (which we'll look at near the end of this chapter), they used table cells to hold different bits of content in position in content boxes, columns, headers, footers, etc., often nesting tabels several levels deep. This was done because CSS support used to be patchy and inconsistent across browsers, and using table cells was seen as an easier option for cross-browser layouts.

But this is BAD! This is not the correct semantic use of tables—it *looks* OK, but is useless or worse to any program trying to make use of the data, such as a screen reader trying to read the page out loud or an application trying to record the data for reuse in some other way. I am urging you not to go down this dark path, now that we have good CSS support across browsers. If I do catch you using tables for layout, I'll send Killer Croc 'round to eat your goldfish...

Advanced table elements

This section discusses the slightly more interesting elements that can give further semantics to our tables. At the moment, it is a bit of an unreadable mess—for both sighted readers and those relying on assistive technology such as screen readers—but help is at hand.

Table headers

One problem is that currently it is very hard to distinguish the table headings from the other rows. This can be easily remedied using table headers—<th> elements. To promote any normal table row to table headings, you simply replace the <td>s with <th>s:

```
<tr>
    <th>Villain</th>
    <th>Main weapons/abilities</th>
    <th>Height</th>
    <th>Real name</th>
    <th>First published</th>
</tr>
<tr>
    <th>Poison Ivy</th>
    <td>Can control plant life and exude seductive
    pheromones. Secretes deadly poison through her
    skin.</td>
    <td>5' 8" (1.73m)</td>
    <td>Pamela Isley</td>
    <td>1966</td>
</tr>
<!-- Same thing done to other data rows too... -->
```

But this is not all you can do. There is also a very useful <th> attribute called scope, which can take a value of row or col. This defines whether the heading is associated with a row or a column, respectively:

```
<tr>
    <th scope="col">Villain</th>
    <th scope="col">Main weapons/abilities</th>
    <th scope="col">Height</th>
    <th scope="col">Real name</th>
    <th scope="col">First published</th>
</tr>
<tr>
    <th scope="row">Poison Ivy</th>
    <td>Can control plant life...</td>
    <td>5' 8" (1.73m)</td>
    <td>Pamela Isley</td>
    <td>1966</td>
</tr>
<!-- Same thing done to other data rows too... -->
```

This gives the visual effect seen in **Figure 18.2** (see `tables_example2.html` for all of the features discussed in this section).

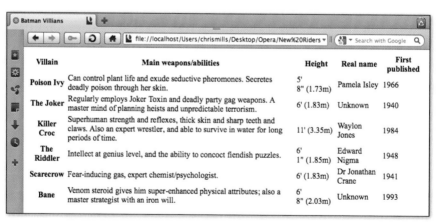

Figure 18.2: The table headings are now in a bold font, center aligned, and have extra padding around them.

The visual effect is helpful, and the different element is useful as a hook for CSS styles, but more than that, the headings are defined semantically as headings, for rows or columns. This means that screen reader users will be told what headers apply to each table cell, so they can understand the information in the table more easily.

Adding a caption to your table

You can also add a caption to your table using the `<caption>` element. This should contain a short summary of what the data is showing:

```
<body>
    <table>
        <caption>Batman Villains: the baddest of
        the bad</caption>

            . . .
```

Figure 18.3 shows the result in the browser.

Villain	Main weapons/abilities	Height	Real name	First published
Poison Ivy	Can control plant life and exude seductive pheromones. Secretes deadly poison through her skin.	5' 8" (1.73m)	Pamela Isley	1966
The Joker	Regularly employs Joker Toxin and deadly party gag weapons. A master mind of planning heists and unpredictable terrorism.	6' (1.83m)	Unknown	1940
Killer Croc	Superhuman strength and reflexes, thick skin and sharp teeth and claws. Also an expert wrestler, and able to survive in water for long periods of time.	11' (3.35m)	Waylon Jones	1984
The Riddler	Intellect at genius level, and the ability to concoct fiendish puzzles.	6' 1" (1.85m)	Edward Nigma	1948
Scarecrow	Fear-inducing gas, expert chemist/psychologist.	6' (1.83m)	Dr Jonathan Crane	1941
Bane	Venom steroid gives him super-enhanced physical attributes; also a master strategist with an iron will.	6' 8" (2.03m)	Unknown	1993

Figure 18.3: Adding a caption to the table.

Extra table structure with <thead>, <tbody>, <tfoot>, colgroup

There are three other elements worth mentioning that can give your table extra structure: `<thead>`, `<tbody>`, and `<tfoot>`. You use these as follows:

```
<table>
    <caption>Batman Villains: the baddest of the
bad</caption>
    <thead>
        <tr>
            <th scope="col">Villain</th>
            <th scope="col">Main weapons/abilities</th>
            <th scope="col">Height</th>
            <th scope="col">Real name</th>
            <th scope="col">First published</th>
        </tr>
    </thead>
    <tfoot>
        <tr>
            <td colspan="5">Data compiled by Chris Mills,
            2009.</td>
        </tr>
    </tfoot>
    <tbody>
        <tr>
            <th scope="row">Poison Ivy</th>
            <td>Can control plant life and exude seductive
            pheromones. Secretes deadly poison through her
            skin.</td>
            <td>5' 8" (1.73m)</td>
            <td>Pamela Isley</td>
            <td>1966</td>
        </tr>

    <!-- ...Rest of data... -->

    </tbody>
```

I have also used the colspan attribute on the table cell inside the footer, to make it stretch across all five columns (rowspan is also available, to make a column stretch across rows, but this is very rarely used, to my knowledge).

This final markup step gives us the table shown in **Figure 18.4**. Note that even though the footer is placed just below the header in the markup, it is rendered at the bottom of the table by the browser.

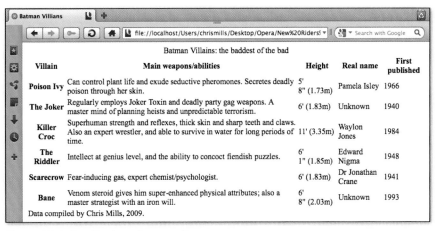

Batman Villains: the baddest of the bad

Villain	Main weapons/abilities	Height	Real name	First published
Poison Ivy	Can control plant life and exude seductive pheromones. Secretes deadly poison through her skin.	5' 8" (1.73m)	Pamela Isley	1966
The Joker	Regularly employs Joker Toxin and deadly party gag weapons. A master mind of planning heists and unpredictable terrorism.	6' (1.83m)	Unknown	1940
Killer Croc	Superhuman strength and reflexes, thick skin and sharp teeth and claws. Also an expert wrestler, and able to survive in water for long periods of time.	11' (3.35m)	Waylon Jones	1984
The Riddler	Intellect at genius level, and the ability to concoct fiendish puzzles.	6' 1" (1.85m)	Edward Nigma	1948
Scarecrow	Fear-inducing gas, expert chemist/psychologist.	6' (1.83m)	Dr Jonathan Crane	1941
Bane	Venom steroid gives him super-enhanced physical attributes; also a master strategist with an iron will.	6' 8" (2.03m)	Unknown	1993

Data compiled by Chris Mills, 2009.

Figure 18.4: Our final markup result.

Styling tables

Our table is basically complete, but it looks horrible! We desperately need some CSS styling to brighten things up a bit. Check out `tables_example3.html` and `tables_example3.css` to see the CSS discussed in this section in action.

> **Tip:** You've already learnt a lot of what you need to know to style a table effectively. You can apply borders, whitespace, text styling, background images, etc., to tables the same as you can to other block level elements. We will see many of these in action again in this section, along with some table-specific techniques. As with everything in web design, experiment and see what works for you the best in terms of delivering well-designed, accessible content to your users.

General layout

First things first: we will start with some general layout organisation. The first thing you need to do when styling a table (in nearly all cases) is to get rid of all the default spacing between the borders of the cell rows. You won't have noticed this yet because the colours are currently all set to white, but if you try setting a background colour on the cells of a default table, you will see white gaps between the cells—not pretty. You can get rid of this spacing using the first property of the following rule:

```css
table {
    border-collapse: collapse;
    text-align: left;
    width: 800px;
}
```

I have also left-aligned the text because I think the center-aligned by default headings look untidy in this case, and set a fixed width on the table, as it would start to look awful if stretched across a really high resolution monitor, or crowded in a narrow browser window.

The next problem to deal with is that the content is all squashed together; to remedy this I'll set some padding on the cells:

```css
th, td {
    padding: 0.5em;
}
```

I'll also force a smaller width on the "Main weapons/abilities" column, as it doesn't need all that space, and the columns could do with being narrower for readability, plus the "Height" values are broken onto two lines, which looks nasty. The following rule will force this column to always occupy 40% of the width of the table, with the rest of the space being shared among the others:

```css
.narrow_width {
    width: 40%;
}
```

(Well, provided you give all the cells in this column the appropriate class—check the source code to see what I've done.)

Lastly for this section, I'll use an attribute selector to add a bit more top and bottom padding to the column headings, i.e., elements that have an attribute of scope="col":

```
th[scope=col] {
    padding-top: 1em;
    padding-bottom: 1em;
}
```

Try it yourself!

Think of another selector you could use to apply this rule to the same elements, which would work in older Internet Explorer versions—i.e. version 6 and before—that do not support attribute selectors.

Text formatting

I'll set a sans-serif font on the whole table, because I think it suits the mood better:

```
table {
    border-collapse: collapse;
    text-align: center;
    font-family: Helvetica, Verdana, sans-serif;
}
```

Next I'll make the data cells' text a bit smaller, and the footer text and row heading text smaller still:

```
td {
    font-size: 90%;
}

tfoot, th[scope=row] {
    font-size: 80%;
}
```

As one last text trick, I'll use a property you haven't seen before, text-transform, to make all the villain names appear in uppercase:

```
th[scope=row] {
    text-transform: uppercase;
}
```

CHAPTER 18

Let's check out the design at this point (**Figure 18.5**).

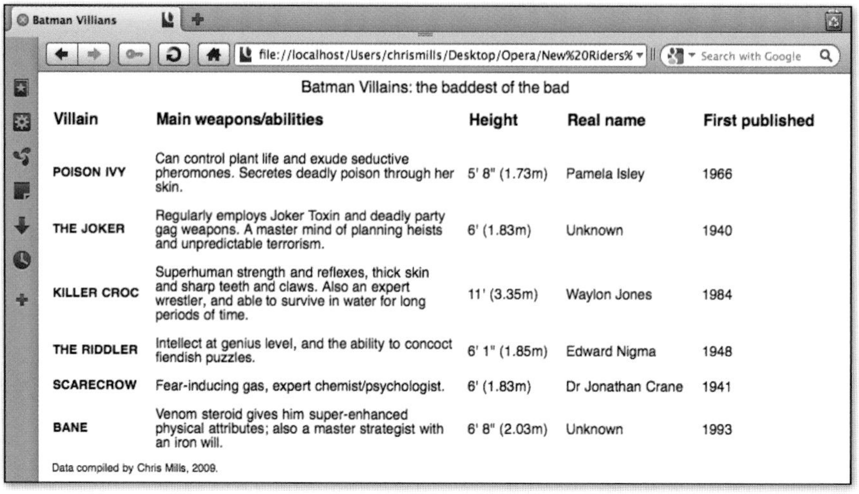

Figure 18.5: The table is already looking more readable.

Adding colour and graphics

Now that we've got our structure sorted, let's move on to adding some colour! First of all, I generated a colour scheme using the online Color Scheme Designer tool (http://colorschemedesigner.com/). Then I converted the hex colours it gave me into RGB colours, for reasons that you'll see later. To do this, I used an online tool found at http://www.javascripter.net/faq/hextorgb.htm.

Adding background colours and graphics

The first thing I did was to apply backgrounds to elements. The `<table>` element has a nice background image added to it:

```
table {
    ...
    background: rgb(7,8,45) url(comic_bg.jpg) no-repeat
    top left;
}
```

The column headings have a gradient applied to them, and the text is set to a lighter colour so it is readable:

```
th[scope="col"] {
    ...
    background: rgb(9,3,29) url(header_gradient.png)
    repeat-x top left;
    color: rgb(99,83,150);
}
```

Lastly, I set a gradient on the footer, and tweaked the text colour:

```
tfoot td {
    background: rgb(9,3,29) url(footer_gradient.png)
    repeat-x top left;
    color: rgb(99,83,150);
}
```

Adding zebra stripes

The next part is very interesting, and explains the need for RGB colours. I set a background colour on all the rows inside the table body. Note the use of the descendant selector to target just the rows inside the body; these are used a few times in this example:

```
tbody tr {
    background-color: rgba(80,58,150,0.3);
}
```

The interesting part is that I am using RGBa colours—I am setting transparency just on the background colours, to let the background image attached to the <table> element shine through. I have then used an :nth-child pesudo-element selector to select only the even-numbered rows, and make them a different colour.

```
tbody tr:nth-child(even) {
    background-color: rgba(99,83,150,0.5);
}
```

CHAPTER 18

Resource // :nth-child

Colouring alternate rows a different colour is known as zebra-striping, and it is often done to aid readability. It is easy to do with CSS3's :nth-child, which allows you to select the odd or even rows (odd or even), or even every third element (3n), or every fourth element plus 1 (4n+1), etc.

It is supported across most browsers now, with the exception of Internet Explorer. If you want to make sure you support Internet Explorer, then you need to use the old method, which is to give every row you want coloured differently a class of, say, even or alternate, and then target that class with the style. The trouble with this is that it is very inflexible: if you add more rows to your table, then you need to manually change the position of your classes so that the effect still works. Note also that :nth-child doesn't just affect tables: you can use it on any sequence of repeated elements, e.g., <li> or even <p>. For more on :nth-child, check out http://dev.opera.com/articles/view/zebra-striping-tables-with-css3/.

Having fun with CSS3 transitions

For a last bit of fun and frolics, I decided to add a CSS transition effect to the body rows, so that when you hover over them, they give a smooth glow animation. This is achieved with CSS3 transitions. The updated rules look like so:

```
tbody tr {
    background-color: rgba(80,58,150,0.3);
    -o-transition-property: background-color;
    -o-transition-duration: 1s;
    -moz-transition-property: background-color;
    -moz-transition-duration: 1s;
    -webkit-transition-property: background-color;
    -webkit-transition-duration: 1s;
}

tbody tr:nth-child(even) {
    background-color: rgba(99,83,150,0.5);
    -o-transition-property: background-color;
    -o-transition-duration: 1s;
    -moz-transition-property: background-color;
```

```
    -moz-transition-duration: 1s;
    -webkit-transition-property: background-color;
    -webkit-transition-duration: 1s;
}

tbody tr:hover {
    background-color: rgba(80,58,150,1);
}

tbody tr:nth-child(even):hover {
    background-color: rgba(99,83,150,1);
}
```

Resource // Vendor prefixes

You may be wondering what the -o-, -moz-, and -webkit- parts stuck on the front of some of the CSS3 properties are. These are called **vendor prefixes**, and these specify the vendor's own specific implementations of those properties (respectively Opera, Mozilla's Gecko engine, which powers Firefox and some other browsers, and Webkit, the engine that powers Safari and some other browsers), rather than the non-prefixed final version.

These exist because the CSS3 standard is still somewhat in flux—they provide a safe playground for browser vendors to implement those properties safe in the knowledge that they won't conflict with other vendors' implementations (which may differ), and the final version, which may end up being different than it was when the vendors originally started to implement it.

So CSS transitions are currently not finalised, but when they do get finalised, all the browser vendors *should* converge on the same non-prefixed implementation. I have included all prefixed versions for now, so I can get this functionality working in all these different browsers.

CHAPTER 18

Let's go through how this works. First of all, you state which property you want to transition from one value to another:

```
    -o-transition-property: background-color;
```

Then you state how much time you want the transition to happen over:

```
    -o-transition-duration: 1s;
```

And that's pretty much it. The transition is primed and ready to go—all it needs is a state change to occur, and a value for the chosen property to transition to. This is provided by the following rule:

```
tbody tr:hover {
    background-color: rgba(80,58,150,1);
}
```

So what this does is transition the background colour's transparency from 0.5 to 1 over 1 second, when the rows are moused over, giving us a nice glowy effect for the rows. Test it out yourself!

Note the selector on the second transition—tbody tr:nth-child(even):hover;. Bear in mind that you can chain pseudo-classes together. Note also that you need to put the state change rule after the one in which the transition is set up; as of the time of this writing, transitions are supported in Safari 4, Chrome 4, Firefox 3.6, and Opera 10.50.

The <caption> element

It was quite difficult to decide what to do with the <caption> element, so I opted for just some basic styling and positioning. I think I'm already in enough danger of "design overkill" on this one.

```
caption {
    font-size: 1.5em;
    text-align: left;
    color: rgb(7,8,45);
}
```

With all this done, our sample table now looks very different (**Figure 18.6**).

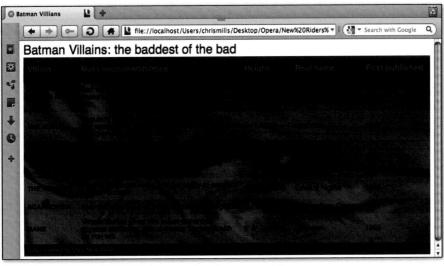

Figure 18.6: Holy styling, Batman! Is this the same table?

Try it yourself!

1. Choose some basic data to mark up, and put it into the three basic table elements. Choose something fun, like your favourite bands or sports players. We can prove that HTML tables don't have to be dull.

2. Add in more semantics—headings, body, footer, caption, etc.

3. Give your table some attractive styling.

4. Write a blog post about your example.

5. As a part of that blog post, justify the colour scheme you used for your table, and comment on the colour scheme of my final example—how could it be improved? (Hint: look in the accessibility chapters for ideas.)

6. Check out the table used for the menu in the Chez Sous Le Vent example site to see how it works (see **Figure 18.7**). This is a simpler example in terms of styling, but effective in terms of fitting in with the overall site design.

(continues)

Try it yourself!

(continued)

Menus

Lorem ipsum dolor sit amet, consectetuer adipiscing elit, sed diam nonummy nibh euismod tincidunt ut laoreet dolore magna aliquam erat volutpat. Ut wisi enim ad minim veniam, quis nostrud exerci tation ullamcorper suscipit lobortis nisl ut aliquip ex ea commodo consequat.

Hors d'Oeuvres

Dish	Description	Price
Soupe du jour	Homemade soup of the day	$6.50
Assiette de fromages	Cheeses and fresh fruit	$15.00
Escargots de Bourgogne	Snails baked with button mushrooms and a traditional garlic and parsley butter	$8.50

Salads

Dish	Description	Price
Salade verte	Mixed greens tossed with grape tomatoes, bell pepper and green onion in a champagne vinaigrette	$7.50
Salade Chez Nous	Tossed mixed greens with seared grapes, smoked duck breast, shaved red onion	$9.50

Figure 18.7: The Chez Sous Le Vent menu—another good use of HTML tables.

Summary

So that concludes our look at marking up and styling tabular data with HTML and CSS. We looked at basic table elements, then added further structure and semantics to the mix to aid the vital cause of accessibility. Finally we added nice styling to our table, including CSS3 transitions and `:nth-child`—it is important so it fits well with your overall design.

We've still got a lot to cover, so let's keep moving—next up are HTML forms, which are also a challenge to make accessible and visually appealing. Take this opportunity to grab a cup of tea.

CHAPTER 19
Forms

by Chris Mills

So far in this book, our interaction with the Web has been pretty much one-sided (unless you count your site visitors or clients phoning you up and criticising your designs as web interaction). We have put our data up on the Web, and our site visitors have received it and made use of it.

Sooner or later, however, you will want to collect data from your visitors, whether it is address and credit card details during online shopping (with proper security measures in place, of course), or customer feedback, or blog comments, or times, dates and locations if they are searching for event details. This is done through **HTML forms**.

In this chapter I will take you through all the HTML form elements you need to know, give you a list of form best practices, then look at the basics of styling forms (which is a real art form in itself and not easy to get right).

This is a book about front-end web design, so it is out of scope for me to start discussing what happens to your user's data after the form is submitted to the server. For server-side programming, I'd recommend a nice beginning PHP, Ruby or Python book.

In this chapter you have the opportunity to **Try it yourself!** *with the convenient sample code downloads found on the book's companion website—*http://interactwithwebstandards.com.

Form best practices

Think about the different forms you have filled in online, when booking flight tickets, signing in to a shopping site, or buying something. You've got to admit that these are not pleasurable experiences. Something small like a login form is not bad, but anything longer can be frustrating. **Figure 19.1** shows a couple of examples.

Figure 19.1: A short form, and a long form. Which one is more fun? Answers on a postcard, please.

As a front-end designer, your job is not to make site visitors weep with joy when they fill in your web form. Instead, it's more of a damage limitation role—you want to make this task as non-frustrating, quick and painless as possible. If a site visitor can't get through your form without struggling, they will be likely to go somewhere else on the Web, which can mean the loss of a sale, or negative feedback and subsequent damage to your reputation and integrity. This section lists some best practices to follow when designing a form, or at least to be aware of (some may not be directly relevant to your role on a website project, but you should still be aware of the bigger picture).

Think carefully about what data you need to collect, and how to ask for it

This sounds obvious, but I've seen a number of sites containing forms where you think "Why on earth do they need that?" or "What are they asking me for here?" Make sure you don't ask for more data than you actually need, and make sure you ask for data using clear language and recognised conventions. Remember also that conventions differ in different locales. If your customers will include Brits and Americans, for example, ask for "ZIP code or postcode" to make sure both will understand what's required.

Break up large forms into multiple pages

If your form is long, break it up into multiple pages. The page layouts will be easier to design, and dealing with small, bite-size chunks will have a positive psychological effect on your users. You can improve things more by adding a progress indicator to the form (e.g., a percentage, or a bar that fills up gradually), or giving each user a backrub after each page. The choice is yours.

Plan your form on paper first

OK, so this should be advice for the whole website, but forms in particular are complicated and fiddly, so start off by sketching out what the form should look like. How big should the form container be, and how far apart should the form elements be placed?

Allow people to select with mouse or keyboard rather than having to type

For example, when they are selecting a country of residence, or choosing an address, give people a drop-down list rather than making them type it out, if possible. This drop-down list could contain the last few choices the site visitor entered on previous visits, or perhaps the five most common choices that all your site users choose, plus an option to enter another choice if desired.

Also, make sure your form controls can be accessed using keyboard controls as well as the mouse, either using browser defaults or custom control keys. These enhancements benefit everyone, but some groups benefit more than others:

- Some web users with mobility impairments find using either a keyboard or a mouse difficult or impossible.

- People visiting your site using a mobile device will find it far more fiddly to enter text into your site, plus they may not have a virtual mouse to use.

Be flexible in accepting different data formats

You shouldn't make your user think too much about the exact format they enter data in. Even if you provide a help message such as "Enter phone number in the format 123-456-7890," different people do it in different ways, so you should allow users to enter the phone number as 123-456-7890, 123 456 7890, 1234567890, 123-456 (7890), etc. You can always get your developer to write code to reformat the entries into the exact format you want on the server-side. But *you* should do this thinking, so that your users don't have to.

In ambiguous cases, such as dates, make it clear what format you expect the data in (e.g. DD-MM-YY, or MM-DD-YY).

Lastly, you shouldn't go against conventions users are used to on the Web. For example, nearly every site expects a phone number to be all entered into one text field, so don't start expecting users to enter the international code, main number and extension in separate text fields.

Make error messages meaningful

Make sure your error messages are written in clear language. For example, if a visitor forgets to enter their e-mail address in a form, and it is a mandatory field, don't give them an error message saying "an error has occurred in the form" (or worse, nothing at all)—print a clear highlighted error message next to the form saying something like "You need to enter your e-mail address here. Make sure it is typed correctly." And highlight the form with a bold outline, for example.

Don't convey information only by colour

Quite often I see error messages on forms saying something like "The fields highlighted in red contain an error." As well as not being particularly clear, this message also relies on colour for the user to find the error and correct it. Some users are colourblind, so this would be no use to them at all—you should supplement the highlight with an asterisk, and perhaps a bold border.

Take proper security measures

Make sure your developer knows what they are doing with respect to form security. A common method of attack that website hackers/crackers use is to enter malicious code into form fields in the hope that it will be executed on the server, perhaps deleting your database or giving them access to your system.

All data coming from external sources needs to be validated so that any malicious code is neutralized—never trust any external data, ever.

Perform data validation on the server-side as well as the client-side

You can use JavaScript to validate the data the user enters into your form before it even leaves his browser, for example checking that he has entered data into mandatory fields, checking that his e-mail address is a proper e-mail address, checking that his phone number has the right number of digits, etc. Doing simple checks on the client-side before it goes to the server is great, because it can get rid of the need for some round trips to the server, saving some time for the user.

However, every browser has the ability to turn JavaScript off, so anyone can just turn off your client-side validation if they wish! Therefore you should check data on the server-side too.

Tip: HTML5 has some features that help a great deal with client-side validation—see the "HTML5 forms" section at the end of the chapter for details.

CHAPTER 19

HTML for forms

In a similar manner to tables, forms are contained within a main wrapper element—everything inside the `<form>` element is part of the form. Then, to create the different form features, you place them inside the form, along with any other elements you need to give the form structure and provide descriptions to help your site visitors fill it in successfully. There are special form elements to use for providing structure and descriptions, but you can also supplement these with standard elements like paragraphs and lists.

The form wrapper

This is what the form wrapper syntax looks like, including all the form-specific attributes you should need:

```
<form action="processing-script.php" method="post">

    <!-- All your form contents go here -->

</form>
```

- `action`: This attribute defines the server-side script that will process the data after it has been **submitted** (see the "Submitting the data" section later on), for example validating the data or storing it in a database.

- `method`: Defines how the data will be submitted to the server-side script—the two possible values are `post` and `get`. The `post` method submits `post` data inside the header of the request that is sent to the server when the data is submitted, while `get` submits the data as name/value pairs inside the URL of the page upon submission. (When you are using the Web next, keep a lookout for big, long chains on the end of the URL you are browsing along the lines of: `country=uk&city=London&shop=hairdressers`.)

Before you go any further, take a look at `forms1.html` from the code download on `http://interactwithwebstandards.com`—this contains the entire HTML from this section. I have built a simple signup-type form that contains examples of all the most important elements you'll need to learn about, giving the form some basic structure using only list elements. This is perfectly reasonable in terms of semantics, as the lists contain multiple related form elements. The basic unstyled form looks like **Figure 19.2**.

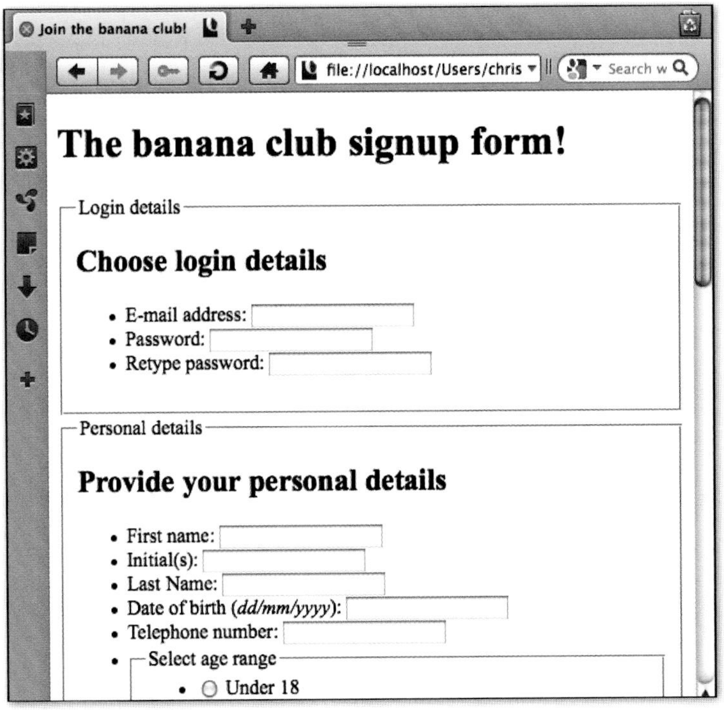

Figure 19.2: A basic, unstyled form.

So I think you'll agree that this form is unspeakably ugly right now. Browser default form styling unfortunately is very ugly, as well as being rather inconsistent across browsers. But never fear: we'll look at styling forms later on in the chapter. At this point, it is important to make sure the form is well structured, usable and accessible. In the rest of this section I will cover in detail all the rest of the form-specific elements contained in the example shown above.

Single line text inputs

The most common form element you'll use is the humble single line text input:

```
<input type="text" name="email" value="">
```

The <input> element can take many different values for its type attribute, which can turn it into many different things; a value of text turns it into a single line text input, as seen in **Figure 19.3**.

Figure 19.3: A single line text input.

This is all it creates—any labels have to be added alongside it using text. In addition, it doesn't allow you to set whether it should be mandatory, or only accept certain character ranges; this goes for all form elements. To add validation features like that, you have to use JavaScript, server-side scripting or HTML5 forms.

> **Tip:** The `maxlength` attribute allows you to set the maximum number of characters that can be entered into a form element.

We've explained the `type` attribute; the others are as follows:

- `name`: This specifies the identifying name of the data entered into this form element after the form is submitted. It will be used during processing of the data, for example when inserting it into a database on the server.

- `value`: Specifies a default value for the form element to contain once the form first loads in the browser. I have left mine blank, as I don't want any default values in this case.

Passwords

A password form element looks like so:

```
<input type="password" name="pwd" value="">
```

This is just a specialised version of a single line text input. The only difference between the two is that with a normal single line text input, the text is displayed as you type it. With a password input, any text you type is disguised as asterisks or bullets on screen, as shown in **Figure 19.4**.

Figure 19.4: A password text input disguises any entered text.

This exists for one reason only—as a security measure. It is a good idea to hide your site visitor's passwords from anyone who might be looking over her shoulder at her screen.

Checkboxes

If you want to give site visitors the option of saying yes or no to different options, you can include checkboxes for the user to toggle between checked and unchecked like so:

```
<p>What banana-related activities do you like doing
most? (check all that apply):</p>
    <ul>
        <li><input type="checkbox"
        name="peeling" id="peeling" value="peeling">
        <label for="peeling">Peeling</label></li>
        <li><input type="checkbox" name="eating"
        id="eating" value="eating"> <label
        for="eating">Eating</label></li>
        <li><input type="checkbox" name="fruitart"
        id="fruitart" value="fruitart"> <label
        for="fruitart">Fruit art</label></li>
        <li><input type="checkbox" name="spin"
        id="spin" value="spin"> <label for="spin">Spin
        the banana</label></li>
        <li><input type="checkbox" name="walkies"
        id="walkies" value="walkies"> <label
        for="walkies">Banana walks</label></li>
        <li><input type="checkbox" name="javelin"
        id="javelin" value="javelin"> <label
        for="javelin">Banana javelin</label></li>
        <li><input type="checkbox" name="salad"
        id="salad" value="salad"> <label
        for="salad">Fruit salads</label></li>
        <li><input type="checkbox" name="fritters"
        id="fritters" value="fritters"> <label
        for="fritters">Banana fritters</label></li>
    </ul>
```

This produces an output as seen in **Figure 19.5**.

Radio buttons

Radio buttons provide the user with many options to choose from for a single value choice—you can only choose one option from those presented in each set. The name comes from old-fashioned radios or TVs, which had physical push buttons to press to choose the channels, only one of which could be depressed at a time.

The syntax looks like so:

```
<ul>
    <li><input type="radio" name="agerange"
    value="under18"
    id="au18"> <label for="au18">Under 18</label></li>
    <li><input type="radio"name="agerange" value="18-24"
    id="a1824"> <label for="a1824">18-24</label></li>
    <li><input type="radio" name="agerange" value="25-34"
    id="a2534"> <label for="a2534">25-34</label></li>
    <li><input type="radio" name="agerange" value="35-
    44"id="a3544"> <label for="a3544">35-44</label></li>
    <li><input type="radio" name="agerange" value="45-54"
    id="a4554"> <label for="a4554">45-54</label></li>
    <li><input type="radio" name="agerange" value="55-64"
    id="a5564"> <label for="a5564">55-64</label></li>
    <li><input type="radio" name="agerange" value="65plus"
    id="ao65"> <label for="ao65">65 and over</label></li>
</ul>
```

There is nothing hard to understand here, although do note that the name attributes all have the same value—you need to do this to associate all the radio buttons together in one set.

This creates the visual output seen in **Figure 19.6**.

- ☐ Peeling
- ☐ Eating
- ☐ Fruit art
- ☐ Spin the banana
- ☐ Banana walks
- ☐ Banana javelin
- ☐ Fruit salads
- ☐ Banana fritters

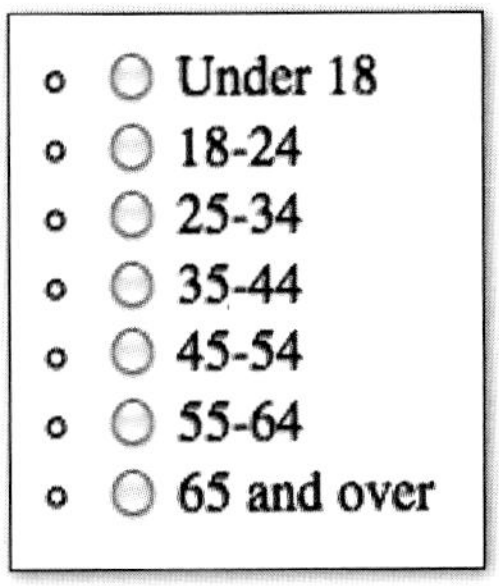

- ○ Under 18
- ○ 18-24
- ○ 25-34
- ○ 35-44
- ○ 45-54
- ○ 55-64
- ○ 65 and over

Figure 19.5: (left) A set of checkboxes. Figure 19.6: (right) A set of radio buttons.

Tip: With radio buttons and checkboxes, there is a way to cause one (one or more in the case of checkboxes) of the choices to be selected by default when the form is first loaded in the browser. You simply include the attribute checked="checked" on the <input> element.

File uploads

This next input type creates a file chooser so the user can choose a file to upload:

    <input type="file" name="image_upload">

Figure 19.7 shows the visual output of this element.

Figure 19.7: A file uploader.

As you'd expect, clicking the *Choose...* button opens up a file chooser dialog for the user to navigate to their chosen file. It is up to you (or your developer) to control what kinds of file you allow to be uploaded, and what file sizes you will allow.

Submitting the data

This is the last <input> element type we'll cover. The classic *Submit* button should always be found at the

Submit

Figure 19.8: A submit button.

bottom of your form, and clicking it will send the data to the data processing file you specified in the `action` attribute of the `<form>` element.

```
<input type="submit" value="Submit">
```

This creates a visual output something like **Figure 19.8**.

In this case, the `value` attribute controls the label on the button. You can have this set to anything you like, even *cheesy bananas* (thanks MailChimp), but it is often a good idea to set it to something intuitive and appropriate to your form, such as *Send email* or *Place my order*.

You may also encounter Reset buttons, i.e. `<input>` elements with `type="reset"`. These serve to clear the form contents. I would strongly advise you against ever using these, as all they seem to do is annoy users who click them by accident when they are looking to submit a form, resulting instead in them having to start all over again!

Multiple line text inputs

Sometimes you will want to collect textual data that spans more than one line, for example a biography, or a comment on a feedback form. The element to allow this—`<textarea>`—looks different from what we have seen so far:

```
<textarea name="banana_col" id="banana_col" cols="30"
rows="6"></textarea>
```

The `cols` and `rows` attributes specify how many columns and rows in size the text input should be. Even though these values only set the size of the `<textarea>` on the screen, and don't limit the amount of text the user

Figure 19.9: A multiple line text input.

is allowed to enter, you should still leave enough space to allow most users to say what they want to say without filling up the space and making scrollbars appear. The text area looks like **Figure 19.9**.

Drop-down selection lists

If you want your users to choose from a list of options, but you want to save space, a good choice is a drop down `<select>` list—by default it appears as a single line, but clicking causes it to expand to show the options it holds. If there are many options, a scrollbar will appear. **Figure 19.10** illustrates this form feature's behaviour.

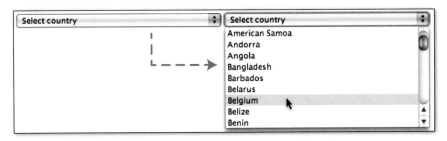

Figure 19.10: A `<select>` *element, closed and open.*

The code for this feature as seen in our form example looks like so:

```
<select id="country" name="country">
    <option value="">Select country</option>
    <option value="AF">Afghanistan</option>
    <option value="AX">Aland Islands</option>
    <option value="AL">Albania</option>

        <!-- Actual code has 245 additional options -->

</select>
```

The `value` attributes contain the data values of each option in the `<select>` list. Note the very top value, which has a blank `value` attribute and is labeled `Select country`. This is a common technique used to provide some more guidance for the user. You can guarantee that this option will always appear by default, as it is at the top of the `<options>` list.

Obviously for a `<select>` list of such magnitude, writing this out from scratch would be a huge task. I would advise you to use a ready-made template from a code-sharing site of some kind (feel free to adapt the one in my example.)

Improving accessibility with <label>

I have included <label> elements in the code, like so:

```
<li><label for="email">E-mail address:</label> <input
type="text" name="email" value=""></li>
```

Every piece of label text that points out what data a form field should contain is wrapped in one of these elements. The for attribute has the same value as the name attribute of the form field, and the effect of that is to associate the label with the form field. This has no effect on the visual appearance of the form, but it is good for accessibility—users of assistive technologies such as screen readers will now be told which labels relate to which form fields, so there is no confusion.

Adding structure with <legend> and <fieldset>

The final HTML feature I have used is a combination of <fieldset> and <legend> elements to structure the form into three logical groups of data: *Login details*, *Personal details*, and *Banana info*. This mainly serves to make data management easier, but it is worth doing for extra styling hooks and extra information also. <fieldset> wraps each logical grouping, while <legend> provides the title, or heading, for each group:

```
<fieldset>
    <legend>Login details</legend>
    <!-- Rest of form section... -->
</fieldset>
```

This creates the visual output seen in **Figure 19.11**.

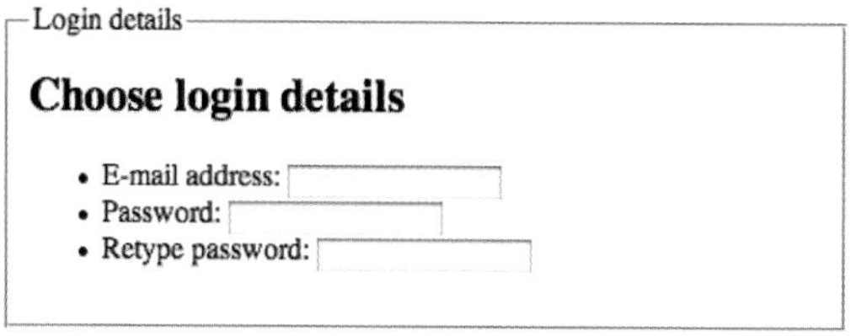

Figure 19.11: <fieldset> *and* <legend> *in action.*

You will also notice that I have surrounded the checkboxes in a <fieldset> with a <legend> and I have done the same for the radio buttons. This is a general best practice for these form features, again providing more structure and a description via the `<legend>`s and associating the descriptive paragraph ("What banana-related activities…") with the checkboxes.

Try it yourself!

1. Create your own form, using some or all of the elements described above. Make it as fun or as serious as you want.

2. Write a blog post about it.

Styling forms

Enjoyed the party so far? Well, now we get to the tricky bit. This is the part of the party where your parents come home early to find that your so-called friends have emptied the liquor cabinet and trashed the living room.

In short, HTML form styling is a real challenge, because there are lots of tiny fiddly bits flying around, there are a lot of unhelpful default browser styles to begin with, and those default styles differ a lot between browsers. If you don't believe me, check out Christopher Schmitt's `http://webformelements.com` resource, a collection of 3,500 screen grabs that document how all the different browsers style form elements by default, and how CSS is applied to form elements in those browsers. This is a very useful resource to keep at hand when styling forms.

In this section I will go through styling our example form in stages—you can find the finished work in `forms2.html` and `forms2.css` in the download files.

General styling

First of all, I will set some general body styles, like so:

```
body {
    font-size: 62.5%;
    font-family: Helvetica, Arial, sans-serif;
    line-height: 1.7em;
}

h2 {
    font-size: 1.5em;
}

li {
    list-style-type: none;
}
```

Nothing special here—in the first rule I've set the font size to 62.5 percent so that it will be 10px in most browsers, a nice number that makes it easier to do further calculations when sizing elements. I've also set the font and the line height to improve aesthetics a little.

The second rule sets an em-based size for the 2nd level headings, and the third gets rid of the list bullets. The next rule is more interesting:

```
#wrapper {
    width: 480px;
    margin: 0 auto;
}
```

Here I've used the content wrapper trick we first saw in Chapter 14, "Whitespace," to center the content on the page. The width of the whole form is set to 480px, and setting the horizontal margins to auto forces them to equally share the rest of the wrapper's parent element's width.

Figure 19.12 illustrates how the form now looks.

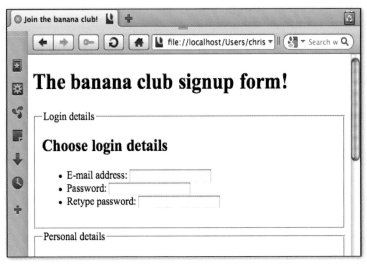

Figure 19.12: We are already seeing some improvements.

Aligning the labels and inputs

The next task is to make the labels and form elements line up. Currently they look squished and horrible and all over the place. The CSS we need is as follows:

```
label {
  float: left;
  clear: left;
  width: 200px;
  text-align: right;
}

input {
    margin-left: 1em;
}

p {
    margin-left: 1.1em;
}
```

The three most important properties are:

1. display: This allows you to force a block level element to behave like an inline element for layout purposes, or vice versa. In this case, we are making all the *inline* label elements display like *block level* elements, so that they now inhabit a box of their own, we can set their width, and other elements next to them will flow around them.

2. float: You haven't seen this property before, and it will be discussed a lot more in Chapter 20, "Floats." For now, let's just say that float allows you to make an element float alongside the content below it rather than sitting above it—for example, if you wanted the text of an article to flow around an image, as illustrated in **Figure 19.13**.

3. clear: clear is another property you haven't seen before that will be discussed in Chapter 20. This property basically tells a float to stop happening. After a float has started you can set clear on a subsequent element to stop any further content from flowing round the element that was floated.

Before adding a float:

Sed ut perspiciatis unde omnis iste natus error sit voluptatem accusantium dolorem laudantium, totam rem aperiam, eaque ipsa quae ab illo inventore veritatis et quasi architecto beatae vitae dicta sunt explicabo. Nemo enim ipsam voluptatem quia voluptas sit aspernatur aut odit aut fugit, sed quia consequuntur magni eos qui ratione voluptatem sequi nesciunt. Neque porro quisquam est, qui dolorem ipsum quia dolor sit amet, consectetur. adipisci velit, sed quia non numquam eius modi tempore incidunt ut labore et dolore

After: img { float: left; }

Sed ut perspiciatis unde omnis iste natus error sit voluptatem accusantium dolorem laudantium, totam rem aperiam, eaque ipsa quae ab illo inventore veritatis et quasi architecto beatae vitae dicta sunt explicabo. Nemo enim ipsam voluptatem quia voluptas sit aspernatur aut odit aut fugit, sed quia consequuntur magni eos qui ratione voluptatem sequi nesciunt. Neque porro quisquam est, qui dolorem ipsum quia dolor sit amet, consectetur. adipisci velit, sed quia non numquam eius modi tempora incidunt ut labore et dolore magnam aliquam quaerat voluptatem.

Figure 19.13: The effect of adding a float on to an element.

In this case I am setting a fixed width on the labels, aligning the text to the right hand edge of the elements, and floating them to the left of the inputs so they line up neatly with one another in a column. Then I clear the floats so that nothing else is floated around each input (without this you would get some really weird layout results).

The second rule pushes the <input> elements to the right a bit, making space between them and their respective labels so they aren't squashed together, while the third rule moves the paragraphs to the right a bit.

After doing this, I went back and added some margins to the `<li>`s to vertically separate them a bit and make them appear more in the center:

```
li {
    list-style-type: none;
    margin-bottom: 15px;
    margin-left: -50px;
}
```

The sample form now looks like **Figure 19.14**.

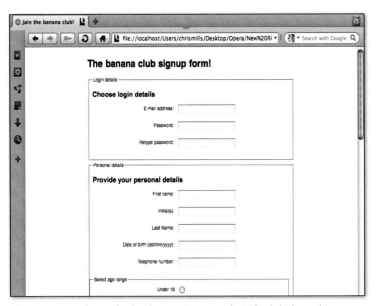

Figure 19.14: Things look a lot neater now that the labels and inputs are aligned.

Fixing the odd ones out

I still have some strange layout anomalies to sort out before I can be happy and move on to adding some colourful bling to the form.

The nested bullets

The nested bullets (i.e., the radio buttons and checkboxes) are a bit far away from one another as they are affected by the earlier rule that moves all the list items vertically apart, so the next thing to do is override this rule just for nested list items:

```
li ul li {
    margin-bottom: 0;
}
```

I have also made the left margin on the <h2> elements smaller so they line up with the paragraphs:

```
h2 {
    font-size: 1.5em;
    margin-left: 0.8em;
}
```

<select>, <textarea>, and the file upload

Being wider than standard <input> elements, these elements also need some extra care and attention to get them looking right, but again this is not that difficult—I just set the same width and left hand margin on all of them:

```
select {
    margin-left: 10px;
    width: 200px;
}

textarea {
    margin-left: 10px;
    width: 200px;
}

input[type=file] {
    margin-left: 10px;
    width: 200px;
}
```

The width makes all these longer form elements line up with one another, and the left margin makes the left hand sides of them line up with the left hand sides of all the other form elements.

A job well done—this gives us a form that we can at least bear to show to our site visitors. The next step, of course, is to add some colour and graphics to make it really sing.

Try it yourself!

1. Instead of the float/clear technique I employed above, you could also use **CSS tables** to align the `<label>` and `<input>` elements. Take a copy of my example files, research how to do this, and make a new version employing CSS tables. Here are some rules to help with your research:

```
li {
    display: table-row;
}

label, input {
    display: table-cell;
}
```

2. The CSS tables method seems to be a lot easier, so why did I do my example the other way? Why wouldn't I do this in a production site?

3. Why shouldn't you use CSS tables to lay out tabular data? Yes, it's a confusing question! Am I joking? No. Is this a shortcoming of the CSS spec? Probably. Nothing's perfect.

4. Write a blog post about your work.

Colour and graphics

The first thing to do is think about a colour scheme. Since it is a form about bananas, I decided that it would be sensible to base it around a banana yellow, so I found a banana picture, loaded it into Fireworks, used the eye dropper tool to find out the main yellow colour value, then put that into http://colorschemegenerator.com to get a complementary colour scheme. I also kept the banana picture to use as a background image!

General backgrounds

So let's get started with adding in that background image:

```
body {
    font-size: 62.5%;
    font-family: Helvetica, Arial, sans-serif;
    line-height: 1.7em;
    background-image: url(banana_bg.jpg);
}
```

Next I will create a rule to add a background colour to the fieldsets, plus some space in between to allow bits of the banana to shine through:

```
fieldset {
    background-color: #fbcb42;
    margin-bottom: 20px;
}
```

Styling the <legend>s and borders

I will now focus my attention on the <legend>s, and the borders that cut through them. It creates a rather nice effect to make the <legend> the same colour as the border:

```
fieldset {
    background-color: #fbcb42;
    margin-bottom: 20px;
    border: 4px solid #a07701;
}

legend {
    background-color: #a07701;
    padding: 7px 10px 5px 10px;
    font-size: 1.3em;
}
```

I've also made the <legend> text a bit bigger to make it stand out a bit more.

Colouring the headings

I also decided to make the headings the same colour as the borders/legend backgrounds. Nothing complicated here:

```
h2 {
    font-size: 1.5em;
    margin-left: 0.8em;
    color: #a07701;
}
```

The form now looks like **Figure 19.15**.

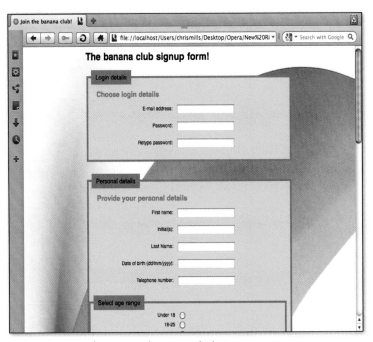

Figure 19.15: We've come a long way, baby!

Styling the nested <fieldset>s

At the moment, we have a noticeable styling problem in that the nested <fieldset>s look rather odd and untidy (look at the bottom of **Figure 19.15** and you'll see what I mean). To fix this, I will add some rules to remove the ugly nested borders and make the <legend>s *look exactly the same* as the <h2> elements. After all, they are acting as section headings for the radio buttons and checkboxes—this will not negatively impact the semantics, and will make the design more consistent.

The rules are as follows:

```
li fieldset {
    border-color: transparent;
    margin-left: 0.5em;
}

li fieldset legend {
    border-color: transparent;
    background-color: transparent;
    font-size: 1.5em;
    font-weight: bold;
    color: #a07701;
}
```

Nothing too surprising here. Note the inclusion of transparent colours to override the current settings for backgrounds and borders, effectively making them disappear so the colours behind them will show through.

A few extra tweaks

This is starting to look quite nice now, but there are a few extra things I decided I wanted to do. First of all, I decided to customize the look of all the form elements, by adding a coloured border round them and setting the background colour to white (I wanted them to be white by default in all browsers; some browsers inherit the background colour from the parent <fieldset>s , and some don't):

```
input, textarea, select {
    border: 2px solid #a07701;
    background-color: white;
}
```

Next, I added a visual clue as to which form element you are hovering over or have selected—you can use pseudo-classes to do this on form elements, just like we did with links in Chapter 15, "Links":

```
input:hover, input:focus, textarea:hover, textarea:focus,
select:hover, select:focus {
    background-color: #f7b704;
```

```
}
```

As with links, it is important to include focus as well as hover, so the feature is useful to those navigating the form using the keyboard.

Last of all, I decided to improve the look of the *Submit* and file upload buttons, as they currently look a bit lame and un-buttonlike. I simply increased the text size and gave them some extra padding:

```
input[type=file] {
    padding: 6px 0px;
    font-size: 1.3em;
}

input[type=submit] {
    padding: 6px 8px;
    font-size: 1.3em;
}
```

As a last little bit of fun, I added subtle rounded corners (an oxymoron, some might say) to all of the form elements except the checkboxes (otherwise they will get confused with radio buttons in the browsers that do allow styling of checkboxes and radio buttons):

```
input[type=text], input[type=submit], input[type=file],
input[type=password], input[type=radio], textarea,
legend, fieldset, select {
    border-radius: 5px;
    -o-border-radius: 5px;
    -moz-border-radius: 5px;
    -webkit-border-radius: 5px;
}
```

CHAPTER 19

And that's a wrap! The final form looks like **Figure 19.16**.

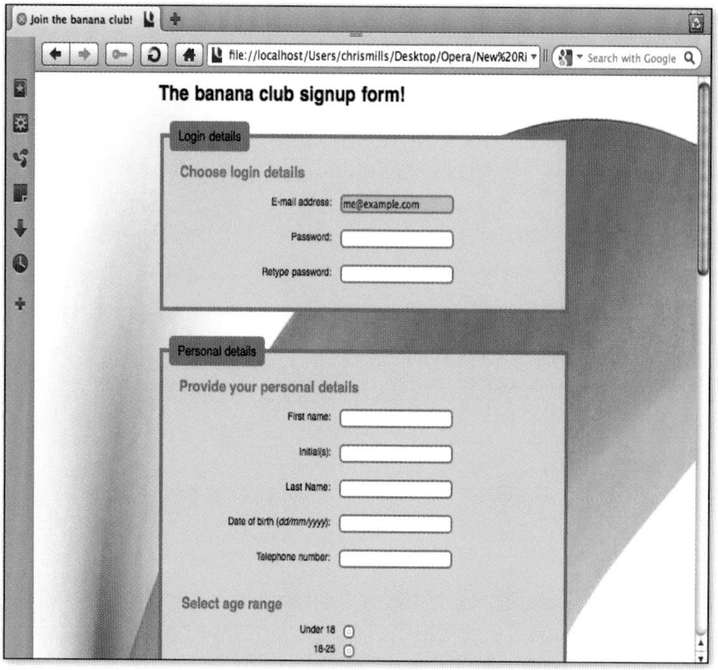

Figure 19.16: Any banana enthusiasts around here?

Try it yourself!

1. Make a copy of my example files (or your own example) and:
   - Replace the *Submit* button with an image to make it look nicer.
   - Replace the <h1> with a more attractive font and icon using an image replacement technique.
   - Replace the <h1> with a more attractive font and icon using a different technique—not image replacement (yes, there is another way, but you'll have to research what it is).

2. Use some other CSS3 features to spice the form up further, trying not to go overboard and make it look too busy (get rid of my rounded corners if you think they are too cheesy).

3. Write a blog post about your work.

4. Which browsers don't support styling of radio buttons and checkboxes, and why would they not support this?

HTML5 forms

The HTML5 spec offers a number of improvements over HTML 4 forms. In this section we will look at a few of these. (You can find a code example in html5_forms.html.)

Bear in mind that HTML5 forms have limited support across browsers (as of the time of writing of this book), so you should still include JavaScript and server-side validation on your real-life forms.

To start with, a common complaint with forms has always been that there is no way to do validation/error handling without scripting. In HTML5 you can make an element mandatory by putting a required attribute on it:

```
<input type="text" name="search" id="search"
required="required">
```

This makes an error message pop up if you try to submit the form without filling in this field, as seen in **Figure 19.17**.

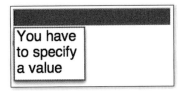

Figure 19.17: A required field in HTML5.

Next, the existing forms spec had no way of autofocusing elements—this also required scripting. In HTML5 this is handled by the autofocus attribute:

```
<input type="text" name="search" id="search"
required="required" autofocus="autofocus">
```

There are also some new <input> element types available, for example url, email, range and date:

```
<input type="url" name="web-site" id="web-site"
required="required">
<input type="email" name="email" id="email"
required="required">
<input type="range" name="price" id="price"
required="required">
<input type="date" name="depart" id="depart"
required="required">
```

These new types create the output shown in **Figure 19.18**.

These types were introduced because they offer a simple way to create design patterns that are very commonly used on the Web, but currently have to be created using CSS/scripting.

Lastly, a brief word about CSS: There are also new pseudo-classes available to style form states such as invalid, valid, checked, etc. For example:

```
input:invalid { ... }
input:valid { ... }
input:checked { ... }
```

Figure 19.18: Some of the new input types available in HTML5.

Try it yourself!

1. Make a copy of my example files (or your own example) and add some HTML5 form features. Don't feel like you have to stick to the ones I've included here—you can look up the HTML5 spec and find other features to include.
2. Write a blog post about your work.

Summary

That concludes our tour of HTML forms—I have taken you through form best practices, detailed all the form elements that you should know about, and shown you how to style your forms so they don't make your site visitors run a mile. I also gave you a brief glimpse of the improvements offered in HTML5 forms.

We'll dig deeper into CSS in the next chapters where we'll explore layout techniques with floats and positioning.

CHAPTER 20
Floats

by Chris Mills

Floats? Clearing? These terms may seem strange to you at first. No, I am not talking about levitation, or clearing your name of a crime you've been wrongly accused of (did you steal this book?) I am talking about the float and clear CSS properties, which you've already seen in action in Chapter 19, "Forms." This chapter will look at these properties in more detail, including some of their most common uses such as floating text around images and creating multiple column layouts.

In this chapter you have the opportunity to **Try it yourself!** *with the convenient sample code downloads found on the book's companion website—*http://interactwithwebstandards.com.

Floating elements around one another

This is the usage that floats and clearing were really intended for: to allow web designers to create documents with text flowing around images, like you see in print publications. **Figure 20.1** shows an example (you could also look in any one of your favourite magazines or newspapers and find several examples).

Figure 20.1: Floats in print publication.

In this section we will create a similar example using HTML and CSS. We will start off with a simple example. Download the code examples from `http://interact withwebstandards.com` and open `floats_clearing1.html` and `floats_clearing1.css`, which you can see in **Figure 20.2**.

Figure 20.2: The starting point for my example.

This includes a simple image and a few paragraphs of text. I haven't done anything special here in terms of styling the page, except for the inclusion of a web font (see resource).

Resource // Web fonts

In my example I decided to spice things up a bit using web fonts. Web fonts are a CSS3 feature that allows you to download custom fonts along with your web page and use them in your CSS—solving the problem I alluded to in Chapter 13, "Headings and Paragraphs," of there being a very limited number of "safe fonts" to use on websites. In my example you'll find the following construct:

```
@font-face {
   src: url(MINYN___.ttf) format("truetype");
   font-family: "Minya Nouvelle";
   font-style: normal;
   /* Larabie fonts license agreement:
      http://devfiles.myopera.com/articles/593/license.txt */
}
```

The first line specifies the URL where the font file can be found and the type of font, and the next lines specify the name of the font and the font-style the file contains (some may include various different files, for the various cuts and weights you can use—such as bold, italic, small caps and other alternatives). This should be included at the top of the CSS so the font will definitely be imported when you go to use it. You use it exactly like you would any other font:

```
font-family: "Minya Nouvelle";
```

Currently Opera, Firefox, and Safari support TrueType (.ttf) and OpenType (.otf) fonts, with Opera also supporting SVG fonts (.svg). Internet Explorer doesn't support these, but it does support a proprietary font format called Embedded Open Type (.eot), so to use the font in Internet Explorer you need to include an extra font declaration just like the one above, which points to an .eot version of the font.

You can convert other font formats into .eot fonts using a variety of converters—search Google for "convert to eot."

Web fonts are a great step forward for web designers, but there is one major caveat: not all fonts are free to use and share. Font designers' work is often copyrighted, and we are only just looking at licensing constructs that work on the Web (with solutions such as TypeKit and FontDeck becoming available). The best bet is to look for free fonts to use, on sites such as http://larabiefonts.com and http://dafont.com, and include the appropriate licensing agreement.

Floating the image

Floating the image is very simple. All you need is a simple rule containing the float property:

```
img {
    float: left;
    border: 1px solid black;
    margin: 0 10px 10px 0;
}
```

I have also included a thin black border on the image to make it look neater, and some right and bottom padding to stop the image from being pushed right up against the text (which looks rather untidy). The result is shown in **Figure 20.3**.

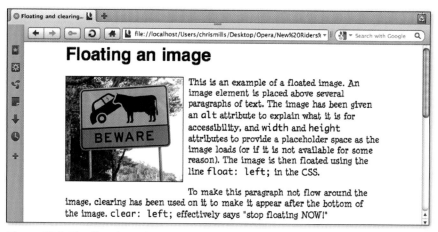

Figure 20.3: The float in action.

Tip: You can also use float: right; if you want the image to float to the right of the content's parent element (in this case, the <div> wrapper).

Clearing a paragraph

This looks pretty cool, but one small problem is that the second paragraph looks a bit messy because of the short line fragment at the top of it. We can make this paragraph appear completely below the image by adding a special class to the second paragraph below the image using the clear property:

```
.clear {
    clear: left;
}
```

What this does is say "stop any floats on the right side of this element." The result is shown in **Figure 20.4**.

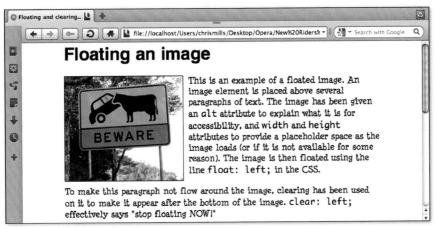

Figure 20.4: Clearing the second paragraph.

The possible values of the clear property are:

- left: stops floats on the left side of the floated element.
- right: stops floats on the right side of the element.
- both: stops floats on both sides of the element.

This is obviously a very simple example; now we will move on to look at some more advanced uses of floats.

Tip: You can use floats on any block level element, not just images (although <img> can actually be block or inline, depending on context. Don't worry about it too much!).

Try it yourself!

Create some of your own content, and experiment with floats and clearing to create some interesting layouts.

Creating multiple column layouts with floats

In the last section we looked at the basic intended usage of floats and clearing. In this section we will look at a float usage that goes beyond the original intended purpose: multiple column layouts! In the bad old days of web design, when web designers used table cells to position parts of their content on the page, it was pretty easy to create a site with a header, a footer and multiple columns. This translated into a three-row table, with the first and last rows spanning across all the columns and containing only a single cell, and the middle row's multiple cells being used for the individual columns of content (**Figure 20.5**).

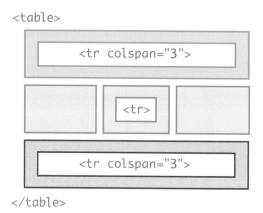

Figure 20.5: Tables for layout. It's a no-no these days, but it used to be seen as best practice.

When we became more aware of the shortcomings of using tables for layout (bad semantics, accessibility problems and more), and CSS became supported better and more consistently across browsers, web designers looked at new ways of creating such layouts. In modern times, it is common practice to float entire sections of content to create multiple column layouts, and in this section I will show you how.

Bear in mind that floated layouts are still not perfect. Because of box model problems in older browsers (see Chapter 14, "Whitespace," for more details), they can sometimes go wrong, plus they can be a bit fragile if you can't control how much content is going to be in your columns (unless you are careful). They are, however, the best cross-browser option we've got at the moment.

> **Tip:** CSS tables, mentioned briefly in the last chapter, are also really good for creating multiple column layouts, but they aren't supported in Internet Explorer versions below 8. In addition, there is a module in the CSS3 spec called **CSS Multi-column Layout**, which provides a useful set of properties for creating such layouts. At the time of this writing, this module has limited support across the major browsers.

It all starts with a single column...

The first thing we will do is create some new markup for an example page. The final layout will have a header, a footer and two columns sandwiched in between. At this stage, however, all of the content parts will pile on top of one another in a single column until we specify otherwise with CSS later on.

This is a very good example to go through, as this is how so many pages on the Web today are constructed. You can see the full HTML in the file floats_clearing2.html, but to save space here I will just give you the structure of the <div> elements inside the <body>—understanding this is the key to the layout.

```
<div id="wrapper">
    <div id="header">
    </div>
    <div id="navigation_sidebar">
    </div>
    <div id="main_content">
    </div>
    <div id="footer">
    </div>
</div>
```

As in the previous example, the wrapper wraps the whole page, but this time it contains the four main areas of the page in separate <div> elements. I have given them fairly verbose IDs to make their function obvious for the purposes of the example. At the moment, all of the <div> elements just sit in order in the normal document flow, as shown on the left hand side of **Figure 20.6**. The right hand side of **Figure 20.6** shows what we are aiming to do.

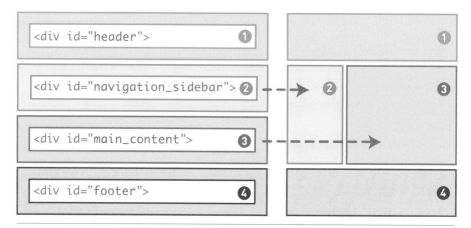

Figure 20.6: The transformation we are looking for—a single column of <div> elements to a header, two columns and a footer.

So how do we do this? The next section explains how.

Floating the columns

The CSS we will discuss in this section is found in the section marked by the *Laying out the page* flag in the floats_clearing2.css file. I have added a number of bits of padding and margin throughout the style sheet to mark out the content boxes more clearly, and neaten the examples up a bit, but you should just concentrate on this section for now.

I have kept the styles very simple in this example, so we can concentrate on the layout. Feel free to take my templates and use them in your designs!

Resource // CSS flags

CSS **flags** are a way of marking sections of your CSS file so that they are easier to search through, especially large files. This is not part of the official CSS spec, just a trick devised by designers that makes clever use of comments. If you look through my files, you will see that some of them contain comments (flags) to make it clear what each section of the CSS does. These are fine if you have an idea of what the flags say (for example, searching for words like *layout* or *image* is often a good bet), but you can also go one step further and add a unique sequence of characters at the start of each of your flags that will never appear in any of your rules (such as =|=), and that can be searched for to cycle through the flags. You could put a comment at the start of the file to say what the search string is. For more information, read Doug Bowman's classic article "CSS Organization Tip 1: Flags," found at http://stopdesign. com/archive/2005/05/03/css-tip-flags.html.

The first rule in this section sets a fixed width for the wrapper—it will always be this width, however much the browser window is resized:

```
#wrapper {
    margin: 0 auto;
    width: 960px;
}
```

Next, we give the header a background colour so we can see the area it covers:

```
#header {
    background-color: #aaaaaa;
}
```

Tip: When you are creating or debugging a layout, it is useful to set a solid background or border on all your elements so you can see exactly where the boundaries of the blocks lie, and work out fixes more easily. You could also use the outline property, which works in exactly the same way as border, except that it sits on top of the layout and doesn't take up space. Some people think this is better because it doesn't affect the layout in any way.

Next, we give the sidebar a percentage width to fix how far it will extend across the wrapper, and float it left so that it comes down to the side of the main content:

```css
#navigation_sidebar {
    width: 29%;
    float: left;
    background-color: #cccccc;
    margin-bottom: 20px;
}
```

At this point we have a problem, as the main content will spill down underneath the sidebar when it reaches the bottom of it. To stop it doing that, we use the following rule, which sets a left margin on the main content larger than the width of the sidebar, so the sidebar is all forced over to the right in a uniform column. In other words, we leave some space free that the navigation can float comfortably into:

```css
#main_content {
    margin-left: 30%;
    background-color: #cccccc;
}
```

The last rule has a clear rule set on it, to make sure the footer stays under the rest of the content:

```css
#footer {
    clear: both;
    background-color: #aaaaaa;
    height: 50px;
}
```

The final result looks like **Figure 20.7**.

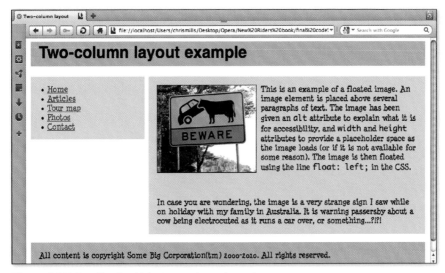

Figure 20.7: Our fixed-width, two-column layout.

Alternative two-column layout with liquid column and faux-columns

The above layout is fine, but what if you want to vary the width of the content as the browser changes width? And what if you want the navigation column to appear to be the same length as the content column? My second example (see floats_clearing3.html / floats_clearing3.css) is very similar from the outset, but the differences quickly become apparent.

The wrapper width is set as a percentage of the body width, so that the content will adjust as the browser is resized:

```
#wrapper {
    margin: 0 auto;
    width: 90%;
    min-width: 700px;
    background: #aaaaaa url(faux_column.png) repeat-y 0 0;
}
```

In addition, a new property—`min-width`—is used to set a minimum width for the content. This is because if the main content goes too narrow, the paragraphs will spill into the navigation menu, making the design fall apart.

You can also use `max-width` to set a maximum width, and `max-height` and `min-height` to set a maximum or minimum height for a content box. Just be aware that these properties are not supported in IE6 or 7. Also be aware that if users resize just the text—e.g. with an older browser like Internet Explorer 6 or with a user stylesheet—the layout will break as the content spills out. It is better to not set fixed heights unless you can control the amount of content in the columns at all times.

The most interesting part of this CSS rule is the `background` property. This is the **faux-columns** part. Faux-columns is a very popular technique, documented in many articles (such as Dan Cederholm's classic "Faux Columns" article at http://www.alistapart.com/articles/fauxcolumns/).

The idea is that you fake it, making it look like the different columns are the same height by applying a background image to the wrapper `<div>` that sits behind the columns and defines the column space. The image is set to tile vertically so it will always reach the bottom of the whole content, regardless of how long each column is.

Next, let's look at the rules for the two content columns:

```
#navigation_sidebar {
    width: 150px;
    float: left;
}

#main_content {
    background-color: transparent;
    margin-left: 23%;
}
```

The sidebar has a fixed width. The main content however doesn't have any kind of width set on it—it will therefore take up whatever horizontal width is left between the right of the sidebar and the edge of the browser window, until the minimum width is reached, in which case the edge of the window will start to cover up the content. The main content has a left margin set on it, as before, so it leaves space for the navigation.

This example looks like **Figure 20.8**.

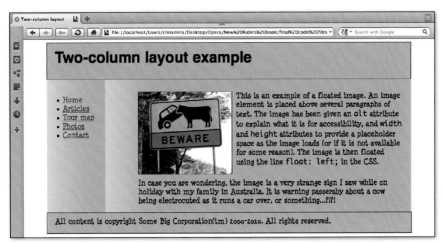

Figure 20.8: My simple faux-columns example.

Try it yourself!

I have deliberately kept the faux-columns example very simple so it is easy to see how it works. I'd like you to create a similar two-column example with much prettier columns, using the faux-columns technique.

A three-column layout

To round off this chapter, I will show you how to extend the last example to create a three-column layout. This is actually pretty simple, although you need to remember to adjust the widths of the columns so that they will all fit in the space without the layout breaking.

In my final example—*floats_clearing4.html* / *floats_clearing4.css*— I have added a third content column `<div>` with an ID of *adspace*. The CSS rules to lay out the content are as follows:

```
#wrapper {
    min-width: 780px;
}

#header {
    background-color: #aaaaaa;
    height: 60px;
}

#navigation_sidebar {
    width: 130px;
    float: left;
    background-color: #cccccc;
}

#main_content {
    width: 60%;
    float: left;
    background-color: #cccccc;
    margin: 0 20px;
}

#adspace {
    width: 130px;
    float: left;
    background-color: #cccccc;
}

#footer {
    clear: both;
    background-color: #aaaaaa;
    height: 50px;
}
```

All the columns are floated to the left. The sidebar and advertising columns are given a fixed width, and the main content column has no width set, and therefore fills up the remaining space like before. The three-column example looks like **Figure 20.9**.

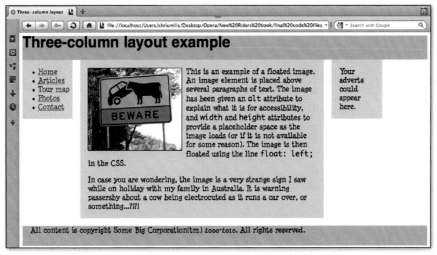

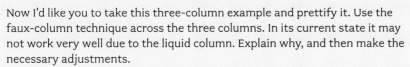

Figure 20.9: A three-column layout, with two fixed-width side columns and a liquid main column.

Try it yourself!

Now I'd like you to take this three-column example and prettify it. Use the faux-column technique across the three columns. In its current state it may not work very well due to the liquid column. Explain why, and then make the necessary adjustments.

A last word about float layouts

You'll probably agree that this chapter has been rather more complex than the last few, but not to worry—floats for layout is among the most complicated of CSS topics. If you don't get it at first, go through the examples again a few times and things should become clearer.

Resource // Float guidance

When you start to experiment with your own layouts, you will inevitably find that some slightly odd behaviour rears its ugly head. Keep experimenting, and look at the following resources for further examples and guidance:

- Floatutorial by Russ Weakley: http://css.maxdesign.com.au/ floatutorial/

(continues)

Resource // Float guidance

(continued)

- CSS float theory: http://www.smashingmagazine.com/2007/05/01/css-float-theory-things-you-should-know/
- HTML Dog page layout: http://htmldog.com/guides/css advanced/layout/
- Quirksmode—clearing floats: http://www.quirksmode.org/css/clearing.html
- Westciv—floated layout: http://www.westciv.com/style_master/house/tutorials/quick/floated_layout/index.html

Try it yourself!

Create a page that looks like a newspaper:

1. Include multiple columns of text.
2. Include a header with an appropriate title, price, date, and edition number.
3. Include an image and float the text around it.
4. For extra street cred, use a web font or two to make the example look more newspaper-like. You should at least choose a nice font for the main heading.
5. Research and create a similar layout using CSS tables.
6. Research and create a similar layout using the CSS3 multi-column layout module.
7. Write blog posts about your work.
8. Check out the layout of the pages on the *Chez Sous Le Vent* case study site. Study how it works, and write a blog post about it.

Summary

In this chapter we have covered floats and clearing, looking at basic usage and purpose, and then going on to look at some more advanced examples of float usage. Multiple column layouts and faux-columns will likely be an often-used tool in your CSS toolbox, so practise these techniques often.

In the next chapter, we will look at another important set of CSS layout properties as we embark upon a study of **positioning**.

CHAPTER 21
Positioning

by Chris Mills

Having conquered the menaces of floats and clearing in the last chapter, we will now turn our attention to the second advanced layout-related topic you should be familiarising yourself with: **positioning**. This feature of CSS allows you to take elements out of the **normal document flow** (i.e., where they are placed by default before any CSS is applied to them) and shift them left, right, up and down, putting them somewhere else entirely. This is useful for a variety of layout purposes, such as multiple column layouts, putting captions on photographs, keeping a feature such as a menu or heading in the same position on the screen regardless of how much the browser is scrolled, and more.

In this chapter, we will look at practical examples of such techniques while exploring positioning.

In this chapter you have the opportunity to **Try it yourself!** *with the convenient sample code downloads found on the book's companion website*—http://interactwithwebstandards.com.

Positioning basics

There are four types of positioning:

1. `static`: The default if no positioning is applied—this simply lays out the element as normal, in the document flow. We therefore don't need to discuss this one much further. You'd use this value to override positioning that has been set earlier in your style sheet.

2. `relative`: This places the element where it would normally sit in the document flow, but then positions it somewhere else—relative to its normal position—depending on the movement values you give it.

3. `absolute`: This takes the element completely out of the document flow (so elements above and below it will appear next to one another as if the positioned element didn't exist), and then positions it relative to the sides of the closest positioned ancestor element (parent, parent's parent, etc.). This is normally the `<body>` element, although as you'll see later you can set it to anything you want.

4. `fixed`: This takes the element completely out of the document flow, just like `absolute` positioning, but instead of being positioned relative to the nearest positioned ancestor element, it is positioned relative to the browser window itself, meaning that the element will always stay in the same position on screen, no matter how much you scroll the contents.

The way you apply positioning is simple. You use the `position` property on the element you want to position:

```
img {
    position: relative;
}
```

You then use the `left`, `right`, `top` and `bottom` properties to specify where you want to position it:

> **Tip:** It doesn't make sense to specify `top` and `bottom` properties at the same time, or `left` and `right`.

```
img {
    position: relative;
    left: 150px;
    top: 150px;
}
```

With relative positioning, the values specify how far away the element should be placed from the left and top edges of the element's *original* position. (The other types work in a slightly different way, as you'll see below.) The effect is something like **Figure 21.1**.

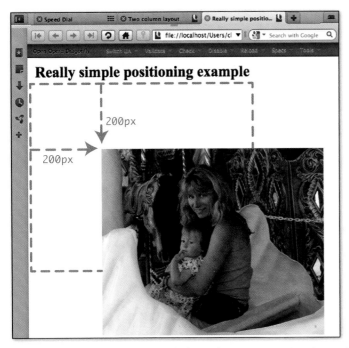

Figure 21.1: A simple example of what relative positioning does, with the original position of the element illustrated for clarity.

Tip: You can use any CSS units you like for specifying positioning values. Note also that you can use positioning on inline and block level elements.

With the basics covered, let's look at each type of positioning in turn.

Relative positioning

With position: relative; you can offset the affected element's position from its normal position in the document flow by the amount you specify (**Figure 21.2**). The movement values you set (using top, bottom, left, right) offset the box relative to the current position of the element you are moving, although they might work in the opposite way to what you'd expect, as these properties refer to the side of the element you are pushing against to move it, not the direction of movement. So, to:

- move the element right, you set a positive value for the left property (or a negative value for the right property).

- move the element left, you set a positive value for the right property (or a negative value for the left property).

- move the element up, you set a positive value for the bottom property (or a negative value for the top property).

- move the element down, you set a positive value for the top property (or a negative value for the bottom property).

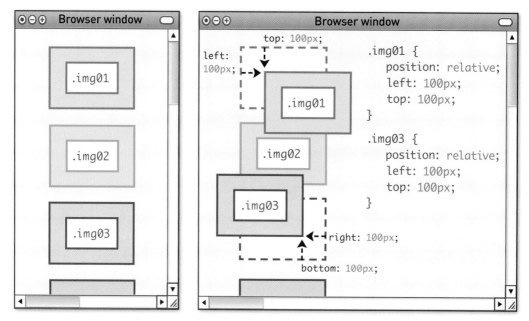

Figure 21.2: A relatively positioned element is offset from its original position in the document flow by the values you specify.

This does seem a bit counterintuitive to begin with, but you soon get used to it.

Bear in mind that the element's location in the document structure remains the same—moving its position is purely a visual effect.

So what is this useful for? Well, you will find it very useful if you want to offset the position of certain elements for the purposes of the design (while retaining the space that the element would normally occupy and preserving the document flow), as I've done with the images and heading in `relative_positioning1.html`, which you can download from `http://interactwithwebstandards.com`. It is a simple single column with paragraphs and images, but I have used relative positioning to shift elements to the left, creating an interesting "out of the box" type effect, which wouldn't be achievable by manipulating padding and margins. The relevant rules look like so:

```
h1 {
    font-family: Futura, Helvetica, Arial, sans-serif;
    margin-top: 0;
    position: relative;
    right: 150px;
    width: 26em;
}

img {
    border: 2px solid black;
    position: relative;
    right: 4em;
}
```

Relative positioning is used to shift the right hand edge of the images and heading over to the left, resulting in the effect seen in **Figure 21.3**.

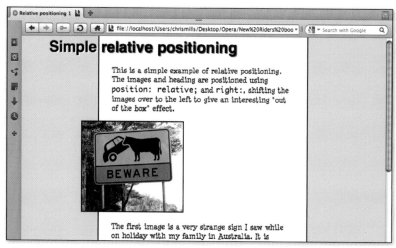

Figure 21.3: Relative positioning is being used to move the images and heading over to the left for a nice "out of the box" effect.

Try it yourself!

1. Do some research on the Interwebs and try to find some good uses of relative positioning.

2. Write these up in a blog post, and discuss them with your classmates/teacher/colleagues.

3. Refer to the Web as *The Interwebs* for a whole day. This comedy affectionate term is bound to annoy the more serious of your coworkers or teachers.

4. Create an example using relative positioning similar to my own, above, but using your own design and content.

Absolute positioning

Absolute positioning works pretty differently to relative positioning, but it isn't really any more complex. When you set position: absolute; on an element, it is taken completely out of the document flow, so it effectively takes up zero space—elements below it nudge up to fill the gap. The top, bottom, left and right values you include specify the element's distance from the four respective edges of the nearest positioned ancestor element (usually the <body> element). See **Figure 21.4** for an illustration of this.

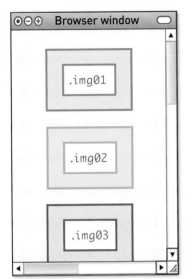

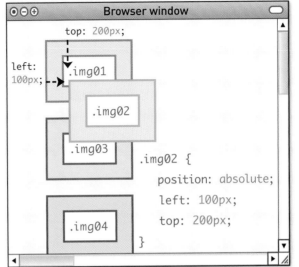

```
.img02 {
    position: absolute;
    left: 100px;
    top: 200px;
}
```

Figure 21.4: An absolutely positioned element is taken out of the document flow, and positioned a set distance away from the sides of the nearest positioned ancestor element. Now `.img02` takes up no space in the document flow, therefore `.img01` and `.img03` now sit right next to each other on the page.

Let's look at an example. We'll create a two-column layout similar to the ones from the last chapter, but using absolute positioning instead of floats—check out `absolute_positioning1.html` on the companion website, `http://interactwithwebstandards.com`. This is a simple layout with a header, footer, menu and main content column. Without positioning, it looks like **Figure 21.5**.

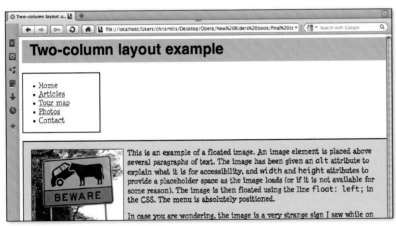

Figure 21.5: The makings of a two-column layout, but we're not there yet.

First of all, let's try absolutely positioning the navigation menu:

```
#navigation_sidebar {
    width: 200px;
    background-color: #ffffff;
    border: 2px solid black;
    margin-bottom: 20px;
    position: absolute;
}
```

This gives us the result shown in **Figure 21.6**.

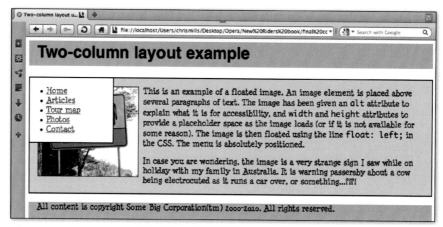

Figure 21.6: Oops—we now have a navigation menu sitting on top of our content.

Setting position: absolute; on our menu has taken it out of the document flow, so the main content has jumped upwards to fill the gap. But there is no space for the menu and we haven't told it to go anywhere else, so it just sits there on top of the content.

To deal with this, we will set some padding on the left hand side of the content, bumping it over to the right a bit to give the menu some room, and set top and left values on the menu to move it down and right a bit, nicely into position:

```
#navigation_sidebar {
    width: 200px;
    background-color: #ffffff;
    border: 2px solid black;
    margin-bottom: 20px;
    position: absolute;
    top: 113px;
    left: 38px;
}

#main_content {
    background-color: #cccccc;
    border: 2px solid black;
    padding-left: 25%;
}
```

This works nicely—the finished layout is shown in **Figure 21.7**.

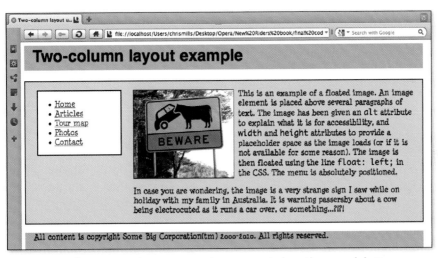

Figure 21.7: The menu and content now have space to breathe—much better.

Try it yourself!

1. Create a sample web page similar to this example, and have a go at using positioning to turn it into a two-column layout.

2. Add another column containing some content, and adjust the design so that you end up with a three-column layout.

3. Add a vertical border between each of the side columns and the main content column. Remember that all three columns are floated, so the wrapper element's height has collapsed to zero.

Making positioning occur relative to elements other than <body>

As mentioned earlier, absolute positioning occurs relative to the nearest positioned ancestor element, which is usually the <body> element but will change if an element further down the hierarchy has positioning set on it. This means that—rather usefully—you can absolutely position any element inside its parent by setting position: absolute; on that element and another type of positioning on its parent.

This is useful—some would say essential—for fine-tuning layouts of various website features, especially intricate layouts of, for example, content boxes or navigation menu items.

Figure 21.8: Adding captions below our images.

Let's look at a basic example to show you what I mean. We'll return to the first example in the chapter and put inset captions on top of the images (check out absolute_positioning2.html in the code download at http://interactwithwebstandards.com for the finished example from this section). First of all I'll add the caption text in paragraphs below the images, as shown in **Figure 21.8**.

We obviously need to position these somehow, but relative positioning is no good for the captions—we don't want big gaps left beneath our images where the captions used to sit. Absolute positioning is what we need here!

But this creates a complication: by default, absolutely positioned elements are positioned relative to the <body> element. Because the images and captions are at different positions inside the <body>, I would have to set different vertical positions for all the captions, and give them all different ids to apply these with. This doesn't sound so terrible for two images, but think of the scalability—what if our site got popular, and we ended up with thousands of images and captions, all positioned in the same way?

To solve this problem I will first add an identical wrapper <div> around each image/caption pair:

```
<div class="image_wrapper">
<img src="weird_sign.jpg" alt="A very strange sign we
saw on holiday in Australia, of a cow being electrocuted
as it runs a car over, or something." width="240"
height="205">
<p class="caption">Weird cow sign</p>
</div>
```

Then I will take the relative positioning off the images, and instead relatively position the image wrappers:

```
.image_wrapper {
    position: relative;
    right: 4em;
}
```

Lastly I'll style the captions. I've set the text size a bit smaller than the standard paragraph font, and given it a border and background. Then we get to the interesting part: absolute positioning is used to position the captions right in the bottom-right hand corner of the images.

```
.caption {
    font-size: 80%;
    border: 2px solid black;
    background-color: white;
    width: 110px;
    height: 17px;
    position: absolute;
    top: 174px;
    left: 130px;
}
```

Figure 21.9: The final result.

The captions are now being positioned relative to the image wrappers, not the <body>, because relative positioning has been put on the #image_wrapper <div>s, which are the parents of the captions. Since the images are all the same size, I can now move all the captions the same distance horizontally *and* vertically to get the desired effect, which requires fewer ids, and fewer calculations. This gives us the final result shown in **Figure 21.9**.

Resource // Internet Explorer bugs

Another good thing about using positioning over floats inside positioned elements is that it sorts out quite a few Internet Explorer bugs. IE8's CSS support is actually very good, but previous versions did very strange things to floats and sometimes positioning. Internet Explorer's layout was controlled by a property called hasLayout, and layouts often failed when dealing with elements that didn't have this property set to yes. Setting positioning on an element does this automatically.

For more about Internet Explorer layout bugs and hasLayout, read the fantastic "On having layout," by Ingo Chao and others—http://www. satzansatz.de/cssd/onhavinglayout.html. Also check out "Explorer Exposed!" at http://www.positioniseverything.net/explorer.html.

Try it yourself!

1. Using a similar technique to the one discussed in this section, create a navigation menu that uses a single unordered list with eight list items, but has them placed in two rows of four. Use a nice background image for the menu "buttons."

2. Research Internet Explorer 6 float and positioning bugs, and write a blog post about them.

Fixed positioning

Now we have got to the final part of the chapter, covering fixed positioning. `position: fixed;` positions elements in a similar way to `position: absolute;` taking them out of the document flow. The difference is that instead of positioning them relative to the nearest positioned ancestor, it positions them relative to the browser window, so they will always stay in the same position inside the window regardless of how much you scroll the page (**Figure 21.10**).

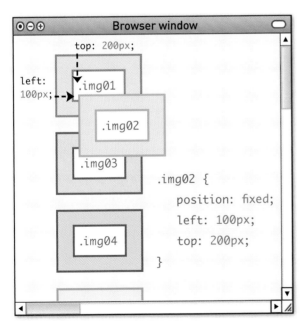
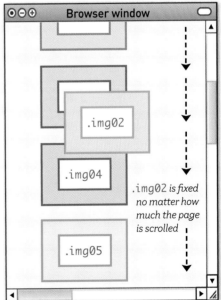

Figure 21.10: Fixed positioning fixes the position of an element relative to the browser window, so now `.img02` will always stay in the same place, no matter how much you scroll the content.

Fixed positioning is very useful for some great effects, but it isn't supported in Internet Explorer 6 and below ;-(

Figure 21.11 shows a good use of fixed position—this is a screenshot of http://www.hicksdesign.co.uk/journal, the blog of designers Jon and Leigh Hicks. The right-hand navigation has been positioned using position: fixed;, so it will always stay in the same position. Check the page out yourself, and subscribe to the Hicks's RSS feed— there's some great content on it.

Figure 21.11: A good use of position: fixed;—http://www.hicksdesign.co.uk/journal.

Let's try to create something similar. I will take the last example and add a navigation menu on the right hand side that always stays in the same position when the page is scrolled. I will also fix the position of the header so it does the same thing. You can see the finished example by loading up fixed_positioning1.html from the code download at http://interactwithwebstandards.com.

Making initial changes to the HTML

To make this design work, I had to make a few changes to the HTML. I first put the header inside its own <div>, outside of the main content wrapper:

```
<div id="header">
  <h1>Simple fixed positioning</h1>
</div>
```

It needs to go outside as I want to scroll the rest of the content underneath this, and I want to stretch it over the whole width of the <body>. CSS is then used to get this the way I want it looking:

```
h1 {
    font-family: Futura, Helvetica, Arial, sans-serif;
    margin-top: 0;
    padding-top: 0.6em;
    padding-left: 0.6em;
    text-shadow: 2px 2px 2px #94d7e3;
}

#header {
    height: 100px;
    background-color: #00A6B9;
    width: 110%;
    margin-top: 0;
}
```

The next thing to do is add in the navigation menu, at the top of the main content:

```
<div id="navigation_menu">
    <ul>
        <li><a href="#">Home</a></li>
        <li><a href="#">Articles</a></li>
        <li><a href="#">Tour map</a></li>
        <li><a href="#">Photos</a></li>
        <li><a href="#">Contact</a></li>
    </ul>
</div>
```

Figure 21.12 shows how this currently looks.

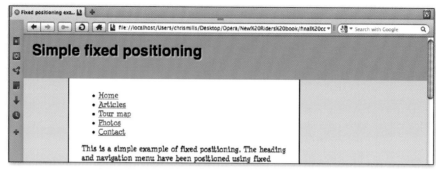

Figure 21.12: Our new additions, near the beginning of the project.

I also added some extra content at the end of the page, to give you some more space to play with the scrolling effect.

Fixing the header and menu position

The next step is to fix the positions of the header and menu. This was done via the following rules:

```
#header {
    height: 100px;
    background-color: #00A6B9;
    width: 110%;
    margin-top: 0;
    position: fixed;
}

#navigation_menu {
    position: fixed;
    top: 5.5em;
    left: 36.5em;
}
```

There is not much to explain with the first rule—the #header rule has simply had a position: fixed; declaration added to it; we don't want to change the position of it at all—we just want it to be fixed in place.

With the `#navigation_menu`, things are a bit more complicated. I've added `position: fixed;` to it, but I've also used `top` and `left` to make sure that it is positioned in the right-hand column.

This gets the elements in the position we want them, but there are a couple of problems (**Figure 21.13**). For a start, setting the header and navigation to have `position: fixed;` takes them out of the document flow, so the top of the content starts off hidden underneath the header! Second, when you start to scroll the content upwards, you'll see that the images actually go over the top of the header!

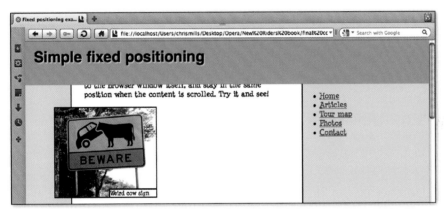

Figure 21.13a: Our content starts off hidden.

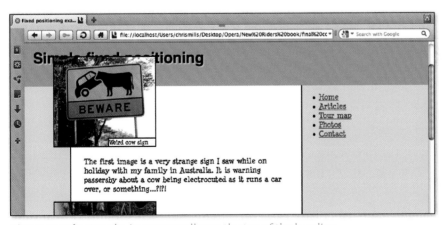

Figure 21.13b: Now the images scroll over the top of the heading.

CHAPTER 21

To start off, let's tackle the content overlapping problem. This is easy to solve—I've added an ID of #first to the first paragraph of the content, and given it top padding to shift it downwards so it starts below the header:

```
#first {
    padding-top: 100px;
}
```

Now we'll address the image problem. This brings us nicely on to the subject of **z-index**. "What on earth is z-index?" I hear you cry. Read on, brothers; read on, sisters…

Understanding z-index—the third dimension

As this is a pretty advanced topic that you'll only really run into when dealing with positioning, it is only natural to cover it near the end of the book. If you thought that HTML and CSS web pages were two-dimensional, then you wouldn't be completely accurate. In fact, different elements sit at different depths to one another, closer and farther away from your nose as you look at the screen; the z-axis, as it were. We are still talking about flat bits of content, but the order in which they're put on the screen (the source order in the HTML) determines which overlaps which by default.

To explain this in a bit more detail, positioned elements (including relatively positioned elements) are rendered within something known as a **stacking context**. Elements within a stacking context have the same point of reference along the z-axis. You can change the position along the z-axis—also known as **z-position** or **stack level**—of a positioned element using the z-index property.

z-index takes a positive or negative integer as a value—the higher the integer, the closer the element to your nose. The default value is auto, which means the element will have the same stack level as its parent. You should note that you can only specify an index position along the z-axis—you can't make one element appear 19 pixels behind or 5 centimetres in front of another! Think of it like a deck of cards: you can stack the cards and decide that the ace of spades should be on top of the three of diamonds.

Setting a really high z-index value will not cause your web pages to poke your site visitors in the eye.

If you specify the z-index as a positive integer, you assign it a stack level in front of other elements within the same stacking context that have a lower stack level. A negative integer value for z-index assigns a stack level behind the parent's stack level. When two elements in the same stacking context have the same stack level, the one that occurs later in the source code will appear on top of its preceding siblings. The browser draws the elements on the page starting from the one with the lowest z-index, going up to the one with the highest z-index.

There can in fact be up to seven layers in one stacking context, and as many different z-indices in those layers as you want, but don't worry—you are unlikely to have to deal with seven layers in a stacking context. The order in which the elements (all elements, not only the positioned ones) within one stacking context are rendered, from back to front, is as follows:

1. The background and borders of the elements that form the stacking context.
2. **Positioned descendants with negative stack levels.**
3. Block level descendants in the normal flow.
4. Floated descendants.
5. Inline level descendants in the normal flow.
6. **Positioned descendants with the stack level set as auto or 0 (zero).**
7. **Positioned descendants with positive stack levels.**

The bold entries are the elements whose stack level we can change using the z-index property.

Tip: To clarify—z-index doesn't actually make the content look bigger or smaller—closer or further away. It just dictates how content will overlap where different block-level elements appear in the same position on screen. The element with the highest z-index value will appear right on the top of the pile—nothing will cover it over.

Going back to our example, to cause our images to behave and stay behind the header, we just need to set a higher z-index value on the header:

```css
#header {
    height: 100px;
    background-color: #00a6b9;
    width: 110%;
    margin-top: 0;
    position: fixed;
    z-index: 3;
}
```

This has solved our problems (**Figure 21.14**).

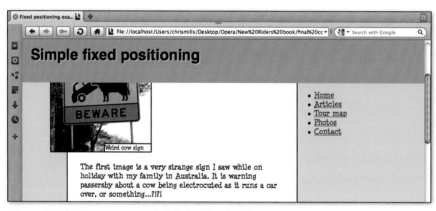

Figure 21.14: Now our example is behaving itself.

Adding extra refinements

There are a couple of other features in the code that I haven't yet covered, so let's go over these now. First, I have given two of the navigation menu list items a class of shifted:

```html
<ul>
    <li><a href="#">Home</a></li>
    <li class="shifted"><a href="#">Articles</a></li>
    <li><a href="#">Tour map</a></li>
```

```
    <li class="shifted"><a href="#">Photos</a></li>
    <li><a href="#">Contact</a></li>
</ul>
```

I then apply a rule to these to slightly displace them to the left, using relative positioning:

```
.shifted {
    position: relative;
    right: 10px;
}
```

I've also decided to style the menu items a bit more by removing the bullets and colouring them a silvery-gray colour:

```
#navigation_menu li a {
    color: gray;
}

#navigation_menu li {
    list-style-type: none;
}
```

This creates the effect seen in **Figure 21.15**. As I've mentioned a couple of times now in the chapter, this combination of positioning inside positioning can be used to create some very precise irregular layout/design features. As always, the best way to find out what is possible is to experiment with these techniques!

Figure 21.15: A jaunty navigation.

The second is somewhat of a hidden treasure. To find it, try narrowing the browser window slowly but surely. If you are using Firefox, Opera or Safari, eventually you'll see the change documented in **Figure 21.16**.

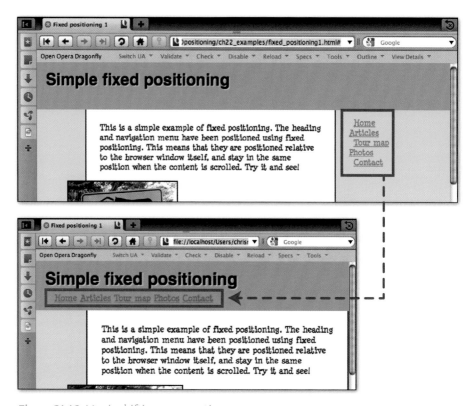

Figure 21.16: Magic shifting menu action.

This is due to the fact that I have implemented a CSS3 media query at the bottom of my CSS:

```
@media all and (max-width: 760px) {

  #navigation_menu {
    top: 2.6em;
    left: 0em;
    z-index: 4;
    min-width: 600px;
  }

  #header {
    min-width: 600px;
  }
```

```
#navigation_menu li {
    display: inline;
}

#navigation_menu li a {
    color: grey;
}

.shifted {
  right: 0px;
}

}
```

This is a CSS3 feature that allows you to selectively apply CSS rules depending on whether a certain criterion is met. In this case, the above block says "If the browser width goes below 760 pixels, apply the rules inside the @media block."

Resource // Media queries

Media queries exist inside their own module of the CSS3 spec. They are basically super-powered media types. Rather than just saying "apply this CSS if the page is being viewed on screen, or printed out," you can set more specific conditions, such as if the page is a certain media type and has a certain screen width, screen height, resolution or aspect ratio. To use one, you insert an @media block into your CSS, like so:

```
@media all and (max-width: 760px) {

    ...

}
```

You place all rules that you want to be applied if the conditions are met inside the brackets. It is really cool to be able to create such dynamically changing layouts using only CSS, whereas in the past this was only possible using complicated JavaScript. And this kind of approach becomes all the more powerful on small-screen devices, where narrow viewing areas can really benefit from an optimised layout.

This feature is supported on desktop and mobile versions of Opera, Firefox, and Safari, and although it hasn't reached Internet Explorer yet, it is well worth starting to use these now, to optimise layouts in browsers that do

(continues)

Resource // Media queries

(continued)

support them. Those that don't yet support them will just silently ignore those rules, and therefore should still display fairly usable content in most cases.

To find out more about media queries and what other conditions can be tested, check out the media queries specification at http://www.w3.org/TR/css3-mediaqueries/.

Try it yourself!

1. Write a blog post about z-index and how it works.

2. Use z-index in conjunction with the :hover pseudo-class to create a "card deck" design in which the cards sit in a stack, and each one comes to the top when you mouse over it.

3. Write a blog post about the different conditions that media queries can test for as written in the CSS3 spec, and what browsers support right now.

4. Write a three-column layout example that uses a media query to change into a single column layout when viewed with a mobile browser that supports them, such as Opera Mobile, Opera Mini, or the iPhone Webkit browser.

5. You'll need to use max-device-width instead of max-width to make your media query work on mobile. Why is this?

6. Have another look at the Chez Sous Le Vent case study site and think about how you could further improve it using the techniques discussed in this chapter. For example, how about adding a media query to make it work better on mobile devices, or adding some kind of useful fixed position feature?

Summary

In this chapter I have covered positioning, one of the hardest concepts to grasp in CSS. Not only that, but I've also sneaked in some words about z-index and media queries for an extra special crunchy treat. If you don't understand all of this the first time around, don't worry—you'll get it soon. If you *did* get it all the first time round, you're already approximately 31.67854 percent of the way towards being a CSS ninja.

Resource // Recommended readings

- Position is Everything
  http://www.positioniseverything.net/

- Five Simple Steps to Designing Grid Systems
  http://www.markboulton.co.uk/journal/comments/five-simple-
  steps-to-designing-grid-systems-part-3

- Faux Absolute Positioning
  http://www.alistapart.com/articles/fauxabsolutepositioning/

- Revised Image Replacement
  http://www.mezzoblue.com/tests/revised-image-replacement/

- Sitepoint CSS Reference
  http://reference.sitepoint.com/css

Ottawa, Canada

Derek Featherstone is internationally known as an inspiring speaker,
creative web developer, and User Experience practitioner specializing in
accessibility. In 2000, he founded Further Ahead, whose team provides
accessible web design and development, UX consulting, and training
courses on all aspects of web accessibility. They recently relaunched
Simply Accessible, a home for their accessibility work.

http://boxofchocolates.ca
http://furtherahead.com
http://ironfeathers.ca
http://www.simplyaccessible.com
http://twitter.com/feather

CHAPTER 22
Accessibility Intro

by Derek Featherstone

Web accessibility refers to the practice of making websites usable by people of all abilities and disabilities. When sites are correctly designed, developed, and edited, we provide the opportunity for all users to have equal access to information and functionality.

The foundation of web accessibility is in human rights and moral obligation. The Web should not discriminate based on a user's abilities. The Web was built on this idea, as stated by the creator of the World Wide Web, Tim Berners-Lee:

> *The power of the Web is in its universality. Access by everyone regardless of disability is an essential aspect.*

Accessibility is an important issue. It deserves very special mention—it needs to stand on its own, as a topic to emphasize. At the same time, it is integrated into every other part of this book. It is part of every topic. It touches everything because it is something that has an impact on *people*—the very reason we want to build websites and applications in the first place. We build them to stand the test of time and to allow all people to participate fully in society. We make them accessible to people of all abilities.

While I have written these chapters on their own as a special topic, you'll find that many of my colleagues have covered some aspects of accessibility in their chapters too. That's OK—these topics are important and worth repeating, and reading them in different ways will help you understand them better, so that you are better equipped to create sites that are exemplars for accessibility. You'll also find that here, in these few chapters on accessibility, we're opening the doors to something much larger. In fact, accessibility is a far-reaching topic that has inspired entire books.

For the purposes of this book, we want to give you enough accessibility knowledge to do two things: 1) create websites and applications that take into account a variety of accessibility needs, and 2) inspire you to reach out and learn more about how accessibility considerations can be incorporated into your work.

So here's what I hope to give you that isn't included in the other chapters:

- An overview of **what accessibility is**, what it isn't, and where the lines between accessibility and usability blur.

- Detail on the characteristics of *people's* **different accessibility needs**, what they mean for how they use computers and the Web, and what that means for us as designers and developers.

- Discussion of **techniques** that work in real life for people with disabilities, complete with some of the pitfalls of implementing techniques that "should" provide more accessibility.

- A detailed look at the **testing tools and tactics** you should employ as a developer or designer to ensure that whatever you are building is accessible.

Understanding accessibility

We all know how frustrating it can be to use a website or application that, for whatever reason, just doesn't work. Have you experienced that with a website you've used lately? Think about it, and let that feeling sink in.

Deeply. Take it to the point where you want to pull your hair out, smash your head against the wall, or throw your computer out the window.

Feeling it?

Now, imagine that feeling magnified by a factor of ten. Or a hundred. Literally. How much more frustrating would it be for you to use that website if you weren't able to see it? Or could only see a small part of it? Or could only type one character every 3 seconds? Or were using the site by dictating voice commands to a computer that, for some unknown reason, cannot interpret what is on the screen correctly?

This is the experience that millions of people with disabilities feel every day when using their computers. Of course, there are varying degrees of frustration—sometimes it may simply be that the site does something annoying like use JavaScript to indiscriminately erase the work that you had done, or maybe it is more complex and frustrating like not allowing you to click on something that you can see on the screen, or perhaps it is something bigger like taking a process that could be completed in one step and turning it into four. In any of these cases though, the lack of "user-friendliness" can be magnified by disability.

Our goal is to ensure that all people can use our websites. As designers and developers we must all remember that every person's abilities lie somewhere on a spectrum from able to do something effortlessly to not being able to do something at all, and everywhere in between.

We can't emphasize this concept enough. Accessibility is not binary, all-or-nothing, black and white. We have every shade of grey in between. How you view this point frames everything that you learn and do about accessibility.

Generally, we think of four key areas when we consider accessibility.

Visual impairment

This can range from complete blindness, to low vision, to colour blindness.

Mobility or dexterity impairment

People may face more severe mobility challenges such as paraplegia/quadriplegia, cerebral palsy, or multiple sclerosis, or they may have difficulty with fine motor control due to arthritis, Parkinson's disease, or simply old age.

Auditory impairment

Someone who has total or partial hearing loss may have great difficulty accessing the content on specific types of websites.

Cognitive impairment

This is the least well-understood issue in web accessibility, ranging from severe learning disabilities to low literacy or numeracy skills, dyslexia, and cultural and language differences. There is incredible range of ability in this area. This makes it more difficult to understand and accommodate in our work.

Try it yourself!

Now that you're thinking about these different types of impairments, take a few moments to think about how not having a particular ability would change your use of a website. What would the Web be like for you if you couldn't see or hear, or had difficulty using the mouse. What would you miss? And are there ways that you would be able to get around those issues?

Make note of it. Blog it, or talk about it with your peers. Do you know anyone who has a disability? Ask them how they use the Web—you may be surprised at what you learn!

What accessibility is

For the purposes of this book, I'm going to limit most of our discussion of accessibility to its impact on people with disabilities, though in reality the reach of accessibility is much farther. As you gain more experience as a web designer or developer, you'll find that many of the concepts and techniques we use for accessibility have a positive impact on people *without* disabilities.

Have you seen "curb cuts" in the sidewalk? You know—the areas near a pedestrian crosswalk or other edges of the sidewalk where there is a built-in ramp to allow people in a wheelchair or using a walker or motorized mobility scooter easy access the sidewalk. They are there for people with disabilities, but many others find them useful too: parents with a baby in a carriage, movers delivering heavy goods that need to use a wheeled cart, even skateboarders and in-line skaters all take advantage of these curb cuts every day.

We must remember, though, that the existence of the curb cut is *first and foremost* for people with disabilities.

As you read these next chapters, keep your eyes out for areas of overlap— where what we're doing for accessibility has additional benefits for other groups. But always remember: the primary reason for creating accessible websites is to ensure access to people with disabilities.

Universal design

If accessible design is the process of creating objects, physical spaces and digital media that are accessible and easy to use for people with disabilities, then universal design is the practice that embraces the idea that designing for accessibility really entails providing better design for everyone. The focus in accessible design tends to be on people with disabilities whereas the focus in universal design is on everyone with a full spectrum of ability.

The concept of universal design seems to have evolved from "barrier-free design" but has additional characteristics: a focus on being accessible and on appearance (http://en.wikipedia.org/wiki/Universal_design).

Universal design also has its limits. There are a few things that we do for accessibility reasons that only benefit people with disabilities. We might add hidden text to provide extra context to screen reader users because they have a very specific need that can't be met with other parts of the design. We would provide versions of videos that offer sign language — something that only benefits people who are deaf or hard of hearing and who also communicate via sign language. In these areas, universal design doesn't quite fit. Those additional features do not benefit anyone else.

Philosophical debates aside, in the digital world this is generally how most experienced practitioners approach accessibility. We want to create beautiful designs that are also accessible. In the past, a typical but less than desirable solution was to provide an "accessible version" of a website. These tended to be seen as "lesser versions" that didn't have the same appeal as the original site. Over time, the accessible versions were rolled into the main site, eliminating the need for a different version that served to propagate the myth that accessible design is ugly.

In reality, it is inaccessible design that is ugly.

Usability

In the first part of this chapter we talked about the frustration that we feel when websites don't work. Something that "doesn't work" generally has some type of usability problem. When websites don't work the way we expect them to, or are difficult to understand, or are filled with processes that are anything but easy, we have a usability problem—a problem that is magnified by accessibility issues.

Usability and accessibility are very tightly intertwined—so much so that some people suggest that they are one and the same. If you ask anyone who has worked with people with disabilities for some time, they are likely to tell you that they work on user experience or usability with groups of people that have a specialized set of needs.

There is no clear line where accessibility stops and usability starts. You need both for a person with a disability to be able to use your website or application. If it isn't accessible, then it can't be usable. It may be accessible, but it still may not be usable.

What accessibility isn't

We've outlined what accessibility is. Now let's turn to what accessibility isn't. During your professional career, you will learn of other areas that are related to accessibility, but aren't accessibility.

Search engine optimization (SEO)

The practice of search engine optimization (SEO) has traditionally been viewed as employing coding, design, and writing techniques that aim to place your websites and content at or near the top of search engine listings. SEO has a long history, and some of its techniques have been criticized. Unethical SEO campaigns have employed techniques to try and "game the system"—to appear at the top of search listings when they don't really deserve to. This topic is something that is best left to other books. For a refreshing perspective on search engine optimization, read Shari Thurow and Nick Musica's *When Search Meets Web Usability* (New Riders, 2009). My favorite quote?

> *Search engine optimization is not optimizing a website for search engines. Rather, SEO is optimizing a website for people who use search engines.*

The reason this comes up in accessibility circles is that often we'll hear that the world's biggest blind user is Google. Let's get something straight:

- Google isn't a user. It is not a person.
- Google isn't blind. It can't be.

The analogy can be powerful when talking to your boss or manager to get them to take notice and to justify the accessibility techniques that you'll use when building websites. Don't fool yourself, though. The bottom line is that many of the techniques that we employ for accessibility's sake also happen to be good for search engine optimization. But, like curb cuts, these techniques are primarily to ensure access for people with disabilities. The fact that they also help with SEO is secondary and a wonderful additional benefit.

Design for mobile environments

The mobile web has exploded and will continue to grow.

As with search engine optimization, there are many features of accessible design that provide additional benefit for mobile environments. Accessible design focuses on simplicity, and ensuring that we have well-structured websites. Attention to detail in these areas for the sake of accessibility also benefits people who are using the mobile Web on their web-enabled mobile phones with older browsers or more modern smart phones.

CHAPTER 22

> **Tip:** For more detail on the crossover between mobile and accessibility see "Web Content Accessibility and Mobile Web: Making a Web Site Accessible Both for People with Disabilities and for Mobile Devices" from the World Wide Web Consortium at http://www.w3.org/WAI/mobile/.

Interoperability

Interoperability is the general principle that our websites should work on any device, with any browser (user agent), on any computer platform (Linux, Windows, Mac OS). In the 1990s we experienced the browser wars—when Netscape Navigator was the most widely used browser on the Web and Microsoft's Internet Explorer was in a significant minority. Frustrated with the way that different browsers rendered web pages, designers and developers began the practice of placing statements like "Best viewed in Netscape" or "Best viewed in Internet Explorer" on their web pages. It became a fragmented Web. You needed one tool to view website A and another to view website B because of the way those sites were written and tested—to work only in that browser.

In large part, this was due to a lack of consistent implementation of standards. Netscape Navigator interpreted HTML, CSS, and JavaScript in one particular way and Internet Explorer interpreted them in another.

Seeing the futility in this, Jeffrey Zeldman cried out to all of us "To Hell with Bad Browsers" (http://www.alistapart.com/articles/tohell/) and the road to consistent implementations began. We won't chronicle that entire history here, but the bottom line is that we now have much better standards implementations. This means that if you write code that works in standards-based, modern browsers, there is little that needs to be done to ensure that it works in other environments. We certainly don't need to write a version of our site for Netscape and another for Internet Explorer.

Yes, the principle of interoperability is related to accessibility. They are not, however, one and the same. Making sure that your web pages work in all browsers, on all platforms, on all devices, is about ensuring interoperability and has very little to do with disability. Think of it this way: If a site doesn't work for someone on the Linux platform, for example, does it matter if that person has a disability or not? No, it doesn't. If it doesn't work for someone because they're using Linux, it has nothing to do with that person's abilities.

> **Tip:** We haven't once said that building accessible websites is about making your website compatible with any particular type of assistive technology. We don't want to make JAWS-friendly sites or sites that work particularly well with Apple's VoiceOver screen reader. Our aim is to follow well-established principles that aren't targeted towards any particular assistive technology.

Summary

There you have it—a brief overview of accessibility and what's in store for you as we move through this section.

Next we'll dive into more detail to see who accessibility really is about, and the different types of accessibility-specific hardware and software that help make the Web accessible for all people.

CHAPTER 22

CHAPTER 23
Accessibility Helps

by Derek Featherstone

It sounds corny, but the best way to describe the people who have accessibility needs is that they are people, just like you and me. They use their computers to do online banking and buy birthday gifts.They write or purchase books. They record, edit, and watch movies, music or other multimedia. They connect and stay in touch with friends on Twitter, Facebook, LinkedIn, or other social networking sites. We have to understand that people with disabilities are the same as each of us.

People first

They may use different tools like customized keyboards or mice or may have specialized software that helps them accomplish the things they want to do. But ultimately, they want to get the same things done that we do, be it work, play, or something else entirely.

This sounds like a very simple way to put it, but it sets the stage and the tone for how we need to approach the topic of web accessibility. Why? Because if we understand a person's motivations, needs, and goals, we can better understand how to provide them with a great experience on the Web.

Understanding this helps us evaluate what we produce not in terms of physical characteristics that a person may have or not have, but in terms of a fundamental need to achieve something.

Resource // People First Language

When we're talking about people with disabilities, we should use People First Language. We don't talk about a blind person. We refer to them as a person who is blind. Simple really: put the person first. For more detail on People First Language see:

http://en.wikipedia.org/wiki/Disability#People_First_Language

In the last chapter we talked briefly about four key types of disabilities. Remember? We want to do our very best work to provide a website that works for everyone, regardless of any visual impairment, mobility or dexterity challenges, auditory impairment, or cognitive difficulties.

Let's look at each of these in a bit more detail. Now, prepare yourself—as we go through this section, we are going to ask you to take the time to think about what it would mean to you if you had some of the physical, sensory, or cognitive challenges that we explore.

Visual impairment

Visual impairment encompasses a wide variety of physical characteristics. A person may be colourblind and therefore not able to accurately perceive differences in certain colours or colour combinations. For a variety of reasons, a person may have a visual acuity of somewhere between 20/60 and 20/160 (considered to be moderate low vision) or more drastic, ranging to the 20/1,000 range (considered to be severe or profound low vision). At the extreme, visual acuity of less than 20/1,000 vision (no light perception at all) is considered total blindness.

Notice that when we're talking about visual impairment, we're not just talking about a binary scenario? It isn't simply a case of someone being able to see or not being able to see—quite literally, it isn't "black or white" but includes all shades of grey in between.

Typical causes of low vision include cataracts, glaucoma, age-related macular degeneration, retinitis pigmentosa, and diabetic retinopathy. At the end of the day, they all have a similar effect: reduced vision.

At its simplest, a person can be born totally blind, or blindness may occur over time as a person progresses through various stages of low vision.

Resource // Visual acuity

There are a wealth of resources and detail on visual acuity (essentially, clarity of vision) and varying degrees of low vision and causes in Wikipedia and other online resources:

1. Eye Health and Research, National Eye Institute (USA):
   - http://www.nei.nih.gov/
2. Low vision:
   - http://en.wikipedia.org/wiki/Low_vision
   - http://www.lowvision.org/
3. Visual Acuity:
   - http://en.wikipedia.org/wiki/Visual_acuity

So, what does all this mean, then, for what you do as a web designer or developer?

What it means is this: A person who is blind can use a computer but they can't see the screen. They can't see the colours you've chosen. They can't see the words that you've typed. They can't see the beautiful imagery you have selected to create emotion, atmosphere, or a certain "feeling."

That does sound a bit scary, doesn't it? Both from the perspective of that person and from yours. What can you do for them if they can't see? Rest assured, they can get access to the text you've written using the tools available to them. Read on and you'll learn more about those tools.

Think about that for a minute. What would your interaction with a computer be like if you couldn't see at all?

What would you experience if couldn't distinguish between red and green? Or yellow and blue? Or couldn't perceive colour at all?

Finally, think about what this means for someone with low vision who needs to have the computer screen magnified in order for them to see anything? What does it mean for someone who experiences "tunnel vision" from retinitis pigmentosa, or whose vision is partially obstructed by diabetic retinopathy?

When we first arrive at a web page, we tend to quickly scan the page to see what it is about. Someone with low vision may only see a small portion of the screen at a time, making it more difficult to visually scan the page.

CHAPTER 23

Try it yourself!

There are many different aids and simulators that help you understand what it might be like to have low vision. Several online stores offer low-cost cardboard glasses that you can use for every day activities to get a sense of what living with low vision might be like. Search for low vision simulation glasses and you're sure to find them.

For an online experience, use WebAIM's Low Vision Simulation found at: http://www.webaim.org/simulations/lowvision.php

You'll experience a variety of issues here and it will help you get a sense of how low vision can impact computer use.

How on earth would those people use computers? Right. As we said at the beginning of the chapter, they use computers just like we do. They just have an extra set of tools to help them along.

Mobility or dexterity impairment

When we think of **mobility impairment**, often the first thing to come to mind is a person in a wheelchair. This has very little, if any, effect on the ability of that person to use a computer. What we're interested in here are scenarios where there is an impact on computer usage.

So, who might that be?

- Someone who has limited movement in their arms.
- Someone who may have the use of only one hand.
- Someone who has difficulty controlling fine movements.
- Someone who experiences trouble holding on to a mouse.
- Someone with a tremor or shake in their hand.

Yes, all of them, and more. Notice that the situations we've described above don't mention any specific reason or disability? If you didn't notice, go back and read them again. They are all scenarios with multiple causes.

Someone who can only use one hand may have had a hand amputated, may have had a stroke, or may have very severe Carpal Tunnel Syndrome. Someone who experiences difficulty controlling fine movements might include someone with cerebral palsy, someone with Parkinson's disease, or perhaps someone with severe arthritis.

Our job is to ensure that we take all of these types of scenarios into account when we're building our websites.

How do these people use computers? Similarly to people with some form of vision impairment, we have a range of hardware and software that helps get the job done—not just used for interfacing with the Web, but interfacing with the computer in general.

Try it yourself!

If you'd like to experience a little difficulty controlling the computer yourself, use one of my favourite tools: an oven mitt.

(continues)

Try it yourself!

(continued)

Put on the oven mitt, and try to control your computer. Browse the Web. Use a web application. Clicking, double clicking, fine movements all become more difficult and frustrating.

Want to experience something else? Try filling in forms with the use of just a single finger. Take it a step further and determine exactly how you might type capital letters, or use shortcuts like Cmd + X on a Mac or Ctrl + X on Windows or Linux—shortcuts that require you to press two keys at once!

Auditory impairment

For years, "people" have made the argument that the Web is a visual medium and that, therefore, our biggest challenges in accessibility exist for people who are blind. Recent years show that the Web is much more than a visual medium.

Look at the success of YouTube, skyrocketing sales of iPods, and sales of content from the iTunes stores. We're becoming consumers of much more than visual content. The Web and the content that we deliver via the Web is more and more about appealing to all of the senses. Video isn't really the same without audio, is it?

Exactly.

And that's the situation that people who are deaf are faced with. Sure, they may be able to watch a video, but what if they can't hear it? Does the video lose its meaning?

What about podcasts or audio interviews? That content that is delivered over the Web presents a challenge to people who can't hear it. It isn't insurmountable, but a challenge nonetheless.

Try it yourself!

Unplug your speakers or turn down the volume. Then go listen to a podcast or watch some YouTube videos.

Can you understand the content?

Was there some type of alternative available for the video or the audio?

CHAPTER 23

Much like visual impairment, there isn't a simple on/off switch for hearing either. People who have partial hearing are often described as "hard of hearing" and have difficulty hearing sounds at certain decibel levels.

Hearing loss may range from mild or moderate to severe or profound. Someone with mild hearing loss may not have much difficulty hearing audio and their hearing may be augmented with hearing aids. Someone with more profound hearing loss may not be able to hear very much at all and must rely on other means of communication such as lip-reading or sign language.

A person who was born deaf may have a different understanding of language than someone who lost their hearing later in life. The "grammar" of sign language is very different than that of American Sign Language (ASL) or other variants like Australian, British, or other Sign Language. Though this has more impact on comprehension of language and text, it is still an issue that we must attempt to address when building our websites.

Cognitive difficulties

If you thought there were shades of grey in visual, mobility, or auditory impairment, wait until you see what is in store for you in the land of the cognitive disability!

When we talk about cognitive impairment we generally mean that something has an impact on the functions of the brain. That "something" may be physiological characteristics of a person's brain, genetics, or it may be due to some type of trauma or injury. There is an enormous range of "conditions" or medical diagnoses that result in cognitive impairment. Look at the following list of clinically oriented terms that you may have heard—each of them with implications for web professionals.

Tip: This is not an exhaustive list of all the scenarios or diagnoses that have an impact on the way in which a person uses the web or their computer. Treat this very much like an introduction to some of the reasons behind the characteristics that we need to account for in our designs.

- **Dyslexia** often results in difficulties with reading and/or speech. Reading can be slower or inaccurate as the person skips words or reads out of order, or experiences difficulty determining the meaning of what they are reading.

- **Autism** may result in difficult social interaction, impairments in communication, and repetitive behaviours.

- People with **Down Syndrome** often have lower-than-average cognitive abilities, and may have delayed development of fine motor skills.

- **Attention Deficit Disorder (ADD)** is characterized by inattentiveness, hyperactivity, and impulsive behaviours.

Did you notice anything about that list? Go through it again and remove the references to the "diagnosis" and read just the end result.

Reading can be slower or inaccurate. Difficulty determining meaning of what they are reading. Difficult social interaction or repetitive behaviours. Delayed development of fine-motor skills. Inattentiveness, hyperactivity, and impulsive behaviour.

Even without the reason behind them, we still see characteristics that have an impact on the way in which people behave or use the computer.

And that's entirely the point when we're looking at cognitive impairment: It isn't the exact diagnosis that matters. It is the functional characteristics that show themselves that are of real interest to us as people that build websites.

Instead of worrying about every possible diagnosis, we can worry about a handful of characteristics. Most cognitive impairments have an impact on one or more of the following functional areas:

- **Memory-related** issues include both the short-term and long-term memory. A person may have difficulty remembering how they arrived at a particular page on your site, or may have difficulty remembering the steps they've already completed in your signup process, for example.

- **Problem-solving** abilities are a critical component for any transactional website. We use these skills all the time to determine what an interface asks of us, what options are available and what we should do next. Someone with difficulties in this area may be prone to making more mistakes or decisions that lead to errors.

- **Attention deficits** tend to result in confusion or distraction from the task at hand. Busy web pages that don't focus on the specific goals of the user can be problematic.

- **Reading, linguistic, and verbal comprehension** difficulties occur for many reasons, including those that aren't disabilities, per se. Someone who is not fluent or a native speaker of the language of the website will encounter similar issues to those with verbal comprehension issues when trying to understand longer passages of text that includes jargon. The person may simply be overwhelmed by large amounts of text, have difficulty reading certain phrases, or may not easily understand how the words they are reading fit into the bigger picture of the paragraph, article, or website as a whole. They may require the use of images to support the verbal content on a page.

- **Math comprehension** has a potential impact on a website, particularly for transactional and e-commerce websites. In the not-so-distant past we used to see order forms on websites that required the user to calculate tax, shipping, and order totals on their own. Someone with difficulties with math would face a significant challenge.

- **Visual comprehension** can also present challenges to people when we present our websites in an overly visual way. Some people have difficulty with spatial orientation or understanding the significance of colour as it relates to the design of your site. You may know someone who can understand written directions to get to an appointment much more easily than they could understand a map to get to the same location. This person may simply have a preference for written directions, but take this to the extreme and we see people that simply can't process that visual information in the same way that they can verbal.

Notice the areas of conflict in that list? Some of the issues that help people with one particular challenge don't help people with others. For example, someone with verbal comprehension issues needs visual aids and graphic representations of concepts to help them understand. On the other hand, someone with visual comprehension issues requires a more verbal explanation.

How do we build websites that cater to both?

The guiding principle that we should use is one of balance. Think of a website that is completely visual on one extreme and one that is completely textual on the other. As you design, find a middle ground that provides simple, clear text that supports, and is supported by, graphic elements. Think back to the brief discussion on Universal Design. Here is a case where providing complementary elements for accessibility reasons actually helps everyone—even people without disabilities.

They say that a picture is worth a thousand words. Some people need the thousand words, some people need that picture, and some people need both.

Assistive technology and tools

We've covered the four main types of disabilities and how they impact a person's use of their computer and the Web. Hopefully, while you were reading you asked yourself some big questions: How do we build sites that take into account all of these differences in ability? What do I have to do to make sure that I'm not closing doors to people with disabilities?

We'll get there.

But, before we do, we need to look at one more crucial part of the equation. We've outlined the challenges that people with disabilities face when using our websites. Now we need to take a look at the tools that they use to make their lives easier.

Assistive technology is a term used to describe a set of tools that a person with a disability will use to help them interface with their computer. That's it. Nothing more, nothing less. These tools generally fall into two categories: hardware and software.

Hardware

The hardware available to help those with accessibility needs is as varied as the population it serves.

Touch screens, head- and mouth-wands, switches, customized single-handed keyboards, keyboard overlays, large and easy-to-use mice, and trackballs are all tools that someone with mobility or dexterity impairments may use. Why? Their difficulties aren't in being able to see or hear or understand. Their difficulties are with the *operation* of the computer.

Another set of customized keyboards exists for people with cognitive impairments. They employ large, high-contrast keys with very clear function labels—think of a magnifying glass or flashlight to represent search, or an image of a house for going to the Home page via keyboard instead of having to remember an obscure set of keystrokes.

Try it yourself!

Time to try some different technology on for size! Research at least three alternative commercial keyboards or mice. What needs do they meet? How do people use them?

To explore this even more, look up your local college or university centre for students with disabilities. They are very likely to have a range of different hardware for you to examine—you'll be amazed at what you see. Take it to the next step and arrange for a demonstration to see how the hardware works with the software you'll learn about in the next section!

Software

All operating systems that run on your computers have settings built in that provide accessibility options to the people using the computers. These settings allow a person with a disability to more easily operate their computer, and therefore work online.

For those with visual impairment, the operating system will provide the ability to customize colour schemes for those who are colour blind, or they will allow a person to enter "high contrast" mode where the background and foreground colours are reversed for someone who has low-vision.

Another feature to help those with low-vision—the operating system provides the ability to increase font size and icon size, and set the resolution of your graphics card, allowing you to set fonts to be twice the normal size and set a desktop of 800 pixels by 600 pixels on a 27-inch monitor. Windows and Mac OS X both include screen magnifiers by default as well—software that magnifies the entire screen or portions of it.

For people who are completely blind, most operating systems include a built-in screen reader—a part of the operating system that literally reads out the screen to the user as they use their keyboard to navigate around the screen. Windows, Mac OS, and Linux-based operating systems all include these pieces of functionality by default. Windows, for example, uses a component called Narrator, Mac OS X includes VoiceOver, and many Linux distributions include the ability to speak content natively or with additional packages. While Narrator doesn't have near the functionality of a full screen reader, it does allow for content on the screen to be read out to someone. It provides at least marginally more accessibility and may be more useful to a person with cognitive difficulties than it might be to someone that is blind.

Try it yourself!

Narrator and VoiceOver are tools that are focused on visual impairment. Take a look at your computer and research its accessibility features that help people with other types of impairments.

To get started, research "sticky keys" on Windows, the magnifier on Windows or Mac OS X, the on-screen keyboard available on any operating system, and visual alternatives to the noise alerts that most computers make when an error occurs.

Many of these operating-system-level accessibility features will help more than one group of people. For example, the screen reading component may have a primary use for people with visual impairment, but may also be useful for people with reading difficulties. Hearing text read out to them in combination with trying to read it themselves may make the text much easier to understand. Built-in operating system voice and command recognition, like that found in Windows, might also be of use to anyone with a mobility or dexterity impairment.

Given the variety of individuals in this world, it should be no surprise to you that the needs of everyone can't be met with the simple tools built into the operating systems. In the web world, we view websites through a browser. Those browsers also have accessibility features built into them, including the ability to resize text, create custom colour schemes, turn images off, or create your own styles to override the web author's suggestions.

The Opera browser, for example, includes an incredible array of keyboard functionality that makes access for people who must use a keyboard much easier.

In addition to browsers, many third party free and commercial software packages exist to help people achieve full access to their computers.

These include screen readers (JAWS, Window-Eyes, Supernova, Orca, and many others) for visual impairment; screen magnifiers (ZoomText, Magic, Lunar, and others) for low-vision; voice recognition software (Dragon Naturally Speaking, MacSpeech Scribe, and others) for those with mobility/dexterity impairment; and software such as Kurzweil 3000 that works as a learning, reading, and writing aid for people with comprehension difficulties.

This is not an exhaustive list, by any means, but it will help you get started in understanding the nature of accessibility and the tools that people use to get their jobs done.

Summary

You now have a sense of the types of people that we're working for when we strive to build accessible websites and applications. We want to be sure that we do as much as we can to enable them to accomplish the tasks that they want to complete, regardless of their disabilities.

In the next chapter, we'll take a look at the definitive resource available to help you plan, design, and build for the web. We'll examine a set of tools that will help you test your work to ensure that you're hitting the mark.

CHAPTER 24
Accessibility Testing

by Derek Featherstone

How are you feeling so far with your journey through the world of accessibility? *Overwhelmed* is a word that people often use to describe how they feel when they start looking more deeply into accessibility issues. If you feel that way, fear not. You are not alone. Accessibility seems to be one of those cases where the more you know, the more you know you don't know. Each time you learn something, you're taken down a pathway with many turns and dead ends. You sometimes feel like you're not getting anywhere. The bottom line?

There's too much to know!

We've spent the last two chapters talking about how people with disabilities use their computers and the Web. Hopefully, you feel like you know a bit more about some of the challenges that people with various types of disabilities feel when they interact with the websites and applications that we build for them.

You should also be asking a lot of questions at this point, the biggest of which is "What does all of this mean for me?" You want to know more about how to ensure accessibility. As we said in the first chapter on accessibility, you've seen pieces of that throughout this book.

When you looked at HTML images, you saw that they needed `alt` text to ensure that people who can't see have a way to get some representation of what is in the image.

When we looked at forms, you learned of the form `<label>` that ties a form control to the text associated with it that also allows for a larger clickable area for someone with motor-control issues.

When we looked at multimedia like audio and video, we saw that we need to provide a transcript and captions for people who can't hear.

We also saw strategies for ensuring that we have a solid semantic structure for documents. This helps break content into more manageable chunks—a critical component for people who have learning or cognitive difficulties.

All of these techniques help to ensure that we create accessible websites. Do they take into account all possibilities? They can't. Shouldn't we be testing with people with disabilities to ensure that we're providing an accessible site to everyone? Absolutely! That is, perhaps, an ideal we should work toward, but it would be impractical to test for every possible effect of every coding and design decision we make on every possible disability. We cannot know everything there is about disability and its impact on web usage. As we said at the beginning of the chapter, there's too much to know!

Web Content Accessibility Guidelines (WCAG 2.0)

Because there is too much for any one person to know, and because we know that not everyone gets the chance to test their designs with people with disabilities, we rely on guidance from others. We can't possibly know everything about user behaviour for every type of disability. Many have stood before us and studied accessibility, how people with disabilities use the Web, and how they interact with their assistive technology.

We need not reinvent the wheel.

When we are building sites and applications, we turn to the most widely recognized guidance available: the World Wide Web Consortium's (W3C) Web Content Accessibility Guidelines (WCAG). The most recent version of these guidelines was released as an approved W3C standard in December 2008 and was designed to stand the test of time—whether we are building HTML-based websites, creating PDF documents, Flash or Silverlight content, or something that hasn't been invented yet.

Resource // A world of accessibility guidelines

Many countries have their own guidelines in place to govern accessibility for the Web for their government sites and businesses. In the United Kingdom we have the Disability Discrimination Act (DDA). The United States has Section 508 of the Rehabilitation Act. Government of Canada websites are subject to the Common Look and Feel requirements, which include accessibility. The Province of Ontario in Canada has the Accessibility for Ontarians with Disabilties Act. The Australian Government Information Management Office (AGIMO) announced that all Australian government agencies will be required to meet WCAG 2. In March 2009, New Zealand adopted WCAG 2 as its standard for accessibility.

Ultimately, almost all of the legislation for each country or even region is based on WCAG to some degree. The W3C maintains a list of policies on accessibility at http://www.w3.org/WAI/Policy/

CHAPTER 24

While many view WCAG as a simple checklist for compliance with accessibility guidelines, it is much more. In addition to detail about requirements and techniques, it also serves as a set of principles that should guide your development. In fact, that distinction is important: this isn't a set of things to check after you've built your site; it is a set of principles that you should be familiar with *before* you start building.

There are four main principles in the Web Content Accessibility Guidelines. These are broken down further into 12 main guidelines for your work. They provide the basic objective for each area of accessibility. Within each guideline, there are several "success criteria." These provide detailed, testable statements that help you to 1) build your websites and applications, and 2) test to make sure that you've provided an accessible solution. Each success criterion states a level of conformance (A, AA, or AAA, with A being the lowest level of accessibility and AAA being the highest). Providing a site that meets the Level A success criteria meets the basic need for accessibility. A site the meets Level AA fulfills additional accessibility criteria. A site that meets Level AAA meets as many needs as possible based on the existing guidance available.

Along with the testable success criteria, you'll find other documentation and guidance to help you to understand the intent of the success criteria and techniques that can be used to satisfy them. Use this additional documentation to help you understand more about the need for accessibility and to discover techniques to provide accessible solutions.

Resource // Guidelines

The main guidelines can be found at `http://www.w3.org/TR/WCAG20/`

Additional useful information can be found in the supporting documents:

- Understanding WCAG 2.0: `http://www.w3.org/TR/UNDERSTANDING-WCAG20/`
- How to meet WCAG 2.0: `http://www.w3.org/WAI/WCAG20/quickref/`
- Techniques for WCAG 2.0: `http://www.w3.org/TR/WCAG20-TECHS/`

Guiding principles

Building accessible sites is founded on four key principles, designed to help us provide an accessible experience to the main types of disabilities we discussed in Chapter 23, "Accessibility Helps," (visual impairment, auditory impairment, mobility or dexterity impairment, and cognitive impairment). Each principle relates to what you've been learning in the rest of this book. Yes, that's right, we've been teaching the fundamentals of what you need to know for accessibility all the way along. Sneaky? Maybe. Effective? We hope so!

With that, here are the brief details on each of the four main principles and their associated guidelines.

Principle 1: perceivable

Information and user interface components must be presentable to users in ways they can perceive.

This ensures that people who have difficulty with their senses—sight and hearing, in particular—can have access to the content.

Your goals for creating content that is perceivable are summarized in the following four guidelines from WCAG 2.0:

1.1 Provide text alternatives for any non-text content so that it can be changed into other forms people need, such as large print, Braille, speech, symbols, or simpler language.

This guideline requires a text alternative for anything that isn't in a text format. Why? Text is incredibly flexible and can be transformed into many other formats such as Braille, large print, and others as mentioned in the guideline. This flexibility means that text-based content is more readily able to meet the needs of everyone. Contrast this with non-textual content such as images, video, and audio. These formats are "fixed" and only available through one sense. Providing an alternative for an image, video, audio, or other form of content removes that barrier—allowing everyone to access the content.

1.2 Provide alternatives for time-based media.

This guideline focuses on the "time-based" aspect of media, meaning that we're interested in providing some type of alternative for the content in cases where timing is important. These include content that is audio only, video only, audio and video, or any of these combined with interaction.

There are different requirements for providing an alternative based on whether the content is pre-recorded or live. Consult the guidelines for the full details. What does this really mean? In a nutshell, the alternative we provide must reflect the content completely. For example, we need to provide a transcript for our podcasts or other audio recordings and captions and audio description for pre-recorded videos. There are many other requirements, depending on the level of conformance you are aiming for (Level A, AA, or AAA). A sign language alternative for audio content would be required, for example, to reach level AAA. As you can imagine, providing sign language versions for all of your content may have significant financial requirements and be beyond the level of conformance your project requires. Remember, a signed version is a level AAA requirement. It definitely helps with accessibility but might not always be required.

1.3 Create content that can be presented in different ways (for example, simpler layout) without losing information or structure.

This guideline is similar to Guideline 1.1 in that its purpose is to ensure that content is flexible enough so that it can be transformed and presented in ways that are optimized for a particular person. You have heard this before: we must write our web pages such that we keep our structure and presentation separate. Doing so means that users can specify their own presentation (with a custom style sheet, for instance) and still make sense of the content because it is specified in the semantics of the document through the use of headings, lists, and other HTML markup. When the presentation changes, the relationships found in the content can still be determined.

We don't want any of our content to be tied closely to a particular presentation format, whether it is visual layout, audio, or otherwise. We don't want to rely on any single particular presentation ("the fields on the left are required" or "one beep indicates your answer was correct, two beeps indicates it was incorrect") because the person may not be able to perceive that presentation. They could, however, get that information if it was provided in a way that didn't *rely* on that presentation and other mechanisms were available to provide the same meaning ("the first five fields in the form in the left column are required," or "a checkmark and one beep indicate that your answer was correct; an error icon marked 'error' and two beeps indicate your answer was incorrect.") The very nature of the Web allows someone to override the presentation that you suggest. Providing content that doesn't rely on any single presentational attribute helps ensure that we're enabling everyone to perceive the content we create.

1.4 Make it easier for users to see and hear content, including separating foreground from background.

While the other guidelines in this section are about providing alternatives for content so that they can be perceived by anyone, this guideline is about ensuring that the content can be perceived *as easily as possible*. This means that we want to choose colour schemes that allow for enough contrast between the foreground and background so that text can easily be read, choose colour combinations that aren't easily confused by people with common forms of colour blindness, and ensure that audio and/or video foreground sounds are sufficiently louder than background noises.

Principle 2: operable

User interface components and navigation must be operable.

This ensures that everyone, regardless of the devices they use to operate the computer (mouse, keyboard, switch, voice recognition, or any other input devices) or how accurately they can manipulate them, can use the interface.

The next four guidelines from WCAG 2.0 help to ensure that what we create is operable:

2.1 Make all functionality available from a keyboard.

This is one of the most critical pieces of accessibility. Quite simply, a person must be able to accomplish all tasks/functionality using only a keyboard. This fundamental requirement allows access to all different types of input devices that emulate keyboard functionality (refer back to Chapter 23, where we examined input devices such as on-screen keyboards, voice recognition software, and others).

2.2 Provide users enough time to read and use content.

Based on what you learned in Chapter 23 about how people with disabilities use the Web—whether using different input devices, a variety of assistive technologies, or having specific difficulties with the act of input itself (think of the person who types by using a mouth wand on an on-screen keyboard)—we have to take into account that people may need more time to read, locate, or understand content or to respond to prompts in a web page.

2.3 Do not design content in a way that is known to cause seizures.

Certain types of content may trigger seizures in individuals with photosensitive epilepsy. Generally we should avoid content that flashes more than three times per second. For further detail, refer to the specific success criteria found at `http://www.w3.org/TR/UNDERSTANDING-WCAG20/seizure.html`.

2.4 Provide ways to help users navigate, find content, and determine where they are.

People with disabilities may require more time or effort to determine what page they're on or how to get around that page. We want to do everything we can to make it easier for users to navigate within a page and between pages as well as make it easy to orient themselves.

Using well-structured, semantically marked up pages goes a long way to help in this regard. Doing so provides headings to help people understand the page's structure. Marking up links and navigation in lists helps to allow people to easily get around the page and understand how many links there are in a navigation bar, for example.

Principle 3: understandable

Information and the operation of a user interface must be understandable.

This ensures that we use the clearest possible interfaces and content so that all people, including those with cognitive disabilities, understand our websites. Understandability encompasses these 3 guidelines from WCAG 2.0:

3.1 Make text content readable and understandable.

We need to ensure that the language in which a web page is written can be determined programmatically (by using the `lang` attribute in the page), that the clearest, simplest terminology is used, and that jargon, abbreviations, and other difficult-to-understand words are defined in the content of the page.

3.2 Make Web pages appear and operate in predictable ways.

The key to this guideline is consistency. Some people's tolerance to changes is less than others', and routines can provide safety and confidence to people with disabilities when using the Web. We don't want to break user expectations nor do we want to "surprise" the user with behaviours that change context—like opening a new window, perhaps? If we do choose to use new windows, we owe it to the people using our websites to at least inform them in advance, or not use popup windows at all unless they make a significant positive contribution to the user experience.

3.3 Help users avoid and correct mistakes.

This guideline asks us to ensure that the expectations are clear for users. Can they easily determine what data should be entered in which form fields? When an error occurs, is it easy for them to understand that there is a problem, and are clear instructions available to correct the error?

Principle 4: robust

Content must be robust enough that it can be interpreted reliably by a wide variety of user agents, including assistive technologies.

This ensures the greatest compatibility possible across browsers, assistive technology and devices from the past, the present, and for the future.

This final WCAG 2.0 guideline ensures that we create a robust solution:

4.1 Maximize compatibility with current and future user agents, including assistive technologies.

The easiest way to meet this guideline is to ensure that the HTML you publish validates. If you validate your HTML, you've written it cleanly and according to the rules of HTML. If you've done that, you've ensured that at a baseline level, your code will be robust and can be displayed properly by user agents such as browsers and assistive technology that have been built with those specifications in mind.

Now that we've taken a tour through the principles and guidelines let's look at actually applying this to your work.

Judgment day

There comes a time when you'll need to determine whether the work you are producing is accessible. In fact, there are numerous times when you need to test your work. Testing for accessibility should not be something that you do at the end of a lengthy development process, rather it should be completed throughout the development lifecycle.

Why?

The earlier you find and correct errors and the earlier you incorporate accessibility into your projects, the less time-consuming it will be. The cost to make changes near the end of a project is astronomical compared to making changes near the beginning.

Resource // Preparing for accessibility testing

The tools and techniques in this section are focused on HTML-based web sites because that is the technology most used on the Web. Remember though, that WCAG 2.0 principles and guidelines are technology-agnostic. Their flexibility allows you to create accessible content with any technology, as long as your implementation of that technology meets the success criteria. Whether you're testing HTML, Flash, Silverlight, PDF, or something else, remember that the success criteria are based on the needs of people with disabilities.

(continues)

Resource // Preparing for accessibility testing

(continued)

WCAG is no longer about using a specific list of techniques that get the stamp of approval for accessibility—it is more about making sure that everyone can easily use what you create. You should always refer to the latest version of "Techniques for WCAG 2.0" (`http://www.w3.org/TR/WCAG20-TECHS`). They aren't mandatory techniques, but they are very informative and provide excellent guidance for ensuring that you're meeting the success criteria in your work and why certain techniques fail the success criteria. This document will be updated as techniques and technology change.

You can avoid costly rework by testing as early in your process as possible. When you're preparing mockups or creative designs for your website you should check the contrast of your colour combinations as soon as possible. The last thing you want is to have someone approve a design that later needs to be changed because the colours didn't have enough contrast.

As you're building your site templates, you should check to make sure that you have used semantic markup with appropriate headers, lists, proper tables where necessary, and employed accurate and useful `alt` text for images.

When you have a functional demonstration version of your website running, you should also ensure that you are able to complete all tasks and functionality with a keyboard only.

The most important tool you need to assess accessibility is your brain. Why? Because you simply must use your judgment in order to determine if the Web page you are building is accessible or not. In this section we'll look at several tools that help you make this determination, but note that these tools cannot make that determination for you. You must interpret what the tools show you. You must think about the intent of the design. You must interact with the web page rather than interacting with the tools. And you must always keep in mind what you learned in Chapter 23, "Accessibility Helps." Users with disabilities actually use and interact with the Web. For the rest of this chapter, we'll take a look at a series of tools and tests that you should begin to employ.

Testing with your browser

All web pages are consumed via a browser. That makes it the perfect tool to test some of the fundamentals of creating accessible websites.

Earlier in this chapter we saw several instances where we talk about people being able to adapt and bend web pages to more closely fit their needs. One such instance is text size. Some users need to resize text so that it is easier to read. In the section on text sizing in Chapter 13, "Headings and Paragraphs," we learned that we should avoid fixing text size to a pixel value in order to allow users to resize the text to meet their needs.

This user need is found in WCAG 2.0 as part of Success Criterion 1.4.4 that states, "Except for captions and images of text, text can be resized without assistive technology up to 200 percent without loss of content or functionality."

In practical terms, that means that you should be able to double the size of the text and not lose any content or functionality—content shouldn't suddenly disappear or links and forms shouldn't stop working properly.

Try it yourself!

Go back through the examples and samples that you've created or review a popular media website. Can you double the text size? Use the Text Size menu item from the View menu in Internet Explorer. If you can't resize the text, then hunt down the culprit—usually fixed font sizes in your CSS. And, in any browser, when you double the text size, do other items on the page begin to overlap one another, obscuring them from view? Does the text wrap to more than one line and suddenly become unreadable? If so, you likely need to get more flexible measurements in your CSS to allow for flexible height containers for navigation, sidebars, or other text.

See how it works? While it may all have seemed like random requirements while you were learning about content being perceivable, operable, understandable, and robust, those guidelines are based on the needs of people with disabilities.

So, be sure to use accessibility guidelines in your work. Review them in detail—we can't cover all of the success criteria here, but we will get you started.

Browser add-ons for testing

Some of my favourite testing tools are browser add-ons. They feature incredible functionality that extends the capability of the browsers to help you easily find accessibility issues.

Chris Pederick's extension for Firefox-the Web Develoiper's Toolbar (`http://chrispederick.com/work/web-developer/`) is not only a great tool for web development, it's useful for testing accessibility too. While it isn't designed specifically for testing accessibility, it includes a suite of tools that make accessibility testing much easier.

In **Figure 24.1**, you can see many useful tools for checking alternative text for images—the toolbar allows you to outline images that don't have `alt` attributes, outline images that have empty `alt` attributes (`alt=""`) or display the `alt` attributes in the page so that you can easily check to see if they are appropriate.

Figure 24.1: The Images options available in Chris Pederick's Web Developer Toolbar.

A very useful feature is View Image Information—a function that opens a new tab in Firefox and shows you all images in the page along with their dimensions, `src` attributes, and `alt` attributes if present. This allows you to easily scan the page to make sure `alt` text is present and is accurate in order to meet Success Criterion 1.1.1 (Non-text content). Remember: A tool like this can only show you whether or not alt text is present. It can't tell you if it is appropriate. You need to make that determination yourself. If an image shows the phrase *Contact Us* but the code shows alt="Comments", we have an accuracy problem.

Another favourite feature for the Web Developer Toolbar is the Disable Styles setting. This prevents the author styles from being used on the page, resulting in a clear view of the underlying HTML structure. This allows you to see headings, lists, blockquotes, and other semantic markup so that you can determine whether the document has a reasonable structure.

Compare **Figure 24.2** and **Figure 24.3**. **Figure 24.2** shows Google's top three search results for the phrase "web standards" with its default look. **Figure 24.3** shows the same page but with the author's styles disabled. Right away you can see that Google has used headings for each search result, and has presented them in an ordered list because this is a ranked list where order matters.

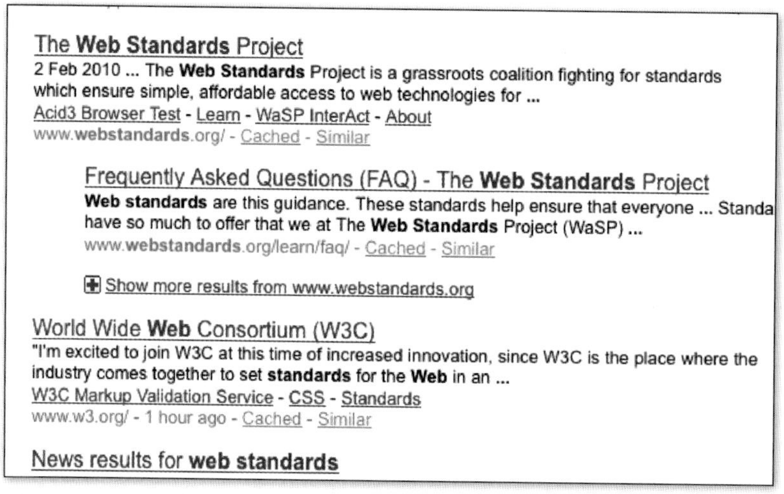

The **Web Standards** Project
2 Feb 2010 ... The **Web Standards** Project is a grassroots coalition fighting for standards which ensure simple, affordable access to web technologies for ...
Acid3 Browser Test - Learn - WaSP InterAct - About
www.webstandards.org/ - Cached - Similar

Frequently Asked Questions (FAQ) - The **Web Standards** Project
Web standards are this guidance. These standards help ensure that everyone ... Standa have so much to offer that we at The **Web Standards** Project (WaSP) ...
www.webstandards.org/learn/faq/ - Cached - Similar

⊞ Show more results from www.webstandards.org

World Wide **Web** Consortium (W3C)
"I'm excited to join W3C at this time of increased innovation, since W3C is the place where the industry comes together to set **standards** for the **Web** in an ...
W3C Markup Validation Service - CSS - Standards
www.w3.org/ - 1 hour ago - Cached - Similar

News results for **web standards**

Figure 24.2: Top three search results for "web standards" with Google's default styles applied.

Compare this view with the same view when the styles are removed (**Figure 24.3**).

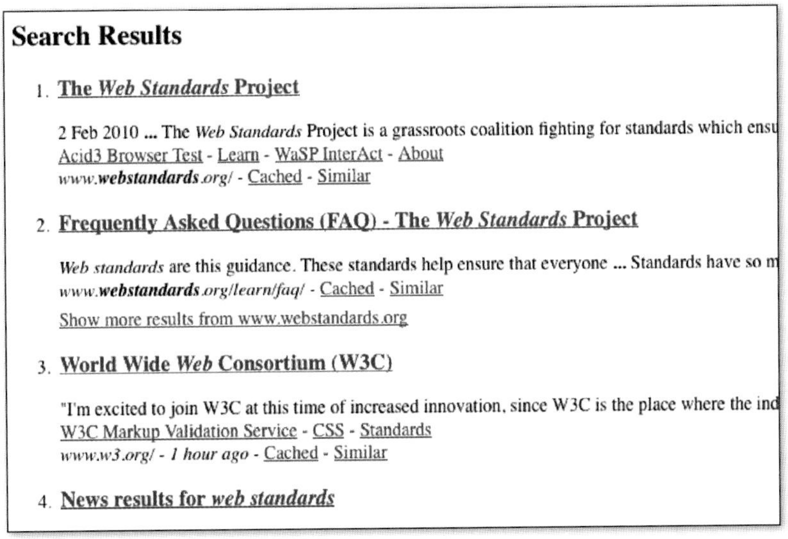

> **Search Results**
>
> 1. **The *Web Standards* Project**
>
>   2 Feb 2010 ... The *Web Standards* Project is a grassroots coalition fighting for standards which ensu
>   Acid3 Browser Test - Learn - WaSP InterAct - About
>   *www.**webstandards**.org/* - Cached - Similar
>
> 2. **Frequently Asked Questions (FAQ) - The *Web Standards* Project**
>
>   *Web standards* are this guidance. These standards help ensure that everyone ... Standards have so m
>   *www.**webstandards**.org/learn/faq/* - Cached - Similar
>   Show more results from www.webstandards.org
>
> 3. **World Wide *Web* Consortium (W3C)**
>
>   "I'm excited to join W3C at this time of increased innovation, since W3C is the place where the ind
>   W3C Markup Validation Service - CSS - Standards
>   *www.w3.org/ - 1 hour ago* - Cached - Similar
>
> 4. **News results for *web standards***

Figure 24.3: Top 3 search results for "web standards" with CSS disabled using the Web Developer Toolbar.

Other accessibility toolbars have similar functionality. Some more popular ones include

- **The WAT Toolbar** from the Web Accessibility Tools Consortium (http://www.wat-c.org/tools/). It includes versions for Internet Explorer and Opera browsers.

- **The AIS Web Accessibility Toolbar** from Vision Australia (http://www.visionaustralia.org.au/ais/toolbar/)

Automated tools

Many of these toolbars also take advantage of automated tools that help you to check accessibility—you'll see these tools in the Web Developer Toolbar, the WAT toolbar, or the AIS toolbar. There are two types of tools in use here: ones that check small pieces of accessibility on their own and ones that run your web page through a number of tests all at once.

Regardless of which tools you use, you need to use your judgment when interpreting the results. Why? We always have to remember that accessibility isn't binary—we can test websites against rules, but that isn't always enough.

Colour contrast

When we put content onto a page we always want to be sure that it is perceivable, as per Principle 1. This means that we need to ensure there is enough contrast between the foreground and background colours so that words can be read, asterisks can be seen, and icons can be distinguished from their surroundings.

As a simple test, envision white text on a white background and white text on a black background as two extremes of contrast. Now picture that somewhere in the middle, you might have shades of grey text on shades of grey background. Some of these combinations may be easy to read, but many will be difficult to read by those with low vision or those who may have different forms of colour blindness. How do we know which ones are which?

Colour contrast can be determined with a mathematical formula, and it is definitely best left to the tools to do so—we want to build websites and applications, not do mathematics. Some of the best tools used to check colour contrast include:

- **The Juicy Studio Colour Contrast Analyzer extension for Firefox** is great for testing pages that are already built. It does the math from the colours that are specified in HTML and CSS (https://addons.mozilla.org/en-US/firefox/addon/7313).

- **The WAT-C Colour Contrast Analyzers** are stand-alone applications for both Windows and Mac computers. These tools test colour contrast using an eyedropper-type tool, allowing you to test graphic mockups of a web page where you don't have access to the hex or RGB colours (http://wat-c.org/tools/).

- Finally, a more powerful tool called **aDesigner**, originally an IBM tool and now part of the Accessibility Tools Framework, allows you to not only test colour combinations, but also visualize how a page may appear to people with low vision or who have varying degrees of colour blindness (http://www.eclipse.org/actf/).

Validation

The toolbars usually provide a shortcut that allows you to send the page you're using to an HTML validator. This is useful for catching errors quickly, such as missing alt text, incorrectly nested tags, and invalid attributes.

- **The W3C Validator** runs as a service enabling you to quickly validate your documents online. It also provides advanced options that allow you to override specific defaults like character sets and even DOCTYPEs to give you more flexibility for testing (http://validator.w3.org/).

- **The HTML Tidy extension for Firefox** sits in the browser's status bar and automatically runs each time you go to a page. It will tell you if the page is valid, or contains errors or warnings. Clicking on the icon in the status bar will then highlight the validation errors for you and in many cases tell you how to fix them (https://addons.mozilla.org/en-US/firefox/addon/249).

- **Validator.nu** is a more modern but somewhat experimental validation tool. It has support for HTML5 and ARIA attributes (http://validator.nu/).

Resource // Accessible Rich Internet Applications (ARIA)

ARIA is an emerging specification from the W3C and is an accessibility effort supported by a number of companies. This work is designed to help provide some degree of programmatic accessibility where it doesn't already exist. Think of it this way: Many of the widgets and advanced controls that we build into our websites are simply made up of <div> and <span> elements that have no semantic meaning. Using ARIA will eventually allow us to reliably tell assistive technology that "this div is actually a dialog box" or "this ordered list of links is actually a menu of choices" or "this collection of divs, images, and spans is a progress bar."

For more details and to explore ARIA further, see http://www.w3.org/WAI/intro/aria. To learn more about how ARIA techniques can help you meet WCAG 2.0 success criteria see: http://www.w3.org/TR/2008/NOTE-WCAG20-TECHS-20081211/aria.html.

Reading level

As we saw earlier, an important piece of being accessible is being understandable. It is generally recommended that content designed for the general public be targeted at a reading level of no higher than lower secondary education.

These tests are not foolproof, but running your content through a Flesch-Kincaid readability test (http://en.wikipedia.org/wiki/Flesch–Kincaid_readability_test) or a Gunning fog index (http://en.wikipedia.org/wiki/Gunning_fog_index) test will tell you roughly what reading level your content is targeted to (at least for English content).

These tests can be run through a variety of word processing tools or you could run them online in a number of places such as:

- Readability Analyzer from Translated.net Labs (`http://labs.translated.net/text-readability/`).

- Edit Central's writing checker (`http://www.editcentral.com/gwt1/EditCentral.html`).

- David Simpson's Readability Test Tool (`http://www.read-able.com/`).

- The Juicy Studio Readability Tests (`http://juicystudio.com/services/readability.php`).

Testing power tools

The tools we just mentioned test very specific and small pieces of accessibility. Now we should take a look at some accessibility testing power tools. These pieces of software enable you to quickly identify known accessibility issues and, more importantly, *potential* problem areas. The reports that these tools provide then need to be analyzed to determine if in fact there are accessibility errors that need to be corrected. Why? Accessibility is not black and white. None of these tools could possibly test for all possible ways to meet a particular success criterion. These tools have to apply their own set of "rules" and as a result sometimes show you areas where something might be wrong, rather than a list of errors.

The automated tests are based on a set of defined rules and are usually variable, letting you test your pages against WCAG 2.0 (A, AA, or AAA), Section 508, or in some cases your own custom set of tests. These tests give you a sense of the overall accessibility of a page. When we run these tests against a number of pages, we get a sense of the overall accessibility of a site. When we run these tests against a number of pages over a period of time, we get a sense of the overall accessibility of an organization.

Starting with a page-by-page testing tool, we'll take a look at a couple of web-based services.

WebAIM's WAVE

WebAIM has a long history and wonderful reputation as an organization that focuses on accessibility. Not only do they believe that everything online needs to be accessible for people with disabilities; they put their efforts into training, advocacy, and building tools that help. The WAVE Web Accessibility Evaluation Tool is an online tool designed to give you a visual reference for the accessibility issues and potential issues it finds in your work.

When you run the service, you'll see the original web page with the WAVE header on top of it. The page may not look identical, but all of the elements will be there. Known errors will be identified with a red icon and error text. Potential errors or areas for further investigation will be shown with a yellow icon and text. Notes and other positive features are shown with a green icon.

Figure 24.4 shows a screenshot of the WAVE service's analysis of the popular CNN.com website. Large-enterprise websites such as this tend to have small issues that creep in from time to time. CNN.com is no exception and included 40 accessibility errors when this test was run. Let's take a walk through what WAVE tells us.

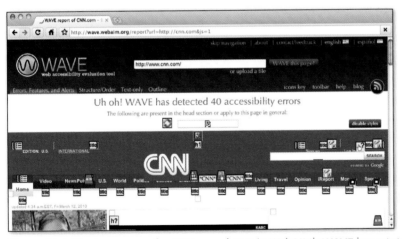

Figure 24.4: The home page for CNN.com shown in WebAIM's WAVE has a total of 40 accessibility errors.

There are a number of blue areas that indicate where certain markup features are present. You'll see in **Figure 24.4** that all of the navigation areas use an unordered list. You can also see where the navigational items provide additional information in the title attribute.

Green icons represent positive accessibility features that have been added to the markup such as null `alt` attributes. These `alt` attributes are set as null, presumably because the images are decorative in nature and don't contribute meaning to the page.

Yellow icons represent alerts—areas that you should look at in a bit more detail to determine if there are truly any accessibility issues that need addressing. Remember that we said that accessibility testing requires judgment? Now is that time. While WAVE identifies areas of possible concern, it is up to you to dig deeper.

Red icons represent known accessibility errors that need to be fixed.

As you hover your mouse over each of the icons as shown in **Figure 24.5** through **Figure 24.8**, you'll get a more detailed explanation of what the icon represents:

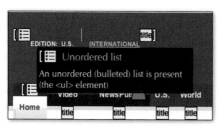

Figure 24.5: The blue icon, with details, shows "An unordered (bulleted) list is present (the <ul> element)."

Figure 24.6: The green Feature icon, showing "Null or empty alt text. Alternative text is null or empty (e.g. alt="")."

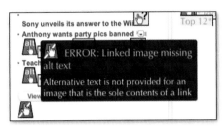

Figure 24.7: Red error icon with text indicating "Error: Linked image missing alt text. Alternative text is not provided for an image that is the sole contents of a link".

Figure 24.8: Yellow alert icon indicates "Alert: Event handler. An event handler is present".

Referring back to **Figure 24.4**, you can see that there are a number of tabs for the WAVE tool. These icons are shown in the default tab "Errors, Features and Alerts." The other tabs include "Structure/Order," "Text only," and "Outline."

The "Stucture/Order" tab allows you to see what the page will look like when it is consumed in a linear order, from top to bottom. This applies to someone using a screen reader, for example. You should look for areas where the linear order doesn't match the visual order of content on the page.

The "Text only" tab provides a representation without any images.

The "Outline" tab attempts to generate a document outline from the page and allows you to see if the page has a reasonable structure. You should look at the outline and determine if you can make sense of the page, just from looking at the outline. If you can, then the page template and the content are likely well written and coded. If you can't, then the writing and/or the coding need some improvement.

Try it yourself!

Go to http://wave.webaim.org and enter a URL of one of your favourite pages. It could be the home page for your school, a government site, or a company down the road from where you live. Run that report, noting the number of errors found. You will see a visual representation of where WAVE found problems and potential problems. Review each area, and, based on what you now know about accessibility, try to determine the best way to address the issues. Refer back to the other chapters for code and other advice.

CHAPTER 24

HiSoftware's Cynthia Says

Cynthia Says (http://cynthiasays.com) is an online version of HiSoftware's AccVerify product. We won't go into much detail here in terms of what it does, but it is a solid tool. It doesn't have the flexibility of HiSoftware's full AccVerify product, but it does give you a sense of what the tool is like. It is less visually focused compared with WebAIM's WAVE, but produces complete reports that help you determine whether a website meets the accessibility criteria you chose when running the tests.

Enterprise testing products

A number of enterprise-level software tools also exist for accessibility testing. You can use them to test a single page, but their real strength is in rapidly performing a large number of tests, on a large number of pages, and then doing so over time.

These tests help you quickly identify problem areas—much in the same way that simple HTML validation lets you see where you have problems with your HTML. By now you should be well aware that accessibility isn't a black-and-white exercise. These tools help you identify possible areas of concern based on examination of the web page or site's code. The reports will prompt you to dig deeper.

Three current tools are:

- Deque Worldspace (http://www.deque.com/products/worldspace)
- HiSoftware AccVerify (http://www.hisoftware.com/products/accverify.html)
- IBM Rational Policy Tester (formerly known as Watchfire's WebXM before they were acquired by IBM) (http://ibm.com/software/awdtools/tester/policy/accessibility/index.html)

All of these commercial products have their strengths. Jim Thatcher, one of the most well known accessibility advocates, authors, and practitioners, has written extensively on the use of automated tools for testing accessibility. You can see the results of his investigations at http://jimthatcher.com/testing.htm.

Working with any of these automated tools will help you on your quest to build more accessible sites and applications.

Summary

You've now seen the details of some of the testing tools you need in your arsenal and are well on your way to creating accessible solutions. Take this foundational knowledge of accessibility and combine it with the techniques you learned in the rest of the book and apply them to all that you do.

Remember, your accessibility testing really should always include real people as well as the tools that we've discussed here. No matter which tools you select to help you complete your testing, always remember that accessibility is, first and foremost, about one thing:

People.

CHAPTER 24

Albuquerque,
♀ New Mexico
USA

Virginia DeBolt lives in Albuquerque, New Mexico, USA. She is a former educator with an abiding interest in the way web design and web development is taught and learned. She's written several books, including *Mastering Integrated HTML and CSS* (Sybex, 2007). Her blog, *Web Teacher*, is full of tips and observations about the teaching and learning of web design.

http://www.webteacher.ws/
http://www.vdebolt.com
http://twitter.com/vdebolt

CHAPTER 25
Bringing It Together

by Virgina DeBolt

In this chapter you will bring together all the information you've learned from the previous chapters to build a small website. You'll step through the process of planning and building a website from the initial planning stages to the uploading and testing of your new site. Everything you've learned in this book from initial planning steps to writing code will be put to practical use in this culminating activity. Here's your chance to demonstrate your new skills.

You'll get some suggestions on an idea for a site, and a bit of a walkthrough to remind you about the process of creating a site from scratch, and some tips for testing and deploying the site when it's finished.

*In this chapter you have the opportunity to **Try it yourself!** with the convenient sample code downloads found on the book's companion website—http://interactwithwebstandards.com.*

The project

You'll create a small website of several pages that will demonstrate the principles and practices of web-standards-based web design that you've learned throughout this book. This will give you hands-on practice with planning, building and deploying a complete, working site that exemplifies best practices. When you've finished, you will have demonstrated your ability to plan, create, deploy and test a web-standards-based website.

Everybody has to eat. Our suggestion is to create a site based around food. Here are a few ideas that might inspire you:

- A restaurant site (the restaurant can be imaginary).
- A food market or farmers' market (it can be imaginary).
- A recipe site.
- A guide to good eating in your area.
- A resource for finding locally grown food in your area.

You can come up with your own food-based idea for a site. Or you can create a site based on a topic of your own choosing.

Project requirements

What do you need to have in your site to demonstrate mastery of the material in this book? Here's a brief list of what you should include. Later in the chapter, you'll get more detailed reminders about the items in the list. In order to demonstrate the skills you've acquired in this book, the following basic requirements need to be met:

1. **Advance planning** to determine site purpose, site navigation, organization of information, audience, and development of content. The planning should culminate in a set of functional requirements, a storyboard or wireframe, a description of the content and page descriptions (see Chapters 6–9).

2. **The site, food-based or not, should meet these standards:**

   A. A home page that clearly defines the site purpose in content and appearance (see Chapter 7, "Site Planning" and Chapter 8, "Content Analysis"). You'll need four or five additional pages of content.

B. Navigation that supports the user interaction in a way that provides clear guidance (see Chapters 7–9 and Chapter 15, "Links").

C. Semantic use of the HTML elements you've learned including headings, paragraphs, lists, tables, links and others (see Chapters 10–18).

D. A form to take reservations, order food, provide a means of contact, schedule catering, or create some other way for site visitors to interact with the site depending on the content you create (see Chapter 19, "Forms"). The form does not have to be a functioning form, since server-side scripting is beyond what you learned in this book.

E. Proper use of div and span elements, ids and classes within the HTML to support styles created in your style sheet (see Chapter 20, "Floats").

F. Presentation rules in an external style sheet that includes layout, colors, background images, link appearance and every other aspect of the site's appearance (see Chapters 11–21).

G. Accessibility is assured (see Chapters 22–24).

3. **Quality assurance testing including validation and accessibility testing.**

4. **Uploaded to a server,** where every aspect of the site functions and appears as intended.

Getting started

You should have all the tools you'll need at hand. If you put off adding the Web Developer Toolbar to your Firefox browser, or haven't yet downloaded an FTP tool like Transmit or CuteFTP, now is the time to get that done.

You'll need to set up a new folder or directory on your computer where you can store the files and materials you'll use in your new site.

Your site content

Your first big decision is what type of site you will create. If you didn't instantly come up with a food-related idea when that subject was suggested, try looking at all the free food images available at http://www. morguefile.com for inspiration. There are images aplenty there that could be used to create a site for a sandwich shop, an organic fruit market, a recipe site or a fancy restaurant.

For this project, you have to develop all the content yourself. In the real world, you would work for a client who came to you wanting a site for their existing topic or content.

It will help you relax about the content to include if you pick some aspect of cooking, eating, buying or selling food you feel comfortable writing clearly about, so you can concentrate your efforts of planning and building the site's pages.

Collect and organize your content. Make sure you are clear about the purpose of the content, your content is outlined and you have a page plan for the content that will be needed on each page of your site.

Your site plan

Review Chapters 6-9 with your content in mind. You originally saw this chart in Chapter 7, "Site Planning." You'll go through all these steps in creating your project. Don't leave any of the steps out (**Table 25.1**).

Project management	
Stages	**Steps**
Start	Define project requirements
Plan	1. Conduct research and analysis
	2. Draft design options and select design
Build	Produce the design
Test	Quality assurance testing
Close	1. Deploy
	2. Maintain

Table 25.1: Project management stages and steps.

Devote some time to thinking about how to structure the site, how to organize the content, how to present the navigation options. For a project this small, a simple global navigation system that includes a link to every page on the site is a sensible option. The navigation text then becomes an important choice in assuring that users understand what each menu option does.

Cover all the potential scenarios for site visitors, using the idea of personas suggested in Chapter 6. For example, assume the site is for a restaurant. What would site visitors be looking for? Perhaps visitors want information about location, maps, phone numbers, reservation forms, menus, reviews, catering or delivery. What if users were searching for a restaurant in a certain neighborhood or serving a certain style of food or for a particular service like catering. Could they identify your site as fitting their needs?

Create a wireframe or storyboard of your site.

Your visual design

With your information architecture, your audience, and your site goals clearly thought out, it's time to start putting a visual face on your information. Your wireframe work will guide you here.

In keeping with the principle of separation of content from presentation, all the visual design decisions are set in place in the style sheet. Your HTML should be semantic HTML with an occasional `id` or `class` to create styling hooks for your CSS. The visual rendering of all your ideas for the site is expressed with style rules.

Working page by page

We'll take a look at page-by-page requirements for your new site. This will help you use individual HTML and CSS techniques and tools that you've learned about in this book. You're ready to start building the site.

Organize the site structure

Set up an organizational scheme for the files that will comprise your site on your own computer. Keep in mind that the file and folder names you use on your computer will be repeated exactly on the live web server. Use descriptive names, with no spaces. Need an images folder? Name it "images." Need a folder for scripts? Name it "js" or "scripts." Need a folder for site information? Name it "about." Need a folder for menus? Name it "menus."

Save individual files with equally transparent and informative filenames. Don't use spaces in filenames, but hyphens or underscores are allowed. For a food site, you might have files saved with names like nut-brownies.html, rhubarb-pie.html, catering.html, about-us.html, produce.html, grains.html, reservations.html, and other similar names. Remember: a filename becomes part of the page URL.

> **Tip:** Filenames index.html, index.htm and default.htm are rendered by default when they are in a folder on a web server. The particular default choice depends on the server configuration. These filenames don't have to be included in a URL. For example, http://www.vdebolt.com/ will automatically open with http://www.vdebolt.com/index.html without including it in the URL.

You won't have very many files in this small project, but imagine the site as if it were a large project with many files and organize it accordingly. Build the site structure now, and as you create the pages of your site, save the various files in the appropriate folders.

As you learned in Chapter 15, links to images, HTML pages, CSS files, and scripts are written as pathways to particular files within particular folders within your site. Plan that structure of folders in advance and keep it set in stone as you build pages and create links. You'll avoid many a broken link if you create the site organization as an initial step and leave it that way permanently.

The hidden decisions

Some of what you decide now will be hidden on the surface of the website. I'm talking about the document head and the information you learned in Chapter 5, "Writing for the Web" and Chapter 12, "<head>."

DOCTYPE

Start with a DOCTYPE choice. You can choose HTML 4.01, XHTML or HTML5. The choice is up to you. Pick one and write the code according to the rules you've assigned to yourself with your choice.

Title

Every page needs a `title`. You probably figured out page titles when you were doing your page planning during the preliminary planning stages. One thing to consider now is how to work the site name into the individual page `title` elements. If your business is the Battle Hill Bistro, and you create a page called "Sunday Brunch Specials," how do you put both in the page title? It could be `<title>Battle Hill Bistro: Sunday Brunch Specials</title>`, or it could be `<title>Sunday Brunch Specials – Battle Hill Bistro</title>`. Make a plan and make it consistent on every page. See **Figure 25.1** for an example of one way to handle this.

Figure 25.1: This popular recipe site, Simply Recipes, chooses to display the page title followed by the site name as the page's title. The page title is visible in the top bar of the browser: Albondigas Soup Recipe | Simply Recipes.

The typographical element chosen to separate the page name and the site name is often a colon (:), a bracket (<), a hyphen (-), or a vertical bar (|).

Meta elements

Keywords, descriptions, and meta elements you read about in Chapter 5 need to be added here. If you use keywords, you want to individualize them for the specific pages they are on, so you need to revisit any meta elements you use as you create each new page.

The home page

Start with the home page. The page is saved as index.html and stored at the top level of your site structure, not within any subfolders.

Now is the time to produce the design that will characterize the entire site and to create the HTML and CSS to achieve the design. The design of this page usually takes far longer to accomplish than that of the inner pages. The inner pages go faster because most of the decisions are already made. Linking to your style sheet and plugging in the fresh content for each new page goes rather quickly by comparison.

The home page also takes more time because you need to prepare the graphic elements you'll use. You'll need graphic elements such as logos, design embellishments, possibly background images. Any images you'll use have to be gathered and readied for the Web.

Naming your images takes some thinking, too. For example, suppose you have a page or section on your site showing three types of pancakes you serve in your restaurant. Give the images names that help identify them— pancakes_blueberry.jpg, pancakes_gingerbread.jpg and pancakes_chocchip.jpg, for example. This naming convention is useful forever, whereas image names like 008452.jpg or gingerpc.jpg are not so helpful.

When the home page is finished, with its linked CSS file, you'll have a layout and appearance that can be repeated on each new page you add. All you need to do on new pages is maintain the structure and CSS you used on the home page. The navigation will already be styled, and should remain consistent through every page of the site. The site's look and feel should remain consistent. Individual pages will have different file names, different titles, and different content in the content blocks, but many of the surrounding chunks like headers, logos, navigation and footers will remain the same from page to page.

In a very real sense, designing the home page is designing the site. The home page establishes certain design elements that will be used for the entire site.

CSS decisions about background color or images, color, line-height, font selections, margins and/or padding for various elements, navigation styles, alignment choices, heading and paragraph font size, list item style displays, and more are determined now. You may add additional CSS rules for specific chunks of information on the inner pages, of course, but many decisions are made here.

The header

At the very least your header area should contain the site name and any identifying graphics such as a logo. You might also include a line describing the site to quickly let viewers know what the site is about. For example, "Battle Hill Bistro: Serving the Battle Hill area with casual cuisine, take-out service, and comprehensive party catering."

> **Tip:** The site name or site logo are often linked to the home page. Web users understand this convention. If there is no link saying "Home" in your menu, users will expect to reach the home page by clicking the site name or site logo in the page header. You can do both: have a "Home" link and use the logo as a link.

The header may include a site search form. This is more important on large sites than it might be on your small project site, but it's often the first thing new visitors look for in order to quickly find what they want.

The header may contain the global navigation. This depends on your design. Will the global navigation be displayed in a horizontal menu across the top of your page, or will it be a vertical menu in a side column? If your choice is to use a horizontal navigation system at the top of the page, then you need to decide if it works best as part of the page header, or if it should be in a div devoted solely to navigation.

Depending on the purpose of your site, you may want to include an address and phone number in the header area.

The content blocks

There are some generalized options for the content blocks. Will you have two columns? Three? Will your navigation be here?

Beyond those general issues, what you do with the content blocks depends on the purpose of your site. What will be the purpose of each column? How will you block out your content into a hierarchy? These decisions should already have been made and planned out in your wireframe exercise.

The number of small content sections nested within the main content area of a page is often different on the home page from the inner pages. On a recipe site, the home page might have several small sections, each one featuring a photo of something yummy and a teaser with a link that leads to an inner page with the full recipe.

On a restaurant site, you might need several divisions within the main content area for things like specials, invitations to join a mailing list, photos of food or the venue, or photos of yummy things with teasers and links leading to inner pages about take-out menus or catering services.

On an organic market site, the home page might have sections that highlight the week's fresh crops or the organic farmers who supply the market or tips for cooking organic produce.

The footer

The footer is the normal location for less frequently used content such as copyright notices and links to legal notices or privacy notices. Recently, site builders have rediscovered footers and used them for much more than copyright notices and webmaster links. You might find displays of photos from Flickr, links to site-related items like Twitter accounts or Facebook Fan Pages, ads, bookmark links such as Delicious or Digg, or all kinds of "auxiliary" content.

Consider including an hCard in the footer area (**Figure 25.2**). An hCard would also be logical in a sidebar column, depending on your design. A place of business definitely should have an hCard on the "About Us" or "Contact Us" page of the site, but it doesn't hurt to include it on every page. Since you will probably have the same footer on each page of the site, it's a good place for hCard contact information. See **Figure 25.2** and the sidebar "More about hCard."

Figure 25.2: The browser display of the hCard example on the book's example website, which you can reach from http://interactwithwebstandards.com.

Resource // More about hCard

hCard is a microformat, the electronic equivalent of a business card. It can be downloaded from your web page to a visitor's address book or phone contact list. Browser add-ons like the Firefox Operator toolbar are used for downloading hCard information. This gives your customers an easy way to get the contact information needed to call for reservations, place an order or simply find your physical address.

Microformats use semantic HTML coupled with some standard class designations within the HTML that identify the information as being an hCard. Every hCard does not need to have every element you see in the example. On a recipe website, for example, you might want to include your name and email address, but a physical street location would not be needed.

Look at the code example for hCard. It contains everything a potential customer would need to call you, find your address, or find your website with a mobile device. It's a standardized way to make your business easy to contact.

```
<div class="vcard">
    <p class="fn org">Battle Hill Bistro</p>
    <p class="adr"><span class="street-address">555
    Battle Hill Blvd.</span>, <span class="locality">Big
    City</span>, <abbr class="region" title="Virginia">
    VA</abbr> <span class="postal-code">00000</span></p>
```

(continues)

Resource // More about hCard

(continued)

```
  <ul>
      <li class="tel"><span class="value">555-555-5555
      </span>
      </li>
      <li><a class="email" href="mailto:bistro@battlehill
      bistro.com">Email Us</a></li>
      <li><a class="url" href="http://www.battlehillbistro.
      com">battlehillbistro.com</a></li>
   </ul>
 </div>
```

Two good sources of hCard information are http://www.ablognotlimited.com/articles/getting-semantic-with-microformats-part-3-hcard/ and http://microformats.org/code/hcard/creator. At microformats.org, you can fill in only the bits of information you wish to share and get code to copy and paste.

The inner pages

As explained in the site requirements, you need to build four or five inner pages to demonstrate your command of semantic HTML. For this project, you need to build *just enough* pages to show that you can use everything you've learned with at least one example. Make at least one of each kind of list, at least one table, at least one form, make working links, add images, write paragraphs and headings, and style it all with a linked CSS file.

Tip: There are examples and tips for creating signup forms for something like an email newsletter at http://www.codegent.com/blog/2010/1/how_to_build_an_effective_sign_up_form.

For a project about a restaurant, just one properly formatted page with a menu—say the lunch menu—will be enough. You don't need to make a breakfast menu page and a dinner menu page. For a recipe site, just one properly formatted recipe page will be enough. You can create a home page that looks as if you have more than one menu, more than one recipe, but you don't need to build dozens of pages to fulfill the illusion.

A table can be used to give store hours, list the weekly specials, or chart the availability of fresh produce. One properly formatted table is enough to meet the requirements. Review Chapter 18, "Tables," to be sure you understand captions, summaries, table header cells and other table elements.

As you read in Chapter 5, "Writing for the Web," web users like to talk back. They want to offer feedback, or complete a task online by doing something like making a dinner reservation. This is accomplished with a form. One form will be enough. It can be used to take reservations, sell a monthly recipe calendar, collect addresses for a mailing list, or solicit feedback from visitors. If you include a search form, with its single input field, that's fine. However, a more substantial form with attention to several types of fields using labels and fieldsets is needed. Review Chapter 19 for information about form elements.

The lowly list

Think about lists. As you saw in Chapter 5, people looking at websites are in a hurry. You have less than 2 minutes to convert a potential user into a user. Lists help with that. They are fast to skim. They can be styled in endless ways. Lists are the workhorses of the Web (see **Figure 25.3**).

*Figure 25.3: Two unordered list stylings can be studied in the book's example website, (*http://interactwithwebstandards.com*). The site's global menu displayed horizontally at the top is a list, as are the three items mentioned in the Supreme Cuisine section. The graphic embellishments in these lists are created with CSS background-image.*

You need to find a semantic way to demonstrate all three types of lists: unordered, ordered and definition. Unordered lists are normally used to create navigation elements, so that's an easy one to include. Ordered lists make sense in step-by-step instructions such as in recipes, checklists for planning party food orders, and best of or top 10 lists such as "top ten ways to serve fresh artichokes." See **Figure 25.4** for more styled list examples.

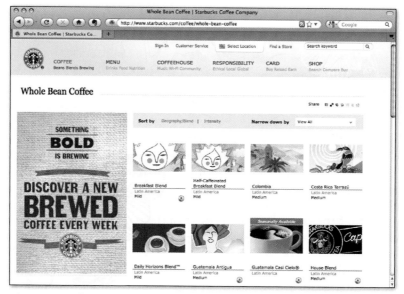

Figure 25.4: This page of valid HTML from the Starbuck's website uses lists for the navigation elements and to create the small images and descriptions on the right for each type of whole bean coffee.

I want to expand a bit on the topic of definition lists, because these seem to mystify many people who want to know how to use them in a semantically appropriate way. A definition list could be used for a restaurant menu. A table is also a semantic way to display data for a menu, but humor me as I make a case for the definition list. A particular food item, perhaps "Turkey Reuben on Rye," would be the dt or definition term. The dd or definition description would be the description of the food item. Since each dt can have multiple dd elements, there are multiple CSS opportunities to style and arrange menu descriptions containing ingredients, calories, price, and other information.

Tip: Some examples of styled definition lists are available at http://www. maxdesign.com.au/presentation/definition/index.htm and http:// moronicbajebus.com/playground/cssplay/dl/files/.

A few potential inner pages are suggested in the following sections. These are merely suggestions. The decision about what content is needed on the inner pages of the site is up to you. If you find the suggestions helpful, make use of them. If not, find other ways of your own to include the various HTML elements.

The main content pages

At least two or three of the inner pages should be filled with content that exemplifies the purpose of the site. As you build the pages, think about presenting your content in ways that allow you to create examples of many types of text formatting, such as various types of lists (and nested lists), headings, paragraphs, emphasis, links and other semantic use of textual elements.

Use good link text for any inline links you include in your pages. Good link text helps your user know what is waiting after the click.

Use typographical entity codes for things like quotation marks or copyright symbols where appropriate.

Use images to enhance the information on the pages. Be sure to write appropriate alt text for images. If the layout you are using does not rely on floating content blocks—or even if it does—images give you an opportunity to show that you can use the float property. The images you use should be sized appropriately and optimized for maximum download speed.

If you don't have one elsewhere, you need to work a data table into one of your content pages. On the book's example website, a table is used to display the menu (**Figure 25.5**).

Menus

Lorem ipsum dolor sit amet, consectetuer adipiscing elit, sed diam nonummy nibh euismod tincidunt ut laoreet dolore magna aliquam erat volutpat. Ut wisi enim ad minim veniam, quis nostrud exerci tation ullamcorper suscipit lobortis nisi ut aliquip ex ea commodo consequat.

Hors d'Oeuvres

Dish	Description	Price
Soupe du jour	Homemade soup of the day	$6.50
Assiette de fromages	Cheeses and fresh fruit	$15.00
Escargots de Bourgogne	Snails baked with button mushrooms and a traditional garlic and parsley butter	$8.50

Salads

Dish	Description	Price
Salade verte	Mixed greens tossed with grape tomatoes, bell pepper and green onion in a champagne vinaigrette	$7.50
Salade Chez Nous	Tossed mixed greens with seared grapes, smoked duck breast, shaved red onion	$9.50

Figure 25.5: A table from the book's example website using `<th>` *elements to identify dish, description, and price data.*

The opportunities for building a form are excellent on one of your main content pages. Anything would work, from taking café reservations for a certain time and date and number of people, to ordering grocery items to be ready for a pickup, to submitting feedback and reviews for individual recipes.

"About Us"/"Contact Us"

Every site needs this type of information. For a small site, you may be able to combine the two into one page. Creating a separate page for each is acceptable, also.

Give a concise description of the site on the "About Us" page. Explain who owns the site—perhaps provide an hCard with contact information.

Does your site feature a business with a supposed physical address? If you didn't put a map to the location on the home page, you might add one here.

The "Contact Us" page is one potential location for a form. Many companies use forms to collect feedback and comments from customers as an alternative to publishing a highly spammable email address in open text on a web page (**Figure 25.6**).

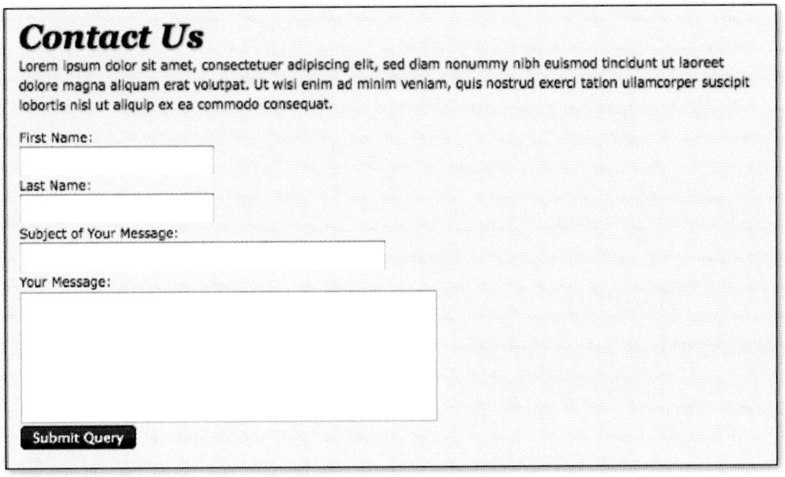

Figure 25.6: A basic contact form can be seen at the book's example website.

The example form seen in **Figure 25.6** does not include a fieldset. Find a way to include at least one fieldset in your form.

The "Contact Us" page does not have to contain a form. The form could be on a different page, with something as simple as an email contact link on the "Contact Us" page.

Reviews/feedback/testimonials

Reviews from (imaginary) outside news sources and customer feedback or testimonials could be worked into a page. This type of page would give you a showcase for headings, links, citations, quotes and blockquotes. Another possible way to display a series of glowing testimonials from satisfied customers would be as a definition list.

Quality assurance testing

Quality assurance tests range from basic-level tests to highly detailed checks on your site. Some tests need to be conducted frequently during the site-building process; others can wait until the project is complete and final debugging and checks are made.

Checks, checking, and checklists

As you complete the building of each page, perform quality checks as a best practice.

Try everything. Check every link. Run every script. Make sure the images show up. This is important both while the site is still on your hard drive and after it is uploaded to the server. Things may work on your computer, but once the site is uploaded errors may appear: a bad link, a mistaken file path, a forgotten upload.

Spelling and grammar

Run a spelling and grammar check on the content of every page. It sounds like such a minor thing to worry about, but spelling and grammatical errors make a very bad impression on site visitors. Such errors yell "unprofessional" to a visitor and cast doubt on the site's credibility. They may even drive visitors away, if users conclude that a lack of attention to such a basic thing implies a lack of attention to even more important things.

Proofreading is important. Spellchecking doesn't catch errors like the use of *your* for *you're* or other commonly misused words.

Validation

Use the validators. There's an HTML validator at http://validator.w3.org/ and at http://validator.nu for checking HTML. Review Chapter 22, "Accessibility Intro" for complete details on validating your pages.

Resource // Validation is important, but not essential

Valid code assures you that the page will work according to web standards in a variety of browsers and situations. Code that validates has met the specifications for the particular type of HTML or CSS that the page is written in. Validation can help you find coding errors like unclosed tags or tag nesting errors. Validity is a goal to work toward, but it isn't a goal that *must* be achieved no matter what.

(continues)

Resource // Validation is important, but not essential

(continued)

Writing valid code does not guarantee that a page makes the best use of elements, that the layout choices and uses of `ids` and classes are the most efficient, or that the proper semantic elements have been used to describe content. Valid code doesn't mean the page is usable or accessible, although usable and accessible pages are distinguished by valid code.

Sometimes you need items on a page that won't validate. You might want a Google map widget on a page—it might be important to the site's visitors and to your business. If it doesn't validate, then choosing the widget you need over the goal of page validation is not the end of the world.

Use the CSS validator at `http://jigsaw.w3.org/css-validator/`. This validator will look at your CSS for errors and mistakes and can help you make corrections.

Both the HTML and CSS validators will run on pages on the Internet by inputting a URL, or by uploading as yet unpublished documents from your hard drive.

Visual and browser checks

Make visual checks of each page in a number of different browsers. Does it look the way you intended? You don't need to achieve a pixel-perfect match in every browser, but the functions and organization of the site should be obvious and usable in every browser.

The Yahoo! Developer Network at `http://developer.yahoo.com/yui/articles/gbs/` has developed a system of graded browser support that can guide you in determining what browsers to use for testing and what to test in various browsers. The Yahoo! grading system emphasizes "progressive enhancement," a method that puts content accessibility at the core of browser support, above visual appearance.

Accessibility checks

Test for accessibility using tools explained in Chapter 24, "Accessibility Testing." Start with the WebAIM testing resources.

The evaluation checklist at http://www.webaim.org/resources/ evalquickref/ is a great aid. Reading through the list reminds you of the checks you need to perform, and the steps that should be taken to make sites accessible. The checklist provides links to resources. Want to know how and where to check your page for color contrast? The checklist has a link for that.

A helpful set of facts about screen readers is available at WebAIM at http://www.webaim.org/articles/screenreader_testing/. Probably the most important information for you on this page, unless you plan to buy and learn to use screen reader technology, is how to approximate the screen reader experience with free techniques. For example, with Mac OS X, you can use VoiceOver. You can download timed evaluation copies of JAWS and Window-Eyes. You can use WAVE or the Web Developer Toolbar for Firefox to generate a text-only version of the document.

WAVE (http://wave.webaim.org/) is a WebAIM tool that helps with accessibility evaluation of websites. Give the tool a URL or upload a page from your hard drive. The tool then displays the page with icons next to each element. If an accessibility problem exists, the error icon is easy to spot. Hovering over any icon on the page gives you more information in a popup tooltip. See the Resource "Glenda Watson Hyatt" and **Figure 25.7**.

Figure 25.7: WAVE in action on my home page. The icon next to the Facebook badge indicates that the image now passes the accessibility test because of the alt text, which is also displayed by WAVE.

In the Resource "Validation is important but not essential," it was mentioned that third-party code you copy to your web page may cause validation errors. Sometimes you can fix such errors, and sometimes you cannot. Missing alt text is an easy fix, but it's an error that might go unnoticed when copying code from a third-party source unless checks like WAVE are run on a page.

Tip: For Dreamweaver users, WebAIM provides a WAVE Dreamweaver extension that can be added to Adobe Dreamweaver software. With the extension, pages can be evaluated with WAVE while working in Dreamweaver. The free extension can be downloaded at http://wave.webaim.org/blog/wave-dreamweaver-extension/.

WebAIM has helped clarify and explain the Web Content Accessibility Guidelines (WCAG) from the W3C with a WCAG checklist at http://www.webaim.org/standards/wcag/checklist.

Resource // Glenda Watson Hyatt

Glenda Watson Hyatt, from http://doitmyselfblog.com, has a downloadable PDF ebook about blog accessibility titled "How POUR Is Your Blog?" It's available at http://www.blogaccessibility.com/. POUR stands for Perceivable, Operable, Understandable, and Robust.

Glenda Watson Hyatt's tip for good alt text in the ebook is this:

> A good test to determine if a text equivalent is useful is to imagine reading your blog over the phone. What would you say when encountering the image to make the page understandable to your listener?

Firefox Web Developer Toolbar

The Firefox Web Developer Toolbar can help you perform a great many page checks. With it, you can disable CSS to see how your content works without styling (**Figure 25.8**). Use it to disable JavaScript and see if the site is usable without any scripting enhancements.

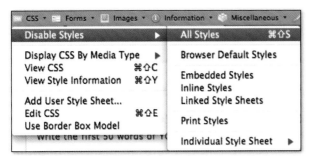

Figure 25.8: An example menu from the Web Developer Toolbar. The CSS menu offers options for editing, viewing, or disabling CSS on a web page.

In the Images menu of the Toolbar, you can check for alt attributes and see how the page looks with images not visible. With the Information menu, you can check any abbreviation elements to be sure the title attribute is providing the full wording of the abbreviation or acronym.

There are several very helpful choices in the Tools menu.

The Web Developer Toolbar Tools menu offers a way to check the site's download speed with a Speed Report. Use the Speed Report to determine how well you optimized images and whether the wait for your pages to download will be a detriment. The results show you the wait time at various connection speeds. The speed check looks at HTML files, CSS files, images, scripts, and multimedia and evaluates the download speed for each individual part of the pages.

In the Tools menu, you find Validate Section 508 and Validate WAI. Section 508 refers to the U.S. government's Disabilities Act, and the requirements websites must meet under that law. WAI is the Web Accessibility Initiative from the W3C. The results for these tests come from Cynthia Says.

The Tools menu contains links to validators for both HTML and CSS.

Once is not enough

It's important to test your pages as you build them. It's much easier to fix errors and keep the building process moving along successfully if you aren't propagating errors from page to page because you failed to do quality checking as you moved along.

That's not the whole story, however. You also need to check everything again after the site is uploaded and deployed. Even when you're sure everything is working perfectly on your own computer, it's common to find bugs and mistakes in a newly uploaded site.

Allowing plenty of time for testing and debugging before a site is shared with the world is an important aspect of professional web work.

Deployment

You're ready. You finished planning, building, and testing on your hard drive. Now it's time to upload this baby of yours to the World Wide Web.

Where will you put it?

With a student project about an imaginary business or using fictional content, it's always a challenge to find some spot on the Internet where the files can be posted. You don't want to buy a domain name for a project that may not be real and won't be left up once the project is finished and you've learned what you set out to learn.

Here are some possible locations. Be careful to get the free plan. Don't sign yourself up for paid hosting just so you can test your project. I don't necessarily endorse any of these, but they provide what you need in terms of free web storage for a project like this.

- Free Web Space http://www.freewebspace.com/
- Tripod http://www.tripod.lycos.com/
- Free Space http://www.free-space.net/

There are many other similar places on the Web, if these don't appeal to you. You need a web location that will allow uploading by FTP, and these three do. Many places let you sign into your account online and use an online control panel (cPanel) to set up email forward and do other chores related to your account. The three sites listed do that. You may also be able to upload files using the cPanel, but for this project stick with FTP.

Find your hosting. Get signed up for the free account. Keep track of the information they send you when you register. This informational email tells you key facts like your FTP address, your sign-in name, where to put your public files and other goodies you need to keep track of.

Set up your FTP software

All FTP (File Transfer Protocol) tools do the same tasks. They all need the same information in order to transfer files from one place to another. Start by setting up your connection to your new hosting space (**Figure 25.9**).

If you can fill in the initial path, it will save you some clicking around and help eliminate the possibility of putting files in the wrong place. Most often the initial path will have a name like `public_html`, or `www`, or `htdocs`. Whatever it's called, it's the place where your files will be stored so they can be seen by the public. This folder (or directory) on the server—`public_html` or whatever it's called—is the folder that corresponds to the folder on your hard drive in which you have stored all the files and subfolders for your site.

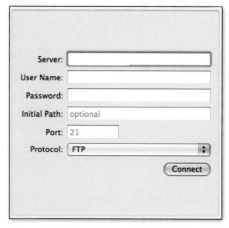

Figure 25.9: A new connection by FTP needs server name (the FTP address), user name, and password. You may also be able to include an initial path (or initial directory) and a port. Most often it's port 21, as shown here. The example shown is from the Mac FTP software application Transit.

Most FTP software gives you a view in one window of your own hard drive. In the other window, you see what's on the server. You're just getting started, so you won't see much on the server. The way things look on your hard drive should match exactly with what you see on the server after you upload (**Figure 25.10**).

Figure 25.10: Some files from the home computer were not needed or uploaded to the server. Otherwise, the directory structure and organization is the same. The example shown is from the Mac FTP software application Transit.

If you double-click a folder in either the home or server window, the folder opens to reveal the individual files sitting in that folder. Usually you just drag and drop to move files from one spot to another. Sometimes you highlight a file and click an arrow to either upload or download it, depending on the particular FTP tool you're using.

Drag and drop with care

Be very careful when dragging files from one place to another in an FTP app. A moved file overwrites an existing version of the file. If you revise your home page and want to upload the changes to the server, this is a good thing. Your new file overwrites the old file. Presto, the home page is updated. If you accidentally do the reverse, that is, download the old index.html file to your hard drive, any changes you made to the home page will be overwritten by the old page downloaded from the server. Your changes will be lost. FTP can put files or get files. Make sure you know which one you are doing each time you drag and drop.

You can add folders on the server side. Normally a right-click or Cmd + click in the server side of the FTP windows will open a contextual menu. The menu allows you to create new folders and do several other tasks. New folders you create should match exactly the folder names on your hard drive.

Upload or put

There may already be a placeholder index page in your server space, one put there by the hosting company. You should be able to see this placeholder page on the Internet in your browser. That is the first page you want to replace.

Before you upload (or put) your own index.html page on the server, go ahead with some other uploads first. Put the CSS file(s) on the server. Upload your images folder. These files are needed for all the pages in the site, so get them in place. Remember, you must recreate the same structure of files and folders on the server that you have on your hard drive (**Figure 25.10**).

Next, upload the index.html page. Look in your browser, reload (refresh) the page, and you should see your own web page instead of the placeholder page from the hosting company.

CHAPTER 25

When you are sure you have things in the right place and that they are showing up on a live web page where you expect them to be, finish the job. In your FTP application, double-click a folder to open it and start dragging and dropping the appropriate files from your computer onto the server.

Upload the remainder of the HTML files and any other files such as JavaScript files that your site uses.

Testing

Yes, again. Test, debug, check.

Use this checklist:

- Do the links work?
- Do the images show up?
- Are the web page titles correct?
- Are there any spelling or grammar errors?
- If you have any scripts, do they work?
- If you have any plugins, do they work?
- Is the HTML valid?
- Is the CSS valid?
- Does it pass accessibility checks?
- Does it look approximately the same in Opera, Firefox, Safari, Internet Explorer, Chrome, or any other browser you have?
- Does it load quickly?
- Is it usable if CSS and JavaScript are disabled?

Fixing errors

You may find errors. It happens.

Suppose you have a problem on the "About Us" page. Maybe an image isn't showing up. Open that page from your hard drive. Look for the error. It could be just about anything:

- A bad filepath.
- A typo, such as a missing quotation mark or equals sign or bracket.
- A human goof-up such as code pasted in the wrong spot or unclosed tags.
- Is the thing you need, such as an image, really on the server in the place the browser is looking for it?

HTML is detail intensive. Check all the details. One helpful tip, if you can't find an error in your HTML in the place where it *seems to be* on a web page, is to look at the code just previous to the error location. Often it's a forgotten quotation mark or an unclosed tag somewhere ahead of the problem that's actually the culprit.

When you think you've spotted the problem here's the process:

1. Make the change.
2. Save the page.
3. Upload the page.
4. Open your browser and check the page on the Internet. If you already had the page loaded in your browser, reload (refresh) it.

If it still isn't right, you're back to looking for errors.

Debugging help from your text editor

Many text editors have aids to coders in the form of color-coding of various tags, attributes, and other parts of the HTML. See **Figure 25.11**, which is an image made of the text editor BBEdit.

```
<p><img src="classwar/greenside_ancestors.jpg" alt="Greenside element
information" width="209 height="255" class="leftfloat" />I can't pick out a div
to use as the ancestor for our descendant selector, because the page is in a
table. The most logical ancestor to use is the table cell holding the
paragraphs, or the <code>td</code> element.</p>
```

Figure 25.11: The colors displayed in the text editor can be a clue in finding an error. Note the missing quotation mark after width="209. *After the error, you see this bit of code in green:* 255" class="leftfloat" />. *It should be red, like the rest of the attributes for* img. *The green is a tip that something is wrong.*

The HTML validator can also help you find errors in your coding.

Getting the word out

A caveat: If your project is an imaginary business or idea that you don't actually want to be found, you won't do this for your project site. But when you make your first real site, use these ideas to get the word out.

Your site is up. You know everything is working and ready for public view. "If you build it they will come" may have worked in the novel and movie *Field of Dreams*, but on the Internet you need to help people find your site.

You first step is to let the search engines know you exist. You do this by registering your site. It doesn't happen immediately; you may have to wait days or weeks before you see the site picked up in the search engine after you complete the registration.

To register at Google, go to http://google.com. Click the "About Google" link. Look for the "Submit your content to Google" link (**Figure 25.12**).

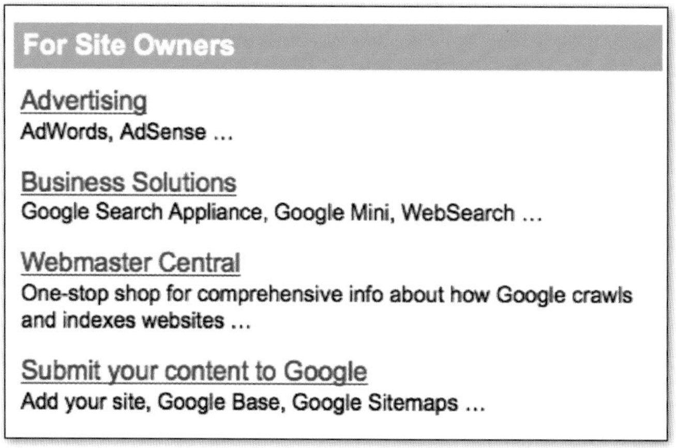

For Site Owners

Advertising
AdWords, AdSense ...

Business Solutions
Google Search Appliance, Google Mini, WebSearch ...

Webmaster Central
One-stop shop for comprehensive info about how Google crawls and indexes websites ...

Submit your content to Google
Add your site, Google Base, Google Sitemaps ...

Figure 25.12: On Google's About Google page you will find a Submitting Your Site link. Use it to register your site.

Click the "Submit your content to Google" link and follow the directions to request that your site be added to the search engine. To register with a search directory such as Yahoo! or the Open Directory Project (http://www.dmoz.org), go to the directory and work your way through the hierarchy until you find the right category for your site. After you find the best category for your site, click "Suggest URL" on DMOZ or "Suggest a Site" on Yahoo! at the top of the page. Fill in your information and hope your site gets accepted into the directory.

Promotions or ads

You can send out press releases or promotional materials. If you have a neighborhood bistro, send a press release to the neighborhood newspaper announcing the services available to customers on the website.

You can buy ads if you have the cash. Put banner ads in places that would be a good source of traffic to your site. Buy Google ads for keywords that lead to your site.

Social media

Use all the social media tools at your command. Tweet your specials on Twitter and include a link to your site. Create a Facebook Fan Page for your site. Promote special events or deals using social media.

Perhaps you are an organic market with links to growers' sites. Partners such as this are usually willing to give you a link in return. Ask for a reciprocal link from your partners.

Traditional advertising

Include your URL on all your traditional advertising materials. Put it on your business cards, put it on your carryout menus, put it in your radio and newspaper ads, put it in your window and on your outdoor signage. Spread that URL around like it was candy on Halloween.

Evaluate your results

Watch what happens after your site is live. Are you getting the results you want? What kind of questions are you getting from people who use the site? What are your stats—are you getting the traffic you need?

Could you make changes to improve your results? One good thing about the Web is that changes are easy and immediate.

Getting a site up and running is the beginning of a long-term commitment to keep it maintained, keep it fresh, keep it relevant. It isn't a one-shot activity that you just walk away from when you are finished.

Summary

Your web-standards-based site should serve you well over the long haul. It should perform well as browsers change and as new technologies are introduced.

Technology does change, however. The curriculum at the WaSP InterACT site (http://interact.webstandards.org) can be a great help in keeping current. This is the first book published by the InterACT group. Keep an eye out for others that will help you create standards-based websites and applications.

Have fun learning, and enjoy all the new websites you are going to make in the future!

WATCH
READ
CREATE

Meet Creative Edge.

A new resource of unlimited books, videos and tutorials for creatives from the world's leading experts.

Creative Edge is your one stop for inspiration, answers to technical questions and ways to stay at the top of your game so you can focus on what you do best—being creative.

All for only $24.99 per month for access—any day any time you need it.

creativeedge.com